The
Letters

Postmark Prejudice in
Black and White

SHEILA WHITE

To Pat & Norm,
Best regards.
Sheila White
Oct. 21, 2023

YORKLAND PUBLISHING

Published by
Yorkland Publishing
12 Tepee Court
Toronto, Ontario M2J 3A9
Canada

www.yorklandpublishing.com

ISBN: 978-1-7390044-0-8

Book Design by Laura Boyle Design

Printed and bound by IngramSpark

To Mom and Dad and racial equality

Prologue

The letters to my mother from 1946 and 1947 are older than I am. I wanted her to write a book about them. They were from her puritanical family circle, part of a campaign orchestrated by her mother objecting to her pending marriage to a black man when, unfortunately, mixing of races was considered taboo.

Had my mother Vivian told the story here of her courtship, of coming from Nova Scotia to Toronto to marry my father, it would have been one hundred percent factual. Both she and Dad were perfectionists.

In the mid-eighties, years after Dad died, I suggested Mom author their story. She never got around to it, but she left all those records behind, eternal saver that she was.

Some people would have destroyed letters that angered or hurt them. My mom made a collection of them, instinctively knowing they were worth saving as significant, archival snapshots of a fledgling evolution of race relations in Canada.

Knowing my mother's stubborn streak, she would have saved them, if for no other reason than to one day prove her detractors wrong. I come from a family of people who like to be right.

So, it fell on me to author this book, patching together a story from the extensive documentation my mother left me. My parents' interracial marriage played out like a novel. Now it is one.

The provenance of *The Letters: Postmark Prejudice in Black & White* is found not only in the racist letters themselves, which heckled me from their plastic storage bag until I gave them this attention, but also in Mom's meticulously detailed five-year diary in her miniature hand, a stack of heritage photo albums, her early year scrapbooks and a shoebox full of poems, letters and telegrams she and Dad exchanged.

This book is based on a true story, but because I didn't ask many questions of my parents about the topic, I was left to guess and imagine the real circumstances in some situations. In a library, it would straddle the fiction and non-fiction shelves.

Some scenes and dialogue are pure fiction while others I extracted directly from my source materials, including one hundred and fifteen individually transcribed pieces of correspondence, the daily diary contents from 1947 to 1951 and my discussions with family members and subject matter experts.

Why a biographical novel? This was the question the wonderfully supportive publishing team of Ed and Rosemary Shiller posed to me. Honestly it was because I didn't have knowledge of the full back story. I didn't question my parents enough when they were alive, nor did I quiz my mother for details after Dad died when we had that talk about a potential book, and before dementia robbed her of her recall.

At the time she said she would want all the featured characters to have departed first before writing such a book. Also, Mom tended to conceal her emotions and personal struggles and had an inherent reluctance to step into the limelight to tell the whole story.

Still the story begged to surface. It held valuable lessons for today about human harmony so pertinent to a troubled twenty-first century rife with racism. It serves as both a microscope on the past and telescope on the future for gauging the distance we have come and how far we have yet to come as a diverse and inclusive society.

I wasn't particularly race conscious as a child. The day I discovered the meaning of the "N-word" was when my mother overheard me outdoors reciting "Eeny, meeny, miny, moe." a children's counting game that included the pejorative in its rhyme, since replaced by the word "tiger."

I distinctly remember her shocked tone as she stood on the outdoor landing and scolded me in front of my friends for using the word and defined it for me. I guess I was six or seven. I felt so embarrassed and ashamed, a reaction I continue to feel every time I hear the word.

No longer a pair of meaningless syllables, now it hurt to hear it spoken. Although the N-word was never once hurled at me, I know too many examples of people who have been victimized by it.

Yet the N-word is used in this book, a decision I did not arrive at lightly. I wanted to put readers in the shoes of the twenty-one-year-old bride-to-be when she peels open each of the letters and digests the full brunt of their contents.

The historical language in parts of the book is raw and real, not used gratuitously, not scripted for maximum shock value as in some idioms. I used a leading newspaper's policy to guide me regarding racially pejorative terms, which advised that they "should be used sparingly and only in direct quotations, when essential to the meaning of the story." I believe readers will agree that the use of the word in this book passes the test, and I do apologize to any who take offence to my decision to include the demeaning word in full where it appears.

In the book I tried to be true to the language of the era. African Canadians weren't "Black" then, they were Negro, another offending term as was spoken at the time that peppers the text, although today is archaic.

There are many stories out there about how horrible those times were for non-whites. It was a shameful period of what we now categorize as systemic racism and colonial-driven white privilege. Minorities were stigmatized and faced almost insurmountable barriers to social and economic equality.

The Letters: Postmark Prejudice in Black & White focuses on change for the better and on the enlightened community of progressive change-makers who welcomed my parents and the movement for world brotherhood, a call never more urgent than today.

There is no place for racism in our world and we must do everything in our power to end it. I'd like this book to be part of the solution to countering nonsensical, race-based conspiracy theories and the poisonous hate that flows from them.

I descend from Mayflower Pilgrims on Mom's side and Virginian slaves on Dad's with a mix of white and indigenous ancestry for added color.

This book is my attempt to square all sides by sharing my parents' race relations success story – their positive experience with the Toronto community and the exciting spirit of race relations they helped to fuel.

For the young adults who read this book, consider a life without instant communication, limited phone, no texting, no email, no social media. Imagine when keyboard meant a clunky, manual typewriter, when pen on paper, writing cursive in longhand was the surest and quickest way to message someone. Letters were such lifeblood that the Canadian and US postal service delivered twice daily and on Saturdays.

Everything my parents stood for would have been lost if care hadn't been taken to save the hard copies. I do wish I had asked them substantive questions and I would advise any person today to consider interviewing the older adults in the family for details about lives lived, highlights, turning points, challenges and lessons learned.

Those familiar with Nova Scotia will see that I have taken liberties with certain site descriptions, being that I'm writing from my imagination and not a geography book. For those licenses I have taken, I hope the reader will take that leap of faith, understanding that I acknowledge any and all deficiencies upfront. This is not the non-fiction version I wish my mother had written.

Another point I need to make concerns my use of some real names in the book. I thank the relatives of these individuals and hope they will oblige me my portrayals, given that I never knew these subjects, and appreciate the roles they played in my parents' lives. They represent a sliver of the overall contacts Mom tracked in her notes and I'm sorry I couldn't mention everyone of import; there were too many.

Here would be a good place to thank the people who helped me starting with my parents, Vivian and Bill White, my version of "ghost writers."

Alex King, my co-vivant, creative partner and life mainstay, lived and breathed this project with me. I owe him a huge debt of thanks for his best supporting role as author's spouse.

The insights of Dr. Sheldon Taylor and his impeccable research; the time and sharing of recollections from the Honorable Arthur Downes, my aunt Dorothy Keeler, Bev Salmon, Judy Hill, Julien LeBourdais, Alan Shiff and Morley Wolfe; thoughtful feedback from cousin Lorna White and her daughter Amanda White; help from cousin Heidi Holysh, cousin Reid White, Marion Wyse, Larry Dawidowitz for his photo restoration, Jim Lawry, Elinor Maher, cousin Gerald Clarke, George Clyke, Greg Gormick, Kathy Grant, Pat Pettigrew, Angie Sist and Sandy Macdonald; support from my siblings, brother Chris, in particular for his afterword, from friends, extended family, Don Heights Unitarian Congregation, all very much appreciated. To my first cousin once removed, Canadian literary treasure George Elliott Clarke, thank you for your words of encouragement to this first-time novelist. I give a huge nod to the comprehensive White Family research work of American relatives Bessida Cauthorne White, Mary Ellen White Dungee and Elaine White Edwards. Thank you to Jack Lakey and Sylvia Hamilton for their kind words.

If not for the interest and faith of Yorkland Publishing's Ed and Rosemary Shiller, I am quite certain the letters in question would still be languishing, lonely awaiting my transcription, their destiny perhaps never to be realized. Finally to my editor, Rosemary Shiller, thank you so much for devoting your time, skills and expertise to this book. Readers will be astounded to know that you cut twenty-thousand words from the original manuscript. So gentle was your touch and care, the edits are indiscernible, the story seamless and intact. As an editor you're an artist. There were more scenes than this book had pages to tell. I guess we'll save those for our Hollywood screenplay.

I wish everyone an enjoyable and interesting read.

"The Dingle"

Chapter 1

To anyone else the sound of the train pulling out of Halifax station was merely that. To one young woman passenger on board this departing train, the chug of its engine gathering speed was the sound of her life changing forever. Finally, the moment was upon her like a long-awaited parcel. Vivian Keeler felt a sense of relief. Rumbling wheels accelerated her toward Montreal to meet Billy. Billy, her husband-to-be, was the handsome, talented, wonderfully mesmerizing charmer who had somehow hypnotized her into leaving her beloved Nova Scotia to join him in Toronto. Today was November 8, 1946. Billy had been lured to Ontario to begin a promising social work job six weeks earlier.

Vivian's school friend Dick had driven her to the station to catch the twelve o-five. Mother had refused to see her off. Devout Jean Keeler, believing she had raised a good Baptist daughter, was fit to be tied. Her lovely, well-bred, only daughter was running away to Ontario at twenty-one to marry a Negro: Billy White. The shock of this discovery had hit Jean like an electric current to her gut. It sickened her to think of it – whites and coloreds weren't made to mix. Intermingling could be tolerated, barely, but intermarriage and interbreeding! Jean refused to fathom this for her daughter's future. Vivian was cheapening herself and descending to the station of street tramp, dooming herself to a life of shunning. Jean had to do something.

Vivian settled into her green moquette-covered coach seat in the passenger car as the memory of last evening's farewell to her rancorous mother drifted to the back of her mind. The wheels were turning. The ritual of counting days was over. Here in the moment, gladness, and excitement, despite feeling slightly off-kilter – probably just fatigue from the frantic pace of the past weeks of preparations and pressures. Wistfulness settled in on her too as she thought of the people she was leaving behind like smoke out of the stack. Mother, teen brother Bernard and her many school and church friends of longstanding, she would miss them terribly. Her workmates at the Wartime Prices and Trade Board and her bosses, the meticulous Mr. Forbes and the forgivably flirtatious Mr. Morrison, they practically begged her not to go. While a few in the BYPU – the Baptist Young People's Union – gossiped like pigeons in the park about her and Billy and whispered sneeringly about the mixing of races, Vivian didn't bear grudges. She would carry all her dear ones fondly in her thoughts as she set out on her new life. Helen was steadfast. Dick and Burleigh were stellar. Her best friend Lillian would never forsake her.

There was a creeping feeling of guilt riding under Vivian's collar, her guilt over not coming clean with her dear pal Dick. When they said their goodbyes, Vivian knew their past engagement dreams were exactly that: past. Dick however was unaware he was being ditched.

They had been friends since grade school. Dick was athletic, easygoing, clever and funny, a good, transplanted – originally from Toronto – Dartmouth boy. He was an excellent scout, artist, writer and nature photographer, who noticed the minute details in things and extracted beauty from them.

When they graduated together from Dartmouth High as accredited students, the school yearbook, *Spectator,* pegged them as the couple to watch.

Richard Hill ... Known as: Dick. Appearance: Dreamy. Ambition: Aeronautical Engineer. Favorite Saying: Fish! Character: Stubborn. Favorite Verse: "Muse not that I thus suddenly proceed; For what I will, I will, and there an end." – William Shakespeare

Vivian Keeler ... Known as Viv. Appearance: Angelic. Ambition: To travel. Favorite Saying: Gosh! Character: Cheerful. Favorite Verse: "Life is a jest, and all things show it; I thought so once, and now I know it." – John Gay

Thirty graduating students signed their names on the autographs page, among them *Dick Hill* in fountain pen. On the overleaf in pencil, he felt compelled to add, "My love forever. Dick." He had just joined the RCAF. That was in 1943.

Vivian looked down at her lap, at the cellophane-wrapped box of Moirs chocolates he had thrust in her gloved hands before kissing her on the cheek. "Don't want to smudge your lipstick," he had said as they lingered momentarily on the platform. "Besides, red's not my color," he joked.

"I wish you every success with this career move of yours, Viv. I'll see you in Toronto when I have my next leave. If I don't see you in the future, I'll see you in the pasture." He winked and smiled his adorably sunny grin, told her to be sure to write and with that they parted. Typical Dick Hill: good natured, easygoing, full of humor Vivian thought as the train edged long out of sight of the station. So lovable, Dick was, but not the Billy White kind of lovable. For an instant, her heart reached for her throat, she had to catch her breath as Billy came to mind, not that he was ever far from it. By suppertime, they'd be together.

He'd be waiting for her in Montreal where they'd spend the weekend and then proceed to Toronto together, their future begging to unfold. *Together*, the word held a whole new meaning for Vivian. Two. Together. Two together. She played with the words. Their decision to unite had not come lightly. It evolved over a period of two years until the inevitability of their mutual destiny was too powerful for either of them to deny.

They met through Billy's brother, George.

If Vivian hadn't gone to Fader's Drug Store on Hollis Street to buy film for her camera that day in 1944, she and Dick would probably be in Lunenburg at this moment, announcing their pending marriage to his parents.

George White worked at Fader's part-time. He was a keen university student training to become a pharmacist, working his way through school. A druggist is all he ever wanted to be. Whatever that took, he'd do it. Soda jerking, stocking shelves, mopping floors, running deliveries, ordering and inventory, cleaning toilets, George took on every facet of his job at the store cheerfully and thoroughly. Mostly he loved talking to his customers, dispensing his opinions as readily as he hoped one day to dispense medications and advice as a licensed druggist.

Chemistry had always fascinated him, both the scientific and the human kind. He felt the latter when Vivian entered the empty store, a radiant beauty, elegant and proper, long, soft and gently curled blondish hair framing her flawless cream-colored face. She spied him at the back of the store behind the lunch counter and floated his way in her sky-blue, all-weather coat. A matching blue kerchief dotted with pastel flowers topped her head to prevent her carefully manufactured curls from flattening in the moistness of the Maritime May air.

"How may I help you, lovely Miss?" George inquired in a gently coaxing tone that awakened Vivian's radar-like detector for kindness. She liked this clerk instantly. It was her first time seeing a person of his complexion working behind a store counter.

"Do you sell film?" she inquired shyly, producing her Kodak Brownie from the depths of her tan leather bag. The black 1934 English model produced to mark the silver jubilee of King George V was handed down to Vivian from her mother's sister, Elsie, as a business college graduation gift. It didn't bother Vivian at all that it was second hand, in fact it meant more to her that it was finding its second life with her.

George came around to the front where twelve curved-back, round-bottomed wooden stools stood anchored on poles at the lunch counter bereft of diners. He whistled at the camera. "She's a beaut," he said, "a special edition import. Yes, we have 120 film, my lady."

"It was a gift from my aunt," Vivian volunteered. She followed George to the far wall of the store. A glass encased counter housed a cash register on top and a collection of pipes, lighters and perfumes below. On the wall next to the multicolored stacks, row on row, pack upon pack, of cigarettes and related tobacco products, a wooden cupboard compartmentalized the boxes of film in its variety of sizes. George reached for two boxes of size 120 film, deciding to test a trick he learned in a year-one marketing course.

"One or two?" he asked Vivian, who was now thumbing the rack of greeting cards in search of a Mother's Day card from the Hallmark turntable stand installed just last week.

Chapter 1

Vivian paused – "You might as well give me two," she said breezily at the very moment the perfect greeting card caught her eye and was selected. It had worked! George was elated that his retail know-how was paying off, but that feeling was quickly overshadowed by a feeling akin to kicking himself in the ass. He hadn't considered that he had just cut in half his prospect of seeing this new customer again. Two rolls of film meant twice as long before she returned for more.

"We develop film here too," he ventured as he proceeded to ring up her charges, "so I hope to see you again here at Fader's. Are you new to the area? We have two locations, you know." He didn't want to make her feel uncomfortable with his questions, but Vivian didn't seem to mind. She was happy to strike up a conversation with the amiable employee. "I've just started my first job," she told him, "On Upper Water Street. Well, my start date is Monday actually, but I was there today to do the paperwork."

"I notice your lunch counter. I suspect I will be stopping by now and then. That lemon meringue pie looks awfully tempting."

George smelled an opportunity and perked up. "Well, let me invite you to be my guest at Fader's 'gourmet counter' on Friday next, Miss. It would be my pleasure ... I'm sorry, what's your name?"

"Vivian. Vivian Keeler. And yours?"

"George White."

A friendship between them blossomed, not that Vivian needed more friends. She had a coterie of companions, but none like George. Now that she thought of it, at the ripe age of nineteen, she didn't have any dark-skinned friends. The colored people in the community lived in different parts of town and attended their own churches and schools, negating everyday opportunities to get to know them.

George's skin was the color of alfalfa honey, his pleasant face conveying a note of distinction, his skin as smooth as a buffed carving from exotic wood. Grounded and focused and intelligent, it was his sympathetic nature and his ability to listen that impressed Vivian. Her new friend's shaded complexion was relevant to her only to the extent that the White family name was embedded in local history and national pride as being a credit to the Negro race, and she always had a keen interest in other people's backgrounds and cultures.

"Ticket, Miss?" The conductor's voice snapped Vivian back from the blur of scenery that paraded past her window seat. She handed over the ticket to the mercy of his paper punch and smiled at the uniformed attendant upon receiving the validated stub – a soon-to-be souvenir of this life-changing trip.

Fortunately, the seat beside Vivian and the two seats facing her were unoccupied at least until the Moncton stop. For now it was space she could use to set down her purse, coat and a canvas tote bag containing a bagged lunch – egg salad sandwich, carrot sticks, pickles, two blueberry muffins, a thermos of hot tea – two books, a writing tablet, sharp pencils and a pocket pencil sharpener in a zippered case, her camera, a Nova Scotia tartan wool scarf with pockets at each end to warm the hands, her winter gloves, her 1946 diary and a collection of important papers bound in a folio. Vivian dug into the bulging satchel and retrieved the folio. From it she lifted a thin, postmarked envelope. She didn't know why she was reading this letter yet again, for the umpteenth time. The only thing stopping her was Dick's box of Moirs staring up from her lap. She set aside the letter temporarily and attacked the wrapping that stood between her and a chocolate.

The cellophane stubbornly resisted her passive attempts to peel open the box. She remembered the nail scissors in her purse, found them and released the chocolate box from its sheath. Lifting the lid, she gasped. The central star – the maraschino cherry chocolate – was missing. In its place, earrings, tiny silver earrings dotted with blue glass in the shape of a flower and a multifaceted, miniature blue sphere in each center.

Dick had unwrapped and rewrapped the box so carefully she hadn't even noticed his tampering. Guilt rushed back over her like a waterfall. A torrent of memories cascaded concurrently as she stared at the box, out the window, back to the earrings in the box, looming larger than any chocolate in the box until she dug them out with her fingers and transferred them to her purse. Subtle smells of bitter, sweet, marzipan and nuts wafted from the open box. She consulted the diagram and chose a soft caramel. Deciding to savor it in the smallest of morsels to make it last, Vivian thought of what she would say to Dick when the time came.

Nothing would change the history between them.

Chapter 1

Innocent days. She, Dick and his dog Tuttles, long walks in the country-side, long talks with Emma and Harry, his mom and dad. His famous Christmas party of 1942 when he announced he was joining the air force. Evolving days. The party at Colonel Powers in tony Marlborough Woods. Their attendance at The Army Show, Canada's all-soldier stage show, plus CWACs, the women of the war effort – wasn't that a thrill to see, especially with the stars, Wayne and Shuster? Dick all highlights. No low lights. Sparks, warmth, but no fire, she sighed. Billy was ablaze. All light. Hot embers.

Vivian reached for the orphaned envelope languishing on the table tray. "Why even open it?" her inner voice tugged at her. "You've practically memorized the contents." She disregarded the noise in her head and let the words on the page play out.

October 5, 1946
Dear Vivian,
I wish you would take these little books and study them. I have had them twenty years. At the five and dime I bought twenty for a dollar. I gave all but these three away and it seems as though I had saved them for you. They will be a great help, if you would read at least the one on Genetics. There you will see unfold the story of your future expectations. Think carefully. Marry not in haste and repent at leisure.

The flowers are from our garden. I want you to take them home to your mother.

She must be a good mother to have brought up two fine-looking children alone. She has worked hard to give you both opportunities. Make her ever proud of you. Don't break her heart.

You're a good girl, just a little mixed up. Go slow and be sure, for the boy, for yourself, for your children and grandchildren's sake.

God bless you dear girl and I pray to see you through.
Sincerely,
M. R. Abbott

Marjorie Reid Abbott, the family's one-time landlady. As a rule, Vivian kept her personal life to herself. But that day, Mrs. Abbott's offer of short-breads and tea and a friendly visit punctuated by a peppering of gently probing questions, temporarily evaporated Vivian's privacy barrier. She confided her plans to the woman days before she intended to spill the beans to Mother, a task she deliberately deferred until Billy had left town, co-conspirators as they were.

Her landlady's letter found its way back neatly folded into the envelope where the three booklets on Genetics, Christian Values and The Meaning of Chastity awaited navigation as the train lumbered on. Vivian had already deemed Genetics unworthy of re-examination. She was saving the ridiculously outdated enclosure on the discredited theory of genetics and race superiority to show Billy. She ferreted out her diary and scratched in an entry. "Train left on time. Dick took me to station. Seeing him I hope not for the last time." Not a word about the earrings.

She returned the diary along with Mrs. Abbott's letter to her bag and rummaged to find something else to read. A month-and-a-half without Billy at hand had been torture despite their contacts by telephone, telegrams and letters. He'd used the compelling power of his pen to entice her with the prospect of living in Toronto. Moving to a big city wasn't Vivian's concept of ideal. She was a country girl at heart whose fondest memories rested in rural Queens County, at the farm in North Brookfield belonging to her mother's parents, Maurice ("Moss") and Dora Harlow.

Vivian found correspondence from Billy wedged in the bottom corner of her bag. Even the sight of the envelope, marked Air Mail/Par Avion made her pulse quicken. Scant hours from now they'd be in each other's arms.

The postmark said Toronto Ontario OCT 30 2:30 p.m. 1946 and addressed to Miss Vivian R. Keeler, 85 Queen Street, Dartmouth, Nova Scotia.

The envelope contained a small, spiralled notebook with a burgundy plastic cover, an apparent promotional item from The Sterling Trust Corporation. It was twenty-four pages in all, including one page with a red feather pinned to it. On the back page was a yearly 1946 calendar and Billy had circled the date of Saturday, November 9 to mark what would be their first day together in one-and-a-half months. He was boarding with a prominent colored couple, Mr. and Mrs. Christian, the flamboyant Curley and stylishly colorful Cleopatra, "Cleo", and their son Doug, in the couple's west-end Toronto home on Lansdowne Avenue near St. Clair Avenue West.

Vivian cast her eyes down to Billy's well-figured handwriting in the booklet and settled in to reread the words of the man she so loved.

October 29, 1946
Dearest Vivian,
Perhaps from the point of view of anyone who doesn't know just how much I love you, there's no perfectly good reason why I can't exist till I go home tonight to write to you instead of using this almost ridiculous mode of correspondence. To me, though, the fact that I do love you as I do is in itself a sufficiently good reason for my feeling that I must write now.

I'm at the Pasadena for the first time since the eighteenth of this month having supper, and for the first time since I've been in Toronto I'm having fried fish – because it's a meatless Tuesday – and, contrary to my expectations, it isn't nearly as tasteless as fish in Toronto usually is. Well, that's neither here nor there, is it?

Last night I went home early because I was not only "wobbly" but a bit tired too. My hope was that I'd go to bed early and get a good night's sleep. I didn't. I was at home when the postman came this morning and felt disappointed when he left mail for Mrs. Christian and Doug – and none for me. However, I'm just leaving the office and I feel better now because I phoned the house and was told that there's a letter for me. I know it must be from you.

No doubt you will be spending considerable time with your Aunt Gladys, won't you? I'm sure she'll be glad to see you. It must be rightfully lonely for her, unless, or course, she has friends there to call on her and keep her mind off herself.

Gee, darling, I wish tomorrow were the ninth, for I should probably be on my way to Montreal now.

Tuesday 11:30 pm – at home
Thanks, my darling, for your letter. I'm particularly grateful to you for writing in spite of your headache. You're wonderful!

The house is perfectly quiet tonight except for the clock here in the dining room. Mr. and Mrs. Christian are in bed and Doug, who works at the Canadian General Electric, is on night shift this week, so he's not home.

I'm reading *Earth and High Heaven* slowly, on purpose. I don't want it to end. It's wonderfully well written. I've been reading it on the streetcars to and from the office because I know that if I were to sit down with it here, well I'd finish it too soon. I'm tempted to present one of my usual dissertations on people who say of such a book, "Oh yes, it's perfectly alright to see the author's point of view while you're reading the book, but after all, you know, it would be the wrong attitude to subscribe to consistently." I won't though darling because in the first place I want this to be a pleasant letter and in the second place there isn't enough paper left in this little book. I played a few of my records last night after I came home. Mrs. Christian, who is quite fond of music, said, "When Vivian Ruth comes we'll have to arrange a musical evening and have some friends in to hear your recordings." She's quite sure that when you come, I'll be and feel like myself again. Gee, darling, you'll like her.

I ask that the infinite good and peace and love that I will for you may better affect any possible contraries that others through their meanness, narrowness or envy may direct toward you.

Vivian, my beloved, my life has never known such wonderful depth, and height of purpose, and fullness of promise as you've brought into it.

Wednesday 9:10 a.m. – at the office
In the mail this morning I received an invitation to write a 1600-word article on racial prejudice for the program annual of the United Church of Canada. The deadline for its submission is December first, so I've written my acceptance with the hope that we – you and I, that is, – might work together on it. Ok?

The Community Welfare Chest's drive for funds is in full swing in Toronto. Red feathers are given to all subscribers. I remember that you've just bought a red suit and hope that this feather can be put to some use as an accessory.

I must go out this morning to see about some materials for our boys department. There's a terrific shortage of woodwork supplies in Toronto so we have to follow up every possible lead with the hope of securing some, at least.

Darling, let me remind you that this fellow, Billy White, is very much in love with you. Knowing him better than anyone else does, I can say with more than a little conviction that if and when you marry him the opportunity exists for you both to collaborate and write a book that will be much longer and far more engaging than *Earth and High Heaven*.

All my love, darling.
Billy

She loved how he expressed himself. She hugged the little notepad to her chest as if cradling a baby before tucking it into its crib.

For the first time Vivian took a hard look across and down the aisle. She studied the other passengers in the train car. Sharing the ride: diagonally across the aisle a harried-looking mother and her sternly postured husband containing two chatty, potentially overactive children who were oblivious to their parents' tension, further down a cadre of cadets and assorted army personnel, two Orthodox Jewish rabbis and, directly across the way, an acne-faced rake of a bespectacled man in an ill-fitting suit reading a Bible and a Nun wearing a cross, her fingers fidgeting obsessively with her rosary.

As a teenager Vivian had begged Jean to teach her how to bake those blueberry muffins. Today on the embarkation of this historic voyage she would savour one.

Surprisingly, although well past her usual lunchtime, Vivian didn't have much of an appetite. That single chocolate couldn't have been enough to spoil it. She reached into her bag to find her thermos. She poured herself some tea using the lid as her cup and deliberated eating half a sandwich. Then again, she could skip the egg salad and partake in a muffin right away. Muffin won out over sandwich and Vivian unpacked one to nibble, employing the brown paper wrapping as a napkin to catch any renegade crumbs. Aunt Doris's recipe, the only item Vivian knew how to cook. Her mother never taught her any housewifely skills or requested any help around the house, believing her precious daughter would eventually leave home to be a missionary, following the footsteps and legacy of the Baptist Keeler women.

One sip of her hot drink had barely touched her lips when the train lurched and groaned to a stop.

Tea jolted out of the thermos lid and splashed onto the brown paper in her lap. Fortunately, she had been diligent in replacing the stopper firmly in the thermos and nothing more than dribbles from the cup spilled in reaction to the train's sudden halt. The locomotive shunted and heaved several more times, then went comatose. Silence in the car ignited a succeeding buzz of inquisitiveness as travelers wondered aloud what was going on.

The conductor didn't leave them wondering for long. Striding to the front of each car, red-faced and looking as though he might explode, he bellowed an apology, explaining that a mechanical failure would delay the train's arrival for an unspecified period as CN personnel ironed out the problem.

With no choice but to accept the reality of the situation, Vivian finished her refreshment. Sinking into the generous seat, she now appreciated the luxury of having both padded armrests. Using her winter coat as a blanket and bunching her scarf for a pillow, she dozed off to the incessant peppering of the chatty children's continued shrieks and utterances.

She dreamed her father Glenn Keeler was alive. He is wearing his First World War captain's uniform. The jacket sports his prestigious Military Cross decoration from King George and his right hand reaches out to Billy, who stands with Vivian in the abandoned barracks inside Point Pleasant Park. "All men are brothers," he says. "I fought for this and now must you."

His words echoed hauntingly behind her eyes as the two men shake hands. Then the stone floor gave way beneath him, and he began melting into a field of mud, leaving Billy with mud on his hand and nowhere to wipe it but on Vivian's white shawl. After that, Vivian descended into a fevered, dreamless sleep.

The lunch counter at Fader's Drugstore

Chapter 2

B illy White's first impression of Vivian was, "she's way too good for my kid brother."

He had dropped in to see George at the store on his way home from work and to pick up some antacid pills for his quarrelsome stomach.

And there she was, seated at the lunch counter at the back, next to the pharmacist's wicket. Her stool swiveled while she rocked it, driven by her knees. Her satiny, soft hair spilling past her shoulders shimmered with each turning motion. The sheen of the curved wooden seatback caught the glimmer of the ceiling lights. George, behind the counter, looked up from his engaging conversation with Vivian, to see Billy approaching. He grinned and waved at his elder sibling. "Hey, brother, here's someone I want you to meet."

The faint scent of lily-of-the-valley wafted as Billy approached. She extended her hand and felt his envelop hers as they briefly joined in a handshake.

"Vivian Keeler. Billy White, my older brother, my much older brother," George emphasized and smiled, "I mean, he is O-L-D! How are you doing, old man?"

Billy laughed. "Oh, I'm old. You're right about that, Junior. I'm here to get some pills for my stomach. Can you help this old fellow out?" He addressed Vivian. "I'm pleased to meet you Miss Keeler. And how is it that you have made my little brother's acquaintance?"

Vivian explained how she'd become a customer since starting her first job that spring. She began coming to Fader's routinely to pick up or drop off film, nursing a soda or a pot of tea at the counter and chatting when he wasn't busy.

She learned plenty about the White Family during those conversations and had heard George wax proudly about Billy and all their siblings. But she hadn't expected his older brother to be this dashingly handsome and strikingly genteel. He had a small broom mustache that punctuated his full, bow-shaped lips and a dimple in his chin. His hair, black, rippled and shiny, lay flat above his full forehead, his eyebrows trimmed in shapely arcs of black velvet. Normally she felt awkwardly shy around strangers, but Billy's relaxed, upbeat demeanour emboldened her.

"Have you tried ginger tea for that stomach of yours?" she volunteered in a helpful tone. "I think the old-fashioned natural remedies that our grandparents used are still the best choice. Pills can have side effects."

Funny, Billy's stomach pain had subsided with the first whiff of her perfume. He looked at George quizzically. "On this matter, I shall defer to my brother," he said faking a dramatic French accent, "a question upon which he will tread, how do you say ... *gingerly*." He paused for Vivian's reaction, and she delivered an amused groan on cue.

George ambled closer and put his arm around Billy's shoulder. "I'm not saying ginger isn't some grand," he poeticized, "but pills is all we've got on hand." Collective laughter followed him down the aisle across from the pharmacist's window where he fetched the product from the shelf as the two new acquaintances remained at the counter. A few customers came and went.

Billy drank in the picture of the young woman two seats over. Casually he asked where she lived, worked, what type of work she did, her schooling, all the while aware of a strange sensation tapping at his solar plexus. A drifting, light-headedness of sorts overcame him as he soaked in pertinent details: a Dartmouth girl, Maritime Business College graduate, a stenographer, a typing award, and her first real job at nineteen as a secretary at the Wartime Prices and Trade Board. He knew the building. It wasn't far from his office at the Halifax YMCA – walking distance. Perfect, he thought, as

George rounded the corner with a bag, a receipt, and a request for payment. Billy flipped him the coins. He looked at his watch. His was always set precisely to the correct time.

"Sorry I can't stay longer," he said to them. "I have an appointment." He was lying. Why couldn't he just say he had a date with Lois? Well, he knew full well why. He had every intention of seeing Vivian again, and he wasn't about to say anything now that would lessen his chances of that.

He felt something the moment their hands had touched. All it took was a second of interaction. Had she felt it too?

He belted his camel-colored coat, tipped his brimmed hat in Vivian's direction, bowed slightly and cooed, "Until we meet again." His chocolate eyes met her penetrating blue gaze and a hint of a smile curled across her lips. "It was nice meeting you, Billy," she replied warmly. He turned and exited, off to meet Lois for dinner at her place.

"I see my brother is interested in you," George had said to Vivian as the bell above the door rang with Billy's exit. "If you want to get to know him better, I don't mind. If you'll always be my friend that's really all that matters to me, Vivian. So don't worry that I'll think the worst of you. That would be impossible. With you, there's only best and better, no worst and 'worster'." They chuckled.

"I'm a hard friend to lose, George," she said. "As for Billy, I'm sure our paths will cross again, but you do know that I'm seeing someone."

Was it relief or elation her words evoked? George was thrilled to hear from a girl not swept off her feet by Billy's charm and relieved that Vivian was committed to a friendship with him that was unique and apart from any future involvement with his brother.

Months passed before Vivian next met Billy. It was in the lobby of the Halifax YMCA building in February. She was at the agency for a Saturday meeting of the Christian Youth Fellowship, whose president, the much respected up-and-comer, Les Vipond, was also executive secretary of the Y. Les had arranged for the multi-faith group to meet at the Barrington Street headquarters twice a year on a weekend.

Seeing Billy wasn't on Vivian's mind as she entered the building as one of two designated representatives of the Baptist Young People's Union. George had mentioned that Billy oversaw the Y programs, but that detail was far from her thoughts. All she cared about this instant was the scheduled rendezvous with her co-rep Burleigh Crozier in the boardroom.

Characteristically she was a little late. Had she been early or prompt, the chance encounter with Billy would have been missed. As it happened, he was striding from his ground floor office to the lobby, having just finished a meeting with Les, when he saw her breeze through the front door toward the foot of the central staircase. Billy rushed his steps to intercept her. "Ah, Miss Keeler," he dramatized. "We meet again. What a delightful chance encounter. What brings you here today?"

"Hello, Billy." She smiled with radiance as bright as the sun outdoors. It cast an involuntary glow inside him. "I wish I could chat, but I'm running late for the Christian Fellowship Meeting, and ..."

After loosening the wool scarf covering her head, she tugged at her gloves, stuffed them in her coat pocket with a furtive glance up the stairs. She rustled through her handbag and pulled out a note pad. "Have you a pen?" Her cheeks flushed more deeply than the cold could account for. *A stupid question*, she scolded herself, as he unclipped the gold fountain pen she could plainly see affixed to the breast pocket of his white shirt. He handed it to her.

"Here, my work phone number and the address," she said, as she ripped off the sheet from her notebook. "Let's arrange to talk another time. Sorry, I have to run. Which way is the boardroom please?"

Billy took back his pen and the sheet of paper and returned both to his pocket. He gestured up the stairs and to the double doors on the left. "You're there," he said. He tapped his shirt pocket to assure her of the note's safekeeping. "I shall call you, Miss Keeler."

"Please, call me Vivian," she laughed as she started to make a rapid ascent.

Billy watched her whish away then strode over to the staff room. He made himself some tea. From the covered plate on the counter, he helped himself to remnants of the birthday cake the staff had given him on Wednesday.

Suddenly, he was glad to be working another Saturday. Vivian had put a new complexion on his day. Six-day work weeks came with the territory, especially leading up to the busy YMCA spring/summer season.

Today he was extra spirited, uplifted by the prospect of a date with Vivian. This was a wonderful development. So was the fact that Les knew her. Billy would tap his boss for information about her. "Project Vivian" would require great research and care.

As a mixed blend, Billy didn't think marrying outside of one's race was an issue. He had been at his father's side and witnessed him garnering the respect of all, from the Albino-pale lights to the comforting deepest shades of brown and black. He never catered or cowed to prejudice but treated those poor souls who suffered from it like a doctor treating the wounded, with compassion and dignity. Yet Pup had wanted Billy to marry a girl of their race to keep the line colored, not intermixed, but in a racial silo. As a minister, he'd been proud to perform a spectrum of intermarriages, yet an eighteen-year-old Billy heard his father tell a convention full of high-ranking white clergymen from across the Eastern seaboard that he didn't see intermarriage as the way to solve human prejudices. He felt each side lost a piece of its identity. Although he knew then and there that he disagreed with his father, trying to please him may in part have spurred Billy to marry Gladys, the mahogany-toned woman who turned out to be the stuff of nightmares.

Hands washed, mouth wiped free of crumbs with his monogrammed cotton handkerchief, returning to his office, refreshed from his break, Billy took a seat at his desk and looked down at the to-do list lying on the desktop blotter. His pending week was jammed. There was his staff presentation and board meeting prep, several counseling sessions with troubled boys and their families, a basketball practice, choir on Tuesday, for which he still had four-part choral arrangements to write for two new songs, plus his church performance on Sunday accompanying his sister June, the scheduled guest soloist, who'd be dropping by his flat Thursday night for a run-through. He'd moved his YMCA jazz band rehearsal to Wednesday night, so he'd be able to attend his monthly political meeting on Friday night with the CCF, the Co-operative Commonwealth Federation, a political party he had joined in 1940 to advance equality and human rights.

Today he would finish proofreading his report to the board about next year's budget needs. Les wanted it ready for Monday's meeting.

At this precise moment Billy was tapping his closed pen on the blotter like a Morse code signaler. His thoughts drifted from work to Vivian and how he should orchestrate his pursuit of her company. An idea struck him. He would put together a package of information and mail it to her like a promo package, and then let her make the next move. He sprung from his chair and headed to the filing cabinet. Opening the top drawer he plucked a few folders, one marked "Acadia" the other marked "Personal" in capital letters, and his aquamarine fountain ink.

From a folder he removed one of three archived copies of the Acadia Bulletin from December 1936 that contained an obituary of his father – Captain the Rev. Dr. William Andrew White. He wanted Vivian to know his pedigree. He glanced over it quickly.

> Baptist ministers from far and near came to pay their tribute of respect and affection to their departed fellow minister. Among the dignitaries who occupied a seat on the platform was the Lieutenant Governor of the Province of Nova Scotia ...
>
> William Andrew White was soon enrolled as an undergraduate at Acadia. He acquitted himself well in his studies and received his B.A. degree in 1903, the first colored man to be graduated from the institution ...
>
> In recognition of his eminently successful pastoral service, his capable leadership of the colored race in Nova Scotia, and his splendid record as chaplain during the World War, his alma mater conferred on him the degree of Doctor in Divinity honoris causa at its convocation last May. Few more popular degrees were ever conferred at Acadia than that on Captain White. It was hailed with general acclaim.
>
> Not long was he destined to wear his well merited honour. Disease had already laid its hands upon him. He passed to his reward on September ninth.

Billy also found a typewritten transcript of his interview about the meaning of community during a guest appearance on the wildly popular Uncle Mel's Radio Hour. He tucked these in with the lengthy obituary.

He was his father's namesake, although unlike "Pup" and Grandfather White, both Andrews, Billy went by his given first name. Doing so avoided confusion in the household. Besides, Billy liked the name William better. He was William Andrew White IV.

Not a day went by that Billy didn't think about his father. One late August day Pup trudged upstairs to bed complaining of tiredness. Diagnosed as ulcerative colitis, pneumonia claimed him in just three weeks. Eight-and-a-half years had passed. Within a year of Pup's death, Mom had remarried. She was Mrs. Edward Sealy now, no longer a minister's wife but still a deaconess ensconced in church life and the backbone to a large brood, living in the Halifax green-painted home Pup purchased for them at One Belle Aire Terrace.

Billy was married to Gladys at the time of Pup's death, living in the rural county of Guysborough where he taught school and was very popular with everyone, except with his wife, as quickly became apparent. Their marriage lasted shy of eighteen months, no children. He wanted to blindfold the entire experience and wipe their trying tryst from his mind.

Pup had earned a modest living but was able to squeak out the funds to acquire Billy enough education at Dalhousie University to qualify him to teach and undertake social work.

Now long unhitched, Billy considered pursuing that elusive degree, possibly enrolling in night courses to finish what he had started. When he had the time, that is. He and his roommate Harry Zappler were deeply involved in the music and drama goings-on at Dal although Billy wasn't a student there anymore. Their next venture, the Halifax County Youth Council variety show, was coming up in March.

Diving back into the files nesting in the cabinet, Billy found a few program covers from their past two shows. He needed Vivian to see the breadth of his interests and talents. These, he was convinced, would compel her to invest some time and attention in him.

He would enclose a poem too, not frighteningly romantic or maudlin flowery, rather something cute and clever that would trademark him as extra special, not run-of-the-mill. His collection of offerings assembled, Billy searched his desk drawer for stationery and an envelope and set out to write his poetic masterpiece. He laid everything in a pile to his left and took his seat, put a sheet of YMCA letterhead in front of him, uncapped his pen newly replenished with ink, and stared at the blank paper.

Nothing flowed.

He recapped his writing implement and picked up the phone to call George at the store.

"Thank you for calling Fader's, George White, pharmacist-in-training speaking, how may I help you," said the voice before Billy interjected.

"George, it's me. You won't believe whose here in the building: Vivian! She's given me her phone number and I wanted to tell you, man-to-man, that I'm going to work to get to know her better. If there's anything you can do, George, I'm asking for that help."

"Well, her birthday is April twenty-seventh if that's any help, her twentieth," George volunteered. "Her father died when she was eleven. He was a decorated captain who served in the Great War with the 85th Battalion. She has a brother, Bernard. He's fifteen. Their mother works at the Halifax Herald, never remarried. Vivian's very smart and very lovely, a real nature girl. Enjoys art, music, literature, she plays the piano. But as far as anything romantic, Billy, forget it. She's not interested, told me so herself. She has a beau. Dick Hill, an air force fellow. Her high school sweetheart."

"I won't keep you from your work, George. Thanks for your insider information."

His brain performed the equivalent of a gymnastic flip. She was seeing someone, of course she was. A Royal Air Force fellow. Well, Billy could never compete on that score.

April twenty-seven, her birthday: that date would ring an ever-sounding bell within him. That day in 1944 he was officially rejected for military duty because of his skin color. December 1943 had been Billy's second attempt at enlisting in the Canadian forces. The first instance was in 1939. On that occasion they didn't even bother to accept his paperwork. The blanched, fat-fingered desk sergeant at the downtown recruiting office saw Billy's well-polished shoes come through the door, glanced up at his face and said, "You're wasting your time, boy. This is a white man's war. Go home."

A man could have felt slighted that National Defence didn't want his ilk. Pup fought vigorously for the right of their people to join the military. Not Billy. He straightened his six-foot-half-inch, one-hundred-and-seventy-pound frame and with shoulders back, did an *about face* out the door. If the military didn't want him, who was he to argue? One had to be philosophical. This policy was the military's problem, not his. Besides, he was a pacifist. His rejection slip became his passport to pursue his passions: music and people.

During the war years he worked in the house band with the Bill Lynch Carnival, traveling across the Maritimes with a diverse and exotic assortment of circus performers. For a time, he worked at the Census Bureau in Ottawa. He played piano in the burlesque houses and movie theaters in downtown Halifax. It was his venture to the YMCA Embarkation Depot where troops came and went that found him entertaining the boys with his golden-throated tones and smooth piano styling, working as a volunteer. He formed the YMCA band, threw concerts and made a bevy of friends. That's where he and Les met and what led to him being offered his current job back in 1942. Les, the administrative wunderkind who hired him, blew saxophone like a barroom player.

"Back to work," Billy barked to himself, putting thoughts of Vivian aside for now. Wanting style tips for his report, he reached for his invaluable Secretary's Desk Book, a gift from Portia two Christmases ago. Four years older than Billy, she was his *famous* sister Portia. By now he was accustomed to saying that. Her impressive classical singing voice had carried her on a path to stardom like she always dreamed it would. Only six years ago she was a schoolteacher in Africville practically starving herself to afford lessons at the Conservatory of Music on her meager salary. A perennial, province-wide, music festival prize-winning performer, director of her father's church choir and soloist who was practically "born singing", she enthralled listeners. They closed their eyes and forgot she didn't have white skin. And when they opened them, they realized it didn't matter. Prejudice that existed didn't deter her. The White family had been taught to rise above it. Now she was clearly headed for the big time with the financial backing of the city of Halifax and the province of Nova Scotia through a trust fund in her name. New York adored her. International destinations beckoned her. Critics gushed. Audiences swooned.

Portia and he were cut from the same cloth and were tailored for greatness each in their own way, of this Billy was convinced. That's what Pup had always told them. They would blaze trails just as he had done.

They had Mom, Izie Dora, to thank for their inherited musical ability. Pup was a fledgling minister crisscrossing Nova Scotia and establishing Baptist churches for the segregated African communities in Nova Scotia when they met. He was first struck that coincidentally her last name was White too. She descended from a mixed lineage of Mi'kmaq, Black Loyalist and white colonist. Izie's ability to play the organ, pianoforte and to sing beautifully as well as fluently read and transcribe notation was chalked up to a miracle. She was playing at the New Glasgow church when Pup arrived at the newly minted hall. While barely a teenager and living in a mere pinprick on the map, Mill Village, Izie possessed knowledge, ability and poise well beyond her years. Her family welcomed Andrew and the commanding preacher's overtures towards her with an eagerness outmatched only by Izie's longing to escape her rural Maritime purgatory.

She relished the vision of being the young wife of this strappingly handsome, six-foot, lionhearted, mature and temperate man, class president and valedictorian at the American seminary in Washington, and an all-star athlete with the grades to match at Acadia University, a man twice her age.

They were married in 1906, the same year Andrew obtained his naturalization papers. They went on to have thirteen children. Three of them died young.

You could say music was the first product of their nuptials. Izie took to organizing and leading the choir at Andrew's new home church in Truro, the town where he purchased their first house and had it moved next door to the Zion Baptist Church. Half their children, including Billy, were born there. She taught all of them everything she knew about music, enlisted them in her choirs and groomed them to embody music integrally and one day assume her baton, especially Portia. They all sang together as habitually as saying grace. Threads of soprano through bass stitched them together in a glorious weave.

Izie's loving influence cultivated Billy's mastery of musical arranging and harmony. His mind didn't get distracted from his melodic intentions and he could juggle and blend any number of harmonies in his head. He could sing each with equal facility while directing other harmony parts with his hands by raising or lowering them by corresponding musical intervals as dictated, often in opposing directions, while singing a third unique part.

Vivian fancied music, George had said. Perhaps she'd like a ticket to their upcoming variety show at Dalhousie. Billy would speak to Zappler about wrangling up a complimentary pass. As the master of ceremonies and director of two choral groups in the show, asking 'Zap' was a courtesy. Billy knew securing a ticket wouldn't be a problem. If he had to, he'd pay for it.

Billy positioned his chair to face the typewriter, which squatted expectantly on a grey, metal table set up at a right angle to his desk. For the next ninety minutes he typed out his report from his handwritten notes, feeling confident of the end product.

That put aside, he reached into his desk drawer, pulled out a pack of smokes, extracted one, threw the pack back into the drawer and lit the cigarette now dangling from his mouth. He opened another drawer below to find the blue Noritake porcelain ashtray Lois had given him for his birthday last week. He set it on his desk and took a slow, thoughtful draw before placing his cigarette on top of the inlaid geisha painted on the ashtray. His exhale billowed against the large, sunlit windows.

He picked up the phone. "Are you free to go out tonight?" he cooed when Lois answered. She was busy. She was sorry, could they do something tomorrow? That suited Billy fine. He hung up and dialed Joan.

"Hello, Beautiful. How would you like to get together tonight?"

She readily accepted and he, just as quickly, ended the call. But the sudden surge of excitement sparked by the impending tryst with Joan, muted as his gaze fell upon the unfinished letter to Vivian. His thoughts turned anxiously to what he would write next. Ask for a date? Arrange a call? He settled on "Yours truly, Billy White" and his office phone number. He'd mail it to her and hope for the best. Surely, she would call and thank him, and he could land a date with her then, an event that would change the course of history, he told himself.

A rap on the glass window of his open office door snapped Billy out of his momentary reverie.

He glanced over to see Vivian, hand on the brass doorknob, her head poking around the door to meet his gaze. A trim, fair-haired, eager-faced fellow edged in alongside her. He was dressed in a khaki drill, cloth-belted jacket over a shirt and tie, a sergeant's walking out uniform, judging from the three-chevron badge on his sleeve. Dick Hill? Billy wondered. He stubbed his cigarette to relight later and rose to invite them in.

"Well, our meeting wrapped up and we came to see if we could find your office and talk to you," Vivian explained without being asked, although Billy's quizzical eyebrows may have prompted her.

"Not difficult since your name plate is mounted beside the door," her grinning companion said, pointing to the brass 'W. A. White' plaque.

"Billy, I'd like you to meet Burleigh Crozier. Burleigh, this is Billy White. We heard all about you upstairs from Les, Billy, about your musical talents and how you lead group singing and about the jazz band you two are in."

She looked breathtaking in her navy full skirt, cream-colored linen blouse and pocketed red cardigan, a red, wool winter coat slung over her left arm, her fringed scarf housed in its sleeve. Her red lipstick matched her sweater.

Drinking her in, he ushered them over to the other side of his spacious office, half of which served as the resource library and social work hub for the entire staff of twenty during the week.

Billy settled into one of two brown, padded, armchairs separated by a beat-up end table near the wall of floor-to-ceiling shelves crammed with books, files and periodicals. Vivian placed her overcoat on the back of the second chair and plunked herself onto the ample armrest closest to Billy.

A couple of hard-backed chairs completed a circle. Burleigh took one of them, flipped it around backwards and straddled it, facing the other two. A heavy, braided, oval rug lay on the floor under a donated, oval coffee table.

Burleigh cleared his throat. "Mr. White," he said, with a hint of nervousness that Billy found amusing and endearing coming from an army sergeant whose name was "burly," "we and many other young people last year attended our Baptist youth county conference on the theme of Christianity and the youth of today. We were challenged to undertake a report to address their needs and we wondered if we could interview you for our research, seeing as you work extensively with youth."

"First, Burleigh, my friend, you needn't be so formal. If you say 'Mr. White' I'll think you're talking about my grandfather, rest his soul. Oh ...," Billy excused himself to dart to his desk, and in a change of plan, pulled only the Acadia Bulletin from the pile of paperwork. "Speaking of my family," he said, upon returning to hand Vivian the newspaper before resettling himself, "I extracted this from my file for you to read at your leisure. George tells me that arts and letters interest you and I hope that includes history."

It struck a chord with her. "Yes, thanks. I'm an avid scrapbook keeper and current events watcher, and diarist. The printed word and accurate records are important to me." She took Billy's offering, set it on the seat of the chair on whose arm she still perched.

"As for your interview, I'd be happy to," Billy enthused. "How about now?" For the next hour they sat in chairs in a circle listening to Billy speak, captured by the sheer preciseness, eloquence and depth of his answers, as much caught up in the cadence of his diction and delivery as in his insights. Vivian had moved over to occupy the wooden chair beside Burleigh and transcribed the whole conversation in Pitman shorthand with blithe competence, in between a peppering of questions from both Burleigh and her.

Their conversation struck a lull. Vivian flipped through the pages, reviewing her notes. "We forgot something," she said to their host. "We didn't talk about summer camps. I have a special place in my heart for your Camp Owen, thanks to the YMCA and Christian Girls in Training."

"CGIT, Cutest Girls in Town," Burleigh joked. Vivian mimed the action of giving him a jovial elbow to the ribs.

"I went there, and my brother and I went to your Camp Big Cove as well. He'll be working as a counselor there soon."

"Bernard, isn't it?" Billy pinpointed, using his instant recall. "George mentioned you have a brother."

"Yes, that's right. I call him Bern, or Bernie. He's five years younger. When I was a girl, I used his initials B.K., and called him Brainless Killer."

They all laughed. "I went to Big Cove in 1940 and 1941, absolutely loved it! Then we moved on to Camp Owen," she said. "A bunch of us still go to old Owen's Lodge."

Billy saw an opening. This was his turf. He was king of the summer camp circuit since joining the Y staff. There wasn't a summer camp in the region he hadn't visited or entertained. It was his job to ensure camp programming was rich and meaningful.

"Let me flip the tables on you," he said to the two of them, a plan already hatched. "Perhaps at a future time I can interview *you* about how to improve our camp activities. How does that sound? Is this something you could do?"

Burleigh's grin looked almost too big for his face. He and Vivian exchanged looks while Billy focused all his mental energy into penetrating Vivian's thoughts, trying outwardly to appear nonchalant and mask how much her affirmative response would mean to him.

It was Burleigh who spoke next. "Golly, Billy, have you picked the right girl. I'm not qualified to assess camp programs but she sure is. Viv here is never reluctant to give her opinion when asked, are you Viv?" he jibed.

"Who says I have to be asked?" she shot back gently. "Billy, we've taken up enough of your time today, but yes, I'm quite willing to give my feedback. Shall we meet at Fader's after work some day?"

She rose from her chair and as if by levitation the men followed suit. Billy handed her the old newspaper still resting on the easy chair. He helped her with her coat. Goodbyes were extended, a hearty handshake from Burleigh, a gentler, but unexpectedly firm one from Vivian. He would call or write to her to arrange their meeting.

When alone he redirected his thoughts to his date with Joan. He'd go home and change first. Then they could go to the Garden View for a beer and a bite and back to her place after that.

Frequent sex was a sport, a release, but deep-down Billy felt far from fulfilled. He wrestled with feelings of abandonment, loss, guilt and failure and longing to attain his place – his place in life and in love. What role would Vivian play in this dynamic?

Chapter 3

Billy thrust a wrinkled two-dollar bill into his roommate's open hand. There were no free tickets for the upcoming show, not even for the cast, Harry explained from his seat at the cluttered table of their cramped kitchen. "If I do it for you, Billy, I'd have to do it for everyone else who has asked me. The show's going to sell out anyway. We don't have a free ticket to spare."

He sifted through an envelope containing a cache of salmon-colored tickets and found the best among them – Section B Row 7 Seats 3 & 4 – and handed it to his friend.

"This could be the best double-buck I ever spent, Zap," Billy stated, putting his characteristic positive tint on the fact that he had to part with the currency after all. When it came to money, bills and budgeting, he trod the margins frequently and struggled to be prudent with finances. He liked to spend, enjoyed dining out, the nightlife and the clubs. If he ran short of cash between paychecks, he'd borrow short term against his next payday and things always worked out.

The envelope addressed to Vivian in Billy's fine handwriting arrived at her place of work three weeks after she'd last seen him. She extracted the note from within and the pair of tickets to the Halifax Youth County Variety Show fell from the sheaf onto her desk. The note consisted of two pages on Y letterhead.

Page one simply said: "With my compliments. See me backstage after. Billy"

It was the second page that stopped her. A smile rose to her lips in response to the personal and pleasant tone of his cryptic communication, a poem he wrote to the tune of Twinkle, Twinkle Little Star.

> Scintillate, scintillate, globule Vivianic!
> Fain would I fathom thy nature specific,
> Loftily poised amid ether capacious,
> And strongly resembling the gem carbonaceous.

A common nursery rhyme turned on its ear using lofty English and even encoding her name in it – how clever! She got the joke right away and giggled.

For the rest of that day every so often Vivian's thoughts traipsed back to the poem and the man who penned it, little aware that she was playing right into Billy's stratagem, living up to his calculation that his creative flair for verse would have her deeming him a person of interest: intriguing, special. In Vivian's head this was certainly the case now.

One of the advantages of her job at the Wartime Prices and Trade Board was its proximity to the ferry that rolled reliably across the basin to and from her home in Dartmouth. The office was a hilly walking distance to North America's oldest saltwater ferry service, founded in 1752. The ferry was a symbol embodying the classic Maritime experience that Vivian couldn't imagine living without. The fabric of her heart was one hundred percent Nova Scotia tartan.

Vivian walked briskly to the wharf this day, fighting a bitter wind that lashed at her face and jaw. Consuming thoughts of Billy had fended off the bothersome chills her slender frame would usually feel from the cold. The freezing temperatures hardly registered.

Aboard the lumbering Alderney ferry, she decided she would tell mother about the concert, but not about Billy. Not yet. *An omission is not a lie*, she told herself.

Mother was very old-fashioned, a straight-laced survivor: of the 1917 Halifax Explosion, of a fall out of a second-story window as a toddler, of a fence post through the leg in a bobsledding accident that kept her off work for three months, where she lost so much blood the doctor couldn't administer any ether for the pain during surgery, of the jarring stillbirth of her second baby in hospital, and the deaths of her husband and her father within a year of each other. Widowed at forty-three with no plans to remarry, she would remain loyal to Glenn's memory until she died.

With a good job of her own at the Halifax Herald and a devotion to supporting her two children as best she could, Jean Keeler was one determined working mom before such a phrase had been coined.

Prim described her best, everything strictly proper, right down to the cutlery in a place setting positioned exactly one inch from the edge of the place mat, which should be one inch from the edge of the table. Her beliefs were rigid, products of a lineage of pilgrim ancestry traced to Plymouth, Massachusetts from the arrival of a relative on The Mayflower. In Jean's world everything had its place and as the tidiness of her house suggested she insisted that things be put away when one was finished with them.

Bernard and Vivian followed their mother's rules obediently and complied with all her requests. They never caused their mother any real trouble. She had made so many sacrifices for them, nursing them through serious illnesses, first Vivian's year off school with tuberculosis in 1935-'36, then Bernie's polio a few years later, paying for their education and privileges, working through all the moves, precipices, hard work and challenges previously unfathomed when Glenn was alive.

What Jean gave to her children – independence, security and her strong, loving Harlow family roots and respected reputation as upstanding community leaders in rural Queens County, where her father ran a farm, owned a general store and was postmaster for forty-two years – was supposed to compensate for her lack of showing emotion and demonstrable affection. She was a bit of a cold fish. The truth is, when Glenn died, part of her died too. For protection she donned self-control as armor and approached life with a steel spine and a square-set jaw.

Though Jean's dream of Vivian going on Baptist missions overseas did not materialize, she was quite content seeing her daughter steeped in church activities and following her footsteps to graduate from Maritime Business

College and secure a decent-paying job. Not everyone working for the Wartime Prices and Trade Board received a full wage like Vivian. Across the country, six thousand people staffed the WPTB, many as civil servants for remuneration of just a dollar a day. And sixteen thousand women sat as volunteers on Women's Regional Advisory Committees responsible for rationing, labeling, clothing conservation, housing shortages, and price checking. Their work inspired Vivian as she cataloged their endeavors for the archives.

Jean felt certain that Vivian would get hitched to her childhood friend and inseparable high school pal turned pilot, Dick. This was still Vivian's intended direction, although on the ferry coming home this blustery day in March, winds of change were sweeping across the deck. Just like the captaincy of the vessel in which she traveled, depending on conditions, one could never rule out a change of course.

Upon debarkation Vivian was surprised to see a familiar Plymouth truck at the landing as she exited the turnstile. Uncle Roy's 1937 PT50 stuck out like a prized trophy, buffed and burnished and denoting bragging rights and pride of ownership. The vehicle's gold leaf lettering across the side door on a paint job in deep cucumber green: "Keeler's Glass Gardens" encircled by a gold cucumber-shaped outline. As heir to the family's reputed greenhouse operation and now its sole owner-operator, Roy was in discourse with a smallish, swarthy fellow in a toque and sweater coat. They shook hands and the man made his way toward the ferry.

"Uncle Roy!" Vivian called out, hoping he was in earshot. The cold was increasingly biting, and the appearance of her father's older brother couldn't have been more opportune. He was there to pick up special seeds for a new test crop this season. He could give her a ride home. When he dropped her off, he reminded her that as usual he'd see her Sunday to drive her to church. She leaned over and kissed the side of his unturned head, and he told her to take the sizeable burlap bag of hothouse vegetables inside for her mother, who would be jarring relishes for the church's spring sale.

"I don't suppose you've learned to cook yet," Roy quipped. "Nothing fancy yet, Uncle, but I'd *relish* the chance to learn." Her pun elicited a truncated grunt. She closed the truck door, fetched the produce from its wagon, slapped the bumper twice and waved to the rear-view mirror as Roy ambled on down Queen Street.

Dragging the bag behind her, Vivian shunted past the knee-high pine tree Bernie had punched into the ground when they first moved into this rental at number eighty-five, walked the bag up the front stairs where their cat, Pal, was waiting. The house was quiet when they both entered, save for the tick of the clock in the hall, but she knew her brother was home. His badminton racquet was propped up in the corner: he was home from his game. "Bern?" she called out. "Mother?"

"She's not home," Bernard called from his room upstairs. As she hauled the bag of vegetables through the door and into the vestibule, the plunk of his sneakered feet danced down the steps.

"We won!" he burst. "One more and Dartmouth High will have a spot in the team finals. Peter and I qualified for the doubles today."

"That's wonderful, Bern," Vivian exclaimed, as they made their way to the kitchen, she with the grocery bag in tow to channel into a corner beside the refrigerator. She opened the Frigidaire. The cat circled her ankles looking for treats. As usual, Mother had tonight's supper ready for heating in the double boiler. Vivian took out the leftover chicken splayed on the rosebud platter, removed the tea towel, threadbare in spots, that covered it and set it on the counter.

In a small glass bowl, she found precooked potatoes, cut in big chunks. There was a tin of green beans on the counter retrieved from the pantry shelves, a storehouse for Mother's canning from Roy's bumper season last year.

"Mother will be so proud," Vivian enthused about Bernard's game. Looking around for something to do, he washed his hands, grabbed a carving knife from the drawer to his right and started navigating the leftover chicken. As he attacked the carcass, Vivian stood over him supervising, watching that he saved all the bones and fat and wasted nothing. After assembling a nice-looking plate of sliced poultry with his sister stationed like a meat inspector a few inches from his left shoulder, Bernard suggested she sit down and just talk to him since he, not she, was the kitchen ace and, frankly, she was just getting in the way. It was then that she realized that she and her brother hadn't engaged in a good conversation since she started her job, and they settled into a genuine gab. By the time Jean got home, Bernard had steaming food ready to put on warmed plates as soon as she was ready to eat.

Jean said grace after which their conversation turned to the sharing of daily events.

In between hastily chewed bites Bernard recited details of his berth-winning badminton prowess at the day's match, his fork serving as a sometimes prop to help him demonstrate the brilliant backhand shot that closed down the set and the block that stymied his opponents.

"Manners, Bernard," Jean said with a disapproving nod toward his plate.

"Eat then talk," his mother said. "I shall be quite proud of you if you win the whole thing. But don't get ahead of yourself. You know what happened last year."

Bernard sank back behind his dinner plate, the victorious pride he had brought to the table deflated by his mother's dig about his painful squeaker of a loss the previous year. Why was she always so down on him? Nothing he ever did was good enough in her eyes and her Vivian could do no wrong.

He tried a different subject. "My camp contract arrived in the mail today. I've been officially accepted as a counsellor." Again, his mother's reaction was underwhelming. She hoped he would save every penny of his wage for school and not do anything foolhardy with his earnings, and perhaps it was time for him to start contributing a few dollars towards his room and board.

Bernard was ready to heave a long sigh of resignation when Vivian interjected. His talk of Camp Big Cove reminded her of last month's conversation with Billy.

"I've been invited to help evaluate YMCA youth camps and offer ideas for improving them. Bern, you should come along when I meet with the chap who's in charge of the consultation."

Jean was curious. "How did this come about, Vivian?"

"Burleigh and I were approached about it the day we were at the Y for the Christian Fellowship meeting with Les Vipond. Burleigh convinced them I was the ideal interview subject, but I think Bernie and I together would be a perfect team that could provide two sets of perspectives: his and hers. What do you say, brother of mine?"

Her brother nodded and opened his mouth to respond, but Jean interrupted to move to another subject. "Speaking of camping, I ran into Emma Hill at the Poetry Club last night and she tells me Dick's next leave is fast approaching. They're expecting him home by May." Then she added: "I have those wonderful photos of the two of you at youth camp. I can't imagine there'd be much to improve at those Y camps."

"An intramural badminton tournament for starters," Bernard ventured eagerly, clearly revved at the prospect of speaking one-on-one with camp decision-makers. "When is this discussion supposed to happen?" Vivian promised she would arrange a date, then, for her mother's benefit, paraphrased the latest letter she had received from Dick. Home by May eighteenth. Some of his photographs will be displayed at the RCAF Arts and Crafts Fair that they were scheduled to attend together on June seventh.

"I'll be going to the Halifax County Youth Talent Show in a few weeks," she added, but Mother was still talking about Dick's mother so didn't hear her, and Bernie was busy slipping Pal chicken scraps he'd selectively plucked from the platter before Mother scolded him.

"Emma told me they're looking at moving to Lunenburg to a country place with a pond."

It was clear to Jean the news surprised Vivian. "They've come to this decision very recently," she hastened to add. "I'm certain Dick will fill you in when he comes home. Perhaps it's in his mind for the two of you to settle there too." She looked intently at Vivian's creaseless, open face and questioning eyes in search of a clue as to the prospect of pending matrimony. "Would you move there?" she wanted to know.

"I should think there ought to be a marriage proposal before I gallivant into a land of fanciful dreaming, Mother. Since Dick has not proposed, I find it impossible to answer such a question. Of course, if I have news of pending nuptials, you will be the first person I tell, I promise."

Dinner concluded with leftover squash pie for dessert, one of Jean's specialties and still delectable despite the absence of whipping cream, its usual topping, due to wartime rationing.

Plates cleared and dishes done by both children, Jean retired to her reading room at the front of the house. Bernard hit his homework and Vivian ascended to her bedroom and took a seat at her cherry wood desk. She pulled the fashioned brass handle and lowered the slanted front on its hinges to its resting place as her writing surface.

She retrieved her monogrammed VRK stationery from the lower desk drawer and reached for her Waterman's pen – the one she never took out of the house for fear of losing it. It lived in one of the little drawers nestled among the desk's organized inner compartments and cubbyholes.

A piece of paper sticking out from one of the compartmentalized stacks stood out to Vivian as an imperfection and she looked to see what was on the paper before tucking it back neatly in line with the other papers. On the day of Vivian's birth, her mother had recorded the event in brown fountain pen ink on a piece of lined paper taken from a pocket-sized diary. "1925, April 27, Monday. Vivian Ruth Keeler was born today at 10:30 p.m. at Grace Maternity Hospital – weight 7 lbs., 14 oz," read the six-line scrawl. A treasured keepsake, Jean had tucked it in with Vivian's sixteenth birthday card.

Before writing a thank-you note to Billy in her stylishly legible hand-writing, Vivian grabbed a stubby pencil to draft a rough copy.

"Dear Billy." That sounded too personal considering they hardly knew each other. She rubbed out "Billy" and substituted "Mr. White" – too stiff, dreadfully impersonal, he had said not to call him that, she thought, eraser at the ready again. She made "Dear" disappear and wrote, "Billy – just a note to thank you very much for the tickets …" She mused momentarily … "and your wonderfully clever poem, which I shared with the girls at work much to their great impress. I shall be pleased to attend the show. I wonder if I could arrange a time to speak to you about camps. I've asked my brother to join me whenever it is convenient for you to see us, and he is very keen to do so. I await word. Regards, Vivian."

Tomorrow was Saturday. She could mail it at the central post office down the street and pick up the craft show tickets at the military services canteen building next door at the same time. They were in Dick's name at the wicket, his letter had indicated. Sensitive, nature-and-peace-loving Vivian didn't like the expression "kill two birds with one stone" and therefore viewed the next day's expedition as "feeding two birds with one seed" instead.

Chapter 3

Words were important to Vivian. Straight As in Latin and English studies, a childhood immersed in poetry, the reading, memorizing, copying, reciting, chronicling and writing of it, she had "a bug for etymology, as much as for entomology," she once joked to Dick on one of their butterfly-chasing adventures. Growing up, language, literature and the printed word sustained her during her year of illness and solitary confinement; kept her company as she quietly grieved the death of her father as an eleven-year-old; nourished her need for worldly knowledge; and cultivated in her a rich and vivid imagination. She thrived on books. They fed her brain, heart and spirit and she felt blessed that her father, the great scribe and storyteller, and mother spawned and nurtured a love of reading.

Had she ever thanked Jean for the stories read to her every night at bedtime and their time spent together over books, especially during those first six years in the family's Crichton Avenue home in a Dartmouth still so rural that the only friends Vivian had were imaginary ones? She made a mental note to do that.

When her father took ill, she spent more than a year living with her mother's parents in the expanse of farm country. She learned to appreciate and apply the quiet art of introspection.

Gramps and Gram Harlow reveled in the love of knowledge, delight in music, the freedom of exploration and the value of hard work. Vivian inherited it all.

During her formative years she grew accustomed to being alone without being lonely, enjoyed solitude because she had books and encouraging, educated parents welcoming her to the world of reading.

On Saturday after lunch Vivian eagerly went in pursuit of the craft show tickets.

"Vivian!" A sweet voice inside the federal building on Queen Street rose above the general din of crowd movement and the milling of military personnel and civilians. When she spun around, Helen Harvey dressed in a blue tweed coat was rushing towards her, gloved hands outstretched, pillbox hat bouncing in time with her steps, her face brimming with the anticipation of hugging her old friend. "Can you believe the coincidence?" Helen asked incredulously after they embraced enthusiastically several times. "We haven't seen each other since the 1944 BYPU convention and we run into each other here, of all places. What are you doing here? Can we go somewhere to catch up?"

Before Vivian could answer, Helen grabbed her hand and started walking in the direction of a bench against a nude concrete wall. "There's someone I want you to meet."

A strawberry blonde chap in uniform stood up, opened a welcoming arm and drew Helen to his side when she was within reach, hugging her at the waist. She reciprocated by putting a hand on his chest and the other around his back, nuzzling into his shoulder, facing Vivian and beaming.

"Vivian," she said. "Meet Harold Kieran, my husband! Harold, this is Vivian, one of my dearest friends."

"How do you do, Vivian?" Pleasantly stunned into speechlessness, Vivian engaged the two of them in a three-way hug, exulting congratulations and gasping that she could scarcely believe her ears.

"I'm sorry you didn't know sooner, Viv, nobody did. This was all very sudden." She looked up at Harold adoringly. "We just had to be married and now we are."

Harold snapped his fingers. "Like that!" he said. "I proposed, she said yes, we got the license, had the military chaplain marry us, and boom! She's Helen Kieran. Mrs. Harold Kieran," he said with emphasis.

"Harold and Helen," Vivian unrolled their names to test how they spilled off her tongue. "Helen and Harold, no, I think 'Harold and Helen' sounds more natural. And you'll never have to think about what monogram to put on your towels. It will be HK either way." They were all smiles.

"Let's find a place where we can talk," Helen suggested.

"You can walk me over to the post office," Vivian said. "I have a letter to put in the mail. Then come home with me, have some tea and say hello to Mother."

Once they stepped outside, Harold took the center position and invited each of the women to take an arm, Helen on his left, Vivian on his right. He whistled a merry tune and encouraged them to skip alongside him, which they did, laughing breathlessly when they reached the oversized front doors of the grand old postal building. The two of them waited outside while

Vivian conducted her business within. She purchased stamps, affixed one to Billy's letter and dropped it through the slot in the mailbox and exited to rejoin her friends.

Home was a short hop and in no time, they were seated around Jean's table enjoying a cup of tea and conversation with her, in the fancy porcelain cups she insisted they use. While there, Harold fixed the hum in the kitchen clock. Among the tidbits of news that arose, Harold and Helen would be moving to Quebec as soon as the war was over, and they were confident that time would soon come. Harold planned to use his engineering and design background to enter the growing field of electronics, but he was also an artist like his father and a talented clarinetist, an upbeat entertainer whose specialty was serving up silliness on the side including dramatic skits for comic relief.

Helen wanted to start a family and Harold's parents were encouraging them to move close to them in the fledgling town developing out of the farms in Beaurepaire near Montreal. Jean didn't miss the chance to reiterate her hope that Vivian and Dick would soon follow suit. Mother was like a record stuck in its groove.

Vivian couldn't tell Helen about Billy or his poem because Jean was never out of earshot. Then all too soon the guests had to leave to meet Helen's sister. "We'll keep in touch by letter," Helen said to her longtime friend with a hug at the door. Harold gave a rigid salute followed by a wink, and off they sauntered arm-in-arm.

Exactly one-week later Vivian's letter arrived at the YMCA reception desk, in the daily pile the matronly volunteer Mary Collins sorted through. "You have a letter this morning," she told Billy as he walked in near midday.

He retrieved it along with a copy of the daily Globe and Mail, which he made a habit of seeking out as much for its cryptic crossword – a ritual obsession – as for its reports on worldly current events, which he also consumed avidly. In the privacy of his office, he set the paper on his desk, sat down, turned his attention to the letter and opened it.

Vivian and friend Lillian Marks, 1944

Chapter 4

"Well, I'll be." He refolded her note after reading it and tapped it on his open palm a few times before tossing it on his desk. His ruse wasn't unrolling exactly as planned, but at least it had succeeded in drawing Vivian nearer even if it meant her kid brother tagging along.

Now Billy had to arrange a meeting in earnest and make it appear legit. He turned to his trusty typewriter, placed carbon paper between sheets of yellow paper and started to type a memorandum in triplicate to camp director Murray Corbett and registrar Hemeon Smith and a cc: at the bottom to Les. On his way out he would deliver the memos to their mail slots. Would they join him in a few weeks' time when he meets with a few Christian young people to hear their ideas about summer camps?

He made a note in his daybook to phone Vivian at work to set the date, ferreted out the ashtray from its drawer and the pack of smokes from his jacket. His plan was to enjoy a cigarette, linger over the paper, attack the puzzle and then take a walk about the hive that was the Barrington Street building on a Saturday. He would assess how things were running, make notes if required and see if any of the activity leaders needed him for anything, before he took off to pick up his car from Old Man Corrigan's son, Gregory.

Wally Corrigan had owned the garage that for a decade serviced the church vehicle provided to Pup. When young Gregory was beaten savagely by street thugs for his paper route money, it was Pup who visited his bedside every day and prayed for his full recovery, then spearheaded a fundraiser for the teen and his father, a widower. Gregory became a friend of the family after that. In his forties and with Wally gone, he owned the business which he had expanded from the carriage business to auto repairs and auto sales.

He had the perfect car for Billy. "She's not much to look at but she runs perfect," he said of the 1938 Pontiac Business Coupe that Billy was inspecting. "You can have it for what it cost me in repairs, Billy."

As was the pattern in the life of Billy White, wish fulfillment came easily. Whatever he needed in life, he was confident, would eventually materialize. This grand lady of a car, despite dents here and there and mismatched paint, was a perfect example of Lady Luck landing in his lap.

"Sold!" Billy hopped into the driver's side pressing his back against the seat and shifting to make his body comfortable. He rolled down the window and Gregory flipped him the key. The beast rumbled then purred. Engine idling, Billy dug his wallet out of his back pocket. "How much do I owe you, my friend?"

He could still see the diagonal surgical scar etched along the left side of Gregory's face marking the place where the metal pipe had smashed his jawbone all those years ago. He'd lost part of his tongue, which made his speech sound slightly slurred.

"Five dollars a week until it's paid off?" Gregory said as though he was reluctant to charge anything at all.

Billy gave him ten bucks.

"This is a down payment. I'll be back next week with another ten. I'll have the balance to you by May," he promised. "I thank you from the bottom of my heart."

He and his friend shook hands before Billy closed the window and breezed his way home feeling exhilarated. Gee, Lois would be surprised. He would see her tonight and they'd go for a drive.

Across town Vivian was with her best friend Lillian Marks in the art gallery whose window showcased a painting Vivian adored. She had rushed in to put a deposit on it the first time she saw it. Today she was paying in full and taking home the first acquisition of her working life, a watercolor by Nova Scotia artist Emma Smith of trees in a shaded forest, various depths of green, brown, grey, sand and tan, brushstrokes applied in such a way as to give a feeling of movement and stillness simultaneously.

"I just love it," she sighed to Lillian, viewing the painting admiringly in her hands. Her friend agreed. "It's a picture of peacefulness, isn't it Viv?" she replied. "Looking at that I'm in the forest right now. Incidentally, we have to start planning our summer trip."

As the gallery owner wrapped the art in newsprint and tied it with string, Vivian and Lillian earmarked July ninth to twenty-third for their holiday retreat. It was customary for them to spend part of their summers together, a ritual formed through their five years of belonging to Christian Girls in Training and a bond dating back to Sunday School.

On the ferry crossing home to Dartmouth they discussed itinerary details, formulated a to-do list and what they would wear to an upcoming classical music recital. They talked about Dick, and Lillian's boyfriend Ron, and their big group jaunt to Camp Owen which they still had to organize and needed an additional twenty-five keeners to sign up. That reminded Vivian of her upcoming consultation at the Y, and she told Lillian all about going there with Burleigh.

Lillian, a brash, bubbly brunette with a statuesque confidence, a fountain of wavy hair cascading past her shoulders, could talk like a whip, one snappy crack after the next. But she was also a careful and earnest listener who could as readily hear another's story and reflect in silence as she could trade wise-cracks with the soldiers coming off the big ships. She knew exactly when to light up and when to lie back. At this moment she was listening intently to Vivian's description of Billy and his role at the Y.

"Is there more to this than you're letting on, Vivian?" she quizzed. "This is more than just getting interviewed about camps, isn't it?" Her intonation made the question sound like a grilling and Vivian felt guilty for no reason.

"Well, I would like to be his friend," she said defensively. "He seems quite marvelous. Granted he's quite a bit older but he seems so young. I will admit to being curious about him. You know my nature: 'If I'm a stranger ...'"

"'... I'm just a friend you haven't met yet.'" Lillian completed her friend's oft-worn pet expression. "You're very trusting, Vivian. Just be on your guard, okay? I suppose if he's as impressive as you make him out to be, I shall be meeting him soon enough."

"And can render your judgment?" Vivian said, faking sarcasm.

Lillian laughed. "Just call me 'Your Honor'." Her father was a practicing lawyer.

When they disembarked from the ferry Lillian suggested they stop at the church and post a notice recruiting candidates for the summer camp retreat while the project was still fresh in their minds. So, they hiked up Ochterloney Street and invaded the Christian youth office at First Baptist to put together a bulletin board poster and sign-up sheet. After posting it, they were content to call it a day. They parted ways with a wave as Vivian made the short walk home. Her turn of the front doorknob synced with her mother's opening of the oven door to remove a sizzling casserole. Jean heard stirrings in the hall. "I'm in here, dear," she called out as she set the dish on the stovetop and tossed aside her bulky oven mitts.

Vivian greeted her mother with a half-hug, her right hand still clutching the newly acquired artwork. She unwrapped it on the kitchen table and handed it to Jean to examine. Jean held it in front of her at arm's length and hummed a note of approval before quoting the chorus from "Song of Nova Scotia":

> We love the sea-tang and sun and mist,
> The forest paths and wood-folk trails;
> Arbutus land, the land we serve
> With loyalty that never fails

"Where first the dawning sunlight gleams, of wooded hill and fruitful vale," Vivian sang a few bars. She took back the painting. "I'll put this in my room. Then I'll come down and set the table. Where's Bern?"

As if on cue the brother bounced in. "I'm home!" he trumpeted. Roy had corralled him into helping at the greenhouse, manual labor that he hated not because of its arduousness but because the penurious uncle never paid him a penny for it.

Bernard presented himself to them in the kitchen. "Smells good," he said as he came in to kiss his mother hello. "I'm starving. I'll go wash up, be right back down."

It was his turn to say grace. He dispensed with that task in short order, facilitating his immediate desire that food make haste into his mouth with a "Thank you, God" followed by a forkful.

His mother clucked at him. "Could you make it any briefer, Bernard?" she admonished.

He looked up from where he was bent over his plate. "Thank God?" he offered cheekily. Jean was not amused. Vivian stifled a laugh.

"We take our faith seriously in this household," Jean lectured. "Grace is not something we skip through lightly."

"I'm sorry, Mother," he said. "It's just that I'm famished and the way I see it, I've done my charity work and service to the Lord today by unselfishly helping Uncle Roy at the usual rate of pay – two grunts of thanks."

Vivian bolstered his protestation. "Mother. Let's talk about something else. What's new at school, Bern?"

"Our class is doing a project on the Halifax Explosion," he said, "in advance of the thirtieth anniversary. Mother, I wanted to ask if you could help me with the research since you lived through it, which amazes me. You were there December sixth, 1917, when two thousand people were killed, nine thousand injured and everything demolished within a half-mile radius of the city." Bernard recited the facts he'd memorized like a newscaster. "A collision in the narrows of Halifax Harbour between SS Mont-Blanc, a French cargo ship laden with high explosives, and the Norwegian vessel, SS Imo caused a fire that blew up the equivalent energy of roughly 2.9 kilotons of TNT," he said while plugging his nose and cupping his mouth to mimic a voice coming from a tinny radio.

Jean lifted her hand like a crossing guard signalling him to stop. He realized that his theatrics had transported her back to that dreadful day and he felt badly when he saw her face cloud. She put down her fork, wiped the corners of her mouth with her napkin before speaking, her voice lowered to a hallowed hush.

"The explosion to me still seems like a nightmare. You felt so cut off from everybody and then you started seeing people cut and in horrible conditions;

then a bad storm started. I had been boarding with The Turners in the North End close to the worst hit area, so there was no point in going there. I went to live with a naval couple, and they opened their home to another young couple who had lost their home and everything in it, the wife badly hurt and pregnant.

"It was all very ghastly, so many eye injuries, cuts by dirty glass. I was shocked to death.

"It was my shoulders and one hand that were cut by flying glass in our office building as I was in the act of hanging up my coat with my back to the windows. I looked around and saw the bookkeeper with blood streaming from his eyes but, like my injuries, his turned out to be not too serious. We tried to phone our relatives and friends, but it was hard to get anyone out of town. They were trying to get through to me from North Brookfield, with no success, and just walking the floor and wringing their hands according to some of Elsie's tales.

"They erected quarters on the Commons for people. I think they were more than just tents but tarpaper shacks or something like that."

"I'm sorry, Mother," said her somber son. "I didn't mean to be flip. How lucky we kids are that you survived!" He reached over the table to find her hand, which was cold and spindly.

"Lillian and I were at the church this afternoon, planning for the big camp excursion." Vivian thought it was time to change the subject but mentioning the church triggered more memories in Jean.

"The original church was damaged beyond repair in the explosion, and Mr. Bezanson worked hard to get the present stone church built," Jean recalled of the minister who was the father of her childhood best friend and the pastor in North Brookfield before moving to Dartmouth.

"Your father was in France at the time of the explosion. He wrote to your Nana Keeler about it. I have his letters. After supper I shall find them for you, Bernard," she promised. "I'm going out with Annie, Mardie and Gladys tonight to see Roy's new pump organ and hear him play it. You're welcome to come."

"I'd rather look at Father's letters, honestly," said Bernard, trying not to wince at the thought of spending the evening with Uncle Roy and the ladies:

his stately Aunt Gladys, the childlike "Aunt" Annie, mother's childhood friend, and Mardie, the persnickety unmarried friend of the Keeler family, who completed the women's social foursome.

"Say hello to Aunt Gladys and the others for me," Vivian said. "I'm going to hang my picture and I'd like to have a look at those letters too, Mother. Bern, do you mind? Can we look at them together?"

Of course, Bernard welcomed her help on his project. It would guarantee him an "A."

The letters from Europe during the First World War from Captain Glenn Harlan Keeler to his mother, Rosa Meina, now hid under blankets at the bottom of the linen chest in Jean's bedroom. Until the evening's dinner table discussion, she hadn't thought of them in years, but she thought of Glenn every day. She hoped her children would experience love as deep as theirs.

Before leaving by taxicab for Roy's, Jean had placed the parcel of *Dear Mother* letters tied with a magenta ribbon on her bedside table.

Seated shoeless on the bed with his sister, workbook at the ready, Bernard cherry picked to find the pertinent ones from December 1917 and January '18 and soon was reading aloud the words of his father:

> Everyone here is talking about the explosion that occurred in Halifax. We got the news through the continental edition of The Daily Mail. The account in it says that a boat was rammed in the harbor and as a result of the explosion, Halifax and Richmond are in ruins and flames – no mention is made of Dartmouth, so I suppose and hope that it was not touched but then again, the paper says that all communication is down for thirty miles around. I do not believe one-half of what the papers say so you will have to write me an account of it. I am very, very anxious to learn what has happened and hope you were far enough away to escape all injury.

Vivian piped in, "Indeed there was widespread damage in Dartmouth," she told Bernard. "An entire community of the Mi'kmaq First Nation in Tufts Cove was wiped out by a tsunami caused by the blast."

"A-plus," Bernie thought, upgrading his imaginary mark as he made a note of what she said in his workbook. He went to the next letter, dated January 5, 1918.

> My dear Mother,
> How anxiously I am waiting for your next letter can better be imagined than described. The last one that I had from home was dated December 2 from Gladys. Of course that was before the explosion – now the next one ought to tell me something about how you fared. I have seen the casualty list and am glad to say that there was no mention made of the name of Keeler – but then lots of things may have happened to property that I may not know about, but time will tell.

Bernie reached for the next letter from mid-January after Nana Keeler's reports from home had caught up with Glenn.

> I have seen towns and cities over here absolutely levelled to the ground after weeks of shelling – to imagine such destruction being done in the twinkling of an eye is very, very hard to imagine even by us over here who have seen and heard a few explosions that were by no means small. What a trial it must have been for you to have had all those people at the house, but still, poor people, they were absolutely homeless.

"Father was an empathetic and caring person, very kind," Vivian said wistfully. "How I wish that he were still alive. He died so young."

Bernard's only memory of his father was a rotten one.

"He took me to a Remembrance Day ceremony. I was five. We were outdoors and it was freezing. When we got home, he pulled down my pants and gave me a hard spanking on my bare bottom for not standing still during the proceedings. That's all I remember about him." His face flushed as he recalled the incident.

"He loved you a great deal, Bernie," his sister assured him. She'd heard this story before. "I'm sorry you missed knowing him. You have to consider that perhaps the brutality of war may have played tricks with him emotionally and disturbed him psychologically to a certain degree."

She changed the subject. "That spanking can't have been as bad as the time you got the strap at school," she half-smirked. Typical Vivian – muting the pain of one bad incident by reminding him of something that would bother him more by comparison.

"That situation was completely unfair," he asserted indignantly.

In Grade Five he'd been off school sick when the announcement was made about a new rule: Students could no longer leave their classrooms to drink from the hall water fountain without permission. Back after a two-day absence and unaware of the new policy, Bernard exited his room to quench his thirst only to learn that a sip from the fountain merited a corporal punishment. The sting of injustice was capped with the belt-wielding principal's words, "I can't believe I'm strapping Vivian's brother!"

"You *would* have to bring that up," he said to his sister dryly. She could be so irritating at times, but he knew she didn't mean to be and would beg ignorance with wonderment if told she was.

They returned to the letters and their father's vivid accounts of military life with the storied 85th Battalion, taking turns reading select excerpts. From the same storage chest Mother had ferreted out their father's handwritten memoirs of the Great War, which he had penned in a diary from his hospital bed in the Kentville Sanatorium before eventually dying of tuberculosis, a consequence of repeated exposure to the enemy's mustard gas.

Vivian left for a while to fetch a hammer and tack and went to hang her new picture. She took his diary with her to her bedroom to read later.

When she came back Bernard inquired about the meeting with Mr. White. He was satisfied to hear that Vivian was waiting to confirm a date and they agreed four-thirty in the afternoon seemed to be a reasonable time for both.

Vivian began organizing by date the letters they'd already consumed. Bernard continued to explore the others, spouting out a choice paragraph or two when he found something colorful, unusual or funny. Eventually they called it a night, retied the bundle and laid it on top of Jean's nubby bedspread for her to put away.

"I marvel at the importance and value of these letters to our family. They reveal and preserve so much." Vivian remarked.

Mother's father, their grandfather "Moss" Harlow, managed the mail service in North Brookfield for more than four decades, and was a committed diarist who kept a lush and articulate daily record of life in the county from 1877 to 1935. So, the printed word carried weight and reverence in the Harlow Family. From girlhood Jean had a picture of a typewriter tacked to her bedroom wall where she could look at it every night before going to sleep. She idolized the idea of learning how to work one, and at sixteen finally did, at the city college.

While not the most affectionate or emotionally invested mother, Jean demonstrated her love for her children by nourishing them with stories, surrounding them with books, encouraging poetry reading, writing and recitation. Harlows were intelligent people, she would stress – smart, skilled and studious. She forgot to mention stubborn, an oft-joked-about family trait. Harlows were also deeply committed to their faith, which went without saying.

Vivian clipped poetry from newspapers, using glue to cement it in workbooks. She copied out copious favorites in longhand. She assembled collections of cut-out postmarks and stamps, saved train and bus ticket stubs and, along with her poems and greeting cards, post cards, memorabilia, and significant clippings, protected them in albums, some might say obsessively, but voluminously would be more accurate.

When Jean came home from her night out, she and Vivian talked while Bernie was moved to wash the kitchen floor after checking no one needed anything in there.

Mother had burrowed through many a pain in her fifty years. Three of her siblings died young. Brother Laurie died at Passchendaele, buried up to his neck in rubble with shrapnel through his head. Willis, ever the brooder, went to Gogama, Ontario to work as a mine supervisor. The family was never fully convinced that his death by gunshot to the head was self-inflicted, but word from there absent an investigation deemed it a suicide. Sister Hattie, a military nurse who moved to her husband's New Zealand to marry him after the war, succumbed to an incurable muscle-wasting disease, leaving him a widower with two young girls under the age of eight.

If there was one thing Jean was used to it was pushing through pain. Vivian felt sorry for her mom and did everything she asked, obliged her at every turn. But Jean didn't ask for much, obedience to God's laws was her only given.

These days, things were much smoother for Jean. No upsets, finances and budgeting were sound, good health, injury free touch wood. Soon she could move the family back to her matrimonial home on Crichton Avenue, which she'd been renting out since Glenn died, an arrangement that soon would be ending. Jean was tired of bouncing around from move to move, first for three years to Roy's on another of the Keeler family's Crichton properties, where she was his housekeeper in exchange for room and board for her and the children, then to Mrs. Abbott's on Annandale when her old job at the Herald opened up, and now here at Queen. She'd be glad to complete the circle and get back to their spacious house on the hill overlooking Lake Banook.

Who knows? Her daughter could be Vivian Hill by then. This evening though, she determinedly bit her tongue and held back another inquiry since Vivian had promised her that if Dick proposed she would be the first to know.

Ten days later Vivian and Bernard were face-to-face with Billy and his cohorts, Hemeon and Murray, in the YMCA boardroom, Billy at the helm of the long table, Murray, the camp director, and Hemeon, the registrar, covering opposite flanks like his wingmen, Vivian and Bernard side by side examining pamphlets spread out on the table, pencil, paper and clipboard in front of them. Bernard had come prepared. He'd been thinking about this for weeks and he was pleased he'd be able to present his ideas, such as the addition of badminton to the activity list, directly to the people who could influence and implement decisions. Vivian concentrated her interest on the brochures, sketched some new layouts, suggested new wording, updated the language, fixed the typographical errors, branded the camp "A Summer Holiday Resort" in a boldly drawn font and proposed new pricing packages for large youth groups like hers. She also offered to design a feedback form and circulate it among senior campers she knew, and then mused about finding a way to bring the camp experience to children and youth who couldn't pay, maybe through a scholarship. Billy's officials were impressed, felt the dialogue had been worthwhile, gathered up the materials, said good day to the young parties and headed back to their offices. As Bernard and Vivian stood up to leave, she remembered something in her handbag.

"Careful, open it gingerly." She emphasized the last word as she handed Billy a folded envelope. He opened it to reveal what looked like shaved chalk. He looked at the contents, then up at her. "Ginger?"

"Special ginger powder from my Uncle Roy, it's good for the stomach. Add it to boiling water. We found some in his larder."

"And" she said, waving a paper at him extracted from her purse, "I'm returning the news clipping about your father. Thank you. Absolutely fascinating. Now I guess we really should be going."

"Listen," Billy said, trying to play it casual, "I could give you two a lift."

As it turned out Bernard was headed to the library. He begged off and parted on his own.

Billy turned to Vivian, "Well, 'you need a lift?" He was finding it hard to keep from appearing anxious and was relieved when she said yes.

"I have to pop home to pick up music for my band rehearsal later tonight," Billy said. "I just live over on Gottingen Street. Then I can drive you to the ferry or home, or wherever you're going, that is unless you want to go get something to eat."

There. He'd said it. His delivery felt natural, but he was nervous. The badminton birdie was in her court. This was the first time he'd ever braced for rejection. He never worried before about an overture of his being spurned. Now here he was suspended in time, seconds stretching like canyons, until she said, "Yes, let's."

Billy grabbed his hat, ushered her to the parking lot and to the passenger door of his awaiting Pontiac, which he had named after his maternal great grandmother Taylor. "Meet my new car, Mary Ann," he announced proudly as he opened the door for her. She used his forearm to steady herself as she climbed in. Vivian laughed. "That sounds like a song title."

His and Harry's place was a short hop away. Billy didn't always bring the car to work. He drove in that day on the miracle prospect that Vivian might be free to linger after the camp consultation, one which ended up being surprisingly useful and making him look like a genius to his peers.

The two-bedroom, second-floor flat was in a stretch of North End buildings that accommodated businesses below, sheltered by awnings and walkups above. There was a barber and hairdressing shop marked by a blue, red and white pole next door and a pub on the corner. Three Navy guys were hanging around outside when Billy coasted to the curb and parked. They eyeballed him as he helped Vivian disembark and as the two began walking toward the trio. The tallest sailor, a freckle-faced carrot top with a shifty demeanour, was forming his lips in a sneer and speaking loudly to his uniformed friends. "You know what they say about a Pontiac," he taunted when Billy and Vivian were close enough to catch the scent of his alcoholized breath. "P-O-N-T-I-A-C: Poor Old Nigger Thinks It's A Cadillac." Snickers. They were past the loudmouth at this point, close to reaching the door of Billy's building.

"Vivian, you wait here for just a moment," he said calmly, and he circled back to the aggravating trio. The surly, marmalade-headed sailor was weaving back and forth, opening and closing his hands, shifting from one foot the other, looking itchy and edgy as he saw Billy coming his way. Vivian stood her ground for about five seconds before deciding to quick step behind Billy to catch up and witness what was going to happen. She feared an altercation as she watched him stride up to the sailors.

"Excuse me, gentlemen," he said. "I couldn't help but overhear your comment." He reached for some mimeographed pamphlets from his inside suit jacket pocket and handed one to each of them, which they studied. He introduced himself. "I run the programs for servicemen at the YMCA here in Halifax."

With that, he launched into an eloquent sales pitch for the upcoming servicemen's dance at the Y and completely took them aback when he invited them to attend. He reminded them there was no cost. It was a popular event with the local girls. Refreshments would be served. He told them his father had been honorary captain in the Great War. He retold a few of his favorite stories about servicemen he had met through the Y and soon had the sailors relaxed and laughing. Looking straight at Billy the instigator of the initial unpleasantness unexpectedly apologized for the slur. They shook hands.

Vivian and Billy proceeded to the front door. Backs turned, they missed seeing the tall sailor form the thumb and forefinger of his right hand into a circle and rapidly thrust the index finger of his left hand in and out of it in a lewd gesture as his buddies chortled and grabbed their crotches in a locker room pantomime. The chubby one let some spit fly.

Harry was home, partially barricaded from view by textbooks on the desk in the front room where he was studying. He looked over the stack and snapped to his feet when he saw Vivian following Billy in. "Vivian Keeler, the illustrious Harry Zappler. Harry this is Vivian, works over at the pricing board. She'll be coming to our show," Billy said.

"So, this is who you got the ticket for," Harry deduced as he welcomed the guest. "Well, I look forward to getting to know you better, Vivian. But you'll both have to forgive me for now. I'm up to here." He gestured with a flat hand raised above his head. "It's reading week."

An Austrian student in England when the war broke out, Harry was interned as a "friendly alien" and shipped to a guarded internment camp in New Brunswick in the summer of 1940. He was one of the "accidental immigrants," the more than three-thousand refugees — among them twenty-three hundred German and Austrian Jews aged six to sixty – who were sent to Canada and incarcerated alongside actual prisoners-of-war, including Nazi Germans who menaced them with threats routinely, promising to cut their throats once Hitler won the war. On Harry's release in 1942 he resumed his studies at Dal to be an orthodontist.

"I'm just here to pick up my music for tonight. We'll be out of your hair soon," Billy promised.

Vivian barely had time to survey their kitchen – neatly kept for two bachelors – than Billy was ready to leave. She asked to use the phone, called her mother and told her she wouldn't be home for dinner.

Walking to the car Vivian spotted a paper on the ground. She bent down to pick it up. It was one of Billy's pamphlets. One of the sailor's had littered it. "Two out of three ain't bad," he said to her, referring to the fact that only one of his three handouts had been tossed. She went to hand it back to him. He shrugged. "Just throw it down," Billy said. "It creates a job for someone."

"Not on your life," said Vivian, who was taught to conserve and not waste anything. She tucked the littered leaflet in her bag as a candidate for her scrapbook, a memento to mark, not just her dinner out with Billy White, but also her inaugural encounter with a blatant demonstration of racial prejudice.

Young Vivian with her father Glenn and brother Bernie

Chapter 5

"How can you carry on as though nothing happened back there?" They were seated at a booth in a restaurant a block away. Billy had donned his round, gold wire-rimmed spectacles to study the menu at The Dolphin. Vivian was reflecting on the ugliness of the drunken sailor's remark.

"I'm not going to let a trio of inebriated anchor-clankers ruin my day, especially when it's going so well being here with you. I have never known discrimination in my life. That's not to say I haven't come upon some ignorant individuals from time to time."

She was unconvinced. "I expected you to sock him in the jaw." She was certain Dick would have, had he witnessed the event.

"I don't believe in violence," Billy countered. "It's no solution."

She agreed. She was a pacifist too. He continued his reasoning.

"I've seen racial discrimination poison its perpetrators and its victims. I can't ignore it. My fists won't solve it."

"Imagine this," he said. "I take a swing at the big guy." He cocks a fist and pantomimes. "All three of them pile on." He shields his face, elbows up, in mock defense as the enactment continues. "Let's say they rough me up and you summon the police. They come, they arrest me, throw me in jail, and you're without a ride to your ferry. Vivian, all things considered, I'd rather fight racial prejudice with psychology."

She laughed despite the seriousness of the subject. He was funny. His lively hand gestures and play acting animated his dialogue. She continued to probe the Pontiac remark.

"Let me say I'm very sorry and I apologize for the conduct of those boys. I think it was very brave of you to confront them. You handled yourself professionally and kept your cool, maybe even changed a mind, but just as easily you could have been seriously hurt, as you point out, and I'm not talking about hurt feelings."

Billy adopted his fallback, carefree stance. "Bah! Those fellows proved that from the biggest mouths come the minutest of thoughts," he quipped. "Mark my words, I'll see those boys at the servicemen's dance, and they'll be no trouble, no trouble at all."

He broke into song, a hushed but lively round of a beloved folk song, "What shall we do with a drunken sailor..." and had her laughing more, music to his ears. His voice, pitch perfect and mellow, lilted with the dynamics of the melody, hers, thin but well-tuned as she timidly joined in the singing.

"Have you decided what you'd like to order? Oh, hi Billy." He was a regular here. Deborah, the waitress waited, notebook ready and pen cocked. He settled on the house special, chicken vegetable stew and a Coke and Vivian said she'd have the same, no soft drink: they already had ice water pre-poured and sweating in the twin glasses in front of them.

"When I was a teacher in Guysborough, the community and all my students referred to me as 'The Reverend'. My pulpit, I discovered, was my voice – talking, singing, teaching or public speaking. I could use my voice in all of these ways to make a difference."

Vivian was listening intently. Could it possibly be that racial discrimination had never affected Billy as he was swearing the case to be? How could this be true when a hotel like the Lord Nelson was a whites-only place, unless you were hired help using the back entrance; when theaters had colored-only sections; when help-wanted signs in store windows barked "No Coloreds" and the only job a man could get was that of a railway porter or dead-end laborer? From the community layout, Guysborough might as well have been segregated.

He steadfastly maintained that discrimination had never held him back, personally.

"I'm two generations away from slavery, Vivian. No one's going to push me backwards."

Of course, discrimination existed, and these policies and beliefs needed to be challenged and changed, Billy conceded. "If you don't say something about it, they'll claim it doesn't exist."

"That's why I got involved in politics and joined the CCF party. And, Vivian, I tell you, I feel particularly at home there. Whoever you are, whatever your background, in that party's vision there is solidarity around social justice and equality for all. I sense you are of the same ilk."

The idea of judging someone based on skin tone was ludicrous to Vivian to start with. Fascinated as she was with a world comprising many countries and cultures, she naturally accepted there would be differences among its people. When her father first took sick in 1931, and she lived on the Harlow farm with her grandparents for a year and a half, she remembered Gramps hired his farmhands fairly on merit, not on color bias, and paid them all the same. He respected and did business with the local Indians and wrote about them glowingly more than once in his columns in Gold Hunter Magazine.

Despite operating in a whites-only world Vivian grew up with a broad world view, entertaining new people and ideas with an open mind. From the Latin and the Greek, she understood that "prejudge" and "prejudice" stemmed from the same root. "You can't judge a book by its cover," her father used to say. She took the expression to heart and lived by it.

How sheltered a life I've had, she thought, as she heard Billy describe the abject poverty jutting out above all else in the distinctly colored communities of Africville, Lucasville and the city's North End, where his father ministered, a catchment area Billy now served through his job at the Y. She hadn't given the question of race any deep thought until it hit her in the face less than thirty minutes ago.

As the meal arrived and they dug into their steaming crocks of mostly vegetable stew, she encouraged him to keep talking about himself, and Billy was only too willing to fulfill. She wanted to hear more tales like the ones he'd spun to the sailors about playing music for the soldiers at the Y and the friends he's made.

He reached for the salt and pepper, sprinkled his stew and between bites rattled off an anecdote about Jimmy the drummer laughing so hard he fell off his stool, an entertaining story made even more interesting when Billy said, "He was laughing at my good friend Harold Kieran who was seated on stage playing clarinet and wearing a head of curly endive lettuce as hair."

Vivian's ears perked up.

"I know Harold Kieran," she exclaimed. "He married a good friend of mine. I ran into them in Dartmouth not long ago, had them to my place for tea."

"Helen," Billy supplied the name. "Fancy that. I played at their wedding."

They marveled at the incalculable coincidence of it all.

He found discourse with her incredibly easy and surprisingly candid for a first sit-down. She'd drawn so much out of him already: the death of his brother and sister barely into their teens and little baby Milton, Billy being left behind in Truro temporarily to live with Charlotte Moxon while the family relocated and settled in Halifax, his riotous growing up in a home overflowing with siblings, his disdain for his mother's second husband. Vivian skillfully coaxed his life into the open by interjecting a few well-placed inquiries of interest. Their age difference meant nothing to him, evaporated in the space of the tabletop that separated them. She was the most beguiling girl he'd ever met.

"Enough about me, Vivian," he decided. "Let's talk about you. I'm intrigued."

She was a Taurus, steadfast, (he a freedom-loving Aquarian). A self-described "child of nature," she preferred rural life over city life, considered beautiful Nova Scotia her forever home. Although reserved, she loved to be at the center of things and frequently orchestrated occasions where that could happen, always projects on the go. Losing her father so young – a terrible pain – she learned to embrace solitude walking in the woods every day. She fancied herself a poet and wrote and kept a diary. She told Billy about living with crusty Uncle Roy for three years, her mother serving as an unpaid housekeeper before re-securing her old job, triggering a long-hoped-for move out.

Billy learned what they shared in common. They were both Baptist.

Both their parents' families were large, and the kids grew up spending as much time with family as they could. A bounty of aunts and uncles, Vivian rhymed off their names and brief descriptions as if she expected Billy to pass a quiz afterwards. Another commonality, they were both fatherless, losing their dads around the same time, and both understood feeling abandoned: Billy as a toddler for those three months in Truro missing his family in Halifax, Vivian not yet a teen keeping the stiff upper lip at her father's funeral.

They both loved music. Musical tastes for the classics and jazz, their favorite songs, popular and folk, were virtually identical coincidentally. They shared a loathing for Al Jolson, his musical thievery and his painted black-face mockery of the Negro person. Vivian sang in a choir and tried to put at least one hour a day into playing the piano. She was a proficient reader and avid collector of sheet music. Their favorite poet currently happened to be Odgen Nash.

"I'm sorry my boyfriend isn't here to see your variety show next week," Vivian said out of the blue.

Somewhere in his imagination Billy heard the faint pop of a proverbial bubble bursting. "Tell me about him," he said in a marked effort to sound interested. After her plethora of positive descriptors about Dick had tumbled to a stop, she predicted they would all meet that summer at the Christian youth camp week that she and Lillian were organizing. "You'll meet my best friend Lillian even sooner. She's using the second ticket."

She reached into her handbag as the waitress delivered the check. Billy wanted to pay but Vivian insisted on going Dutch. "This isn't a "date". I have to be stay true to my boyfriend. You do understand?"

Billy didn't protest. He let her plunk down her carefully calculated half, the clunk of coins dull, like his hopes, his fantasy fading fast, feeling futility with the forlornness of a vanquished knight.

"Alright, have it your way." He checked his watch, time to go. He didn't want to be late for practice.

"Come on, I'll drop you at the wharf." He helped her on with her coat. A rush crept up his neck from the electricity of being close to her as she slid her arms into the coat sleeves. What was happening to him? Lust was no stranger to him, but the accompanying inward tickle more suited to a giddy, little boy caught him off guard. *Get your head out of the clouds, White! Holy mackerel, give your head a shake.*

When Billy opened the door for her and a stinging shot of early spring air burst in, they missed a pair of cold stares piercing their backs, judgmental clucks and disapproving whispers that followed them out the door.

"See you at the concert," were his final words to her before she climbed out of his car at her destination, and he roared off to join the band.

. . .

The gymnasium was buzzing on the big night when Vivian and Lillian arrived, behind schedule because Vivian wasn't ready on time as usual. Most of the crowd was already seated and leafing through the six-page mimeographed program. The girls had time to steal away to the ladies' room to powder their noses and touch up their lipstick before finding their section downstairs in the hall, squeezing past two pairs of knees to reach seats three and four with minutes to spare before the curtain rose and Billy strode on stage to a rising rhythm of applause. He hadn't told her he was emcee! An array of acts awaited the audience's sampling, divided by two five-minute intermissions. Every number shone and Billy was magnificent. She could hardly wait to tell him so backstage. He commandeered the crowd with a robust "Good Evening," ever the captivating host, witty, poised and well-spoken, and the variety show "Featuring Youthful Talent of Halifax" was rolling.

Vivian was pleased to see Harry Zappler brandishing a baton for the "Dalhouse" Glee Club – misspelled in the program, Vivian noted among other typos, which she corrected with a pencil while Lillian went to scope the lobby during the first intermission. Then she studied the program further, reading up on the Halifax Youth Council's origins and mission.

"The general purpose of each group is to plan for the post-war welfare of young people."

"The primary function of the Council is to act in the interests of young people, through investigation of problems, which affect the young especially, and through recommendations which will help to bring about an improvement in existing conditions."

She liked the sound of that.

During the second intermission Vivian and Lillian hiked to the lobby to stretch their legs.

"I'll be going backstage afterwards to say hello to Billy," Vivian said casually.

Suddenly Lillian blinked hard, and her head gave a slight shimmy. "Is this the Billy you and Burleigh met with at the YMCA that day?" The penny dropped: eyebrows raised, she realized the Billy hosting on stage in front of her was the guy from the Y, one and the same, a man she had presumed was white-skinned.

"You never told me he was colored!" Lillian's phrase reduced to a whisper so none among the throng would hear as they milled toward the double entrance doors on their way back into the auditorium for the third and final act.

There wasn't a single moment of the show Vivian didn't enjoy from the moment the Halifax Conservatory Orchestra sounded the opening of a Gilbert and Sullivan medley to the two choirs' joint performance of "United Nations on The March," which was a particularly uplifting and hope-filled closing that had conductor Harry on the podium mimicking full flight, leading up to its crescendo finish. Then everyone stood and sang "God Save the King."

The show wrapped up, hoots and applause showered the performers as they all crowded the stage to take their synchronized bows, Billy White and Harry Zappler fronting the chevron-shaped cluster. Vivian thought Billy's gaze settled on her momentarily as he lifted his bowed head.

She and Lillian remained in the gym to allow patrons to thin the hall. The beginning of the third act had interrupted their conversation about Billy's race and Vivian wanted to set the record straight.

"I wasn't trying to hide Billy's skin color from you, Lillian. To be honest, it just slipped my mind. I shouldn't think the tone of his complexion would be particularly relevant."

She was feeling slightly defensive, and Lillian could sense it. "Hey, Viv, everything's jake. It's not like you're going to marry the guy or anything!"

Stragglers and volunteers aside, the gym was empty. The steps up to the stage seemed to point them to the source of a din of assorted shrieks and laughter and indiscernible babble. Coats on, the two women threaded their way up, through chairs and music stands pushed to the wing. Vivian tripped on some coiled rope but recovered by bracing herself on a fortuitously placed lectern.

Lillian pointed to the propped open fire door and yawning hallway beyond it. The festive sounds, spontaneous bursts of song, giggles and hand claps, a weft of violin lines, flute bursts and trumpet shots, sounds of the after-party wafted from the inner sanctum. "Shall we?" Traditionally, Lillian led. Vivian, the shy one, would be a couple of paces behind. Tonight, Lillian's hand gesture said it was Vivian going first.

Her walk down the hall was slow and hesitant. Lillian ushered her forward like a nanny pushing a baby carriage. There were three doors on their left, all open. The first was the make-up room not in use. Next to it the music rehearsal room, a hodgepodge of blue velvet-lined instrument cases lay gaping on the floor. Coats hung three-deep from brass hooks on the wall. A table housed the overflow.

A flautist cleaning her instrument saw them, smiled and pointed, "Party – that way."

From the final open door, a party atmosphere wafted. Vivian summoned her most confident air, grabbed Lillian by the arm and pulled her into the lively room with her.

The room was jammed, obscuring their sight line. "We're looking for Billy," Vivian enunciated into the ear of a girl wearing a tunic sporting a Bloomfield High School crest. She pointed over a sea of bobbing heads. "By the far wall."

Lillian was waylaid by a table offering punch glasses full of Kool-Aid and patterned porcelain plates decked with sugar cookies and shortbreads. She melded into the lineup of takers waiting their turns while Vivian jostled her way through the chatty celebrants closer to the front of the room.

She could see him now, his tie loosened, and suit jacket open, appearing far less relaxed than anyone else in the room. Instead of rushing up to him, she paused and observed, camouflaged by a small grouping of people in front of her. A small nest of choir girls thrust programs out for his autograph. He indulged them.

A woman stood next to Billy looking striking in a tight-fitting, hot pink satin skirt and a blouse with a river of ruffles encircling the neckline and running down the front. With silver bangles on both arms and in her ears, her extended nails in polished maroon pawed Billy's shoulder like a black cat needing attention. From her gestures, directing autograph seekers, she was acting like his manager. Her coal black hair had the curl ironed out of it, pulled back tight on her head and a bun topping it. Billy didn't appear to be enjoying the vibrant woman's fussing.

His eyes furtively scanned for a sighting of his invited guest. She was partially obscured behind a group of people, but then he thought he caught a glimpse of her in navy and white. Their eyes locked fleetingly. His pleading gaze cast in her direction, he held his place, frozen, as if bound by unseen ties. Vivian pretended she didn't see, gave him a look as one would give a horizon, turned and went back to where she'd parked Lillian, who was having a grand time chatting up Harry Zappler.

"Hello, Harry." Vivian had joined the ensemble.

"Harry was telling me about his internment," Lillian raged. "It's awful what you endured. You were persecuted," she decried.

Vivian idled up to the crumby cookie tray and salvaged a few broken remnants. "I have to diverge from this somber subject to say I enjoyed your choir very much Harry. I sing, read and play myself but nowhere to the degree of excellence that your group put on display for us. Congratulations."

The diminutive maestro clearly delighted with the praise and the change of subject, threw his arms open to Vivian. "So nice to see you again, Vivian, when I'm not buried in books. You can see what I look like below my eyebrows," he laughed. She viewed his visage now – slick brown hair, no part, bushy eyebrows, a square face, a large arched nose and a broad smile.

"It's good to see you too, Harry. I'd like to invite you all to my house sometime. We have a piano you can play."

Vivian looked at Lillian. "You ready to go? We don't want to miss the ferry."

Her friend agreed and Harry bid them a good crossing and continued to mingle.

They hadn't made it to the cloakroom before Lillian asked, "Did you speak to Billy?"

"Actually, no," Vivian replied. "He appeared to be …" she paused, "occupied. And then I lost my nerve."

On their way to the ferry Vivian described what "occupied" meant. Lillian bit her tongue. They talked instead about the concert and its inspiring message of looking to the future. For them it would involve marrying their sweethearts and having children, never losing touch. Their lives would revolve around the CGIT motto: 'Cherish health. Seek truth. Know God. Serve others.' The Allied boys would come home victorious. The war would end.

April twenty-seventh, Vivian's twentieth birthday, fell on a Friday night. Dick wouldn't be home for this one, soon though. In another year, peace achieved, they could concentrate on writing the story of their lives as one. His leave was imminent.

When June rolled around and they were reunited, she and Dick were taking a break from the RCAF craft show and sale where his pictures won judges' choice; there was an expectation hovering at the front of Vivian's mind. They huddled at a small round table, he drank her in, rubbed his thumbs across the tops of her hands that reached across to his, a look of deep purpose in his enigmatic hazel eyes.

"You know I've loved you since the beginning of time, Viv," he said. The ring finger of her left hand seemed to be getting extra strokes. She was sure that his next move would be to relinquish his hand patting for a dive into his pocket. He'd flip open a velvet covered jeweler's box; a small diamond would wink at her and her answer to his question would be "yes,"

Little wings beat across her heart.

His hands stopped drifting and clasped her fingers firmly.

"Viv, I don't know quite how to say this, so I'll just go ahead and speak from my heart." She leaned forward thinking that however he said what he had to say, it would be followed by a kiss. "I'm not ready to get married. I think we should wait." She sat back.

Dick's rationale made perfect sense to the pragmatist in her. He wanted to complete university, get himself established in teaching or weather forecasting, he wasn't sure which, and to save before they settled down. His plan did appeal to Vivian, although not enough to cushion her hurt feelings at that moment.

He saw her partial pout. "Hey, kiddo. Nothing's changed. Never doubt for a minute that I love you. I don't want to rush our marriage. I want to prepare so that I can be the best possible husband to you when we do marry. Trust me, Viv. We'll be glad we took our time." After his soliloquy he sought a kiss and she felt better after delivering one.

• • •

By June Billy was going out of his mind. Since the variety show there'd been no word from Vivian, not even a thank-you note. He knew she had enjoyed herself. Harry had been quick to mention seeing her that night and how enthused she was.

"Didn't you two talk?" Harry was only now quizzing him about what happened that night.

"It was complicated. Lois was there and Lois is the jealous type and Lois and I are in a rocky phase right now and …"

"So, your answer is 'no,'" Harry countered. "Look, Billy, that girl Vivian is too good to lose track of. It's been ages since the show. You've got to figure out a way to meet her again, find an invitation she can't resist. You'll think of something."

How long had it been since his wisp of a sighting of her in that crowded party room? Only an eternity could stretch longer, he figured. The buzzer to their flat hummed him into real time and he surged down the stairs to answer the door. A uniformed CN attendant thrust forward a special delivery envelope for Mr. W. A. White. He asked for a signature and Billy obliged with his best scrawl. Unable to wait until he climbed the stairs, he tore into the envelope and was delighted with what it contained – a note from Portia. His sister was singing at Dalhousie in just over a week. Enclosed were two tickets. Thank you, God! Billy bolted up the stairs two at a time.

"Zappler, you're a conjurer," he beamed. "Here's the irresistible draw you were recommending – second row seats to a Portia White concert on June eighteenth." He waved the tickets like a fan. "And Lois won't need to know a thing about these. I'll just say I'm with my sister that night."

He swore Harry to secrecy. Done. Lois was too cloying and superficial a dame in Zappler's opinion. He felt his roommate and comrade deserved better even though his girlfriend was a dish, no two ways about it. Like Billy, she had been married before. Her husband died in a hunting accident barely a year into the marriage. An investigation concluded that he had slipped in a creek, which caused his firearm to accidentally discharge, killing him.

Billy couldn't wait for the work week to start. He had a reason to phone Vivian now, and he couldn't get his finger to the rotary dial fast enough come Monday morning. Her office switchboard connected him. "Good morning, rental division." The unmistakable voice warmed him like soft angora. "Ah, Miss Keeler. It's Mr. White speaking." He hadn't planned to begin with such formality, and it sounded a little ridiculous when he heard his words aloud. At least he could obtain a read of her temperature this way. If she was open to his call, she would respond using his first name and suspend the formality, he reasoned.

"Hello, Billy." Bingo! He cut to the chase. "I have a spare ticket to Portia's concert a week today. Will you honor me with the pleasure of your company?"

She lowered her voice. "I can't talk long. They've changed the rules around here. Best we mostly communicate by letter from here on in."

This was a hopeful sign. She was ruminating about continuing to correspond with him. Interesting.

"Vivian, I'm sorry I didn't get to speak to you at the show back in March. I'm hoping to make it up to you with this concert ticket. Please give me the answer I want to hear." And she did.

She consented readily. Plans quickly solidified. Their call ended. He was over the moon. Vivian's self-esteem was surging after the dampening it weathered during the letdown date with Dick. In a week she'd be hearing and meeting Nova Scotia's darling of classical song fresh from New York City in the company of the singer's tall, dark, handsome brother.

Promptly at six on the Monday of the concert Billy came to pick her up in "Mary Ann", which he spent part of Sunday afternoon polishing with extra elbow grease. His second-hand automobile sparkled as best it could as its driver glided the car to the curb in front of Vivian's workplace, saw her waving at the entranceway, smiling as she made her graceful approach. Summer's warm wind whistled up her skirt as she walked down the stairs, creating a billowing effect under her slip and patterned full skirt, accented by a form-fitting, almost sleeveless peach blouse and a lacy wrap over her arm. Their plan was to go out for dinner first.

Ever the organizer and strategist, Billy had rehearsed what he would say about Lois if Vivian asked. Maybe he was being presumptuous for imagining the subject might emerge. Oh, she looked lovely. It suddenly struck him that this was the first time he'd felt this level of excitement since he landed his job at the Y, and that was a different kind of excitement. The very vision of Vivian stirred him. Her presence beside him in his car was an awakening of a sensation long buried. Uncharacteristically, he was dealing with something beyond his control, and it was richly delicious, exhilarating and life affirming to feel swept up by this personification of wonderfulness sitting next to him.

They were going to Nanking first for Chinese food. Billy did all the ordering after checking for any food aversions – none. He took control as was his routine with every girl he brought here. His dates always seemed entertained by his finesse with navigating the menu, and Vivian was no exception, if you could call her a date. Billy still wasn't sure.

Soup was followed by steamed rice, vegetable stir fry with chicken, sweet and sour shrimp and an egg roll. They followed their food adventure to the final grain of rice pudding and the last sip of green tea. The conversation was spicy, never dull, nary a lull. Her laughter was pure and unforced like a spring brook.

Vivian told him about Dick and their deferred wedding plans, acting as though it was a mutual decision.

However, Billy saw a door opening, regarded the postponement as an opportunity to step up his pursuit of her, but slowly, delicately, so as not to scare her. Vivian he would handle with care, "too good to lose" in Harry's words.

He asked for her review of the variety show. "Did you enjoy the concert?"

"I enjoyed it a great deal," she said. "I was going to speak to you afterwards, but I saw you were busy and …" She changed gears, "was that your girlfriend?"

"I've been a bachelor for nigh on nine years waiting for the right woman to come along," Billy said. "I was married once before," he volunteered. He was skirting her question and her silence spoke to her desire for an answer.

"I was with Lois that night," he acknowledged. "Lois Jackson, a beautician friend of mine."

"She looks like a pretty good friend," Vivian exclaimed in an open-ended way. "I really didn't feel right about interrupting the two of you. Your interactions seemed quite intimate."

"I doubt we're as close as you and Dick," Billy countered.

Her eyes seemed to bore into his soul and read it like the current month's magazine. He might as well have been lying on a psychiatrist's couch. She was his truth serum. Nothing was secret anymore, everything out in the open. There were traits in Lois he loved, but she wasn't his be-all-and-end-all. He was a wretch, a lout, for not being willing to give her up, for leading her on, stringing her along while knowing deep down there'd be no long-term future together.

Pompously he convinced himself he had to stay with Lois because it would be too hard on her to lose him, a great justification for biding his time until the right girl happened along. Then he hoped to settle down. He wanted to be sure he wouldn't fail his second time around. Lois didn't give him that certainty.

The check arrived. This time Vivian made no attempt to pay her portion of the bill.

On the way to the campus in the car she told him about turning twenty and then over-estimated his age by two years, which ruffled his vanity. "I'm thirty," he told her.

"My mistake," she apologized. "I'd be very ill-suited for a job as an age-guesser at the carnival."

Portia's concert was glorious. The ambience in the gymnasium was quite different from Vivian's visit there in April. Then it felt folksy. This evening there was an air of opulence. Vivian felt underdressed as she surveyed the women in the mixed crowd in their flowing sleeveless satins, summer organza, fancy hats, fascinators and ornate costume jewelry, although they were the ones looking out of place in the stuffy gym, high heels navigating a basketball court floor.

Attendance far exceeded the turnout for the youth variety show. It was standing room only tonight, chairs densely packed in impeccable rows and lining the walls under the banks of immense arched windows climbing up the twenty-foot ceiling. The rafters were full. Like a work of crowd choreography, patrons fluttered their programs to fan their faces and move some air around the stuffy room.

A few dignitaries delivered speeches first. The mayor issued a welcome and there were brief words from the event sponsor, Nova Scotia Talent Trust, the foundation established by the city and province to fund Portia's career.

Someone ordered the unplugging of the fans on stage. They groaned to a stop as the accompanist assumed his position. The smattering of applause for the pianist suddenly swelled to a crest to greet Nova Scotia's chosen child. Portia took command with a repertoire spanning four languages and a tasty platter of classics.

At one point during "May-Day Carol" by Deems Taylor her note was so full, clear and bold the power of its reverberation against Vivian's rib cage caused her to jolt. Her hand clutched Billy's forearm in a state of involuntary thrill in reaction to the soaring vibrato of his sister's richly shaped high E.

He waited to see what would happen next. She let her expectant hand rest on his suit jacket sleeve. His sister's music was moving through Vivian and drawing her closer to him, a seductive lure that he answered by enclosing his warm, eager paw over hers and holding it there until the end of the song.

Thunderous ovation subsided, and the paper's music critic departed to file his review while patrons continued to mill about. Bill and Vivian didn't stay to greet Portia backstage – Billy would be seeing her at their mother's the following evening. He had a long drive ahead of him to get Vivian home by car, going by way of the winding roads around Bedford Basin.

The drive through the hills and long shadows of bough-filtered moonlight created an atmosphere of unintended romance in both their minds. Uncharacteristically he took his time driving, wisely. Marked by candid disclosures, personal secrets and revelations dialed up during the dark ride to Dartmouth, their night was enhanced by the exchange of trust building between budding friends. By the time he inched up near, but out of sight of her house, his urges were overpowering.

He turned his car off. Neither of them moved. Billy, looking straight

ahead, said "I'm sorry you couldn't meet Portia this time. There's another recital the first Thursday in August, same location. I'd like you to be my guest.'

He turned to look at her beautiful face, smiling, head nodding. She'd
like that very much, she said. She wasn't attempting to leave, and in that
instant, his manly compulsion took over. "Vivian," he said lowly, in a gentle
growl.

"Yes?"

"I have this incredible urge to kiss you." Her smile, her slow-motion lean
forward towards him, lips parted ever so slightly, eyes closed, she welcomed
him. His lips savored hers, drank in their softness with thoughts of strawberry nectar and wild honey during one determinedly sensitive kiss before
their lips slowly broke apart.

"I'm sorry," Billy said. "I couldn't help myself. Maybe you better go."

Somewhat stunned by what she had allowed to happen Vivian fumbled
with the door handle. When extricated and standing she looked at him
through the open passenger side window.

"You didn't tell me the date of Portia's concert." She could hardly formu-
late a sentence because a tickle in her solar plexus was making her breathless.

"Thursday, August second, but you'll be hearing from me before then!"
He was flying high. He was light-headed and happy. Vivian was the embodi-
ment of the music he heard in his head. Maybe he will write his next song
to express how he felt right now.

After a hasty goodnight, she walked the block home aware that Billy was
still parked there watching her. It had been his decision not to park directly
in front of the house, partly to spare her being peppered with questions when
she got in the door and partly to protect the tender gains he had just made
establishing a bond with her.

Vivian concentrated on the sound of her footsteps treading the pavement
and hoped her legs wouldn't buckle and send her sprawling. She didn't look
back and wave. It was all she could do to put one foot in front of the other
after his all-consuming kiss.

Once inside the house she made a direct beeline for her bedroom and got
ready for bed. Bernie, in the living room curled up with the cat on the sofa,
was absorbed in a book and didn't look up. Seated in front of her vanity table

and three-way mirror she stared at her face, cheeks tinged with rosiness, eyes with added sparkle. She touched her lips with her thumb and forefinger and traced the imprint of his kiss. Mother was in bed already, thankfully. One look at Vivian and she would know something was up, the flush crawling up her neck an indicator of stimulation, like a thermometer measuring heat.

A solitary kiss from Billy carried the impact of one hundred from her reluctant fiancé. It lifted her to a higher plane. She loved Dick Hill dearly. Yet, in this moment on this evening, she felt her love discovering new facets. That her love capacity was greater than realized was an unexpected revelation and not necessarily welcomed since it led to an accordion of complications. First and foremost, she still had a committed boyfriend, but now this statuesque, striking man with a dimple in his chin was in the wings poised and triggered to make his entrance.

She tried multiple times to create a moving picture in her head – her confessing to her mother that she'd kissed a colored, older, divorced man on the lips. But the scene always ended badly no matter how many times she reran it. While she couldn't keep her secret forever, for now, mum was the word.

Billy's father William "Andrew" White in uniform

Chapter 6

W hen Billy next telephoned Vivian at the Wartime Prices and Trade Board it was in response to her timely thank-you note. As they connected on the line, he was abruptly reminded of the leash on office girls lingering on personal calls.

"I hate to give you the brush-off. Could you drop me a note? Bye." These few words were just enough to quell his need to hear her voice. His reply on Y letterhead arrived postmarked Halifax with a timestamp of "Jun 25 1:30 a.m. 1945 N.S." Over lunch at her desk, she read it privately and was coming to grips with the fact that she had a problem most girls of her age would never face. Her new friend was older, he was divorced, he was from another race, and she had to acknowledge the memory of his branded kiss and the feelings for him that dogged her.

My dear Vivian,

May I ask you a few questions, although my common sense tells me I'm being unfair to ask them?

What has happened to me to make me feel, in spite of my knowledge of existing circumstances, that just seeing you, even if only for a few minutes, is a strangely, pleasantly disturbing experience? Why should I find myself thinking of you in terms of the reason for my wanting to express myself in poetry? Why should I want to tell you that I think you're wonderful?

This is very important, too: When shall I see you again?

Vivian, if I make this any longer, it won't be a note, it will be a letter. And you did say a note, didn't you? So, I'll stop right here.

Sincerely,

Billy

"What are you reading?" The query was coming from Vivian's office mate Peggy Evans. While "none of your business" was the first response that Vivian contemplated, she was too polite and collegial to behave in any way that would be perceived as disrespectful to a colleague. "Is it from that colored pal of yours?" she nosed. Her neck craned to see the notepaper Vivian was sheltering from her view.

"As a matter of fact, it is," she said. "We're pen pals." She turned her attention to her lunch pail after tucking Billy's letter in her desk drawer. Peggy wasn't ready to let up.

"Let me see," she badgered. "What flowery words is that boy laying on you now? They're only after one thing, you know. They're animals. You're naïve if you think otherwise."

Vivian pursed her lips. "Apparently you've had no exposure to the Negro race," she stated matter-of-factly, heels digging in, "or you'd know they are just as human as you and I."

Peggy scoffed and countered with a retort that tested Vivian further. "If I want to see a darkie, I'll watch an Al Jolson movie. Anything I need to know about Negroes I can get from a minstrel show."

Vivian was appalled although not yet rendered speechless. She squared herself in her chair and took aim at the remark. "Peggy, Al Jolson is a horrible mimic who only found success after he put black polish on his face and ridiculed another race. Ruby Keeler, the Hollywood dancer and movie star who married and later divorced him, is a relative of mine. According to family stories he was a monster to her." She paused. "We are all equal in the eyes of the Lord."

"Sure, we're all equal," snorted Peggy, unrelenting. "It's just that some of us are more equal than others. Look, Vivian. I didn't write the rules, I just live by them, and you should too. Likes stick together. That's all there is to it."

Vivian was relieved to see her supervisor Ellen appear at that moment, her presence ever the leveller. The contentious conversation had its wearying effect and had gobbled up most of Vivian's lunchtime. Peggy instinctively slunk back to her desk.

Throughout the afternoon Vivian harnessed the anger that Peggy had fomented to speed through a stack of typing, her flying fingers producing a flurry of sound patterns from the striking keys, the return bell and carriage return. Typing, for Vivian, was an escape, a time when she could read and transcribe from the raw notes yet allow her mind to mull. She burrowed through all her assignments and helped relieve some of Ellen's backlog before quitting time.

Billy, Billy, Billy: his name like an alarm clock she couldn't turn off. She recalled Peggy's crass comments. Testing Billy's advice she had engaged in a dialogue with Peggy, not that she reckoned it had done any good.

She retrieved Billy's letter and reread it at her desk, then tucked it in her purse. The idea of resisting his overture was akin to asking an orchestra conductor not to turn to the next page of the score. She wrote a response suggesting they could go for a drive to Point Pleasant Park or for a walk through the public gardens in Halifax after work before she boarded the ferry home. She indicated he could call her at work any day between noon and twelve-thirty because Mr. Jacks in the executive branch, the proponent of the ban on personal calls, and its only enforcer, took his break then.

A daytime rendezvous with Billy would be all she could squeeze in as summer rapidly engulfed her calendar. Ellen would allow Vivian an extended lunch, on request, to compensate her for readily volunteering extra hours without pay to help with whatever task came along.

Vivian's datebook was burgeoning with trips, club meetings, church and family obligations, CGIT special projects – in particular, the Victory Garden, the wartime effort to grow fresh food to supplement rations, reduce pressure on the food system and boost civic pride – and most pressing of all, the youth week at Camp Owen. She and Lillian had it all lined up – twenty-five Christian youths heading to St. Margaret's Bay at the end of August under the special group rate they had secured through Vivian's newfound connections at the YMCA. Twelve girls, thirteen boys, separate lodgings, of course, but co-educational activities. More immediately she and Lillian would be vacationing in New Glasgow and then Charlottetown on Prince Edward Island in less than two weeks. Dick had been called back to his station in Labrador: weather monitoring. His parents hosted a farewell dinner for him.

Vivian's workplace datebook drove home to her that with twelve days until her holiday departure there was insufficient time to arrange to meet with Billy by mail. Instead, she rustled up the courage to telephone him at his office near the end of her workday.

He answered. She cupped her hand around the mouthpiece of the clunky handset to muffle her voice from any outside ears.

"Hello, Billy?" was her soft overture.

"Are you whispering?" he asked.

"Yes, I'm keeping my voice down because I don't want Mr. Jacks to hear and scold me for it, but I would like to set a date with you to discuss the questions you raise in your letter, Mr. White, because I am due to leave for my vacation in little more than a week," she said, adjusting her posture, dropping her secretive demeanour and finishing off the sentence in a bolder voice.

"That's more like it," he coached. "Your private, after-hours call needn't concern the national trade board. You're entitled to reasonableness. We're not breaking any laws."

Maybe it was her guilty conscience, undue concern about workplace spies or disciplinary measures, but Vivian couldn't quite relax on the phone with Billy. She quickly rattled off three possible meeting dates, to which he replied, "Why not all three?"

Two days later Billy presented himself at 77 Upper Water Street. Such a beautiful day, radiant in every way, he thought as he whistled by the front steps and waited for Vivian to appear.

She obtained special dispensation from Ellen to overstay the limited lunch period and enjoy the splendid afternoon as payback for unpaid hours.

Peggy could barely conceal her resentment. "Are you going out with your Sambo?" she needled when everyone else in the office was out of earshot. Vivian ignored her. Clearly Billy's way – talking it out – hadn't worked with Peggy. Vivian remembered his approach of not letting other people drag him down and she applied his wisdom of not taking it personally where poor Peggy was concerned. She wasn't worth ruining one's day. The important people in my life would never be like that, Vivian assured herself as she rushed past her colleague to meet a waiting Billy and a Maritime summer breeze that cleared the air of anything but positive thoughts.

They walked to the public gardens, Halifax's prized patch of flora, stopped at a hot dog cart and purchased two sizzling dogs with a generous ribbon of mustard and onions for him, none for her. A camera dangled from Billy's neck, often an accessory since photography was a hobby. Today he brought it to snap staff profile pictures for the Y newsletter and was glad to have it on hand. Vivian was pretty as a picture. She knew a great deal about art and literature, he discovered as their frankfurter summit progressed. He learned about Wallace MacAskill the Maritime photography pioneer, Emma Smith, a remarkable female in Nova Scotia's art world, the history of Maritime folklore, indigenous stories from Lake Keji – absorbed her fascinating fountain of fresh facts.

It was time for a walkabout. Always with two clean handkerchiefs on hand, he offered her one for wiping away mustard from the corners of her mouth. She felt foolish that she'd been talking all that time with a mustard blob on her face and now she apologized for the yellow spot on his linen as she handed it back to him, knowing that mustard stains.

Calls of "Hi Billy" peppered their jaunt. It was commonplace wherever he traveled to be stopped by someone he knew. Vivian felt she was in the company of a celebrity, his popularity reflected on the enthusiastic faces of the people they encountered on their stroll and who wanted to shake his hand and chat. With every greeting he made sure to introduce her as his good friend. His power of name recall was quite uncanny, she noticed, and his magnetism was intense.

Vivian luxuriated in the free time she had earned from Ellen, feeling no pressure to hurry. Billy injected so many extra hours into his career that no one questioned his timetable. Every weekend through to September was booked for camp tours, weddings or church work. Regrettably he'd be out of town when Vivian and her gang were berthing at Camp Owen. Maybe next year.

He found himself inexplicably reveling in her knowledge of wildflowers, in the silliness of hearing her recite all the floral names to him in English and in Latin as they passed each species in their various beds. At one particularly lush floral display he asked her to pose for a few snaps. Looking up from behind the viewfinder as she fit herself into the frame before a bounteous rose bush, illuminating her optimum smile, he said, "I don't know whether I'm photographing Vivian in a field of flowers, or a flower in a field of Vivians!"

Inside he felt ecstatic. She was doling out a hope that he could win her over.

"How's Lois?" Reality came knocking.

"I imagine she's as well as your fiancé," Billy replied. Vivian didn't pursue the topic further.

Their next rendezvous was over a soda at Fader's. George was working the store, popping back when he could. Surveying Billy and Vivian on side-by-side stools, he could see a relationship had progressed between them. They leaned into each other when they spoke. Billy was still showing off like a peacock in mating season. Big brother Billy – bewitched, and who could blame him? George harbored a worry in the back of his mind, though. Was she destined to be one of Billy's many conquests? Somehow Vivian being one of them was unfathomable.

Every dialogue between the bonding pair exposed another fascinating facet or coincidental commonality. They both possessed a zeal for etymology, word play and solving crossword puzzles, particularly the cryptic kind, but there was Billy going one better yet again – he designed his own cryptic crosswords from the creation of the hand-drawn diagram to the invention of all the clever clues and the placement and insertion of their solutions. Vivian was awed and impressed by the original puzzle he gave her to solve, but not stumped by it, and this, in turn, impressed him.

Over a snack they talked about their mothers. Vivian started that conversation by asking Billy what his was like. If how a man speaks about his mother is a test of character, Billy passed. He adored his mother. To hear him describe her she was a loving, earthly angel, his biggest believer and booster, an even more impactful example to her children than their legendary father.

They all worshipped their mother, giver of their first breaths, sharer of her inexplicably advanced gift of music, possessor of a golden voice that thrilled to the marrow, seamstress of the harmonic threads that held them together and which distinguished them as a family of note.

Mom was a shoulder, an ear and a backbone, the glue, the able teacher, the giving hand, consoler, counsellor and comforter, who stayed strong throughout many trials and pains without hardening, made a place at the meal table for the hard done by and the hopeless, trusting that the family's scant cupboard always would render enough sustenance to feed all in need, loaves-and-fishes style.

Too bad she hadn't prayed a little harder before remarrying, Billy bemoaned. He thought his mother remarried too soon and made a poor choice. But she had her security to think of, he supposed, and Mr. Sealy was handy, as in convenient, if nothing else. He had been a tenant at Belle Aire in what they called the Little House, a barn-like structure out back behind the Big House. He didn't have far to travel to consummate the relationship. He was a CNR linen clerk, a widower, who married for the first time at forty-three.

He pursued Izie by sneaking up the back staircase, according to Billy. In his opinion his mother deserved so much better than a man who could never hold a candle to his father.

Edward Sealy, sixty-eight, a native of Barbados, served as a sergeant in Pup's No. 2 Construction Battalion. Sealy was oddly morose, withdrawn and distant, difficult for Billy to be around, he told Vivian. Perhaps he had experienced an undermining incident during his time overseas. Billy remembered Pup citing an example of the racial prejudice commonly inflicted in Canada's segregated military.

A riot broke out between No. 2 Construction Battalion personnel and a group of CEF (Canadian Expeditionary Force) infantrymen after a white soldier made a racial remark. The white unit had stepped in front of No. 2 Construction soldiers who were waiting their turn in the bath line. Sgt. Sealy ordered the man arrested for his comment. A sergeant-major from another unit ignored Sealy's orders and instructed the offending soldier's buddies to break him free. "And all hell broke loose," said Billy. "They attempted to remove him from the guard house. A riot broke out and a number of soldiers ended up in hospital. Sealy was humiliated and degraded, but he wasn't written up."

"You need to feel empathy for that man," Vivian told Billy.

The topic switched to Vivian's mother, whom she described glowingly as "strait-laced, hard-working, good-hearted and devoted, from a large family descended from arrivals on the Mayflower."

"White as the driven snow," Billy said. "I wonder what she would think of you being here with George and me." He wasn't expecting Vivian to answer, and she didn't. She'd been asking herself the same question. Mother tended to be critical anyway.

Whereabouts in Africa is your family from?" she wanted to know. It was one of those rare occasions that forced him to say, "I don't know."

"It pains me that I may never know," he replied. "Slaves had their origins ravaged and histories erased. In Richmond a fire wiped out records up to the mid-nineteenth century. Whatever records there were went up in flames. But thank you for that question, Vivian. No one has ever asked me that. I've only ever regarded myself as Canadian. I do speculate about my fate had slavery never happened. Most certainly I would not be sitting here with you, and that would be classified as a great modern tragedy."

He saw his remark had pleased her then launched into his paternal grandparents' story:

They lived on an active Civil War corridor in Virginia. King and Queen County saw frequent activity since it lay on the route from Richmond, the capital of the Confederacy, to Gloucester Point.

"When my grandmother Isabella and grandfather Andrew were freed at the outset of the Civil War, with the help of their former owners they shepherded themselves and their six children out of harm's way to an island some sixty miles to the southeast, Mason Island off the coast in Mathews County, where they lived safely throughout the war. There the mistress of the household taught the Whites' eldest child to read, who in turn taught literacy to all his siblings since neither parent could read.

"My father was the first of their eleven children to be born free," Billy said. "Remarkably, none of them went to an auction block. His family remained whole, was spared the forced separations and slave auctions of those terrible times."

New freedom for Andrew and Isabella enabled them to purchase and assemble three hundred and thirteen acres between 1870 and 1877. A farm and enduring homestead in the county, it was a springboard for a White family legacy of community builders made up of secure, confident and well-grounded offspring.

Andrew Sr. was a skilled tradesman, builder of the finest homes in Richmond, a carpenter, a gardener, woodworker and coachbuilder. He took pride in his station, co-founded a church and became its first deacon and treasurer. A servant to his faith, he lived the example. When Isabella's former slave-owner fell on hard times and came to call, they put him up and fed him.

"When I consider what my grandparents achieved in spite of slavery and how they conducted themselves, I have to believe no barrier can impede me unless I let it." Billy paused.

Vivian felt tinged with regret that she could trace her lineage back ten generations and Billy – only three. But as she knew from the plant world, from cuttings spring new life and roots can re-establish themselves even when hidden.

From family, the conversation turned to future. Billy revealed that he could read tea leaves and minds. Vivian gave him a cute, sidelong look. The mention of tea reminded him to tell her that her gift of ginger had worked wonders on his sour gut, and he thanked her again for it.

"I have studied numerology," he said, staying in the psychic vein. "Looking at the numbers, Miss Keeler, I can tell you it is no accident that we met in this year of 1945.

According to Billy this was a *one* year. He found his pen and something to write on, and scrawled: 1+9+4+5=19, 1+9 =10, 1+0 =1.

He was cupping his hands over an imaginary crystal ball and looking into her skeptical face. "The year 1945 has a value of one. A *one* year is a time for new beginnings, a time for progress, for pioneering and new ideas, self-determination." Vivian waved off his reading dismissively.

"Hocus, pocus," she said, feet-on-the-ground type that she was. Secretly, though, she admitted to being intrigued, beyond just the amusement of his numerology notions, to know what the future held for her.

"My mother would call it 'the Devil's work,'" she laughed.

"You would do well to look into numerology," Billy told her. "The letter 'V' is the most powerful letter of all – number twenty-two in the alphabet – and you have two of them in your name. That's special," he said, raising his arm in a flex. "In Keeler, you also have a 'K,' the eleventh letter and second most magical. Someday I shall do your numerology chart. I read tea leaves, playing cards and palms as well." He reached for hers, studied the open palm she presented into his waiting hand, turned it to better investigate its creases, and made his pronouncement.

"I see a new man in your life and big changes coming." Vivian quickly withdrew her hand and looked pensive.

George came to join them, quipping, "Don't let him feed you that malarkey."

He and Billy swapped news about their siblings: most notably Portia's concert in August (George and his new girlfriend Elsie would be going), word from Mildred in Sandusky, "baby" Lorne's latest athletic achievements on the high school basketball court, Jack's struggles with Mom and Sealy.

Their familial candor made Vivian feel like part of the family. She looked at her watch and realized they'd have to leave soon or wait around for the next departing ferry.

There was no kiss goodbye when he dropped her off this time. After his palm-reading comment at the store Vivian had signaled she wanted to keep things casual, and Billy dared not push the boundaries. Their goodbye was warm and pleasant. He was in no hurry. Inevitability would catch up with her.

The next time they would see each other was for his Music Appreciation Night at the Y two days before her holiday with Lillian.

The piano room at the Y was also the reading room in the boy's department. A beat-up lectern, with a folded piece of cardboard wedged under the front foot to prevent it from rocking, stood to one side of a table housing a phonograph and a half dozen phonograph records generously provided by Billy's acquaintances at nearby Phinney's Music Store. Billy's personality and his entertaining, skillful communication style made him easy to like and therefore a superlative acquirer of donations.

An ornate but abused upright piano had its lid open awaiting hands on its keys. Tonight, a healthy crowd, about seventy, each person paying ten cents to be there.

For Vivian it was an all-inspiring evening, she would even deem it a turning point, for it was a first in two regards. It was the first time she heard Billy play piano and sing, really sing, not like he did in the restaurant clowning around with the drunken sailor song, but with a captivating resonance, passion and flawless execution she hadn't expected.

Then she witnessed something unlike anything she had ever experienced. Astoundingly, Billy conducted this group of unknowns, of random strangers, and had them singing in four-part harmony in six minutes, stimulating a glorious, communal sensation, music that amazed everyone it seemed, except for Billy. He led them in a few folk songs – "I's the B'y" and "Molly Malone" along with a spiritual, "Swing Low, Sweet Chariot," one of his favorites. Following the choral uplift, Billy showcased his choice of recorded music and talked about the composers Weber, Stravinsky, Tchaikovsky and Felix Mendelssohn, another of his idols. Charlotte Moxon, his early guardian in Truro, gave him a book about Mendelssohn for his twenty-first birthday which he had read with great relish.

Vivian was charmed. She couldn't stop herself from absorbing the attractiveness of his being, from his shiny, rippled, ebony hair held tight to his head, marked by that distinctive widow's peak coming to a point at the center of his forehead like an arrow tip above arced brows, full but trim, not bushy, down to his tamping foot on the piano pedal.

She was trying to resist the lure of him, which was challenging. Despite days ago, indicating that they maintain an element of distance, her emotions were telling her something quite different. Rather than guilt, fear and sinfulness she felt virtuous, excited and unapologetic. Was this the palm reading ringing true? She would do her best to fend off the weakness that was taking hold, control the flutters that flitted inside when her awe overtook her level headedness.

At the end of the evening Billy did his customary glad-handing, soaking in compliments and chatting people up until the final stragglers had shuffled out of the building, at which point he took Vivian over to the staff kitchen. In the cabinet above the sink, he found a couple of cups and a tea caddy. He proceeded to fill up a kettle.

Hot beverages prepared, he reached for a solid red, round tin on the counter, pried open the lid with his fingertips and tilted the tin for her to see inside.

"My homemade pound cake," he said triumphantly. He set out two small plates, placed a slice on each one and presented hers.

"Mademoiselle," he said, with a French accent as he served her the cake with a wide sweeping gesture and the finesse of a classy waiter. Vivian giggled. Suddenly he was in full flight with his character voices, pouring the tea, mimicking a West Indian mother-in-law, and serving it with the mannerisms of a British lord. Then in a thundering bass voice he played the preacher saying a grace before indulging. The flush in Vivian's cheek and the continuing, cascading, warmth of her laughter told the show-off he was making the desired favorable impression.

By the end of the evening, she took his arm when he offered it as he walked her to the wharf. She promised to write him while on holiday, which she did one week later, a descriptive letter and some postcards from Lillian's aunt's place in Stanhope, PEI.

While she was away, an eternity in Billy White's time zone, her essence consumed him like a haunted man. He believed he must be falling in love. His inner overseer slapped down his ego for wishful thinking.

After reading her PEI letter, he used his pen to pour out his soul on paper, crumpling several miserable attempts before the flow of his ink spilled freely, emboldened by his memory of her willingness to accept his lips against hers in the car. Letter perfected and wanting her to read it before their next face-to-face encounter, he sent it to the return address she had written on the envelope in her tiny, perfect script.

My dear Vivian,
This is the beginning of my third attempt at writing to you. My two previous efforts were abandoned in utter despair, as I realized in each case that I was laying my heart

bare before you, and in so doing, was painting a picture of gloom, longing and loneliness, which would have made you feel, perhaps, that I must be on the verge of complete spiritual disintegration. Fortunately, I recognized a direct contradiction, or, seemingly, an absolute disregard for our determination to maintain the element of casualness in this relationship of ours, which, as we both know only too well, in reality reaches to far greater depths than either of us imagined.

Gee, Vivian, thanks very much for your letters and postcard. I won't say any more than, "It was marvellous hearing from you," and leave it to you to interpret that statement as you know it should be.

It's really too bad that Charlottetown was not at its best for you. I think that you found it quiet because it was Sunday when you arrived there. Usually, the place is quite alive. On your way back, I'd suggest that you pay a visit to either the *Old Spain* or the *Orchid* for dinner. You'll enjoy it.

Last Saturday I discovered that the Mendelssohn Violin Concerto *was* in the library when I returned the "Beethoven." Gee, it's a marvellous work, which you must hear sometime.

Vivian, dear, I'm finding it very difficult to write this letter, because incidentals are not just the things I want to write and, having committed myself to remaining within the borders of casualness, I'm going to have to stop here. First of all, though, let me write a line or two:

Thou art my lute; by thee I sing;
My being is attuned to thee;
Thou settest all my words a-wing
And meltest me to melody.

"My song" although bereft of words
Grows sweeter (so it seems to me)
Than all the songs of all the birds;
It whispers "I am one with thee."

Think of me occasionally, won't you, Vivian, and remember that for each of your thoughts there is an accompanying one at this end.
    As ever,
    Billy

Chapter 7

Home from her holiday, refreshed and eager, Vivian returned to work with renewed gusto and dug through a backlog of secretarial correspondence in record time her first day back. Two letters that had arrived in her absence she put aside for later. The logo on their envelopes identified them unmistakably as Billy's.

July 31, 1945

My dear Vivian,

The purpose of this note is really twofold; first of all, I want to let you know that I am becoming more and more disturbed, inwardly, about you. Gee, Vivian, it is most surprising to me that I should feel this way; but it is true, nonetheless, and I have no desire to discourage so wonderful a feeling. I think you're wonderful! Seeing you always is utterly perfect as a means toward making my day worthwhile and although I know it is definitely not good for me, the more often I see you, the better. I really don't think I need to tell you that, do I?

My second reason for sending this note is to tell you that a guy named White was in my office recently and insisted that I send you the enclosed ticket. He assured me that it was quite alright, and that you would know why it was sent and what you were to do with it. He looked very much like a dope to me. Anyway, I'm sending it to please him just in case he knows what he's doing.

Vivian, I'm going to stop this note, because I want to say more that would be better unsaid, and that at this moment I don't trust myself! And that's bad!

He signed, "As ever, Billy" in his customary ink.

His approach tickled her. There was no other way to say it. Beyond amusement, his words triggered in her a profound delight and a longing for more, followed by waves of self-admonishment and guilt for allowing sentimentality to take command of her sense of propriety. Thoughts of loyalty to her present boyfriend retreated all too willingly, ceding to her fantasy of exploring what this exceptional new man had to offer. She banished her guilt to the sidelines.

She was doing nothing wrong. Dick had advocated taking their time to be sure they both were ready for marriage. Maybe she wasn't. If mere words on a piece of paper from Billy could prompt her imagination to run hot, perhaps Dick's reticence about their engagement was justified. He had wanted her to soak in new cultural experiences and friends and be open to what life had to offer. Who was she to argue? Dick was her best friend and the most important man in her life, and she would respect his advice.

She studied the ticket to Portia's concert and tucked it in her purse, first marking the date in her daybook. Then after handwriting a quick thank-you note in her well-formed, compact cursive and preparing it for mailing to Billy on the way home, she tidied and organized her desk before leaving for the day.

Examining the unopened second letter, she noted sequentially this one was written first. She took it with her to read on the ferry.

July 23, 1945

My dear Vivian,

To say that the past two weeks have been most unusual would be stating an astounding fact very mildly. Had I completed the several letters I started to you while you were away, they would certainly have reflected the element of unusualness to which I've referred, and would, perhaps, have made your vacation anything but the pleasant experience I hope it was. The truth of the matter is that I have been miserably confused and unsure of the ground I've been treading during that time, which necessitated my remaining silent until I had gleaned an appreciable degree of definiteness from the almost countless trends of thought which presented themselves.

Consequently, my vitality has reached a new low from having attempted to withstand more sleepless nights than I should have, and I feel as though I'm "all in but the buttons." In spite of this physical set-back, I feel somewhat like the warrior who returns victorious from a long battle, for I have found the truth concerning these two "most unusual" weeks, and that alone is sufficient compensation for having spent unpleasant, but seemingly necessary hours, searching my soul for this truth which I knew lay hidden there.

Perhaps you've wondered just to what startling revelation this is a preamble, so I shall tell you in as few words as possible exactly what is on my mind.

Vivian, I haven't been mistaken about your having taken a very important place in the life of one Billy White. In all fairness to you, I'll say merely, "I think you are wonderful" and ask you to call me when you find yourself with a spare minute or two.

I've missed you terribly but, at the same time, I was greatly relieved that you weren't here at the time of the explosion. It would have certainly been a terrible ordeal for you to withstand. Still, you must have been worried, weren't you?

Yes, the explosion could have been so much worse. Vivian had telephoned her mother long distance – worried that Jean would be reliving 1917 – and heard firsthand from her details of the event, a situation fortunately far less grave than the historic obliteration of the city during the First World War.

It happened at the Canadian Naval Ammunition Storage Depot at Bedford Basin, two or three miles up the harbor. Sailors offshore saw it unfold; the munitions cracked in exploding illuminations with breathtaking frequency like some horrific drum symphony. Reverberations blew out every window of the dockyard buildings. Flames licked the night sky and curtains of smoke shrouded it as the ammunition dump smouldered for days. Fearful city dwellers, fifteen thousand people in Halifax and another ten thousand in Dartmouth spent the night in parks. Jean was not among them. She carried on in the face of it, having learned through the many pains handed her the importance of remaining calm and level-headed in a crisis.

A foghorn sounded, and Vivian emerged from her thoughts to finish reading.

> You'll laugh when I tell you that I missed my train on the morning I was to leave for Sackville. As a result, I didn't reach there until late in the evening. The conference was interesting, but to be very candid, my heart wasn't in it.
>
> Now that I'm nearing the end of this note, I think I'll say, *Au revoir, ma chérie* and remind you that nothing will be more welcome than a call from you, except the thrill of seeing you again.
>
> As ever,
> Billy

She was glad for the skeletal slats of the boat's wooden bench against her back as she absorbed the words and her spine turned to jelly. What felt like a rock was weighting the hollow of her stomach and the pace of her breathing changed from shallow to deep. Were her cheeks flushing? She glanced up from the letter to study the other passengers to see if she was attracting looks. All were oblivious except for a girl around six who was sucking the end of one of her pigtails while staring at her. When their eyes met the girl smiled, the braid tip still clenched in her teeth, and Vivian gave her a teensy wave then put the letter away. The power of its contents did not leave her mind, however.

This all seemed so sudden, but not really. The magnetism had been there way back to their first encounter at Fader's. Now the power was gaining strength as she reconsidered some of his key words in his letter like "thrill," "sleepless nights," "wonderful," "*ma chérie.*"

All that repelled her forceful attraction to Billy was the dictate of propriety and convention that said that races should be kept separate. She didn't believe that to be true: her motto was kindness, giving, loving and respecting all of God's creation. On that particular ferry ride home, to the backdrop of the engine's steady hum, the more she pondered Billy's declaration of love the more certain she became that those old-fashioned ideas presented no reason for her to hold back friendship or feelings for this man. Their next date was mere days away.

Billy and Vivian had agreed to meet at the concert venue and Vivian was determined not to be late. To that end she had a plan. She would stay in Halifax after work and had pre-arranged to meet her mother downtown for supper. Tonight was the night she was going to tell Jean about Billy. That decision came when she realized the pointlessness of trying to conceal knowing him and liking him. It's undeniable his importance in her life was surging. For all she knew, Bernard may have already mentioned Billy to Mother after their meeting at the Y.

So face-to-face at supper that evening at the newspaper's cafeteria, over melamine trays of the turkey dinner-plate special and after exhausting other topics of familial interest – Aunt Elsie's pending visit from Massachusetts with her upright, son-of-a-minister husband John, a weekend jaunt planned to Aunt Doris's in Pleasant River in September where the three surviving Harlow sisters would reunite for the first time in years – Vivian introduced the subject of the evening's concert.

"I didn't tell you who I'm going to see tonight," she began. "I'm attending a Portia White concert."

Jean purred her approval and commented on her daughter's luck in having procured a ticket. Everyone in Nova Scotia was aware of the rising star.

Working at the newspaper, Jean followed Portia's career like everybody else, but had the added advantage of having a daily Halifax Herald to digest close at hand. She didn't miss the headlines boasting of packed houses, the rave reviews and feature stories, the photo highlights of Portia's command performance for the Earl of Athlone and Princess Alice at Government House the previous year. Had Vivian invited her, Jean gladly would have accompanied her daughter to take in the evening's recital.

They spent so little time together these days.

"I'm actually going with Portia's brother," Vivian said. "Billy White – he works at the Young Men's Christian Association."

She deliberately chose to use the proper name for YMCA to emphasize the word "Christian." "That's how I came to have a ticket. Bernard and I met with him concerning camps and we've become friends. I know his brother too."

Jean felt the need to repeat what she'd heard. "You're attending the concert with Portia White's brother." Her voice trailed off slightly into a pause, followed by, "I suppose that will be all right."

Vivian was tempted but decided not to point out that she wasn't seeking her mother's permission. She could see by the movement of Jean's pupils that her mother was calling up images in her mind and judging the perceived scene. Fair woman, dark man, in a mixed crowd and dimly lit hall, the optics of them sitting together should be okay. The tumblers in Jean's head continued to turn as she calculated what her church friends might think.

Vivian gave her mother a measured look, allowing an acceptable lapse in time for any projected worries or fears to fall away and a normal flow of conversation to resume.

Mother looked lovely and more at ease than usual. She was wearing her favorite color combination: yellow and purple, an omelette yellow suit against a mauve blouse in the new rayon fabric Eaton's was selling, accented by Gram's string of pearls.

Jean's rigidly upright posture and sharply defined jaw line seemed to characterize her approach to current life circumstances, a disciplined and confident woman, both a landlord and a tenant, with a career, a vision and a financial plan for returning to her marital home and controlling her destiny again, master of her own house. By then her daughter would be Vivian Hill and on her way to giving Jean longed-for grandchildren. Why hadn't there been any news about an engagement? She dared not ask.

An impulse struck her. She unclasped her pearls and handed them across the table to Vivian.

"Wear these," she said. "Your blouse is begging for an accent."

Vivian gratefully accepted the strand and immediately lowered her chin to fasten them behind her neck and admire their resiliency against the deep blue hue of her top.

She looked up and into Jean's eyes. "Dick doesn't want to get married yet, Mother. I've been meaning to tell you. We're going to wait. He wants us to be prepared and I agree."

Jean was surprised but not devastated. Postponing probably did make sense. After all, she waited for a proposal until she was twenty-eight.

"Apparently this is God's plan for the two of you," Jean responded, "as it was for me. My years with your father were the happiest, but we didn't rush into marriage. We were sensible."

"Did you know right away that Daddy was the one?" Vivian wanted to know.

"My heart would never lie to me," Jean replied.

The conversation moved to the Independent Order of Daughters of the Empire and Jean's current activities with them and then to First Baptist gossipy tidbits.

The Osborne baby has croup; Verne Gilligan is in a bad way after losing his hand in a farm accident and the church is passing the hat, poor soul, no one knows how he'll make a living now; the 85th Memory Club published a nice tribute to Glenn recently; Brenda Bickford broke off her engagement with Gordy McCullough – a big uproar in her family over his lack of station and means. Her father absolutely forbade it.

"Save the concert ticket for your scrapbook," said Jean, herself a serial documentarian: reading, saving, arranging, compiling and placing information in keepsake books. "That ticket will be quite a novelty item someday, Vivian. A Negro singing the classics: who would believe such a thing possible?"

Vivian's watch said it was time to go. Her mother's characterization of the great singer as a display case oddity made her uncomfortable. The gentle weight of Gram's pearls around her neck stabilized her as she kissed Jean goodbye and thanked her again for the loan of the necklace.

She had plotted a trolley route that would deposit her at the university thirty minutes before the concert start, which turned out to be fifteen , ending with a markedly rapid foot flight to the front doors of the venue, where Billy stood waiting for her, heaving on a cigarette.

"Come," he said, as he steered her by the elbow toward the open doors and into the heavy scent of perfumes and cigarette smoke.

He ushered her to their seats, dispensing nods of recognition and the odd wave to the teachers he knew in the crowd. Front row with the VIPs, thank you Portia!

The evening's program borrowed from Schubert and Brahms with a smattering of Bach, Verdi, Handel, Dvorak and Tchaikovsky plus a piece by Gretchaninoff, a composer Vivian had never heard of, and a Portia rendition of "May-Day Carol." There were folk songs and spirituals to accompany the classics. When it was over, Vivian timed the thunder of clapping hands until the diva returned to the stage for the demanded encore: a full fifty-seven seconds before it began to diminish.

"This time we're going backstage," Billy said. "I really want Portia to meet you."

Vivian felt flattered. She was eager to meet the legendary Portia, but Billy had placed the emphasis on Portia meeting her and that made Vivian feel like she actually belonged in the VIP row. The excitement remained in the air. It must have been contagious because Vivian had butterflies in her stomach as they made their way back to the dressing room where months before she and Lillian had hung up their coats at the variety show after-party.

The room was bubbling with admirers. George and his girl Elsie were there but couldn't stay. A throng of well-wishers, a Herald photographer, Portia's agent and a representative from the management company were crowded around while Portia gave a reporter an interview. She saw Billy as he entered, and her face lit up. "I'll be five minutes, Billy," she said, indicating the five with her fingers held up like a stop signal. Her hands were beautiful, French manicured, nails polished and buffed to a sheen the day before by her friend, Lois, a beautician, friend and student of Viola Desmond: Viola, the expert hair stylist who had fashioned Portia's stubborn, thick hair for the evening, taming it with her latest products; Lois, the woman who had served as Billy's love interest for the better part of six years, off and on. Lois, the woman he knew would be away visiting her aunt in Preston on the date of this concert. No chance of accidental run-ins this time. He had made sure of that before inviting Vivian.

Several years apart from each other, Portia and Viola attended the same high school at Bloomfield. Billy directed the choir when younger sisters June and Yvonne were students there. Portia made the introduction to Lois, knowing full well her brother's proclivity for not only chasing brother George's girls but his own string of them as well. She had warned Lois from the outset not to pin her heart on Billy. On the farm he'd be what they'd call "free range." He had quite a reputation as a lady's man, cut a fine figure, was funny, smart, all-around fun to be around – how she loved this brother of hers. But women were his weakness, or he was theirs.

He and Vivian stood around waiting for Portia to wrap up.

"You received my letters, *ma chérie?*" He took her hands and turned to face her. "I meant every word, Vivian. My heart is in this for keeps. You may think my ramblings are flights of fancy to be written off as wishful thinking. I believe they are dreams yet to come true. Please say you will share more of your time with me and that you will allow me to share more of mine with you."

His outpouring was blunt and overt and in such a public place as this, Vivian felt as a woman feels pulling the curtain tight in the fitting room at Eaton's to make sure nobody sees. Faintly she said, "your letter affected me greatly and I shall be glad to discuss this when we can be alone together."

"Nothing I'd like better," he said, clapping his hands and executing a soft shoe shuffle step to indicate elation. "Remind me later to show you my trademark tap dance move. I call it, 'Chicken in the dough tray.' I'm the only person in the world who can do this step."

Her response was wry. "Is there anything you can't do, Billy? Be honest."

He considered her question momentarily. "I can't swim," he said sheepishly, "at least not very well, and I'm afraid of dogs. I had a close call with a German shepherd when I was a kid."

"If a dog is mean, it almost certainly has been mistreated. Poor thing needed to be rescued," Vivian said.

"I was the one in need of rescuing," Billy said. "That dog tore my shoe off as I scaled a wall to avoid it."

He saw Portia waving at him and interrupted himself to announce, "Come, *chérie*, the moment for which we have been waiting." Vivian clutched her program and at least had the presence of mind to plan to ask Portia to sign it. A shallow sea of people around his sister parted as Billy strode forward with Vivian on his arm. "Hi, hi, hi" he cheered jubilantly. He and Portia embraced. Billy stepped back to introduce the two. Vivian Keeler? Portia White.

"Hello, Portia."

"Hello, Miss Keeler," there was a regal air to her voice and a hint of haughtiness as well – no first name basis in return, more of an iceberg off the coast of Newfoundland than a warm Nova Scotian welcome, Vivian thought, and wondered why the cool exchange. She was tongue tied for an instant by Portia's formality but mustered a "pleased to meet you," and a request for an autograph.

"'May-Day Carol', I've only heard one other version, and may I say you sing the song even better than Nelson Eddy."

"Well, thank you very much, Miss Keeler. I've never been compared to a Hollywood tenor before." Portia was a classical music snob who felt popular music styles had degraded the pure and strenuous art of vocal music generally.

She autographed the program while laughing with Billy over Vivian's remark. Vivian felt the blush of hot cheeks creeping across her face, compounding her feelings of awkwardness.

"Oh, I've embarrassed you," Portia said. "Forgive me. I should have stopped after 'thank you very much'. It is such a unique compliment although I'm not sure I want to be compared to a man," she mused.

"Unless it's Pup," Billy piped in. "Here's to Pup," Portia agreed.

Sizing up Vivian, she was mulling: who is this one now? Every time I turn around, he's juggling Lois and an array of other girls.

This one looks so young; has a most noticeable effect on Billy. Portia, a profoundly sentient and visionary being, couldn't ever recall seeing her brother this happy. She sized up Vivian's features: lithe and lovely with high cheekbones, a winning smile and sapphire-blue eyes that were keen and kind. But Portia suspected his interest for Vivian might be to the fairness of her skin. Portia reckoned Billy was like her, looking for that key to guarantee participation and acceptance in a lily-white world. So far, they were accomplishing that, but no one had said it would be easy. In neither case could it be done without the committed assistance of white people. That's just the way it was.

The siblings laughed about old times while Vivian, still flummoxed by Portia's formality, looked attentive while silently reprimanding herself for being so gawky, inarticulate, and misunderstood. Her self-flagellation ended and her funny bone sprang into action as her attention was grabbed by Portia recounting how she once put pennies on the eyes of a corpse at a funeral home on a dare. They all roared, and it was toward this uproarious trio that a polite publicist was moving to say it was time to wrap up – Portia still had obligations to patrons and a late rendezvous with her dear friend Ruth Wilson after that.

A Thursday evening, it was already a late night as far as Vivian was concerned. Usually, she was home by 11 on work nights. Tonight, she didn't care about the time. Billy indicated he wanted to talk to her, which suited her fine. He, and only he, could help her sort out the feelings that were combusting in their communal kettle. She wanted to explain that his love did not scare her – she had feelings for him too, but she wanted to be sensible about a relationship between them, set boundaries, and respect the social rules they would agree to establish.

Good nights with Portia were exchanged. That distinctly cool and distant "Miss Keeler" was the only note of the evening that wasn't perfectly in tune.

"I don't think your sister likes me very much," she said as she and Billy stepped into the air, strangely still and sticky after a rare humid day when traditional breezes took a hiatus.

He stopped to light a cigarette, first checking whether she wanted a smoke by thrusting the open pack and jiggling it in her direction with quizzically raised eyebrows. She waved it off, watched him grasp and flick open his lighter to ignite the Export A, and in one smooth motion click it closed with a snap of his wrist before tucking it into the right-side pocket of his jacket.

He took a deep draw and exhaled a blue cloud into the night sky. He started out by assuring her not to worry about Portia because he had five other sisters and, all kidding aside, it was impossible for Portia not to like her because there was nothing about Vivian that he could see —and he was very perceptive – that could possibly deem her as unlikeable to anyone.

"Portia has always behaved as though she ruled the roost and some-times her mother hen comes out. You know how big sisters are," he chided. "Please don't let Portia spoil my chances with you. I assure you if I'm happy, she's happy, and Vivian, my dear, I declare to you, I am happy!" His voice emanated jubilance. He threw his arms open to the sky and sang the word "happy" convincingly to the stars.

As they made their way to his parked car, a thought struck Billy. "Hey, Vivian. What are you doing for Natal Day? Will you celebrate with me?"

"A bunch of us are going to Point Pleasant Park for the day," Vivian replied. "You should come."

Not the answer he was hoping for, but what the heck? Would Dick be there? No, he was told, but Burleigh, Lillian, Ron Simpson and a bunch of the regulars would be. Dick was due back from Labrador at the end August at which point he would be entering Dalhousie, having enrolled himself there to pursue a science degree.

Billy wanted to know whether Vivian's friends would mind him tagging along. He would be welcomed, she assured him. All her friends were nice people.

They had reached the car.

Billy opened the passenger side door and ushered her into her seat, then dashed to his side, first removing his suit jacket that, although light, was too warm in the heat and then slid in smoothly behind the wheel. This was the night he intended to lay it all on the line, splay his heart like fruit on a platter and serve it to her in carefully prepared portions. His words of luscious sweetness would linger long after their goodnights and would move her closer to him in every way despite the seeming impossibility of it all, he hoped.

They drove off in the direction of the ferry dock. He would have gladly driven his date all the way home, but she insisted the ferry was the better option.

She promised they could linger and talk at the wharf for a time.

They had forty-five minutes to kill, a lot can happen in three-quarters of an hour, Billy was thinking. He didn't intend to waste a minute.

"Vivian, I may be totally out of place and if I am, please forgive me. Tell me if I am treading on forbidden territory and I swear I shall not continue."

"I'm listening," she said, as she turned to face him, "and then I'd like to say something to you."

"Vivian, my darling, at this very moment it seems as though it would be a very simple matter for me to forget everything and everyone else and devote my every minute to loving you. I thrill at the mere thought of it," he continued in her rapt silence.

"You are very dear to me, and it is only my recognition of your profound sense of duty that represses the urge to say, with all the warmth and sincerity I can command, 'I love you!!'"

She felt frozen like a porcelain figurine by the hypnotic passion of his soliloquy. For an instant she felt faint, her heart was beating so fast. His eyes, soft as suede, seemed to be combing her soul, as if searching for a reciprocal glimpse in her of the emotions he so keenly felt.

While Billy eagerly awaited her response, she impulsively lunged toward him, her parted lips meeting his. Her intensity and boldness startled both of them. They pulled apart, fell into still silence – two statues alone in the darkness of the car under the waning crescent moon.

In the absence of light, Billy dissolved into the background of dark shadows while Vivian's skin appeared luminous, opalescent. Together, a picture of contrasts but an essential pairing, like salt and pepper, sugar and cinnamon.

He consciously tried to control his hair-trigger arousal, afraid of where prolonged kissing might lead. He suggested they abandon the stuffy car and walk to the water.

They ambled toward the water, and she felt quite at ease putting her arm around his waist in the semi-darkness offset by boat lights skimming the water and low lamplight bathing the fenced perimeter. There was a lookout point and an inviting bench stationed as if waiting for them. Seated he faced her, studying her visage like the artist studies his model, thoughtfully, artfully, appreciating the nuances he will commit to shape and form, sculpting each delicate detail into his memory for life.

Her hair cascading like a waterfall down her shoulders, gently curled, and made blonde by the sun, a linen-like sheen giving her crown of locks depth and softness, made him eager to touch it, run his fingers through it and so he asked if he could.

She smiled a yes and his big hands leapt at the silent consent to stroke her golden strands. Her eyes were surveying the landscape of his hair, tight to his head, richly black and shiny, and rippling like the wool of the black lamb from Gram and Gramps' farm that frolicked with her when she was a girl.

"How do you get your hair like that?" she asked. He tucked his dimpled chin down and leaned forward so she could touch his hair, which she had been yearning to do but didn't dare ask.

As she patted his corduroy-like head he explained his curl-control method to her:

"I apply lanolin to my hair at bedtime and I wear a mojo."

"A mojo?"

He explained that it was a tight-fitting stocking cap he sleeps in to keep his hair controlled overnight. He straightened himself on the bench. She stood up, smoothed her skirt and faced him head-on.

"I have feelings for you, Billy," she said. "I do believe I love you. Then I think of the realities of our situation, the futility of entertaining the thought that we could ever unite as anything but friends. On one hand I want to be spontaneous and be open to changes and on the other, I tell myself I should keep a cool head and behave in a way that is expected of me."

She paced as she spoke, sounding like she was either rehearsing her lines or arguing with herself. When she'd finished, she was standing directly in front of him with her hands on her hips and an exasperated look that suggested she wanted him to fix something.

"What do you want me to do, Vivian?" he asked. "I'm afraid I can't help you unless it is to say that whatever you decide on this matter is entirely up to you and your conscience and I will support you. Recognizing all the barriers that may confront you in pursuing our romance I would understand completely if you were to surrender to convention and relegate me to the 'just friends' department. If that's what you want, *ma chérie*, I will accept your verdict most regrettably, but accept it I will if you were to give me no other option. And should you tell me to leave, I will, although I am certain I would never recover."

She was fingering her pearls one by one as she considered his words. He continued.

"When I think of the paradigm trap that society contrived for the members of my race, my living to those expectations would have sentenced me to the servants' quarters. I had to aspire. It's what I was taught. Vivian, you need to live for yourself and meet your own expectations, not others. That's how you will find your harmony and happiness. As for spontaneous, you say ..."

In a distinct change of pace, he stood up. A bronzed god, Vivian thought. He was glowing, mischievous, looking down at her, his extended hands now clasping her waist, moving forward to get the grip he needed to scoop her up into his arms. Her legs spilling out, arms instinctively clutched to wrap around his shoulders, head thrown back laughing, an interspersed whoop and a slight shriek as he twirled around a few times before setting her down.

"For me, there's no turning back. Don't fault me for wishful thinking, darling Vivian. Tell me we can manifest the future I see ahead for us. Tell me my psychic sense isn't wrong. No," he backtracked. "Prove it."

This time Vivian's passion leapt forth. She would leave the rationalizing for later. For now, her libido propelled her into a hungry exchange of kisses, from hard to wet, steamy to tender, staged like musical notes on a score, some in a flurry, bunched together and others long and sustained. When they broke apart a beam from a flashlight was pointing their way and a uniformed port official was approaching.

He shined the light in their faces, first zeroing in on Vivian, who screened her light-sensitive eyes from the glare, and then to Billy and back to her again.

"Everything alright here, Miss?" he said. He sounded Scottish. "Is this here man bothering you?" He beamed the light up and down Billy's figure. As Billy took a step forward to introduce himself, the guard jumped back in alarm. "Don't move, or I'll be calling the coppers," he said. "You, miss, what are you doing hanging around with the likes of him? You're asking for trouble. Why don't you go on your way?"

"I will do no such thing," said Vivian. "And you have no business interfering with us. Please leave or I shall be reporting you to your supervisor."

The broad-shouldered, seam-bursting official was taken aback by Vivian's assertiveness. Much to Billy's delight, the pompous security guard withered in the presence of her defiance. "Consider yourselves warned," he grunted under his breath and slunk away like a scolded puppy. They shared a giggle over what had transpired as Billy walked her to the ferry, during which time Vivian outlined her terms.

They could date in private, but in public they had to adopt a cooler persona. "Private time" versus "in public" – Vivian had rules for both scenarios. They said goodbye until the following Monday, when on Natal Day, a celebration of Halifax's birthday, they would face their first in-public test under her new edict.

Billy went home where, elated to the point of insomnia, he made use of his sleeplessness by writing her a poem to give to her down the road, now that he was assured there was a road.

Loving You

The meaning of "love" has always caused
A great deal of confusion;
But after giving it some thought,
I've come to this conclusion:
If "loving you" means
Wond'ring where you are,
Or feeling that you are
Supposed to be close to me,
If "loving you" means

Thrilling thro' and thro'
To have you only smile at me,
If "loving you" means
Dreaming that I hold you,
Oh, so close to me,
And that you don't care to say,
"This is not supposed to be."
If "loving you" means
Wish you were mine
Then, by the stars that shine,
I love you.

Vivian atop Martello Tower, Point Pleasant Park, Halifax

Chapter 8

"What did you do while I was away? Did I miss anything?"

Lois's long, sculpted and varnished fingernails clawed systematically through Billy's tin of recipe index cards in the cramped kitchen of his flat. Their first rendezvous since her return, she had promised to cook dinner and was hunting for Portia's sauce recipe, then found it filed under "P" for Pasta instead of "S" for Sauces. "Aha!"

She whirled around with the card clutched in her pincers – "Tomato Sauce with Clams" – looking cute in Billy's big apron knotted around her petite yet buxom body. He hadn't missed her, and he felt guilty admitting that to himself. Her mauve sleeveless dress hugged her hips and bust alluringly, and its purple matched her nail polish exactly. It cut in too tightly at the arm holes causing indented marks and a fleshy flap spillover, telling of her recent weight gain.

Harry had said he'd be back around nine after the library closed so it was just Lois and Billy for dinner. Naturally she wanted to catch up on everything that had transpired during her absence. He handed her a story that closely resembled the truth.

There was Portia's concert, of course. Lois had been sorry to miss it. "I gave her your regards," he fabricated. What was he supposed to say: He attended with a gorgeous young girl whom Portia treated haughtily perhaps out of allegiance to Lois? Billy didn't have to be clairvoyant to predict that no such admission would be in the cards, not tonight, not ever. Why spoil a grand thing? He could lead this double life quite comfortably. Two women worlds apart, two women each with the ability to satisfy a different set of his needs, so what was the harm? He did like her a lot, like a man likes a favorite pair of slippers for being warm, predictable, reliable.

A divorcé cavorting with a friendly widow and an endearing, chaste maiden simultaneously – there was no infidelity here, he reasoned – and he'd end it all with Lois and any others in an instant to be with Vivian exclusively and eternally. In the meantime, he convinced himself, he could enjoy the best of both worlds unencumbered.

"I went to Point Pleasant Park on Natal Day to meet up with a bunch of young people through the Y connection," he told her, as though this statement of fact would erase his previous lie. While careful not to mention Vivian's name, there was no point in concealing the event. It had been a complete flop, in Billy's opinion.

While Lois worked the cupboards and drawers of his kitchen like an octopus, Billy complained about that day to her turned back. He hadn't anticipated the crowds and the difficulty he would have rendezvousing with this new group. In long-sleeved shirt and slacks, camera slung around his neck and a straw hat shielding his head, he was dressed wrong right down to his socks and shoes. He surveyed a landscape of bodies in bathing suits and shorts, a sea of pale pallor and sunburned pink, mayhem in the swimming area, cheers rising periodically for oarsmen in rowboats racing across the bay, a mosaic of picnic blankets, an obstacle course all its own.

In the heat of high noon's glare all the white people looked the same to him. He'd been instructed to find the group next to the lifeguard tower. Upon arrival he saw there were four towers, two to his right, two to his left. By the time he hit the first one, his shoes were gritty inside with sand. Before heading to the next tower, he removed them and his socks, rolled up his pant legs, stuffed his socks in his shoes, which he carried. Not finding his party at the second tower, he was forced to turn around, retrace his steps, and trudge all the way back. Being the only authentically dark person on the beach certainly got you noticed, even by the sunbathers with deep tans, he thought, as heads turned, and eyes followed him. By the third tower he could have given up, but it didn't make sense to have come this far and quit. When he reached the fourth tower, he concluded he was in the wrong place and went home sweating and grumpy, having wasted the afternoon.

Lois had been laughing heartily at her boyfriend's description of his failed meet-up, sandy socks, sore feet and the overall runaround. "That's what you get for trusting white folks," she chortled. "They're always going to let you down. I know you like mixing with them, Billy, but it's not right that you're traipsing after them like that. White folks are always setting up traps for us, leading us on and letting us down. Welcome to Nova Scotia!"

Onions sputtered in the fry pan. In went the tinned tomatoes, market-fresh clams, no garlic since Billy wasn't a fan of it, some herbs, salt, black pepper – not too much – and stock, setting it to simmer.

"I will remind you, Lois, that my father was head of the entire Maritime federation of Baptist clergy, which was comprised entirely of white men, but for him. He was leading them, not the other way around, and I intend to do the same. Big change is coming and I'm ready to embrace it." Billy saw himself at the front of any parade.

"Portia told me once that your father was a follower of Marcus Garvey. She said his ideology was all about self-determination for the descendants of Africa – a 'do-for-self' approach not reliant on whites."

Lois was proud to be following the self-sufficiency model in her new life as a beautician without a husband.

"Well, yes, he did tell the white preachers back in 1934 that he didn't believe the answer to discrimination was to be found in intermarrying between the races," Billy conceded. "He believed it would dilute the ability for people of our race to fulfill their own destiny and would eventually erase us out of existence. That thought sickened him. On the other hand, he boasted about performing these intermarriages, so I think he was pandering to his white audience to an extent, maybe saying something they wanted to hear in the context of his musings about Garvey. After all, my Negro mom is also part white and part Indian, and after thirteen kids it's clear my father didn't oppose mixing.

"Lois, ours is a new generation and I have to believe change will come. When it does, I'll be there. I believe prejudice can only dissolve when we work with the white majority and show by example how to unite and cooperate."

She tossed the pasta sticks into the boiling water, pushing them down with a wooden spoon as they bent in the steam. "I don't blame you for playing the white man's game," she said, "so long as you acknowledge that's what you're doing and admit that you crave their acceptance."

"That's cockeyed, you dizzy dame," Billy said in his best James Cagney, using humor and theater to deflect a comment he knew may be true, at least where Vivian was concerned. He craved her acceptance. He hadn't heard from her since the messed-up rendezvous. He'd called her the very next day to explain and apologize, all too aware that personal calls at her office were taboo. A reedy-voiced woman on the other end of the line told him that Miss Keeler was unavailable and took his name, promising she'd relay his message requesting a return call.

Billy squeezed around Lois to reach the breadbox on the counter and extract from it the loaf of homemade bread he had baked the previous evening. "Surprise!" he said as he floated it in front of her. She waved her spoon in the air like a flag in celebration: just what they needed to soak up the sauce.

"I have something else for you," he said, groping in the upper shelf of the cupboard.

"Is it bigger than a breadbox?" she joked. He handed her a nondescript envelope holding two tickets to the Halifax Community Concert Association's first show of the 1945-46 season on October eighteen, the General Platoff Don Cossack Chorus, Nicholas Kostrukoff, Director.

"You're a prince. How thoughtful, Billy. Thank you. I'd love to go."

She scrutinized the ticket and emitted a low whistle. "Hoity-toity, the Grand Ballroom of the Nova Scotian." A cloud passed across her eyes and briefly stole the eagerness from her face as she looked askance. "Will they let us in?" she wondered skeptically. Billy quickly put her mind to rest. "Most definitely yes and I mean through the front door," he said. "You're thinking of the Lord Nelson," he said, referring to the notoriously whites-only hotel. "At the CCF meetings I'm attending we're talking about planning some kind of action to fight the discrimination there."

Lois was having difficulty accepting that a CN-owned hotel like the Nova Scotian would be any different from CN, the railway employer, where her brother worked and got treated badly. "I'd like to see your CCF do something about the plight of railway porters like Reggie," she said. "He's a genius with his hands and a brilliant fixer, but they barred him from applying for a job as an engineer, kept him kissing up to the white man, kept him down, shining shoes and cleaning toilets. Reg though, he was smart enough to escape that fate and elevate himself to the position of inventor and entrepreneur, but he's a rarity."

Lois was splendid that night, put out a lip-smacking meal, washed the dishes with Billy drying, gabbed an unending string of nothings, giving his mind many opportunities to wander through dinner, and then produced a fifth of her brother's whiskey. They sampled a generous shot before leaving for her place and the second part of their evening.

Having not heard from Vivian in more than a week, he concluded that it was vitally important to take the hint and rein in his deep feelings for her, try to disembark from his fantasy train. Ever since childhood he had been good at distancing himself from his emotions and remaining aloof. Not talking about his feelings became his protection and allowed him to keep control. Getting too personal was a barrier to his wish for universality. Billy was a big-picture guy who preferred to approach situations from on high: cool, calm, composed and detached; it was the same with his dealings with women.

Why couldn't he sublimate his thoughts and feelings about one Vivian Keeler? How many times during Lois's soliloquies tonight did he find himself escaping to respite thoughts of Vivian as one might drift to the thought of a luscious fruit hanging just out of reach? He was consumed with an uneasy restlessness and yearnings that served as underlying, inner distractions.

As for Vivian, when Billy failed to show up on Natal Day, she was disappointed. She figured there was a good reason for his absence and proceeded to become immersed in a beach volleyball game. Had she specified the red tower? She wasn't sure, but she wished she hadn't mentioned his anticipated arrival to her gaggle of friends, because now she had to field questions about his whereabouts, opening the door to a comment from the objectionable hanger-on David-Michael Baxter, who scoffed at Vivian's "newfound wonder boy" and sniffed that "wasn't it telling and just so typical that it's the Negro fellow who can't get himself anywhere on time." Some in the group laughed until Ron Simpson told them to shut up. Unexpectedly, Vivian found a reason to be glad that Billy wasn't there.

As days bled into a full week of not hearing an explanation for his absenteeism that day, doubts began to visit her. Her cautious self screamed at her, the noiseless shriek of judgment. She and Billy had been moving too fast down a tricky road. They needed to put the brakes on and slow the pace. Was he of the same mind and was this the motivation for his disappearing act?

The poetic verses, the candid conversations, intimate moments, and declarations of passion: were they a hoax, a cushion for him between rough patches with Lois?

She would wait to hear from him. In the meantime, she would get on with her life.

August was winding down. And so was the war: Japan had announced its surrender on the fifteenth. All the boys would be coming home. Dick would be back in Dartmouth for September and the much-awaited Youth Week at Camp Owen would be over and done, save for writing a final report. Jean had recruited her daughter to help her and Roy's sister, Aunt Gladys, with the fall fundraiser for the Halifax Philharmonic. Autumn harvest was right around the corner too, the Victory Gardens and Uncle Roy's bounty ready to benefit from Vivian's unwavering help.

Billy assumed a slot behind a whole list of events spilling over one another on her calendar, promising to consume the remainder of Vivian's summer and a chunk of September. Still, thoughts would drift to Billy, like a waft of lilacs' scent, causing her to pause as would a passerby inhaling the perfume and memorizing the aroma. No doubt Billy's schedule was as tightly compressed as hers. He had camp appearances and conferences every weekend. The summer season moved all programming into high gear and Billy along with it. Plus juggling all his hobbies and extra-curricular diversions, understandably he was too busy for her, she accepted.

Partly out of reserve, partly out of stubbornness, contacting him was out of the question. She didn't want to intrude, and she certainly didn't want to appear needy. Etiquette dictated that he should make the next move. On this she was firm. Besides, hadn't she planned to slow things down? She waited.

The idea that Billy could banish Vivian from his consciousness was of course impossible. He was becoming increasingly bothered that he hadn't heard from her. He was gripped by the vision of her in his arms, of stroking her hair, the kiss – arousal, he had to stop this, and he picked up the phone.

He dialed her number and abruptly hung up. This was so uncharacteristic of him, to have the poise knocked out of him, but he had to calm down and rehearse. He dialed again, this time he reached another voice through the switchboard – Ellen's – not the oboe-like sneer he heard through the receiver the last time he called.

"I'm sorry. Miss Keeler is not available, but may she return your call, Sir?"

"Well, this is my second message, actually and thank you, yes, it's William White calling. Yes, she has my number."

He hung up, feeling like a pubescent schoolboy preparing to ask the class sweetheart to the dance. When his office phone jangled a few moments later, his thorax leapt like a frog – there was no mistaking who would be on the other end of the line.

"Hello, *ma chérie!*"

"How did you know it was me?"

"I'm a mind reader."

"If you're a mind-reader, why am I calling?"

"Ahh, to apologize for not responding to the post-Natal Day message I left at your work?" he ventured cautiously.

"I'm sorry, Billy. I didn't know you called. No one gave me a message. I'm phoning because Ellen just gave me one now. I can't stay on the phone long though."

"It was a woman with a voice that sounds like a mosquito in your ear," he said. "I called the very next day, I felt so bad about not finding you when I came to the beach that day."

"You were there?" She leaned into the phone. Peggy had entered the office area and took a seat at her desk within earshot.

"Can we talk?" Billy suppressed any urgency in his voice.

"Yes. Where?"

"I'll come and pick you up at five. We'll go to Fader's."

Vivian hung up. Grabbing her notebook, she scrawled in shorthand a reminder to talk to her supervisor about the wayward telephone message. Then she set back to concentrating on her work, relieved that she and Billy would be reunited, the air cleared.

It turned out she didn't have to approach Ellen. Ellen herself was curious how a message went astray in a workplace under her management. "Someone took a message here from a William White the first week of August," she called out sharply to the girls in the steno pool. "Who took that message?"

A pin could have dropped, but Peggy eventually broke the silence with a small display of theater, pretending to find the message, which she had hidden under her desk blotter.

"I found it, I think," she faked. "From Billy," she virtually spat. "I'm so sorry, Vivian. I put it aside and forgot about it," she said ingratiatingly.

Ellen was having none of it.

"We don't pay you to put things aside and forget about them, Peggy," she admonished sharply.

"It was a personal call," Peggy replied obstinately. "I was merely following Board policy."

"Our policy limits personal calls during work hours, excluding lunch and after hours. However, it does not limit the receipt of incoming messages and it's our job to ensure that all messages are relayed in a timely fashion. I should like to see you for a further discussion before you leave today, please."

Ellen only used formality when she was annoyed. Her words settled over the room like a pall and Peggy stormed to the washroom red-faced. Later the boss would inform Peggy that she was being written up for certain inappropriate comments of late and non-collegial conduct and that she should consider this a reprimand.

Vivian left on the dot at five. Billy was waiting in the car. It was one of those moments when two people feel no time has passed since their last meeting. Weeks, years, it mattered not, they were with each other now, and both felt like companion jigsaw puzzle pieces, cut from the same mould, together again and picking up where they left off. As she approached, he jumped out of the car to ensure an open passenger door was waiting to welcome her. Once his precious cargo was safe inside, he resumed his position behind the wheel. Before starting the engine, he looked at her happily and queried, "Do we really want to go to Fader's, or should we take a swing down Dingle Road where we can really talk?"

Vivian gave him the answer he expected, willingly disregarding that "The Dingle," as the place was affectionately named, was code for a lovers' lane. Delighted with her response, Billy fired up the car. A walk along Dingle Road would allow them a heart-to-heart. He was desperate for one of those and it ensued, beginning seamlessly en route as he headed west out of the city towards Spryfield.

"I missed you, Vivian. I assumed you didn't return my call because you were angry with me for not meeting up on the holiday, not that I didn't try. I still have sand in my socks to prove it. I'm sorry I stood you up. I felt badly." He recounted his attempt to locate her that day, including his mortification that a thousand pairs of eyes were staring at his skinny legs exposed by pant cuffs furled to his knobby knees.

"Peggy didn't give me your message. I swear she deliberately withheld it. It doesn't matter now." Vivian positioned herself in the seat to face Billy and study his artfully etched profile as he commandeered the vehicle. "I was never angry with you, Billy. I assumed something more important called you away, but when I didn't hear from you, frankly, I began to question whether we should be seeing each other. I started to have doubts ..."

"Why didn't you telephone me or post me a letter?" he said between glances at her lovely presence and the road leading to their destination. She was wearing a patterned cotton dress with a buttoned-up lace front opened at the collar under a pink sweater that matched the barrettes securing her silken tresses off to the side of her face.

"I had no idea you called my office," she stated. "Not hearing from you caused me to question your sincerity, to be honest. All the reasons why we should not be together began tumbling over in my mind. Then I got busy with so many tasks and projects – well, you know how that is!"

"I guess I'm like you," he said. When my call to you went unanswered, I thought that was your way of saying 'Vamoose!' You say you think something more important came up for me on Natal Day? Nothing's more important than you, *ma chérie*."

And he meant what he said like he'd never meant anything more in his life. To the core of his being he felt if he could just have her bond in friendship this would satisfy him for the near term, would still his restlessness, anchor his thoughts and steady his life's direction.

They sailed through the city toward Purcells Cove Road, hooking around the Northwest Arm to head to the waterfront park. Vivian savored the vistas of her home province, somehow even more stunning on this special evening, her head and heart relieved of stress she didn't even realize she had been harboring these past months wrestling with the Billy factor. She didn't want to term it a dilemma because as they chased the waning sun it wasn't one at all. For both of them, their togetherness was a solution akin to drawing excellent letters in Scrabble but taking an agonizing while to see and play the game-winning, eight-letter word. Or being a move away from a checkmate and, what seems a lifetime later, victory. The chess pieces seemingly come to life and show you the right move to make.

Something felt ordained about their stroll through the birch trees and their visit to the monumental tower where they climbed precarious stone stairs to the top lookout over the ocean.

The salt mist enraptured the circling seabirds judging from their dips and swirls and declarations. The ebb and flow of crashing waves provided a natural soundtrack, conducive to talking revealingly about their feelings, something neither Billy nor Vivian did very well.

However, their dialogue in Martello Tower had the ring of a confessional.

Billy talked about being four and his ten-year-old brother Romney dying the day after Christmas, falling out of the back of an open truck and hitting his head on a rock. After that the city passed a law that no one could ride in the back of an open truck, which kids used to do all the time.

He lost a darling younger sister to liver cancer. She was only 14. A third sibling Milton died at age two. Grief over losing his father arose as a topic too.

All through childhood Billy stored his emotions tightly inside for the good of the family and for Mom's sake. He cloaked his bereavement knowing Mom was hurting more and his best course of action was to wear a brave face.

He remembered misery as a three-year-old feeling rejected and lonely when he was left behind for a time in Truro, but through separation and family tragedies he learned to mine his inner resilience and avail it whenever needed. Did Vivian believe events in her childhood had affected her in a lasting way? Billy wanted to know.

She could readily relate to what he was saying. She likened the tragedies in her life to ink spilling on a blotter. Traumatic experiences absorb into the human fabric and stain it and oftentimes one can never be scrubbed clean, and it would be a mistake to try. He was causing her to think out loud. "As much as sorrows hurt us, they are there to teach us too," she said. "Being sick for a year at home right after being hit with my father's dire illness, I learned to be stoic, self-sufficient and to keep my own company. I suppressed my grief. I never shared my troubles with my poor Mother, who had enough to endure. I did everything my mother told me, to make life after Daddy's passing as bearable as possible for her."

Vivian couldn't remember the last time she had allowed her feelings to flow so freely. "I doubt she will ever remarry," she said, adding after a hint of a pause, "how about you?"

"If you're proposing, the answer is 'yes,'" Billy chimed. She blushed. He took both her hands and drew her near, not to kiss but to view her against the panorama backdrop of land, sea and sky.

"Vivian, I have declared my love for you. My feelings are not going to change. Should you find it in your heart to accept me as a suitor, I shall take my cue from you. For now, just to be with you is the fire I need."

What could she do, this maiden captive in the tower? What could she do but succumb to her dashing, bronzed hero and melt in the ardor of his strong arms? Resisting the urge to throw herself on him, she administered a soft, quick hug, gave him a peck on the cheek and said, "Gee, Billy, I'm relieved to know we can take our time to get acquainted as friends, test the waters."

Vivian recited her terms. Their friendship could continue as a slow build. They could meet at Fader's. They could go on walks, meet at YMCA-sponsored activities and anything camp-related. She didn't mind coming to his flat if Harry was there because he could serve as surrogate chaperone when she and Billy were in close quarters. Things had to be proper, she insisted. And she and Dick would continue to be very close friends.

Yes, yes and yes. With a "c'mon" he led her as they descended the staircase to the picnic tables by the waterfront. His heart was filled with the zest and fire of a young buck.

As they sat facing the sea, oblivious to the strolling couples and families with children, he returned to Vivian's earlier question. Would he remarry? Up until a certain chance drop-in to his brother's pharmacy, he considered himself a committed bachelor with eyes trained on his career after proving himself a failure at marriage. But now?

"I'm still seeing Lois," he admitted unintentionally, "and I perfectly understand that you want your beau in your life as Lois is in mine."

Vivian had reopened his mind to the idea of marrying again. It was Vivian who stirred his hopes, emboldened him to imagine a forever union. All he needed was a sign from her and he could break free of his holding pattern and devote himself to her.

They kissed out in the open, and then again. She couldn't resist. A taste of love makes you hungry for more. His moustache hair tickled her top lip. She giggled like a brook.

Driving home to the ferry he put his arm around her and steered with one hand, contented.

They had each just found someone with whom they could entrust their oft-sheltered feelings.

From then on, they resumed semi-regular contact under Vivian's pre-set conditions. Letters between them were frequent, personal visits less so. She was elbow-deep helping Jean and Aunt Gladys with the fall fundraiser. And along with her work friend, another Jean, she had volunteered for a special welcome-home project for the troops.

Billy was wrapped in a whirlwind of social work and political meetings, band and basketball practices, coaching kids and corralling them into choir singing, and seeing Mom and the brood on Sundays.

Lois was a willing and dependable vessel for his desires. To say she was excited about the Russian concert at the ritzy hotel was an understatement.

The evening had finally arrived. She was over the moon, dressed to the nines, fussing last-minute with an atomizer that Billy pleaded with her to stop spraying. He should have spoken sooner.

They left on a cloud of "Evening in Paris". He immediately opened his car window to dissipate the overkill of fumes. "They're going to smell you coming a mile away, Lois," he coughed. "Here, light me a smoke."

"I always wear this scent," Lois harrumphed. "Somebody's over-sensitive tonight. Don't blame my perfume." She took his lighter and smokes, fired one up and handed it to him, then lit one of her own. "If you weren't so handsome, I could throttle you sometimes, Billy White. Here we are on a nice evening out and you start it out on the wrong foot by insulting me. What's gotten into you lately?"

"Well, sugar, I never liked your perfume," he confessed. "It's just I love you too much to hurt your feelings," he fibbed. He was recalling the subtle fresh floral scent of Vivian's hair.

"I forgive you," Lois said as the hotel's majestic outline by the water came into view.

Billy looked terrific in his black, Sunday suit. His crisp, over-starched, white shirt made his neck itch around the collar. Lois looked like spun gold, her body wrapped in a satiny taffeta number that her seamstress sister made, her height elevated by gold high heels that warranted a hazard sign. They entered the regal entranceway and were enveloped by the bustle and bigness of CN's flagship hotel. As busy as it was, sounds were muffled by plush broadloom and thick walls. As they made their way to the grand ballroom's double doors, a figure moved in front of Billy to stop them from passing. "Excuse me," a baritone-pitched, jowly man with knitted eyebrows and wearing a hotel uniform barked, while a flow of other patrons moved freely in and out of the doors.

Lois, who was clutching Billy's arm, squeezed in closer, fearing the worst.

"May I help you, my friend?" Billy's steady, calm voice tempered the perceived tension. The man was ruddy and brawny. He cleared his throat.

"You're White, aren't you?" the man said haltingly. "William White?"

Billy nodded, not ceding any ground. The man broke into a grin and thrust out his hand. "I recognize you from the Y. You helped my son. He was having some troubles, but you saw promise in him and got him playing basketball and put him on the team. We'd nearly lost hope on him until you came along. I want to thank you."

"You're Mick Jones's dad." said Billy. "Well, let me tell you, Mick did all the work himself. My job was to twig his motivation. He's a fine youngster."

The father, who introduced himself as Joseph, plumped with pride. "You're going to the concert, I gather," he said. "Follow me, I'll take you straight through to your seats" and he ushered them in, VIP style.

Such a grand entrance was bound to turn heads. One of them was Vivian's.

Chapter 9

They could have been figurines on a wedding cake, Vivian thought as she saw them stride in like royalty, being led to their chairs by the burly floor captain in his brass-buttoned, maroon suit with matching cap and gold detailing. Lois, flouncing partway down the aisle to the indicated row, adjusted her fox stole in a slightly exaggerated fashion before easing into the chair. The fox head lay glumly on her chest. Billy took the aisle seat, delighted he would have some leg room and equally glad Lois had positioned the stole as she had, so he wouldn't be staring into the beady eyes of a dead fox all concert.

Vivian was near the front sitting with her mother but surveying the back double doors on the lookout for Aunt Gladys, who was due to deliver opening remarks for the fundraiser they'd all worked on so diligently.

After observing them strutting to the far side of the ballroom, Lois latched possessively on Billy's arm, Vivian whipped her face forward and hoped he hadn't spotted her. The first thought that struck her was a desire to avoid any awkward situation, whether with his girlfriend or with Mother. The second thought was to imagine herself as the woman on Billy's arm. To see them together was disconcerting, she had to admit. Despite the love letters and poems from him that lived comfortably in her desk drawer at home, Vivian's doubts nibbled away at her. Did he really love her as his writings professed? Or was their budding friendship just a mirage, a trompe l'oeil – beguiling and beautiful but deceptive. She and Dick were going out this weekend. That thought comforted her in the moment, evened her keel. Billy was living by the rules she'd established, committed non-commitment.

Once composed, slowly and subtly she would turn for sporadic looks back to watch them interact. Billy had forgotten his reading glasses and Lois was reciting details to him from the program, which Vivian had typed and collated as one of her volunteer assignments on the project. Had she been closer to the couple she would have known he was suffering from Lois's butchery of the Russian names and song title pronunciations.

Vivian's voyeurism was soon interrupted. A middle-aged woman in a brown suit and exuding an air of authority appeared through the back doors and approached the front of the room, clipboard in hand, moving as hastily down the aisle as her sore back allowed. Billy happened to notice her as he scanned the room. He studied the arriving woman as she gave a small wave to two ladies beside the empty seat she would occupy. From the aisle, she reached over a few seated concertgoers to hand her purse to the pretty girl next to the vacant chair, a girl who looked a lot like Vivian. Billy did a double take that confirmed this was her. Who was she with? Her mother? Was Dick here too? No. Evidently, she was without a male escort and that gave Billy the squirm of a guilty party despite having committed no crime. He wished the older woman's vacant chair was his, he thought, as he watched her labor to the stage and approach the lectern positioned stage left. A warm ripple of applause welcomed the stately lady. After a few throat clearings, coughs and rustlings from the audience had subsided, she began:

"Welcome everyone. Thank you for being here. My name is Gladys Baker, representing the women's committee of our wonderful Halifax Philharmonic Orchestra and our local chapter of Independent Order of Daughters of the Empire." A burst of robust applause ensued. "We worked together to make this inaugural concert the perfect kick-off to a post-war concert season, and I say this with utmost pride and in celebration of the extensive hand our brave boys had in bringing peace to the world ..." Applause. "... as well as in commemoration of the sacrifice of those who gave their lives so that we could have the freedom so essential for all peoples of the world. Your purchase of tickets enables us to continue to present the very best in the world of music through this remarkable concert series." More clapping. "All of us here believe that music is a universal language supporting unity among people. Tonight, you are in for a real treat, I assure you," Gladys said, quoting from Vivian's careful wording in the script.

"Now, without further ado, I give you Mr. Nicholas Kostrukoff and his General Platoff Don Cossack Chorus."

And with that, the exquisite mastery of the Slavic singing troupe commenced. It was a display of vocal acrobatics that mesmerized the audience and kept it absolutely transfixed. Except for Billy, whose eyes cast through the dim room light to Vivian's spot, his concentration on the performance broken by his mental plotting on how he would navigate through the evening with two girlfriends under one roof. Once he arrived on a plan, he settled in to appreciate the spectacle onstage.

Vivian could feel his eyes on her. In the low light between numbers, she did glance back and to the right to validate her intuition. He had her locked in his sights.

She appeared to look right through him, not at his eyes but to some point beyond his left shoulder – a cool, impassive look of a distant stranger. Then she turned away and focused her attention on the singers commencing their next selection. Not a hint of recognition, her coolness froze him. Then he recalled her rule about how they were to behave when in public together.

As the sonorous bass soloists Andronoff and Grigorieff boomed incredibly in "Save Thy People, O God" by P. Tchesnokoff, Billy reflected on his Baptist roots and the text of this familiar song, the last of the show's liturgical segment.

The house lights came up signalling the first intermission. Predictably, Lois wanted to find a mirror and look at herself. Billy stood up to let her out. "I'm going to work the room," he told her, and she knew she wouldn't see him again until Act Two.

Billy hustled over to where Vivian was clustered with her mother and aunt.

"Good evening, Vivian," he said with a broad smile. "What a magnificent musical evening this is! I saw you here and wanted to say hello. How do you do," he said to Jean and Gladys, not waiting to be introduced. They rose from their seats, and everyone shuffled into the aisle.

"Mother, Aunt Gladys, meet Billy White, the program director at the Halifax Y."

He extended his hand, which Gladys shook warmly, palm-to-palm. Jean, in contrast, let the fingers in her gloved hand go limp when Billy clasped them as she uttered a weak "good evening."

"I knew your father," Aunt Gladys said, "a fine example of your people, he was. In fact, the woman who helped him enter university here is a dear friend of ours: Helena Blackadar, a member of our Nova Scotia mission. She was his teacher at a seminary in Washington. Vivian, your mother has a photograph of you at the age of three holding Miss Blackadar's hand outside Nana Keeler's house."

Another astounding coincidence, Vivian thought, even more peculiar than when she and Billy realized that they both knew Harold and Helen Kieran. She had no idea that she'd held the hand of the woman who had encouraged Billy's father to come to Canada. Billy once mentioned that his oldest sibling Helena was named after his father's favorite teacher, neither he nor Vivian could have put two and two together. "Well, I'll be!" Billy was amazed and delighted to learn of the connection. Providence, he thought. Yet again a sign he and Vivian were destined for each other.

"My late husband had wonderful things to say about the YMCA during the first war," Jean volunteered. "I shall find the letter that he wrote to his mother where he spoke of it and I'm sure Vivian will be glad to transcribe it and pass it along to your agency for posterity. Won't you dear?" Vivian nodded with a smile.

"That would be most kind of you Mrs. Keeler," said Billy. "And may I say that I am very sorry for the loss of your husband? My father has been gone nigh on ten years and thoughts of him are as fresh as yesterday." He turned to Vivian. "And thank you, again, Vivian, for all the help you and Bernard gave to our Inclusive Camps Project." He prided himself for inventing that name spur-of-the-moment to describe the meeting more than a year ago that he staged to get to know Vivian better. He figured he should extend the harmless ruse a bit further and close the subject. "At the Y, we're continually reaching out to serve all segments of our youth and adult communities regardless of their income, status or race. You should be very proud of Vivian and Bernard for helping to move this forward. Changes should be in place for our 1946 summer season at Camp Owen."

The conversation flowed naturally, and Vivian finally piped in.

"Lillian and I are planning another Camp Owen bonanza for next year. We'll have everyone from last summer and then some."

Ceiling lights flickered to indicate five minutes to the close of intermission, prompting Billy's "nice meeting you" to the elders and an easygoing "see you, Vivian." He hastened back to his seat where Lois's facial expression was as glum as the fox head on her fur wrap.

"I could have used you out there," she said dully, with a backward nod to the lobby. Billy sensed her distinct change of mood. "What happened?"

"I was at the center of an unpleasant scene, that's what happened," she sniped. "Some uppity white woman complained about my using the hotel washroom. Imagine! She demanded in a loud voice that the hotel matron sanitize the stall right down to the door handle after I exited the cubicle, made me feel this tall." Lois opened her thumb and index finger to the approximate width of a pencil.

"What did I tell you, Billy? Where white folks are concerned, there's always trouble."

"I'm sorry that happened to you, Lois. What did you do?"

"Well, I didn't slug her, but I wanted to. I was so angry and embarrassed I was at a loss for words for a second. I just went to the sink, washed my hands, then dried them with the plush cotton hand towel, nice and slow, and I waited for her to emerge from the stall. When she did, I looked her up and down disapprovingly and with all the other hoity-toity white women listening I rendered my judgment, and said, 'You should do something about that hair.' I gave a shudder and a huff, and I tell you I left with my head held high."

Billy chortled. "That's priceless, Lois. You sure took care of that crabby apple, but don't let one bad apple spoil the whole bunch."

Lois wasn't ready to be cajoled out of her indignation. "*One* bad apple? I know you love your white folks, but don't expect me to feel the same way. I will always have my guard up."

Billy shrugged. He wasn't going to change her mind. There was no teaching her to believe and trust whites. In Billy's analysis, this was one of the reasons why he and Lois weren't fated to be a permanent pair. He wanted to cross the great racial divide. She didn't. But before the lights lowered, as concertgoers resettled for the second half, he put a consoling arm around her, and whispered, "Don't let it ruin our night, beautiful. I'll fix this," he vowed, considering possible courses of action, one of which involved bringing the matter to the attention of Gladys Baker.

The explosive second act of folk songs, war songs and classics left it impossible to nurse inner hurts and grudges as the sounds emitting from the thirty-five athletic Russian singers would allow only the exultation of glory and uplifted emotions to enter the listeners' hearts.

Billy had to admit to feeling professional envy of chorus director Mr. Kostrukoff, whose all-male chorus lay title as the greatest singing organization of its kind. They traveled throughout Europe, North and South Africa, the Far East, South America, Australia, New Zealand, Honolulu, Mexico and the West Indies and now were embarking on a seventh transcontinental American tour. Would that I could make as big an impression someday, he thought.

The impact of the exquisite range of impeccably conditioned voices, from the lowest timbre to the soprano-sphere purity of the falsetto, constituted a religious experience for Billy that night. While he caught Lois yawning a few times during part one, she stayed awake and hopping at times in part two, emitting shrieks with the crowd in awe of the closing number, Lezginka, a Caucasian Cossack dagger dance.

One dancer gives an exciting exhibition of knife juggling while he whirls about the stage with ever-increasing momentum, finally projecting each dagger with unerring aim to form a straight line on the stage floor, like so many pins in a bowling alley.

Part three roared to its finish with a performance of Kozatchok, a riotous free-for-all of thrilling, agile stunts. Concertgoers thundered their appreciation.

No mingling afterwards, Billy shepherded Lois out of the hall, first casting a hopeful look in Vivian's direction where a hive of happy well-wishers surrounded her.

He took Lois home. He swore to God, this one last time.

• • •

Billy detected the faint smell of lavender and Ivory soap in Gladys Baker's parlour. The October sun streamed through the drapery-festooned window of her old Dartmouth home, bathing the potted geraniums that lined the sill in welcome light, and casting a glow on the small trolley where a teapot and matching fine china cups awaited their ritual of service.

Vivian initiated the pouring, starting with Aunt Gladys's customary clear tea in the yellow rose cup, what used to be Nana Keeler's favorite. Billy was indebted to Vivian for arranging this meeting the week after the concert. After he told her what had happened to Lois, she was more than willing to facilitate a conversation with her aunt. The IODE and Gladys had been most obliging. That the complainant was Billy's girlfriend didn't stand in the way of Vivian's readiness to help, which heightened Billy's admiration of her.

"A most unfortunate situation I grant you, Billy," Gladys agreed between sips. "I'm not persuaded that our organization can nor should be held responsible or accountable for the conduct of one unidentified patron. To be clear, we at the IODE do not condone such objectionable conduct. However, it is not our place to police the community concertgoers and I don't see how I can be of much help."

Billy set his dainty cup on its saucer and made use of the end table to free up his expressive hands. He held them out, palms up. "How about a compromise?" he inquired, and when he saw he had her interest he rolled out his suggestions.

Would Gladys write a letter of apology to Lois on behalf of the IODE expressing regret for the uncomfortable interaction she encountered? Would the executive committee consider writing a letter to the hotel to inform management of the incident so that staff might be trained on managing similar unpleasantness?

He told Gladys he had considered going the political route and working on resolving the problem with his CCF party, to perhaps lodge a more public protest, but felt diplomacy would achieve more.

"I'll write the letters," Vivian volunteered. "Then all you'd have to do is sign them, Auntie."

While not as quick to consent as Vivian would have liked, eventually after a moment staring into her teacup, Gladys looked up and said, "All right. I will do it."

She knew that not complying would put her headlong into conflict with Vivian's stubborn streak and incessant pestering until she acquiesced. Growing up, Vivian was never able to leave well enough alone – always involved in causes, always trying to bring people together and make things perfect. Such a dear girl, she thought as she absorbed Vivian's grateful look.

"This will mean the world to the complainant, Mrs. Baker," Billy said, "and I thank you most sincerely from the bottom of my heart, both of you."

He stood up to leave. "Again, my gratitude and a good day to you both, Mrs. Baker, Miss Keeler."

Gladys moved to the front door to see him out. Vivian stayed behind to help her aunt assemble thank-you notes and wrap gifts for committee members and volunteers. She gave Billy a smile and a mild wave goodbye from her seat before remembering the folded paper in her purse, her typewritten transcription of her father's account of the YMCA during the First World War. "I almost forgot," she called out, as she retrieved the paper from her purse, stood up, stepped toward the doorway and handed it to a smiling, receptive Billy.

He looked forward to reading it on the twelve-minute ferry ride across the harbor to Halifax. On his walk to the terminal, he felt self-satisfied. Not only had he secured a measure of restitution on Lois's behalf, but he had been given a private key to enter Vivian's family life. He also reflected on Vivian's unblemished kindness – helping him, helping Lois, unfazed, always friendly, goodness personified.

As the ferry chugged from its slip, he unfolded the paper, and put himself in Captain Keeler's shoes:

> You speak of the work that the Red Cross is doing – and it is undoubtedly good – but I want to tell you about an organisation that is doing bigger and better work for the men over here. It is the YMCA. If I ever have any money to give to any organization the YM will get it. Let me tell you about a little of their work.

They have – as you know – writing rooms all over the place where they provide paper and envelopes. Also, wherever possible they have reading and recreation rooms. This is a great thing for the men who would otherwise have nothing to do.

I remember one time I was sent out of the line, to arrange for billets for my company, who were being relieved that night. I got out about six o'clock and did my work, then began to think about something to eat for supper. I had no money – not a franc – so gave up the idea of eating and went to the YMCA for a cup of water. The man in charge asked me if I would like a glass of cold lemonade (it was in the summer). Well, to make it short – I said I was broke – he got the lemonade and a package of biscuits and would not even allow me to promise to pay him later.

Once again, I was coming out after a particularly hard trip and was just near exhausted as possible when I met a chap who was directing everyone to the YMCA for hot tea and biscuits. You can't imagine what that hot tea did for the boys that night – it cheered them up, gave them new vigor to carry on. Oh! I can't begin to tell you all about it – it all looks so tame on paper.

They are not safety-first people either – I have seen them carry buckets full of hot tea around a battlefield looking for wounded men, cheering them up and saving many lives of men who would have died had they not had some stimulant – they are great, good men these YMCA people and have my everlasting thanks and sympathy.

Les would be thrilled with this, Billy thought, knowing that his boss was Y to the core and a history buff to boot, who tracked the years of YMCA War Services from 1866, when it first began providing support in the form of recreation, religious, educational, and entertainment services to troops serving abroad. YMCA staff was a welcome sight and became known for offering moral support and comfort. Vivian had proffered a firsthand testimonial to this.

Initially he missed noticing an arrow in pencil drawn in the bottom right corner indicating he should turn the page. He did and his attention jumped to her handwritten words. His heart plummeted: he could hear her gentle voice like the wind spiriting away his hopes as he read the lightly pencilled words:

> Dear Billy,
> Dick asked me to be his study partner (sorely needed) so I will be quite busy with him over the next while. I think it would be wise for you and me to use our time apart to consider the realities of our situation.
> Regards,
> Vivian

Her pithy sentences pierced him like a pitchfork in hay, thrashing his earlier optimism to the ground. Was she dumping him? He reread and dissected her note. "Consider the realities of our situation" – that could mean anything and didn't necessarily mean she was ending it. But he had to face the possibility that Vivian could be slipping from his tenuous grasp. In a matter of half an hour he'd gone from elation to near devastation.

He found himself admiring her forethought upon realizing that she probably used pencil for writing instead of pen so he could erase her words and still give the typewritten story to Les for his file. Vivian was a very deliberate thinker and a planner, and oh, so considerate. How Billy loved her.

Being a Saturday, he headed to the Y. But instead of working, he decided to compose a masterwork for Vivian, an ode, a plea, a vow. Clearly something changed the night she saw him with Lois at the concert. Now, his plan was to compose the heavenly strains from the very fibre of his heart and soul to woo Vivian to be and stay by his side.

Once inside his Barrington Street office he virtually flew to his desk to conjure the sonnet that was coiled and poised to leap from his body onto the page.

When I found you, dear one, I reasoned thus:
the Fates no longer bent on toying with my heart
to bring me pain and bitter discontent, were moved on
seeing
that the light of love therein long since flickered out.
And being moved to deep compassion, grief and self-re-
proach,
avowed their wrong and pledged themselves to make
amends,
commensurate to my loss. They chose for me,
from Venus' treasured store, a spark of light which,
though a million years before had found its birth
in God's eternal Light of Perfect understanding,
yet shone a million times more bright.
They laid it on my heart and by its light
I found the road to Perfect Love.
The road to thee, my love, had opened up to me for all
Eternity.

He titled it "Recompense" and recapped his pen. Then he found an eraser in his desk drawer, retrieved Vivian's note from his pocket and rubbed out
her comments and decided to behave as though she'd never written them.
He typed out his poem, released it from the machine and made strides toward the music room, sonnet in hand.

There were four places Billy could go to play the piano: Here at the
YMCA, at the church on Cornwallis Street, at Mom's, or at his own
apartment on a harmonium – a pump organ in a box – that he purchased
for eighty cents. He also had access to one at the Dal music department
through Harry, who had assumed the presidency of the Dalhousie Music
and Dramatic Society. Their next show, "A Dream of Love," a musical ex-
travaganza under Harry's direction, fortuitously sponsored by the IODE,
was slated for the end of November.

Like magic Billy was hopeful again, such was his character that he never
stayed down for long. A single optimistic glint was all it took to springboard

him out of the doldrums. As director of scenes three, four and seven, he cheered himself with the vision of featuring his new composition, to end the finale. Vivian would be there in the audience at his invitation of course, swooning over the original masterwork he had created for her. Later he imagined her accepting the handwritten manuscript, which he would fashion with precision nib strokes of India ink. His music and artistry would clinch it for him, he told himself, and he began to compose music to his sonnet, "Recompense".

Chapter 10

"I don't care about their stinking letter." Lois tossed the IODE apology letter in the direction of her living room waste basket. She'd had a terrible day – an argument with her bank manager, an upset client and a broken heel on her favorite pair of shoes leading to a twisted ankle. Her swollen right foot elevated on the coffee table between immersions in ice water, she eyed Billy from the couch. "What does one Gladys Baker know about how it felt to be me in that moment? How can she say, 'I can certainly appreciate your concern'? I guarantee you, that woman will never know how it feels to have a skin color that lets her get treated like dirt. She and her IODE types live in a world of privilege all their own. I don't believe their apology is going to change one damn thing!"

Billy was impatient with her petulance and disappointed that his move to make things right hadn't been well received.

"You know, Lois, you could at least be gracious and accept an apology when one is offered," he counselled. "And the hotel will be notified and can train the staff."

"Oh, you shut up, Billy," she cranked. "Always cozying up to those whites and taking their side. Why can't you side with your own people once in a while? Are you just a Negro on the weekends?"

He was disgusted with her, clicked his tongue sneeringly, and shook his head hopelessly.

"I've had enough. Lois, I can't be with you anymore. Let's just admit we are on different paths and be the friends we started out to be."

If there was one thing Billy couldn't stand, it was leaving on bad terms. He did that once – with his ex-wife – and it nearly did him in.

Lois wasn't fighting him. She was resigned to the fact that Billy was slipping away. She'd seen this coming for months, ever since his affair with Joan, even before, but especially recently. The distance between them had grown, so a formal unhitching was not totally unexpected. Had Portia not cautioned her from the get-go?

"It hurts," she said, misty-eyed, and not referring to her bruised ankle, "but you're right, of course. It's time we admitted we're not made for each other." She shrugged. "Come here and give me a kiss then and get out of here. I'll see you around."

She was being a good sport, perhaps believing this would be like any of their other separations, temporary.

Leaving Lois was refreshing, a splash of cool water on a flushed face. Billy sailed down the sidewalk, light-footed, his weightless heart freed of its concern about fallout with Lois and buoyed by the nearing concert night with Vivian in attendance. Harry had set aside complimentary house tickets this time and arranged for both Lillian and Vivian to come as his and Billy's special guests.

Billy's walk to his car was interrupted by an accosting from a rumpled sack on the sidewalk. On closer examination the muffle emanated from a woozy and wizened, charcoal-faced man, wool blanket pulled up to his chin as a minimal and inadequate buffer against November's chill.

"Spare change?" he slurred, his scant eyebrows arched quizzically as he peeked out and up at Billy, whose hands rattled his pockets for change. "What's your name, my friend?" he prompted, tossing five cents in the dented can that squatted on the sidewalk. The ring of the coin hitting the tin seemed to snap the beggar to attention and he made an effort to gather himself on his battered piece of cardboard. He wore a beat-up, broken-zippered fall jacket, his flimsy shirt made visible and a torn breast pocket, revealed. As he sat up and adjusted his blanket around his bent shoulders, he introduced himself as Stewart Reed. His friends call him "Bones" as in stew.

"Guess my middle name or give me another penny?" he asked, trying his best to maintain a level head on a rubber-like neck. He had a rheumy right eye that wandered involuntarily like a bobber in the water. "Three guesses?"

Billy couldn't resist the challenge to his psychic powers and was entertained by Bones's creative panhandling. He guessed "Otis," then "Michael" and finally "Cornelius." Bones shook his head, delivered the answer cagily. "It's Cant," he said, raising his hand to draw an exclamation point in the air, "Stewart Cant Reed." His look was deadpan until it curled into a scamp's grin and then they both roared. A penny plunked into its new home.

Concern held Billy in his place. Stewart was in terrible shape, dirty, undernourished and gaunt. There was an acrid smell about him mixed with fumes of cheap wine. Joining him on the sidewalk were an orange crate and his burlap sack, filled with a haberdashery of items, some sharp-cornered belongings bulging from their bag.

Billy reached for his pack of cigarettes, lit two, and handed one to the man.

"Stewart ..." he began.

"Call me Bones."

"Bones," he restarted. "I have a proposal for you. What if I told you I could get you a nice bath and a hot bowl of soup, and a place to stay? Is this something that interests you?"

Bones considered the proposition, twisted his pursed and largely toothless mouth from side to side as if trying to solve a difficult problem. "Can I bring my stuff?" he wanted to know.

"Yes, of course, bring your possessions. My car's right here."

Bones stood up, put his potato sack in the inverted crate and shuffled to follow Billy, goods in arm, his sockless feet in bedroom slippers, the cigarette hanging from his lips.

They reached the car. Billy unlocked the trunk.

"Bones. My name is Billy. This is "Mary Ann". Come on, load your belongings and let's go. I'm going to introduce you to Mrs. Marjorie Walker, and on the way there I'd like you to tell me about yourself and what Stewart Cant Reed *can* do."

Bones eased into the passenger seat, in a partial state of disbelief that a kindness had befallen him. Billy wasn't quite ready to drive. He untied and removed his shiny brown shoes and black wool socks, then handed Bones the socks one at a time.

"Here," he said. "Put these on. You need these more than I do."

And with that he re-shoed himself, cranked the engine, as Bones adorned his feet with the warmed-over socks, and chauffeured the hobo to the rooming house, one of the private billeting arrangements the YMCA-run hostel in Halifax struck up with churches and community members like Marjorie Walker, the tireless president of the Helping Hands Society. The church and she personally had sheltered many a hard-done-by man while the Y helped them back on their feet. Billy stopped at a telephone booth – the great new marvel that had mushroomed in Halifax since arriving in Canada last year – to say they were on their way.

A tall, lithe woman with skin the color of burnished walnut, chin-length hair sculpted with the use of chemicals and curlers into a pageboy, tucked behind largish ears of ample lobe, an angular face, high cheekbones and all-embracing eyes, she had a sweeping, take-charge welcome awaiting them when they rolled up to the black door of her grey, frame house.

The hot bath was steaming ready for Bones to pour himself into, a towel laid out atop an assortment of mix-and-match hand-me-downs for him to examine and choose for himself, a toothbrush with some baking soda there too. Boots and shoes, there was a boxful of donated footwear in the spare room where he'd be sleeping. He could pick out the best-fitting pair to keep. She explained it all to Bones as they stood at the door to the bathroom, and then left him to the privacy of his personal business.

On the drive over Billy learned that Bones was one of the boys who had signed up in 1916 to serve in Canada's segregated unit during the First World War. He was born in Preston in 1898, the son of a rag merchant and a laundress. His parents drank and fought constantly, didn't pay him much mind. They weren't cruel or mean. They were indifferent, which can be a cruelty all its own. He felt insignificant, felt it in the fact that they never cared whether he went to school, so he rarely did. They were frequent yellers, and their raucous, high-volume arguments affected Bones like toxin. He felt weakened by his poisoned parents and couldn't wait to strike out on his own, join the military, make a contribution to his country and acquire the skills to build a better life on his return home. His homecoming made him feel shunned and insignificant all over again. The only job he could get back home was cleaning latrines at the shipyard. Over time his repeated exposure to raw sewage and fumes led to terrible side effects including an eye infection that left him partially blind. He was in and out of hospital, treated more like a prisoner than a patient. The company accepted no responsibility for his illnesses or the working conditions and fired him for absenteeism while he was still struggling to pay the doctor's bills. His plight drove him back to his widowed father and into a spiral of drinking and gradual self-destruction. He made money fixing things for people. Everyone marveled at his mechanical know-how. There was never an occasion where he couldn't figure out what was wrong.

Billy calculated the odds of meeting a panhandler who not only knew Pup, but served in his battalion, as about a million to one. For the son, the current scene harkened memories of being at Pup's elbow as they offered assistance to the feeble and the needy. Food, clothing, a job prospect – somebody Pup had lobbied was hiring for the next day. Billy at Pup's side proffered hope to people trapped in the jaws of poverty and in so doing witnessed both the transformations and the transgressions of people in dire straits. It led him into social work.

The aroma of chicken stock filled the kitchen. An iron pot gently simmered on the stove. Marjorie gestured at Billy to take a seat at the table where she joined him to be filled in on Bones' circumstance.

Stewart Reed's First World War story was just as Pup had sermonized in retrospect a few years before he died.

"I have seen on the streets of London colored men from America, the West Indies, the Indians, the Chinese, the Japanese and men from all quarters of the globe dressed in the uniform of the Allies doing their bit in the cause they called the cause of freedom and democracy," he told his all-white cleric colleagues. "For a time, all barriers of race and color were broken down. They were comrades in arms. On the return to their homes, they expected to find the same conditions existing. Instead, they found other barriers they had never known before."

When Bones emerged scrubbed, shaved and outfitted, the two others had already made some decisions and were eager to test his reaction. He came to join them in the living room, giddy with lavender freshness from using Mrs. Walker's homemade soap.

Mrs. Walker led with an invitation for him to stay with her temporarily, then to the Y hostel, while they searched for a decent rooming house for him. In the meantime, she had repairs that needed to be done and while she couldn't pay him much, she could pay him something and could recommend him to members of the sizable church congregation. Billy followed up with one condition: no alcohol. If Bones wanted this opportunity, he'd have to change. That meant reporting to the Y once a week for a check-in and a counselling session with Billy. They waited for his answer, sitting themselves down at the supper table.

The table set with spoons, plates and a basket of biscuits, Mrs. Walker ladled the chicken-laced vegetables and broth into bowls which she delivered one at a time to their places. Bones hadn't said a word yet – his nose following the steam rising from his bowl. He inhaled.

"Mrs. Walker, Ma'am, I swear the smell of your soup just sent me straight to heaven and back. God is giving me the chance to be a new man. I'd be a fool to turn it down. May he give me the strength to avoid temptation and not disappoint. I promise to do my best."

"Perhaps you would do us the honor of saying grace," Marjorie suggested.

They bowed their heads as Bones articulated a heartfelt prayer. By the end of the meal, his hands were shaking as his thoughts turned to drink. Marjorie gave him two aspirins with water, showed him to his room, and told him to rest. The afternoon mostly spent, Billy had time to swing home to pick up his music and don a fresh pair of socks before heading to meet Harry for tonight's rehearsal. He bid adieu to Mrs. Walker who asked in parting that he relay her regards to his mother, the founder of Helping Hands. He was seeing Izie and the family tomorrow for Sunday dinner and planned to treat them to a preview of his newly composed song for Vivian. Just a few touches needed beforehand to complete the composition.

Routinely Saturday night was glee club night. With their show a faint two weeks away, rehearsals adopted an air of heightened intensity and anticipation. Harry had parked himself at the back of the hall, scribbling show notes, marking cues and working out a musical arrangement seemingly simultaneously. Billy, the masterful, humor-imbued choral leader, ran his well-oiled choir through its paces, his screw-together, ivory-handled baton waving a spell of disciplined synchronization over the group such that they finished before eight.

"No Lois tonight?" Harry wanted to know, assessing his chances of a ride home with Billy.

"Lois and I have parted ways," Billy said. "We've reverted to friendship status, and yes, I'm going straight home. I can give you a lift."

"Sorry, I can't say I'm broken up about your breakup," said Harry honestly. "Now you can devote yourself to the woman you're really after. Time doesn't wait, Billy, and neither will Vivian. I consider Vivian my friend too, and I see her clock ticking and you missing the beat. Look, I know the inter-racial aspect must be a factor, but the way I see it, you're letting her slip through your fingers."

"Hey, by the way," Harry said, "I found us a piano for the apartment belonging to the parents of a kid in my class, free if we move it. The university weightlifting team agreed to haul it up to our place because one of the guy's has a girlfriend in the show and her father owns a truck. I can't believe our luck!"

"Don't worry, the boys can handle it," he said in response to Billy's dubious look. "Four of them were pallbearers at Humphrey Davy's funeral," he said, referring to the school's former heavyweight star felled famously by a heart attack during a lift. "They can handle the weight and I'll rearrange the front room to make space."

On their way home in the car, Billy returned to his friend's inter-racial comment.

"My father was asked to speak on the topic of 'race re-adjustment' to an all-white group of preacher men in the early 1930s. He told them his theory: that the chief cause of misunderstanding may be found in the haughty air of superiority, grown out of the fact that we are prone to see the worst in the other race rather than the best, Harry."

Billy delivered his father's point as he remembered it: "If a white man beats us in a bargain, we shake our heads stoically and say, that's a white man for you, he is always up to some sharp practice. If a colored man commits some crime, we immediately brand the whole race as criminal. We forget that there are good and bad in all races."

Harry clicked his tongue in agreement. "That just about sums it up, Billy. I wish I could have known your father."

Back at the flat and fueled by Harry's observation that the sand in his romantic hourglass could run out soon, Billy set about finishing the manuscript for "Recompense," a song for Vivian. More than a song: a masterpiece, an intermezzo, seven pages of intricate notation.

Seated at the small square table shoved into the corner of his bedroom he switched on his desk lamp, uncorked his well of India ink and unscrewed the fountain pen he used exclusively for music calligraphy, which he executed with scientific precision to complete the final passages. Now all that was left was a cover design. He got up to retrieve photos in an envelope from his dresser drawer and found the one of Vivian among the flowers at the public gardens. This he would use as his model for replicating a pen and ink etching of her face on the cover. Then he had the idea of using poster paints to add a background color to the cover. Before he knew it, he was immersed in drawing, coloring, lettering and completing the manuscript to the letter. By two he went to bed tired and satisfied, his final thoughts floating to Vivian like the tune in his head and then, oddly, to Bones. Mr. Sealy *must* have known him. Billy would ask him tomorrow at Sunday dinner.

George was there with Elsie, as well as Jack, Lorne, Yvonne, June and Nettie and kids, plus Mom and Mr. Sealy – a full house when Billy arrived with homemade cornbread for the table and a hail of hellos, handshakes and hugs.

Around the dining table Izie had worked her usual magic, stretching groceries to their absolute best and most savory uses to feed the familial army.

"Certainly, I knew him," Mr. Sealy said of Bones when Billy said the name Stewart Reed. "Private Reed had a mechanical mind and able hands. He was a good and earnest man who enlisted to escape a difficult home life. I think he was one of those teenagers who lied about his age so that he could join."

"He's not doing so well now, but I'm trying to help him through the Y services. Mom, I took him to Mrs. Walker's. She asked me to relay her greetings."

Mom nodded pleasantly.

Dessert of canned backyard pears pleased their collective palates and sibling banter peppered their family time together. After dishes were done, in between the flurries of conversation, Billy walked Izie to her pillowed armchair, seated her and announced he had written a song for the girl he wanted to marry.

"That's lovely, dear," she said before hearing a single note or posing a single question about his latest girlfriend.

Once he unrolled his musical tapestry, aided by the keys under his fingers and the bell-like clarity of his vocal execution, Izie intuitively understood what her son had uttered was gospel truth. He would marry whoever this woman was.

The cover of Billy's original song "Recompense"

Chapter 11

The debut of "Recompense" hadn't worked the magic Billy had expected. Thrilled as she was by it, Vivian didn't automatically drop everything to be with him. Her life was full and rich with activity: choir on Tuesdays, an hour a day practising piano, BYPU on Thursdays, still dating Dick. To his parents, she was the daughter they never had. Between them, her own relatives and pals, she didn't need to venture far to find all the stimulation and companionship she needed.

Her separation from Billy had allowed her the distance and the time to think and regain her good sense. She vowed to take a dispassionate approach where Billy was concerned. No more kissing, that was for certain. Friendship was possible, and desirable: romance wasn't. Society made that perfectly clear. No mixing. Until now Vivian hadn't considered it strange that at school, church, in college and now on the job, everyone around her was white. These days she was acutely aware of racial injustice and an unfairly divided community. Still, she was raised to play by the rules, honor her family and its good name.

She would sublimate her emotions and meet Billy on an intellectual level. That way they could be together, and she wouldn't run the risk of hurting or offending anybody. Meeting after work, long walks together, endless talks about life, philosophy, current events, the arts, and literature, discussions about race, religion and a favorite, exploring the meaning and origins of words, sharing letters and poetry. As friends they wouldn't be rocking any boats, she reasoned.

Vivian's new resolve had Billy spinning like a yo-yo. Through phone calls, letters and face-to-face encounters their contact continued, but not in the way he had imagined. He realized the way to her heart was through her mind, and he went to work on it, advancing his best debates and arguments to her patient, listening ears and intelligent questions and insights.

For Vivian, the arrangement was ideal – intriguing, interesting, involved – yet safe. She'd already tasted backlash and judgmental slaps from people like Peggy and Mr. Morrison at the office. He had taken Vivian aside to tell her he'd prefer if Billy waited in the outer lobby when he called on her, rather than loiter at her desk in the inner suite of offices, which he felt could "cause discomfort" in others.

It was hard to know whether to take George B. Morrison seriously. Many of the girls in the office catered to their handsome boss and were accustomed to his cavalier remarks.

This was the same Mr. Morrison who, when prompted by a few drinks (rye and water), could easily fall into a drawling southern accent and disparage darker-skinned people, calling them "darkies," only the way he shaped the derogatory word it was "dawkies."

Vivian was more uncomfortable than ever with this side of Mr. Morrison and hated herself for keeping quiet about it.

Billy advised her not to do or say anything that would put her job at risk. From then on, he made a point of presenting himself in front of her desk when calling on her, disarming anyone in his path with his elevated charm.

"The United Nations General Assembly just met for the first time in London," he once said. "Since nations from around the world can meet around the table, I expect your Mr. Morrison will come to accept the idea of equality and acceptance in due course. In the meantime, you needn't sacrifice your employment on his account."

As usual Vivian agreed with Billy. He was so much older and wiser than she and she respected his judgment and his knowledge.

January bled into February, the season of hearts – Valentine's Day. Vivian had lunch with Dick, and later dinner, Chinese food with Billy at the Nanking. Billy's day was the reverse: supper with Vivian and lunch with Lois.

Yes, the on again, off again with Lois was on again. He hadn't intended it, but with Vivian vacillating between skepticism and rejection over the idea that the two of them could be anything more than friends, well, what was a man to do when a certain ex-girlfriend came to call?

"Look, Billy," Lois implored. "I have needs. You have needs. I'm doing well, and you are free to be who you are with no strings attached. What do you say we just love each other as friends, intimate friends, and enjoy what we have between us? Why fight it?"

The way Billy saw it, he couldn't answer Lois's question fully over the telephone from his office chair. This conversation needed to happen in person. They could have a drink at "their" bar – a mistake. He had forgotten how alluring her feminine wiles could be and he was back to his juggling act, but not trying to hide it from Vivian this time even though he knew he could. She was everything Lois was not – innocent, naive, trusting and shy, agreeable, clever and worldly in knowledge, sophisticated yet earthy, at one with nature. Lois was brash and flamboyant, loud, argumentative and driven, self-assured and comfortable with her smouldering sensuality. She was an old habit, like the cigarettes he was so fond of but knew he shouldn't afford. Eventually he would tell Lois about Vivian. When Vivian was prepared to take a stand, he would be all hers.

Valentine's Day dinner with Vivian was entrancing, divine, rapturous, giddying for Billy. For her – another baby step closer to indulging her fantasy about having this man as her boyfriend. That night she wanted to know how a married relationship between them might work. It was not the first time they had discussed the issue. They'd debated all the aspects from interracial to financial before, like philosophers, probing truths. This time she was approaching the question from a practical standpoint, and Billy suggested they think about moving west. They could sell their possessions and start saving.

The following day after work Vivian wrote him a letter that inched them further along that course.

Dear Billy,

I would phone you if I could be sure you would want me to. But as I told you, I like to be sure of my welcome, and then too I seem to have a positive genius for choosing the wrong time to call.

It's five o'clock now. Everybody else has gone now. The building is very, very quiet. This is as good a time as any, I suppose, to quote for you, Sara Teasdale's poem "I Shall Not Care."

> When I am dead and over me bright April
> Shakes out her rain-drenched hair
> Tho' you should lean above me broken-hearted
> I shall not care.

> I shall have peace, as leafy trees are peaceful
> When rain bends down the bough;
> And I shall be more silent and cold-hearted
> Than you are now.

Especially now, darling, it's 5:21 p.m. You're supposed to be psychic, then you should know that I'm waiting here for you to call me. Perhaps you do know, but don't care.

Numerous difficulties must present themselves to the man who is attempting to carry on two love affairs simultaneously.

Yours,

Vivian

Her words struck Billy like an anvil. He dumped Lois shortly thereafter, only this time he levelled with her, told her he hoped that he and she and his new girlfriend could all be friends, if not right away then eventually. He donned his program secretary hat: he told her he'd been thinking for some time about an idea she broached about personally training young men to become barbers and at the same time teaching them how to dress, groom, present themselves and form good habits.

"We're in a position at the Y to move on your idea, and there's a part-time job in it for you this summer, if you're interested."

That seemed to smooth the transition considerably. Lois relinquished all claims on Billy. Most significantly he had the two main women in his life on the verge of knowing and respecting each other, or so he hoped.

• • •

Vivian turned twenty-one in 1946 and her mother determined she should host a party at the house. Jean promised she would pay for it as well as help with the planning and preparations. April twenty-seventh was a Saturday. Perfect timing, a weekend. The first task was sending invitations. As she surveyed the fifteen names on her daughter's guest list some of them leapt off the page – Harry Zappler and Billy White.

"Zappler – what kind of name is that? Where's he from?" Jean quizzed.

"He's Jewish, Mother, from Austria. He was interned. Now he's working on his degree at Dalhousie."

"And Billy White? Why is he on the list?"

Vivian felt impatient. "Mother these fellows are friends of mine and because of them we're going to have some wonderful music in the house. This is supposed to be your gift to me. Why are you being so overbearing?"

Jean wasn't deaf to the edge creeping into her daughter's voice nor to the argument that the party was a gift and should be as Vivian wanted it to be, nor was she dumb to the fact that having live music would be an asset to the party, so she silently decided not to protest the idea of strangers in her house, although she was tempted to put her foot down. She would welcome them for their entertainment value.

Guests also included Dick, Lillian, Ron, Burleigh, BYPU cohorts Greta Mosher, Mary-Susan Greenfield and Donna Baker, childhood friends Carol and Muriel Beeman, sisters, and their brother Geoff. Muriel's husband, Arthur, Vivian's supervisor, Ellen, rounded out the roster. Bernard would be there too, as would Dick's younger brother Chuck. Jean added their names to the list, along with Aunt Gladys' and Uncle Don's. They lived on Queen Street too, but because Don had a golf date the same day, he and Gladys would stop by that evening.

It was an afternoon affair from two until five. Jean's friend Mardie was there to lend a hand. While Vivian received the partygoers in the front room, Jean and Mardie took turns welcoming new arrivals at the front door.

Some guests were already there when Billy and Harry arrived together at two-fifteen. It was Jean's turn to answer the knocker. Billy remembered the first time they met and how "cold fish" her handshake had been at the Russian concert evening. He was determined with this second meeting to counter any standoffishness with exceeding warmth. He extended his hand and coaxed hers forward, then enveloped it in both of his for a secure pause, the sincerity in his eyes and voice conveying to her he was pleased to meet her again. And then he introduced Harry, the boy wonder and genius president of the Dalhousie Music and Dramatic Society.

Jean exchanged greetings and ushered them toward the direction of the voices in the party room with her good wishes, her hands still buzzing from Billy's all-encompassing handshake. Mardie had been watching from the kitchen. When Jean re-entered, her friend nodded in the direction of the sink with a slight sense of urgency and a grimace. Jean headed there, turned on the tap and thoroughly washed her hands with soap.

The party was a success. They played charades, ate tiny sandwiches and birthday cake and drank iced tea. Harry had them in stitches with his impromptu skits and Victor Borge imitations. Then Billy took over with a song leading session that filled the house at 85 Queen Street with the heartiness of music. Everyone had a chance to share a joke or talent. Vivian flawlessly played a classical piano prelude by Chopin. Dick told a story about the icebergs in Newfoundland and his adventures on a floe. Then the birthday girl opened her gifts, a wildflower identification book, a Nature Canada magazine, lipstick, a paperweight. In that room were three men who fancied themselves as Vivian's future spouse: Dick, Billy and Geoff – Geoff, whose bodybuilding photos and comical marital overtures she never took seriously. Billy gave her a tin of butterscotch candies. From Dick she received a journal and from Geoff, a photograph of their Camp Owen group set in his handmade birchbark frame.

Chapter 11

Billy sat himself at the upright, ready to strike the beginning chords of the happy birthday song. Harry stood poised, an invisible baton between his thumb and index finger, to conduct everyone in the singing as Vivian readied to blow out the flaming candles on Mardie's homemade chiffon cake. The scene was of friends having a good time.

Billy and Dick hit it off right away and from then on Billy stopped viewing Dick as competition. Jean was another matter. She could pose trouble, he sensed. She felt the same way about him. This had been a milestone day for her, beyond seeing her daughter turn twenty-one. It was Jean's first time having a Jew and a colored in her home.

Spring blossomed into summer and with it signs of change. They met discreetly, Vivian and Billy, and reveled in the natural delight they found in each other's company. Sir Sandford Fleming's gift to the city; Point Pleasant Park, grand and glistening; their road nicknamed "The Dingle"; the Citadel; the gardens; their jaunts combined walking and talking, trading dreams and what-ifs for budding possibilities and plans. Their exchange of letters to each other's workplaces became even more frequent. Nanking and the Garden View Restaurant became two of their favorite haunts, where they could lounge in a booth and sip cokes, share a meal and dwell in each other's spheres, immune to the looks and stares sometimes directed their way.

She was white with upper middle-class roots, descending from Alfred the Great and William the Conqueror, according to Vivian's grandfather. Her suitor was non-white from unknown and dirt-poor origins. Vivian was pure, obedient and devout, Billy a renegade determined to break a mold.

It was Vivian who put the infernal question into words after a memorable trip they made at the end of June to what the locals called Lover's Lane. Vivian had relaxed her kissing rules and there'd been some passion on display. They were leaning against the car looking up at the stars.

"What's going to become of us? Our stories are so different," she said.

"I have an unshakeable conviction that I can depend on the absolute efficacy of love," he pronounced.

Vivian wanted to believe him. "Unlike you, I can't put stock in a flight of fancy with a storybook ending. Set emotionalism aside, Billy and one sees the reality that a union between us is not allowed even though my heart says otherwise."

They bid goodnight a block away from her door and upon his return home to Halifax, Billy put his thoughts on stationery and Vivian received them in the mail a few days later – his synthesis of what he called their "glorious night."

> "I believe that love will provide some means of eradicating the many obstacles and hindrances that prevent our taking the course that seems obvious and desirable. I believe, too, that the genuineness of my love for you will eventually be revealed so plainly to you that your present inclination toward skepticism will disappear. I honestly pray for that – because I love you."

Like a wedge in a slightly open door, Billy went to work on the assumption that Vivian would conclude unequivocally, as he had, that they were destined to unite.

• • •

That spring he received word about a job prospect in Toronto through his mother. Izie had received a letter from Curley Christian, a war connection of Pup's, written at the behest of his wife, Cleopatra. Cleo Christian was friends with Leona Brewton, who sat on the board of a Negro community center in downtown Toronto, and the search was on for staff to assist the newly hired American firebrand executive director, Vyola Miller. The board thought he'd be perfect for the position of program director for the Home Service Association. He had visited the center once in 1943 and wowed everyone. After coming in for an interview at their Bathurst Street offices he was quickly offered the job and by August he penned his letter of acceptance.

His last day at the Y was September twenty-fifth after wrapping up the traveling summer camp and conference season.

Chapter 11

Les and a throng of Y associates, social work colleagues and kids were there for his goodbye party. Vivian was there, as was Lois, the two having had a brief discussion when they were both at the Y building one Saturday in June. Vivian had volunteered that day and was tapping away at the keys when Lois dropped in after conducting one of her youth esteem sessions. She strode into Billy's office without knocking and was surprised to see Vivian behind the desk and Billy nowhere in sight. "Where's Billy? Who are you?"

"I'm Vivian, Billy's friend."

"A white woman? You're a white woman? That rascal, I should have known. I've always accused him of favoring white eggs over brown. Well, how do you do? Finally, we meet. I'm Lois. I used to date Billy."

Vivian felt herself blushing. "I suppose I'm more reddish than white right now," she said shyly attempting humor.

She paused and stood up and from behind the desk extended her hand to the saucy beauty across from her. "Hello, Lois. Actually, I know who you are. We almost met a couple of times, and I'm glad to meet you now."

They shook hands.

"I think the program you devised here is marvelous. It ought to be a permanent part of the Y curriculum, in my opinion."

Lois squeezed out a thank you as she began looking around the room.

"Billy's in with Les," Vivian explained.

"Well, please tell him I was by. I'm looking for staff volunteers who will let my boys cut their hair."

Lois left equipped with the new realization: Billy's new girlfriend was a white girl, a "pasty face." That explained a lot. With his appetite for working his way up the white man's ladder, it was small wonder Billy chose to cleave to a woman who could facilitate his acceptance into the white world, Lois rationalized. So what? She liked Vivian, who didn't seem to have a mean bone in her body. It just didn't feel right to hold her skin color against her.

In the summer Billy made good on his previous year's promise to spend a day with Vivian, Lillian and their friends weekending at Camp Owen – boating, swimming and water play, singing, sunning on the dock – with Dick part of the gang. He and Vivian had drifted apart in a gentle way – two compatible but meandering streams intersecting now and then before heading their own way again. Dick devoted his off-school time to his parents at their new home in Lunenburg. He'd be changing residences in Halifax when he returned to university in the fall for two more years. Billy's sister June and George's girlfriend Elsie were at Camp Owen too. The place was burgeoning with all ages of campers, the day trippers, the week-longs, the disadvantaged kids from the North End skids who were sponsored by the colored Baptist churches of the region. That day onlookers would have seen a phenomenal glimpse of the incoming generation: youth of mixed races chumming around together and acting like it was nothing out of the ordinary.

Billy would be leaving Nova Scotia in a month. Most of what needed doing was done. He had a place to live in Toronto with The Christians, extremely willing landlords. His summer itinerary packed, train reservations made, plans established – first a Y conference in Belleville, on to Toronto to sign his contract with HSA, a stay with Harold and Helen Kieran in Montreal on the way back, then to Maine to visit his sister Mildred for the first time in eight years in early September before his Halifax YMCA wind-up and starting at Home Service in October. The only thing left to nail down was Vivian's absolute commitment to join him in Toronto.

She kept mixing signals and shifting her position on the fence. Yes, she loved him. Yes, she could see exploring new possibilities in Toronto, but no, when viewing with objectivity, she didn't see marriage as a realistic prospect. "We'll see."

Late in August he wrote to her from Belleville, yet another attempt to coax her along. His letters of persuasion were difficult to ignore:

> As I told you last Thursday night, if I can't marry you, I'll never marry anyone. And I mean that more than ever.
>
> My attitude as I write to you now is quite different from any that I've ever experienced before. Very sanely, calmly and clearly, I think of you as the only person with whom my existence and all the accompanying experiences from now on should be shared. Answers to the questions, "Where," "When" and "How" may be still somewhat

remote, although I have no reason to despair of finding them, but as far as the question, "Why" is concerned, it has been answered, in every detail, to my satisfaction.

Darling, will you talk to your Aunt Gladys again about "us"? Will you think of the situation again very carefully from every conceivable aspect, and will you let me know the result of your thinking before I return to Halifax? You see, my darling, this is the "inevitable" that I mentioned in a letter several months ago, and it appears quite plainly to me that your decision will be the great determining factor as far as my future course of action is concerned.

No doubt, you're quite amazed by the directness of this letter as compared with former ones.

Back home Vivian was feeling quite anxious throughout August. While Billy was away she did what she had been taught to do before making a difficult decision: she made a list of the pros and cons.

> Cons:
> Hurting Dick's feelings
> Society disapproves
> Billy's past marriage
> Our age difference
> Finding a new job in a new city
> Leaving Nova Scotia and friends
> Difficulty being accepted
>
> Pros:
> I love Billy
> Have children, a good father
> Be part of a new era, contribute
> Expanded vistas and experiences
> New friends and opening doors
> Mature, ready to make own decisions

I don't believe in racial prejudice
Courage of my convictions

She counted the items under each column, which showed where the weight lay: seven minus, eight in favor. Her decision landed on the plus ledger, and she would pay a price for it.

Chapter 12

Billy's trip to Toronto was as smooth as a train rail, just like his trip in August when he was there to seal his employment deal. Only this time, instead of staying at the King Edward Hotel when he arrived he settled immediately into boarding with the Christians. They welcomed him like family, making for a seamless transition to his new role as second-in-command at the Home Service agency. He'd arranged shipping for his books and phonograph records and hoped they'd catch up with him soon – he could resume hosting music appreciation nights at this new venue. Within his first few weeks he felt at home in his new city.

"I'm beginning to see, darling, that Toronto is the place where I – we – should live," he trumpeted in a letter to Vivian. "I like it for its bigness and for the possibilities it has to offer in terms of variety. One never knows what to expect. The element of surprise is always present and keeps one's curiosity at a high peak. It will be so much nicer when you come because we can share such experiences and find many things together that will add tremendously to our enjoyment."

The only missing element was Vivian, he rued. She was the clincher. Despite her intended plan to join him, he still wasn't certain she would consent to be his wife. Would she even be there for the planned rendezvous in Montreal?

At least they had letters to bridge the distance. He filled his with news he hoped would bring her closer. There was the warm, pastor's welcome he received at the door and from the pulpit of Davenport United Church, the fancy ladies' tea he attended at the behest of Mrs. Christian, and his surprise phone call from Les Vipond, who was passing through town, to tell Billy how much he was missed in Halifax.

In mid-October Billy fell ill and lost fifteen pounds in two weeks.

Just before he took sick, one letter from Vivian shook him to his core, as his reply to her made apparent:

October 16, 1946
Dearest Vivian,

There are some experiences, I guess, that are best for-gotten, especially if they are particularly unpleasant.

For hours I lay awake thinking of the one sentence in your letter, "I do not want to go to Toronto." It struck me so forcibly that I found myself shaking from head to foot. On Sunday I stayed in the house and kept myself confined to my room. And with every hour that passed my feeling of impending doom grew more ominously terrible.

What would I do? I couldn't sleep. I tried to read but couldn't. Nothing interested me except finding out wheth-er or not that one sentence that has been virtually burned on my mind was meant to convey the meaning that seemed to jump out at me spontaneously when I read it. Monday came. I got up at seven-thirty, borrowed the Christians' car and went driving. It was one-forty when I returned. The next morning shortly after sending you a wire I felt a sensation very much like an electric shock passing through my body that left me feeling as though I were drifting from consciousness into unconsciousness.

I watched the dawn of day arrive – I was afraid to lie down again because I had tried to go to sleep after my first shock and had experienced the same sensation. Finally, I propped my pillow up against the head of the bed and lay back on it.

Sometime after five-thirty I dropped off to sleep. Yesterday morning, needless to say, I felt so miserable that I wished I had died. I got up, washed and dressed. I decided to go to my office, although I wasn't due in until one o'clock. When I arrived at the office I decided to go and consult a doctor. The one who is nearest the Home Service Association happened to be Dr. Michalovsky, so I went to see him after I had walked up to the C.N.T. office to send you a wire. It was difficult for me to tell him how I felt then and how I had felt the night before without telling him all the details, but I managed it somehow. He told me that I had been either overworking or "perhaps vorryink about somesink" (He talks very much like Harry.) and that it was affecting my nervous system. My pain, he said was another manifestation of nervousness. He gave me some tablets to induce sleep and advised me to take it easy.

Mrs. Christian had told me that she'd call me if there happened to be any mail for me, and, when she hadn't called at eleven-fifteen, I called her. There wasn't any mail. Then, my darling, about three-fifteen she called me and announced the arrival of a telegram. I asked her to open it and read it to me and just hearing the second word "darling" made me realize that my weekend of utter horror had been entirely unwarranted. Then, last night, although I missed your call by less than five minutes, I knew that you wanted to talk to me. I slept well last night because I felt immeasurably contented and deliciously tired.

This morning being an early morning for me, I was up at eight and in my office a few minutes past nine. Mrs. Christian called at about eleven-fifteen and told me that a special delivery letter had come.

Darling, I'll go on now to tell you of the importance of your letter. I can see now that what I must do is remember that there is no reason for my having any misgivings about other people and that the one important consideration is that you must be made to see and believe that you can place all your trust in me and feel every assurance our future together will be as full of happiness as we would have it. Then, I must, by example – or demonstration – prove that I love you beyond the very bounds of my life and that making myself the perfect complement to your existence is the goal toward which I shall always aspire. Remember this too, darling: you're the person who has brought real significance to my life; it's you who inspired me to find the great purpose there is in living. And having found these important elements through you, I want to express my love, my appreciation, my actual worship of you by doing those acts that will bring you an appreciable sense of satisfaction with me. I do love you, Vivian, darling, I know that I shall always love you.

Always yours,

Billy

Seated alone in the board's cafeteria, Vivian refolded the letter and hugged it to her chest, then held it to her nose to inhale the smell of the vellum and ink. For some reason the scent brought her closer to him. His letters were copious that fall, each one of them a lifeline for Vivian, whose life had grown increasingly complicated. She had stolen a private corner to soak in his thoughts. He had misunderstood what she had meant about not wanting to go to Toronto. "Want" was the wrong verb: she could never *want* to leave her beloved Maritime province. She didn't want to: she was driven by compulsion like a bee to pollen. There was no reversal. Billy had relocated and they had agreed that she would join him there.

He knew she had booked her train ticket, and while in Lunenburg weekending with the Hills she had established that Dick could drive her to the train station. His whole family was excited for her heading to Toronto to find better job opportunities. The war in the rear-view mirror now, the pace at the Prices and Trade Board would wind down. Eventually the board would cease to function. Dick, plowing towards his degree, was still open to pursuing a post-war career with the air force and was quite satisfied to know Vivian's expectations of him had eased. Love could survive the distance and their differing ambitions if their love was meant to be, he reckoned. He had no reason to suspect what was to come or feel any anxiety about their pending separation because loving a friend like Vivian was a love forever anyway. A former Toronto boy himself he had nothing bad to say about the city. "I can't hold you back," is how he responded when she first told him of her decision to go. "I'd never forgive myself if I kept you from doing something you wanted to do. I'm all for seeing where this takes us, Viv."

She hadn't expected Billy to come unglued as he had upon reading her Lunenburg letter, but it made her feel unexpectedly powerful to realize that she could reduce a controlled, confident, unflappable person like Billy to a crumpled, fearful and broken-hearted wretch at his very thought of their not uniting. Billy emboldened her. Oddly, his weakness strengthened her and gave her purpose. And strength and determination she needed in large measure following all that had unfolded in the three weeks since his departure for Toronto.

When few colleagues showed up for her farewell party at work, Vivian's letter to Billy dripped with despondency. He tried to console her in pen.

> I envision you after the party sitting in the chesterfield chair, your lovely eyes filled with tears of disappointment – wishing that "the darned thing had never materialized." I wish I could have been there to take you in my arms and tell you that the only people who had any reason to feel disappointed were the guests who weren't there. Never underestimate yourself, Vivian. You are the most important person in the world, that in no terms can your full value be estimated, nor your wonderfulness be expressed. There is no future for me without "Vivian".

As she and Billy were becoming closer and visibly more frequent companions in Halifax over the past year, Vivian had detected an air of disapproval in stares and haughty sneers from people unknown to her and no limit to the bald comments of acquaintances and friends.

Her mother didn't know the extent of the relationship, of course: didn't know Billy was part of the weekend trip Vivian took to Moncton in late September and was unaware of Billy's seminal visit to Toronto to sign his employment contract. That trip had been punctuated by a reunion with his sister Mildred for the first time in eight years. Vivian purchased stockings for him to take to "Mil" as a gift. En route to her home in Ocean Park, Maine, Billy visited the Kierans. ("I told Harold about us," he wrote to Vivian, and Vivian immediately wrote to Helen.)

Jean had dropped enough disapproving comments after the birthday party to signal a decided intolerance toward one Billy White. Vivian decided not to mention any of their trysts. In her own time she would break the news to Jean gently, tell her about the real motivation for her Toronto move. Undoubtedly Jean would offer blessings once she overcame the shock. Vivian had faith in her mother's ability to reason, but that belief torpedoed out the window on the evening of September twenty-seventh, the night after she bade Billy farewell. Twenty-one, still living at home but paying for room and board as she did, Vivian did not expect the sight that greeted her when she arrived home from work that Friday.

Mother was already home, seated in the tufted, high back chair in the front room, her hands composed in her lap, right fingers drumming the back of her left hand, underneath which was a small book, deep brown, hard-covered and leather-bound. Vivian recognized it right away and felt pale – her 1946 diary. She steeled herself for the onslaught. Bernard was there seated on the chesterfield looking very much like a schoolboy being disciplined and wanting to be anywhere else.

"There appears to be a lot you haven't told me lately, Vivian," Jean said. "I read your diary. I wish to God I hadn't."

"Well why did you, Mother?" Vivian was indignant. "That's my personal, private property you've chosen to invade!"

"I suspected you and he were up to something, but I never dreamed you would even contemplate entering a coupling. You can't. It's just not done.

Intermarriage is a sin. I won't allow it. You must cancel your trip, Vivian. That's an order."

Jean's voice croaked with her rising volume to resemble a small terrier barking because her vocal cords tightened as her neck strained against the buttoned collar of her white blouse. She brought her words down to a whisper, "Can't you see this is a disgrace to your family?" Bernie had never before seen her eyes flash with such anger or heard her voice drip with disgust.

"What I see," Vivian emphasized, "is that you've abused my trust and you're not willing to listen to me or listen to reason. Mother, I have a plan to which I've given much thought and I'll be following through with it. That's my decision to make, not yours. You'll just have to accept it. I love Billy and he loves me and that's the way it's going to be."

Jean had her hands over her ears at this point, moaning "no, no" and her head shook as it hung low, her misery on full display. Her daughter's words were unbearable to hear. But like a developing storm cloud, she gathered herself up, stood determinedly to face Vivian and wagging her spindly index finger threatened, "if you go through with this, I promise you, Vivian, you will regret it, and don't come crying to me when the walls come crashing down on you. I won't be there to save you. This is an awful thing you are thinking of doing. How can you ask me to accept it? You must put an end to your recklessness. I demand it!"

Out of the room she marched, leaving the diary on the seat of her abandoned chair and imagined scorch marks on the Persian rug.

Vivian exacted a deep breath and sighed, fanning her brow with her hand to indicate heat. Bernard slapped the top of his legs as he stood up, stretched and shook himself down. "You're on your own on this one, Sis," he said. "I'm going out."

Dinner was a stiff and silent affair. Jean and Vivian ate to the clink of silverware and the sound of their own chewing. When Jean eventually spoke, her voice cracked in the air between them like ice dropped in tepid water to chill it.

"What about Dick?" she minced.

Vivian put down her cutlery, finished chewing and swallowed before replying.

"Dick will be driving me to the station. You needn't concern yourself with what Dick thinks, Mother. I'm thinking for myself."

"Not very clearly," Jean snapped. "You can't change the fact that I'm still your mother, and I swear as sure as I'm seated here no daughter of mine is going to marry a Negro. I refuse to see you abandon your station and lower yourself to that level. You'll be throwing your life away. My heart can't bear the thought of it."

Her voice began to tremble. She removed her spectacles and used her cloth napkin to clean them and wipe her moistening eyes before returning the eyewear to her face. "I can't talk about this now. Honestly, Vivian, I can hardly bear to look at you, my dear. We will have another discussion when you are prepared to listen to reason."

But there was no glacial thaw. The famous Harlow stubborn streak governed both of them. Vivian retreated into herself and her myriad tasks for getting ready, refusing to be badgered by Jean's arguments or by her futile administration of the silent treatment. The iciness between them hardened as fiercely determined Jean fixated on her pledge to stop the union and bull-headed Vivian successfully tuned Jean out, although the chasm between them was killing her.

Home wasn't the only place where atmospheric changes were evident.

October was frosty. As soon as the grapevine seized on her intentions, in short order Vivian was fighting her way through the grasping tendrils of gossip and stigma. For the first time she experienced the sting and humiliation of being called a horrible name, the diminishment of personhood from the whispering as she walked by and the simmering infuriation of being forced to listen to undoable falsehoods. People she liked were disappointing her. Their opinions saddened her. But it was Constance Page who blindsided her with a body blow that convinced Vivian it truly was time to go.

Constance Page, a member of Vivian's choral group, assistant director in fact and the accompanist. In her late teens she sang competitively as a mezzo soprano in the Nova Scotia Music Festival, forever coming in second to Portia White and sounding woefully amateurish comparatively – bottle glass next to finely cut crystal. Had she gone into community musical theater, she would have been the shining star. As for the classics, Constance was good but never good enough, and she grew to resent the fact. Her abundant hair was the color of corn silk and shiny like sateen, heaped on her head in perfectly pinned rolls, not a strand out of place, often adorned with expensive combs. Her background, Dartmouth upper crust, relegated her to private school and finishing school. Everything about her from posture to politeness was lifted straight from etiquette books. She wore only one shade of lipstick. Vivian and Lillian named it "Pepto-Bismol Pink." Behind that doctored smile fixed to her face like plaster, Constance was gifted at masking her true thoughts.

She knew all about the Whites. They were haughty and uppity, she thought, judging from a distance – as close as she wanted to get. When she heard that Vivian was involved with Billy, she couldn't wait to unload the information she had on him at the first available opportunity after he'd left town.

Lillian had to miss choir practice that week. After rehearsal Constance pounced on an available opening. "Vivian," she trilled, her Pepto-lips upturned at the corners, "may I have a word with you?" and she gestured they should sit on the front row pew of the church hall.

Innocently, Vivian obliged. Constance waited until the last of the choir members filtered out of the hall echoing their goodnights then wasted no time.

"I hear you're leaving us to run away with Billy White. It's all over town, Vivian. You must know."

Vivian regarded her impassively, having decided that silence was the best way to respond to people's newfound interest in her life path.

"Do you know what you're getting into, Vivian?" Constance took the approach of a concerned choir mistress. "I know some terrible things; saw them with my own eyes." She let the mystery dangle.

"What on earth are you talking about, Constance? Terrible things, like what, for instance?"

"Philandering," Constance blurted. "I saw him on a number of occasions this past summer in the companionship of his ex-wife. You know she was a singer, don't you? A very nice lady and a nice voice to match. I saw them concertizing together and I couldn't help seeing how cozy they looked together.

I know he was very much in love with her back then. And I thought to myself, when I heard the rumors about you and Billy, 'isn't that just typical of the Negro man? part beast, part infidel who sees nothing wrong with being unfaithful until he gets caught?' So I worry for you, Vivian. Don't waste your life on one of them." She smiled sympathetically and stood up to signal she'd said all she had intended to say and would leave a dumbfounded Vivian to sort it all out on her own.

Seeing his ex-wife – Constance was so much more familiar with the characters in this scene. Vivian was blindsided from the wings. Head spinning, she felt sick about the betrayal, like she'd weathered a punch to the gut. That night she quickly relayed her distress in an air mail letter to Billy, who roared back his airmailed response postmarked "Toronto Oct 12 8:30 p.m. 1946 Ontario."

> Vivian, my darling,
> Before I actually get underway with this letter, let me ask you to pause for a few minutes – or longer, if necessary – and look as deeply as possible within yourself for the answers to three questions that I'll pose for you.
> First, "is Billy the person who can make my future what I hope and expect it to be?"
> Second, "am I satisfied beyond all doubt that I love Billy, all there is, and that his love for me is equally as great?"
> Third, "am I prepared to spend the rest of my life as Billy's wife, to give what I can and accept what he is able to offer toward making our marriage the perfect union he is convinced it would be?"
> There you are my darling. Now, when you feel that you have answered all three questions definitely, then, and not before please, you have my permission to read on to page two.

Chapter 12

Vivian turned the page.

I've lived through that period when I've sensed on all sides the presence of a million of convention's policemen. The only adequate means of working out a plan for living lay in relying on my own concept of what was right in terms of the will of God. People who allow themselves to be submerged in the darkness of tradition, prejudice and stupidity are menaces to those like you who are not interested in artificial goodness or hypocritical sanctimony. My annoyance with such virtuous souls tempts me to damn them without compunction.

Vivian, darling, don't let them get you down – even if you like them. You're too big, too noble for them; and your unaffected goodness of heart and healthy attitudes are so foreign to them.

I certainly have no objection to people who, like your Aunt Gladys, are reasonable. Here, of course, it's wrong for me to even attempt to draw a comparison, because such people are very rare. But, if outsiders would keep their noses out of other people's affairs and concern themselves with making their own lives more genuinely powerful, all society would be much happier.

If you have answered yes to the three questions on page one, there's no point in discussing the matter further with these people. If the word friend carried any definite meaning for them, they, like your Aunt Gladys, would be *for* you in any circumstance.

I'm just convinced that Miss Page, with all due respect for her, is all wet. Her knowledge of the accomplishments, personality and qualities of my ex-wife is quite amazing. As for her being very nice, I have my own opinion. If her nice voice refers to her singing, well, darling, that's one of the qualities in her I could have appreciated and admired – had she revealed it to me. As for my being very much in love with her, I needn't say anything contradictory to that for your benefit. You know the story. I never went anywhere with her; we had nothing in common; our spheres were entirely different in every respect. I'm afraid Miss Page has been thinking of June, with whom I went to almost countless places in Halifax to accompany her on the piano when she sang. June, I fear, wouldn't think of the mistake as a compliment. I'm sorry if I seem impatient, but Miss Page is responsible for your being upset.

Vivian, I've come to Toronto and have been glad to make the change, because I believed not only that you would be glad to come too, but also that you would welcome the opportunity of being with me, as I with you, to go where we should wish and do all the interesting things that Toronto offers without having to worry about hurting anyone. Darling, I still believe what I believed before I left Halifax. I've pinned all my hopes on meeting you in Montreal in three weeks and beginning to live in the finest, fullest sense of the word. There's nothing else I want from life except to be with you.

Vivian, you *must* know that! Please, please, please! darling, don't take that hope from me!

I can't write anything else – except that I love you.

Always,

Billy

Seated in the basement canteen, Vivian reflected for fifteen minutes or so before heading back upstairs to the office at the conclusion of her break, her spirits fanned by today's correspondence from Billy halfway across the country. She only had to endure the external pressures for a few dozen more days.

For every veiled barb, every unsolicited and unwelcomed opinion there was a comforting word to follow from Billy in his letters and their prearranged phone calls countering the ugliness. But not eliminating it entirely.

They couldn't undo the stress and torment these multiple inflictions of unkind opinions had caused for Vivian. Stubborn as a mule, her Aunt Elsie had once said of her. Having that trait was a godsend now. She plowed ahead with her checklist in readiness for the move, determined not to let her mother or any others interfere.

Back at her desk Ellen approached with an armful of files which she deposited on Vivian's desk. "These all need to be catalogued," she said, "and I think you'll be particularly interested in this one." She pointed to the file on top. "Mr. Morrison came by to tell you that your reference letters will be available at the end of the month." She paused. "Golly, I'm going to miss you, Vivian. I'm sorry you're leaving under such a cloud."

"Clouds are temporary, Ellen. Don't worry. I feel my forecast is sunny. And I thank you for being the sunshine and not the gloom."

Vivian put her nose to all the work she knew had to be completed by day's end, but first she went to the top file and perused its contents: the Desmond-Kane case! She must write Billy to update him this evening. Their meet-up in Montreal was imminent now, soon to be immortalized in a Billy White epic limerick.

• • •

"There you have it, *ma chérie*, my poem titled 'To Vivian – With Apologies to Ogden Nash.' You see I left the last line for you to complete," Billy said in concluding what he considered to be a masterful recitation of his work, his dramatic delivery interspersed with cascades of Vivian's laughter ringing like a wind chime responding to the cadence of a breeze.

Standing facing her in his bedsitting room at the Lansdowne duplex in Toronto, his outstretched hand offered her the typewritten sheets. Taking it from him, she examined the limerick delightedly.

"It's terrific, Billy. It really is. I will treasure this," she paused to count, "all eighteen-and-three-quarter stanzas of it." The poem was missing a last line.

He had summarized their recent reunion rendezvous beautifully: how "he wanted to marry 'er and throw every barrier to the farthest ends of oblivion", his mounting nervousness waiting for her delayed train, how "for two days and two nights they explored Montreal's wondrous sights" – dining at the Old Mill on Saint Catherine Street, seeing mist hover over the land from their view atop Mount Royal, Billy's attempted proposal with a dime-store ring. The poem hit upon Vivian's hesitation and the conversation she initiated about race.

> Then she mentioned a point quite genetic
> She had learned from a would-be homiletic,
> Which to her disparagement
> Said their intermarriage meant
> A future just too, too pathetic.

The next stanza had Billy declaring "there must be a clearance of this wrong interference."

She hugged him and kissed his cheek. "Thank you, darling."

"And your last line?" he asked hopefully.

She paused to reread the final stanza and considered his challenge that she end it. Her eyes looked up as her brain searched to find the right line.

> The wish of his life
> Is to make her his wife ...
> *And hers was for hair that would curl.*

They laughed.

"It was exactly one year ago today that you heard 'Recompense' at the variety show," he reminded her.

So much had happened since then. Stops and starts, pushes and pulls, twists, turns, stresses and elations were hallmarks of their 1946. Numerology deemed it a *two* year last January when Billy had predicted to Vivian – partnerships, cooperation, union, duality, "the year for us two: for me and you."

Chapter 13

Mrs. Christian insisted they stay for Sunday dinner: roast pork, oven roasted potatoes, canned peas, homemade applesauce and apple pie. The kitchen scents wafted upstairs where Billy and Vivian were cloistered in his room rereading old letters she had written to him. Although Billy had them assembled in chronological order, they chose at random from the fanned-out pile, displayed on a small table. They sat snugly in front of it, each on a fold-out chair.

Vivian held the sheets of one of her most recent letters. "Here's where I wrote you about the Desmond-Kane case."

Vivian saw the case listed at work in the trade board's gazette. The story had everyone at the office talking: Philip Kane, a white car dealer, was found to have violated a board order on price controls when he overcharged for the 1940 Dodge he sold to Miss Viola Desmond, a black businesswoman. On that basis the feisty Viola hauled Kane to the Supreme Court where, remarkably, she won. As Portia's friend and hair stylist, a former classmate at Bloomfield High, and as Lois's mentor and Billy's introduction to Lois, Viola was more than a passing interest to both Billy and Vivian. In Halifax, alongside Joe's Barber Shop, Vi's Studio of Beauty Culture in Halifax was a landmark and a hive.

"I remember my reaction," Billy said. "I wrote you back wondering whether or not Vi ever got her eleven hundred dollars back. And I remember thinking to myself, 'people are going to remember her name. She's breaking down barriers with courage.' And so are we, Vivian," he said tenderly, "fighting for a principle."

For a moment he flashed back to his own beloved car, Mary Ann, which he sold before leaving Halifax to raise much-needed cash. "Victory minus restitution equals half a victory at best," he mused. Vivian understood what he meant. A moral victory without true justice and reconciliation left unfinished business on the table.

It would pain them both to find out later that on the very afternoon that Vivian left Nova Scotia for Montreal to meet Billy, Viola was being forcibly dragged by her wrists out of a movie theater in New Glasgow, arrested and thrown in jail for not budging when theater managers told her to leave the whites-only section on the lower floor and sit in the segregated balcony. All she was doing was killing time on a business trip by taking in a matinee.

Toronto was a whole different scene – seemingly no limits to where they could venture, no areas they needed to avoid due to an unwelcoming air. On the contrary, Billy as if by osmosis, rapidly became a known commodity, a community essential. He was gifted at making himself visible and wasted no time in doing so. Vivian was settling in nicely in the weeks following her arrival. Through the YMCA, Billy helped her find an upper room in a home on Oakwood Avenue in midtown, and she enrolled with the Underwood Temporary Agency where she could jump into a secretarial job immediately.

Freedom was palpable in this big city and the openness, a relief. But Toronto's tenor would take Vivian some getting used to. At first, she found it a place where passersby didn't look you in the eye, overwhelming, intimidating and gritty, a smell of slaughterhouses and soy mills replacing the invigorating, salt sprayed air of her maritime home. The Christians served as a counterbalance. They were warm, wonderful, remarkable people, animated and accommodating Toronto boosters, who instantly took Vivian under their wing.

Curley Christian's story could have been the script for a feature film. His life was encapsulated beautifully in August's Chatelaine Magazine in an article penned by journalist Isabel LeBourdais, a white liberal member of the Home Service board.

Born to black parents in Virginia in 1884, Ethelbert Christian earned his nickname "Curley" from the black tussle of locks his sentimental mother left uncut until he was six. After his schooling in Pennsylvania and Michigan, a trio of in-demand skills took Curley across North America from Alaska to Cape Horn – steel, bricks and cooking, what that young man couldn't do with his hands! His finesse as a steel forger guaranteed him employment traveling mill to mill. In between times he'd be snapped up for his fastidious efficiency as a brick layer. To get farther afield he farmed himself out as a cook on ships and was famous for his steaks. He was hired as chef on a ship from Seattle to Alaska. Then his travel itch ushered him through Canada to explore province after province.

In 1915 Curley enlisted in the Winnipeg 78th Grenadier Guards of the Canadian Army during the First World War and headed overseas for his introduction to gruelling trench warfare. He was a runner.

Two years later, on April eighth, he had just returned from running supplies to the line. Bone tired at Vimy Ridge, he was too weary to be roused to join his two compatriots, who warned him "the big ones" were coming before they hastened on an errand to pick up periscopes. But when a shell burst behind him, Curley started off in a hurry in what he called his "big run."

It was also to be his last run, April 9th, 1917, the first day of the Battle of Vimy Ridge.

He raced as hard as he could to his destination, clearing trenches, tree trunks and debris as he flew. He fetched the periscopes and hitched a ride back on a transport truck, on his return passing his amazed mates still making their way there.

"It was my last run, but it sure was fast," he recalled.

When a shell blast hit, it rained rubble on Curley, mincing his arms and legs. A tree fell in such a way that, miraculously, his torso was shielded. When they found him the next day, his rescuers did not know whether he had survived or died until they held a mirror under Curley's nose. A faint mist appeared on the glass.

He cheated death at least twice that day because the first rescue attempt failed. Two of his stretcher bearers were killed by enemy fire while carrying him from the battlefield and they dropped him.

It took three nights to get him to Boulogne Hospital and three weeks more to reach Bethnal Green Hospital, London, gangrene having overtaken all four of his limbs by then. His chance of living was slim to none, his limbs were amputated, first the arms, then the legs, by an Australian surgeon. An American doctor bet twenty-five dollars on Curley pulling through. After the surgery the doctor brought the patient the money with the words, "you won."

Before his surgery the nurse who cared for Curley hoped he'd die. She said, "I didn't see how life could be bearable for him after those amputations, but do you know what he did? He sang. The morning after the arms came off, I came down the corridor and wondered who was singing 'It's a long, long way to Tipperary' like that. It was Curley. 'I'm not dead after all,' he said to me. And he was just like that all the way through."

In hospital he was the life of the party, employing his uncanny knack for changing patients' outlooks, making the worst-off blokes feel better. He came home to Canada in a basket.

Altogether his recovery spanned two years and four months, first at Red Feather Cottage, the Ontario Military Hospital in Orpington, England, and then for the bulk of the time at Davisville Orthopaedic Hospital in Toronto, where he met his Cleopatra. Cleo was his full-time attendant at the Davisville Hospital.

Curley's wooden legs were manufactured at Christie Street Military Hospital. "I chose the kind fitted with heavy braces over my shoulders running from a leather corset laced to the stumps," he told Billy and Vivian that night at dinner, as he negotiated his meal with the knife and fork he designed for himself that fasten on what was left of his arms. "And you know even now I can feel the tickle in the arm that isn't there and sometimes my invisible leg aches."

Relying on prosthetics below his elbows and knees for mobility guaranteed that getting around would be more challenging, but when he didn't feel like wearing his legs he scooted around on a handcrafted board with wheels attached to its underside. He remained cheerful and optimistic, explaining, "If I thought moaning would grow me another pair of arms or legs, I'd sure try it."

Being the only surviving quadruple amputee in the entire British Empire added celebrity to Curley's status. He became heavily involved in the War Amputation Association.

"They call my Curley their mascot," chortled Cleo. "We've only missed two of their conventions."

"They have traveled all over Canada," Billy chimed in. "Vivian, they've been to England, France, Belgium, South America, the West Indies and of course the United States."

"Having no arms and legs has its advantages," Curley insisted. "I'm so well-known I've been getting free admission to every racetrack in Toronto for the past twenty-five years. I can just walk in, and everyone salutes me and welcomes me by name."

"He was asked by a woman seated near him to remove his hat during the playing of 'God Save the King' before the races began one day," Cleo recalled. "He says to her, 'Perhaps you'll remove it for me, Lady. You see I lost both my arms fighting for the King.' The lady made a quick retreat."

Another cascade of laughs as Curley – a handsome, oval face, sturdy neck, high forehead and a shock of thick, black hair, a mere hint of its wave still evident, wire rimmed spectacles perched above the flared nostrils of his broad nose, tucked around alert ears ready to receive his endearing grin at any moment – held court around the supper table, captivating Vivian with his tales.

"We're making progress on a number of fronts," he said optimistically, "on obtaining allowances for wives and children, the right to work without losing the pension, and getting an Amps clubhouse in Toronto. We just have to keep pushing."

"Curley attended the Vimy Reunion of battle veterans in 1936 and was recognized by King Edward, who shook his "hand"," Billy remarked to Vivian. Mrs. Christian picked up the story from there.

"My husband loves 'King Eddie' as he calls him. We were in our room at the hotel when the phone rang. I answered it and a voice identified as the King's secretary said he had a message from His Majesty. I thought it was one of our veterans pulling my leg and opened my mouth to tell him to go jump in the Thames, and then I stopped, and oh dear was I glad I had. The

King had ordered a special wheelchair and an attendant for Curley's visit and the call was made to provide us with a special phone number to confirm arrangements as well as early, preferred seating at the Palace Garden Party."

"Curley was one of the more than eight thousand veterans who returned to France when the new Canadian National Vimy Memorial was dedicated by King Edward in July 1936." Cleo loved boasting about her husband, but not about herself. A woman with flair, her demeanor was surprisingly low-key in the public eye. Curley was the star. Throughout the meal, Vivian found a homespun comfort surrounding her, a feeling she'd forgotten and found lacking back home since the controversy about Billy had erupted.

Looking at her host, she was thinking of her father now. Same war, different men; how she wished the two of them could have met. How amazed and impressed he would have been with the spirited Mr. Christian and his wife.

Cleo wasn't done. "There is one other fellow in all of North America who's in the same situation as my Curley. He's in the United States, no arms, no legs, home from the war. You know what they did? They gave him one hundred thousand dollars in cash and the Ford Motor Company built him a special car! What did Canada give Curley? Salt peanuts, that's what."

"Now tell us about you, dear girl," Cleo urged, her rant having run its course. Vivian obliged, first dabbing the corners of her mouth with a linen napkin monogrammed with an embroidered "C."

"My father was a captain in the Great War who served the entire course of the war. I lost him when I was eleven."

"My mother lives in Dartmouth along with my sixteen-year-old brother. I'm here without her blessings, I'm afraid. She disapproves of my decision to marry Billy." She hesitated, "because of his race," she added as though it needed explaining.

"The smartest thing I ever did in my life was to get married," Curley said. He had Billy light him an after-dinner cigarette and insert it in the holder now clasped between his lips. He would roll it from one side of his mouth to the other as the conversation ensued. Billy grabbed and lit a smoke from his own pack.

"Vivian and I are working on an article and lesson plan for United Church youth across Canada that will be like a handbook for dealing with racial prejudice," he told the couple. "Our deadline is fast approaching."

"Well, it sounds like the type of article your mother should read, you poor thing," Cleo said, looking at Vivian with characteristic nurse-like compassion. "I'm sorry this is what you're going through, dear. We believe in standing up to bigotry in this house. Why, I can't tell you the fight we had getting our son Doug into the navy. He's the same age as you: you're twenty-one, aren't you?" Vivian nodded. "You'll meet him soon, child."

"His skin color got him rejected and we were having none of that malarkey. Any unit would be lucky to have our Douglas. So, Mr. Christian chased down an appointment and the two of us went to Hamilton to meet with the navy minister. It was through that meeting that our son became the first one of our race from Toronto to be admitted into the Royal Canadian Navy. Someone had to be first. We made sure of it."

"Your mother will come around. You'll see. Give it time," she counselled.

"I sure hope you're right," Vivian said, her voice trailing off in uncertainty. With dinner concluded she volunteered to help with the dishes in Mrs. Christian's modern kitchen – their lovely, modest home financed with savings culled from Curley's meager pension, and income derived from Cleo renting out rooms, each decorated with her personal flair. Her cousin Arthur owned a rustic cottage up north in Waubaushene where she, Curley and friends were welcome to vacation anytime. He asked her to help him decorate the cabin. She installed a chandelier in the bathroom.

Vivian saw in Cleo a beautiful, creative and engaging older woman who handmade her wardrobe of vibrant clothing. The two of them carried on at the sink with cleanup and chatter while the fellows smoked and joked. Then Billy took a seat at his landlords' beautiful piano. The only one of its kind he'd ever seen, it was made in England, by Ajello & Sons, London. It stood about four-and-a-half feet high, was regulation length and finished in light mahogany. It performed like a dream despite being slightly out of tune. He played everything under the sun, feeling like his old self again finally, after having overcome that terrible bout of influenza last month before Vivian arrived.

Now that she was here, he felt like a champion running through a roster of tunes in a victory lap. Playing music soothed his worry about the effect her mother's campaign was having on her. Vivian wouldn't open up about it fully. She tended to keep her innermost feelings to herself and rarely disclosed deeply personal information, preferring to process and deal with her emotions privately. Her diaries contained names, events and places, not intimacies, confidences and innermost confessions: facts, not feelings. Her mother was able to glean some details from spying into her daughter's 1946 diary, but Vivian being who she was omitted juicy and blatantly revealing bits such as the times she and Billy kissed and the unique thrill of that arousal and awakening.

Letters from family members began reaching Vivian shortly after her arrival in Toronto. As quickly as Vivian had forwarded her Toronto address to her mother, Jean was equally fast to redirect letters to her there. The post office, as advertised, delivered them without fail one by one. Vivian read them behind the locked door of her second-story room at 582 Oakwood, the owner-occupied home of George and Margaret Phillips, near Eglinton Avenue. That's where she digested the grit. The first letter to arrive was from Uncle Roy.

> November 7, 1946
> Dearest Vivian,
> I am praying our loving Heavenly Father will guide you and help you. May he give you wisdom and strength of purpose to so order your life that it will bring honor and glory to His name.
> I have never wished for my dear Grace's presence so much as I have for the last two days. I have had little sleep since, and the burden of your problem is crowded into every waking moment. I have recalled many memories of the days we spent together at 210 Crichton. I wish I could have been more to you than I have been. I have been very proud of you as I watched you develop into such a fine woman. You mean much more to me than you can perhaps realize.

Your dad's picture is looking down at me as I write. You lost a great deal when he was taken out of your life. Your words haunt me that you would have "no way of knowing what he would think." Oh, if you had only known him a little longer and a little better!

You can look into his eyes in his photo and try to read there what his wish would be for his daughter, the daughter that he longed to live for, so he could guide her footsteps in the pathway of life.

You are right, dear, when you said nothing should be done to sully his memory. Let us both honor it in our hearts and lives.

Pardon errors. I am quite tired. Pardon the errors through the years that I could not in some measure have taken your father's place in your life. I love you dearly.

Uncle Roy

Uncle John, the minister's son who married Aunt Elsie, wrote next.

November 15, 1946
Dear Viv,
When I got home this evening I received an awful shock, in fact Elsie is about crazy over the letter she received from your mother, telling us that you had gone to Toronto and that certain nigger is up there. Viv, I never thought that your mind could run in such channels. I am sure that if your father were alive he would get out his gun and go nigger hunting, in fact I'd like to do it myself, and according to the white code of living I would be fully justified, black is black and white is white, the world over, your father and I fought for those ideals in the last war. I had nothing against any colored person, I only believe in what I have seen in my travels. I know that love is a queer thing and that it does queer things to you and sometimes will warp your mind, I have known

some very cultured Negroes, but to see them mixing socially with white people, there is always a line drawn. Intermarriage with them only results in misery on both sides. Viv, I might say again that perhaps you love him, or perhaps you only think you do. I wish I could take you into the nigger section of Boston. It alone would convince you of what only could come of your marriage to a colored person. It will mean the cutting off of yourself from all your relations and kinfolk, and in later life you will deeply regret it. Ask Mary just what she thinks of them. She has lived amongst them and should know more about them than I. I have seen plenty in Canada, the U.S.A. and England and France, so Viv please search your mind and conscience before you disgrace yourself and your family. Why even the white girls in North Brookfield would have better sense than to run around with any of the Harper family, much as they were admired and respected in the community. If you want to work, why not come down here. I can get you a pretty good job in G.E. where you will forget this foolish infatuation of yours, so if you value my friendship and relationship please reconsider.

From your loving
Uncle John

P.S. Please don't take offense at what I have written. I am only giving you my point of view, also that of millions of others. Again I say I am not dictating to you but giving you my views and those of your father, who if he were alive would say the same, and only for your own good. We all have to live our own lives and what we make of them is our own personal business, so long as we don't intrude upon the moral code and injure those we love. John.

Vivian's beloved Aunt Elsie, her kindred aunt to whom she felt exceed-ingly close, enclosed her thoughts within John's letter. Two years younger than Jean, outgoing Elsie was far warmer and oodles more fun than her practical, understated sister, full of spunk, spice and an adventurous spirit. Now Elsie lived with John in Lynn, Massachusetts and was trying to support her closest older sister from a distance. Their son Charles, now married to Mary, was a close cousin of Vivian's growing up.

> My dear Viv,
> I want you to know my dear if you want to come here you will be very welcome. Uncle John thinks a lot of you, and I love you. I cannot think you will marry a colored man; we would consider it a big disgrace. The colored race is alright so long as they do not want to marry white people. It is the way I feel and every other white person I know that amounts to anything feels that way too. The colored people will think of you as white trash. Please dear, do think of your mother and us and do not do such a thing. Think of Bernard. His life will be just about ruined too.
> I do want to keep you if you will come to us. You hold in your heart and hand the chance to put the blackest mark on all our lives. Please I plead with you, do not do it. Do think of us. Your people.
> Vivian you will not be happy. You may pretend to be, but you never will be if you bring this horrible disgrace on yourself and your family. Colored people need to marry their own color.
> Love from Your Aunt Elsie
>
> P.S. I'm not telling Charles or Mary anything about this. They would be so upset. Aunt E

A letter after that from Bernard hardly surprised Vivian. She could imagine Mother standing over him dictating every word with a rolling pin in her hand. Dated November eighteen, it read:

Dear Vivian,

I am going to put in my two cents worth, but I want you to understand that I don't think that you haven't thought of the points nor that I am the only one to bring them to your attention. The following are the reasons why I beg and plead with you not to marry Billy.

1. No one person can make up to you for all the other people in the world, and if you marry, most of your friends and relatives will forsake you. There will not be half a dozen people who you can call friends.
2. Mother, especially, has said that if you marry Billy that will end all connections between you and her.
3. If Billy is selfish enough to ruin your life by marrying you he is not good enough for you anyway.
4. You will harm him in his work if you marry him.
5. It will ruin any possible social life for you, and you will be so lonely you won't know what to do.
6. You will give anything, in a few years, to have it undone, when you realize that you cannot be happy together.
7. Your children will not have a happy life if the home is not happy, which, if you marry him, it will not be.
8. If you don't marry him, you will find someone much more suitable with whom you will be able to have a happy marriage.

I am afraid that, unintentionally, I have encouraged you by not making myself clear before. I hope that this will clear up any misunderstanding on your part. I also hope that you realize I am trying to save you from an awful fate – an unhappy marriage, as well as looking at it from my own selfish viewpoint.

In any case please don't marry him at least until after New Year's 1948.

We got your card today and will send along your trunk
and key soon. I'll write a letter either this week or next."
Love,
Bernie

Vivian's hypothetical imaginings didn't stray far from the truth, barring
the rolling pin scenario. Jean did sit her son down and order his pen to paper
after force-feeding him the points his letter should cover. He did as he was
told. After all, at sixteen he had years to live with her still. The following
Sunday he walked to church ahead of his mother and Uncle Roy, who always
drove her, and got there in time to witness something that made him wish
he'd never written the stupid letter.

He had volunteered to be a youth greeter so he was stationed at the
huge cathedral doors to welcome parishioners, guests and newcomers with
a smile, and give any assistance the older ones would need to get to their
seats. The young protégés took their cues from Mr. Evans, who supervised
their affairs. He was there to greet Bernie just as the first comers ascended
the wide set of stairs separating them from the entrance.

Bernie stationed himself at the top with Mr. Evans, shifting from one
foot to the other and clapping his hands together to beat the morning chill
while waiting for more worshippers. Uncle Roy and Jean, among those who
arrived, were welcomed and ushered inside. They came in waves. One con-
gregant came solo, an older Negro man dressed in a brown suit and white
shirt, his burgundy bow tie slightly askew under a topcoat one size too big
and a bowler atop his head flattening his puffy, greying black hair that
matched his overgrown eyebrows. The ingrained scuff on his shoes had been
polished and buffed – no disguising how well-worn his footwear was. Aided
by the handrail he reached the top, squared himself and straightened his tie.
Bernie could see that the stranger's thick lips were chapping, and the skin
had split. His inclination was to offer the man some water before showing
him to a seat. That thought was short-lived.

Mr. Evans inserted himself and his considerable height between the man
whose hand was about to reach for the ornate brass door handle, blocking
his entry.

"You can't come in," he said, looking down on the man. "Your church is up there." He pointed to a hill in the direction of the African Methodist church, an extra thirty-minute distance by foot at least. "On a cold day in his shoes," Bernie thought as he observed the pathetic scene. He could see a roulette wheel of expressions in the man's eyes starting with a look of relief at having reached his destination to one of abject wounding, resignation and sadness over being turned away. At first he opened his mouth as if to protest but perhaps recognized the pointlessness of that against Mr. Evans' imposing shadow. He shot a look to an uncomfortably stunned Bernard as white congregants filed past them and into the church building. Bernard had seen that look in defeated opponents on the badminton court, knew firsthand the sting of disappointment when something prized is denied, unattainable, a thankless uphill trudge.

The stranger bid them both "God bless." Bernard watched him leave and followed him with his eyes until he was out of sight. An overwhelming sense of guilt engulfed him. Vivian would have spoken up on the man's behalf. "That man's going to be late for church," was all he could muster to say to Mr. Evans.

"Oh, don't you worry about them, young man," Mr. Evans said dismissively. "God waits for all men," he chuckled. "It's never too late for the Lord."

He could tell by Bernard's impassive facial expression that the lad was neither impressed nor convinced.

"Look, Bernard, I didn't make the rules. These are God's laws. The Lord made the races, and he made them separate. Separate but equal, you understand. They have their church: we have ours, and that's the way it was meant to be."

He paused, and seeing a moment with no one around, spoke candidly. "We're all very concerned about this Negro-sympathizing sister of yours, Bernard. You're not going the same way on us, are you?" he chided, not waiting for an answer. "Of course you're not." He gave him a paternal backpat, as he held the door for the shame-laden young Keeler and ushered him through the entrance. "Now let's go hear today's sermon."

It was on loving thy neighbor.

Chapter 14

November's flurry of disapproving letters had Jean's fingerprints all over them.

To Vivian it was painfully clear now that all of the letters, including Mrs. Abbott's were sparked by Jean's maniacal determination to derail her daughter's plans.

She was desperate to draw on the willing support of family, friends, associates and even the clergy to end a pending mixed marriage. Such a relationship was unthinkable. Of all the pains Jean had suffered – the loss of a husband, a baby, three siblings and both parents – all the injuries – multiple teeth extracted as a child, stitches to her mangled leg as a young woman, both without anaesthetic, the fall on her head at age two – nothing felt as excruciating as the wounding from Vivian's fall from grace. Jean was prepared to do whatever it took to redeem her daughter's previously unsullied reputation.

After reading the letters Vivian responded the same way each time. She read them not once, but several times. The first time through she felt like a shock absorber weathering the impact of content that made her gasp in places, some parts upsetting her with a breathy sickness that stuck like a pit in her throat or forcing an involuntary jump in her Adam's apple. She swallowed hard before continuing.

On second read she deliberately dissected the diatribes and deadened herself to them. By the third time around she was carefully composing mental arguments to include in her written replies. She refolded the letters, storing them in the chocolate box that once held the Moirs that Dick had given her at the train station. Like a postmaster's granddaughter, she dutifully answered all letters promptly with care and logic. Not once did she consider burning them or ripping them to bits in a bid to banish the anguish they caused her. Her natural inclination always leaned toward preservation and collections. Someday these letters would be archival relics of a bygone era, of this she was convinced.

Until then she'd be contending with naysayers using words like knives, performing cut and thrust from a distance, attempting to cut away at the fabric of her beliefs when there was no chance they could actually shred them.

Her perceptive landlady, Mrs. Phillips, who occupied the main floor with her husband, noticed an effect on Vivian when she brought her mail postmarked Nova Scotia. A cloud of hesitancy dusted the girl's face when the second one came, and the landlady ventured to inquire. Thus began an open and trusting relationship between the two of them, Vivian being frank about the pressures her family was applying and Mrs. P. lending a sympathetic ear, on occasion inviting Vivian to talk in the downstairs kitchen. She could open up to her landlady, a stranger, more readily than she could to Billy, whom she didn't want to burden with the distraction of her pitiful family situation. Margaret Phillips was a wonderful listener, and neutral; she dispensed advice only when asked and avoided passing judgment.

Besides renting furnished rooms, Mrs. Phillips taught Sunday school at the local Anglican Church, and hubby George was in the insurance business. Vivian's room was a dormered room overlooking Oakwood Avenue, at the end of the upstairs corridor. A second bedroom off the hall belonged to Reg Walton, a loud, acne-scarred Albertan in his thirties, a machinist by trade, who hoped coming east would change his luck. There was a bathroom at the other end of the hall and a shared kitchenette – a sink, an icebox, a table and three chairs, a hotplate and toaster on the counter, cupboards above and below in addition to the real kitchen downstairs. Simon McNaughton, a shift worker who kept odd hours, lived in the basement. Vivian rarely saw him, but Reg was around a lot, talked too much and often smelled of booze.

Chapter 14

Snow blanketed Toronto's dirt the day Aunt Gladys's letter arrived. On seeing the sender's name Vivian was hopeful that this piece of mail would be different. She and Billy had been looking for Gladys's unqualified backing and Billy worked hard on a letter to her pleading their case. It was understandable that Vivian's heart was longing for comforting words from her only aunt on the Keeler side. There was a letter and a magazine clipping enclosed. Vivian set the enclosure aside for now and delved into the correspondence, seated on her bed in the privacy of her chilly room, a blanket covering her legs.

> December 1946
>
> Vivian Dear:
>
> I have been looking each day for a letter, but so far in vain. In fact last Saturday morning, I was so sure there would be a letter from you that I slipped my bathrobe on and rushed down to the mailbox when the postman rang. Don had gone to the Valley on Friday, but the car driving hurts my back so much I stayed home. We are very disappointed about that, the car driving, I mean, as it certainly limits my activities. However, I can just keep hoping that by next summer there will be a big improvement. As far as I know now, I have to go back for a check-up about the first of the year. I think Don has a conference in Toronto about that time too, so perhaps we shall see you then.
>
> There is really very little news to write about. Don and I were down to dinner and supper Sunday with your mother and Bernard. We enjoyed it but missed you very much. I thought your mother looked dreadfully. She is worrying herself sick about you, I know. You are hardly ever out of my thoughts either.

At this point, Vivian breezed through several pages of small talk before reaching the nugget that explained the clipping.

I am enclosing a clipping taken from the new Ladies Home Journal for December. It is on the page "If you Ask Me" by Eleanor Roosevelt. She certainly expresses my views.

With a strange combination of eagerness and reluctance, Vivian unfolded the enclosure and absorbed the words of America's First Lady.

Under the headline "Do you approve of intermarriage of Negroes and whites?" Mrs. Roosevelt replied:

> At the present time I think that intermarriage between Negroes and whites may bring to both of the people involved great unhappiness, because of the social pattern in which we happen to live. If, of course, two people, with full realization of what they are facing, decide they still want to marry, that is their right and no one else can interfere, but it takes very strong characters to face the kind of situation in which they will find themselves in almost any part of the world. For those I love, I should dread the suffering which must almost certainly lie ahead.

That crestfallen feeling invaded Vivian's heart yet again as she continued reading. Aunt Gladys was supposed to be her ally and had come up short. Mother's influence was too tenacious.

> Vivian dear, you cannot know how much I think of you and your problem – all through the day, and night too, as there is scarcely a night that I do not dream of you. I know it is your problem, but I cannot bear to think of the inevitable unhappiness that is bound to follow. Darling, don't marry Billy. It will not mean happiness for either one of you, but the greater burden of unhappiness will fall on you. If you will only try to look at things in the light of the future, instead of just the present, I am sure you will see that you have everything to lose if you do marry Billy, and

everything to gain if you wait until you meet someone with whom you will have a greater chance of happiness – not only for yourself, but for your children.

Do not think that you cannot love again, but that your love can be greater than you even dream of now. Your mother had the impression that you thought I could understand the fascination, but I think she misunderstood you. I have tried to look at it from a broad-minded view-point, but I always feel, like I told you and Billy both, that you are standing on a dreadful precipice and as if I must reach out and grab you back from destruction.

This is Monday evening, and I shall just add a few lines and mail this when I go out tomorrow. It has been really cold today – a touch of winter in earnest, with snow flurries. Your mother, Madge and I are going to Mardie's tomorrow night for supper. I feel it is too much for Mardie as she has taken on extra work in the evenings. However, she seems to want us to come, so that is that. This is my reading club night, but decided it was too cold to go.

Do please excuse all the various blots and marks on this letter. It does not look fit to send but I would probably not get another written before Christmas. Wondering what you would like for Christmas. I have not done any shopping yet – well, yes, I did buy a pipe for Don and a scarf for Roy. Do not seem to have much heart for Christmas this year.

Tell Billy that I still plan to answer his letter and sorry that it has been so long delayed. Wondering if you have a position yet. Do write soon, dear – and often. You seem so far away now.

Love as always,
Aunt Gladys

Around the same time a letter from Bridgetown, N.S. from Jean's older brother Walter landed in the mailbox. Walter, the dentist, was the fun-loving father of Vivian's cousin Martha.

> Dear Viv,
> We've just recently heard of your approaching marriage, and I'm sorry we can't rush the best wishes and all that. Yes, you've guessed it – Aunt Lou and I don't approve. You have no doubt heard this so many times that you're very tired of it. Aunt Lou and I have always admired you so much and we'll feel so sorry if you make a move that you may regret later.
>
> I don't want to appear narrow-minded but feel that although the present infatuation seems a wonderful thing to you now, I'm sure it can't last. My marriage is a give-and-take affair, especially after the first glamour wears off, but it seems to me that you will have so many extra difficulties and complications in yours, that it can't possibly work out. Aunt Lou and I, as well as most couples, have had ups and downs a-plenty in married life, but when you go out of your own race and color, there will be so many times in years to come when it will be intolerance for you. You are a social outcast in your own race in any part of this world and are considered a "poor white" among his people. It will be so hard to give up all of your white friends and all of your relatives (though maybe we're not so hot after all), and I just can't think of never seeing or recognizing you again myself – maybe. I am very clumsy about showing affection, but I've always felt that you were so sweet, accomplished, clever and smart looking that I can't give up such a fine niece.
>
> At your age most of us were in love and out of love every few months – could be yours is the same. I've always liked the colored race a lot, but intermarriage presents such

problems that I can't see how it would ever be right. I'm wild about colored babies, but can't see you as their mother, and it wouldn't be fair to them either.

I wonder how you are liking "Tronna" by now, and if you've heard them call it that yet. I liked the city a lot in the short time I was there.

Biggest news I have is that Martha is lousy. Aunt Lou is dousing her head with everything she can think of. Poor Marth', of all people!! She is so fussy about her person.

I hope that you'll write soon Viv, and that your problem can be worked out so that you'll be very happy always; and I want to do anything I can to help.

Best love from us all,

Uncle Wal

In a postscript he asked his niece to search the Toronto record stores for the album titled "Call Me Mister" and ship it to him COD if it wasn't too much trouble so that he might receive it in time for Christmas. Of course she would do him the favor.

Her relatives were good, decent, loving and well-meaning people. How could upright people be so downright wrong? It surprised her that she could respect them and not their perspective. She still loved them despite their views, but she needed those views to change.

Working with Billy on the article for the program annual of the National Young People's Union of the United Church kept her fueled and focused on creating something that could do exactly that: open minds. The article would be part of the book's Christian Citizenship chapter and would include a course outline and lesson plan.

She'd spent hours with Billy dreaming up scenarios and exercises that reflected upon and challenged the prejudicial attitudes of the day and worked out lessons lauding an appreciation of differences and acceptance of others.

He originated and composed the narrative, she edited to perfection. It was around this time that professionally Billy became Bill White, William A., or W.A. All of a sudden, he decided that Billy sounded too girly, a nickname reserved for use, in future, by those closest to him. Bill sounded stronger and would command more respect. Timed with his relocation to a new city, dropping the "y" made sense to him.

His job as the newly minted program director at Home Service was an all-in affair. He eagerly introduced Vivian to the place, a converted house at 556 Bathurst Street that was always abuzz. He couldn't wait for her to meet executive director Vyola Miller, the exacting taskmistress, the board members and community centre staff. Most of all he wanted her to meet the people who used the agency's services. Most especially, he wanted her to get to know the volunteers at the lively center, hoping she would join their ranks. This was one of the few places in Toronto that his community could trust to provide the right help, guidance and solace. Another place was the UNIA, Universal Negro Improvement Association, the more radical of the two, whose roots grew out of the activist Marcus Garvey movement of self-determination.

Friends and connections were easily made, and the city was rich with events and experiences. Bill and Vivian visited a cluster of local churches, shopping for the one that was right for them and collecting more acquaintances along the way. Toronto was starting to grow on Vivian.

There was plenty going on to keep her mind off the disquieting murmurs from afar – learning the city's grid layout and street names and navigating Toronto's streetcar network, for example. Temporary work was a cinch for her to land as Billy had predicted. Benefitting from her impeccable references and dogged work ethic, her employers gained far more from Vivian than their puny wages reflected on her paycheck. Six dollars a day.

She and Billy were at Home Service after hours one evening, ten days before the agency Christmas party, the place festooned with Christmas decorations. Vivian released the final page from the office typewriter she used to finesse their article before submission to Reverend Alvin (Al) Cooper, the brains behind the program annual.

"Done!" she exclaimed with a sense of triumph, waving the final sheet in Billy's direction before separating it from the duplicate copy and the carbon paper sandwiched between the two. She collated the original and the copy and set the latter aside for filing.

"Have a look, W. A. White." She handed the original to Billy with a jubilant smile.

He examined it proudly like a hard-earned trophy. His catchy heading and the concepts he was set to unleash had him on the edge of gleeful.

Pardon Me, Your Prejudice Is Showing!
A Program on Race Prejudice and World Brotherhood
By W. A. White

Built around the idea of small groups discussing questions of race and prejudice in the home, community, country and world and then reporting their findings to the whole group, the program was a complete package. Everything from prepared remarks for session leaders, scenarios and dilemmas to put to the group, the course rationale, procedures for follow-through and the way forward, was provided in the neatly presented essay. He scanned segments of his preamble:

> The problem of race prejudice is, without a doubt, the most thought-provoking dilemma in the world today. The peace and security of the entire human race depend upon its solution. Before we can fully appreciate the great import of race prejudice, we must first examine it for the purpose of finding out what it is and where it comes from.
>
> Since there are as many different attitudes toward race prejudice as there are thinking people, it is impossible to apply any one set of immutable principles by which a solution that would be satisfactory to everyone may be reached. The matter, then, of approaching the problem has more personal than general implications and must be worked out on an individual basis. The value in our discussing the problem as a group lies in the fact that the mere exchanging of our ideas and opinions allows for great possibilities for each of us to evaluate our attitudes more accurately.

The question of world brotherhood seems to be uppermost in the minds of Christian thinkers today. They reason somewhat in this way: Scientific development in the fields of travel, communications, and other technical inventions have made a virtual neighborhood of the world. In the realm of human relations, our horizons should seem much closer, and our attitudes more all-encompassing when we think in terms of world brotherhood. What can we as individuals do toward lessening the prevalence of racial prejudice, and toward making world brotherhood a reality?

Actually, prejudice is the passing of judgment upon a person, group, or idea without giving sufficient thought to it. In most cases it springs from our selfish desires to feel a sense of superiority. Any difference may be used as a pretext for our prejudices – color, religion, customs, language, economic status, or ability.

It is impossible to determine accurately the amount of harm we can do to others – and ourselves – by allowing racial prejudice to take root in our lives. On the other hand, we cannot overestimate the value of our individual contribution toward making the world a place where, in terms of inter-racial relationships, understanding and appreciation will replace ignorance and thoughtlessness, brotherliness will take precedence over racial prejudice, and where all people will be accepted.

The text was laden with suggestions for follow-up projects, community liaising and promotion:

Have the group draw up a set of rules for better race relations, based on the discussion throughout the evening. These might be printed on small cards and distributed in the community.

Publicize programs of this nature. Invite young people of minority groups to attend. Send detailed accounts of discussions to the local newspapers.

Arrange to have a series of discussions on race prejudice, each one to be led by a representative of a different minority group. Discuss the fallacies of racial superiority and means of successfully refuting them.

Have several members of your group visit homes of members of minority groups, and at your next meeting give an account of the similarities and differences they noted in the ways of life as compared with their own.

Vivian liked helping develop the discussion topics:

If the following situation arose in your home, how would you remedy it? A friend of your family, during a visit, speaks contemptuously of a minority group.

How would you deal with the following in your community? A club, of which you are a member, refuses membership to your friend who is a Jew.

"*Ma chérie*, we have created a masterpiece." Billy faked a French accent.

"Well, monsieur, you had better proofread that masterpiece carefully before you give it to Al."

Billy put the papers aside and swept her up in his arms, hugging her affectionately while twirling her around a few steps on an imaginary ballroom dance floor.

He stopped and faced her.

"You are marvelous. I love you." His smooth words took on a more urgent tone. "Marry me," he said, boring into her eyes with that lean and hungry look she found so attractive. "Let's not wait."

He thought he could hoodwink her, but she was having none of it.

"Oh no, I couldn't possibly," she laughed. Her adoring eyes looked up at him. "Our plan last June was to wait a year. I need time to make arrangements, not just the wedding plans but finding us a place to live Billy. We said we'd work and save as much money as we could in the meantime. I want our wedding to be perfect. It's not something I'm prepared to rush."

Secretly she hoped Jean would be over her pickle by June. As any bride would, she envisioned her mother in the front row of the church witnessing her only daughter walk down the aisle.

Billy saw he was beaten and gamely abandoned his overture momentarily, turning his attention once again to the manuscript.

"My darling, thank you for everything you did on this." He thumbed through the pages. "This essay of ours could change the world," he proclaimed boldly.

Then, as she took a seat in a nearby revolving wooden chair, he grabbed his chance at a soliloquy, played to her like an actor on a stage.

"Vivian, I love you because you represent all the human goodness I was seeking, and because you reveal your goodness in practically every conceivable way. I love you not only because you're good to me, thoughtful and considerate of me, but also because you're good for me. You make me conscious of the favor in which I must be held by the fates.

"I only want to prove it to you."

Billy had this habit of making her jaw drop. The way he spoke, the way his honeyed voice rolled like a lullaby, his phraseology and phrasing, she had to convince herself this was her he was talking about. How could this perfect man be moved to speak so lavishly about her imperfect self? She caught herself gaping at him and quickly converted her mouth into a smile.

"Prove it to me at the end of June," she teased. "Let's go eat."

"Mrs. Christian wants us at the house for leftovers with Curley and Doug," he said. "They are having someone new stay with them. His name is Sonny Bell. He's the son of a family friend, whom you've yet to meet. I kinda, sorta promised, okay *ma chérie*?" Of course it was. The open door at 1472 Lansdowne made it a place where Vivian loved spending time.

Billy grabbed the world brotherhood article and course outline and found an envelope in his desk to contain it. On the front he wrote "Rev. Al Cooper" and stuffed it in his gaping briefcase. They'd be spending Christmas and New Year's Eve with the Christians too. On one of those occasions Billy envisioned himself springing to his feet to announce an early wedding date. Though lovingly spurned this night, he wasn't about to give up on trying to accelerate the process. There were several reasons for that: he wasn't one for wasting time, he felt the marriage would derail Jean's steamroller, but the overriding reason was persistent and sexual; he desperately wanted to consummate his relationship with Vivian. The sooner he could snag his reticent bride the better, and he vowed not to quit trying.

Vivian writing a letter in Billy's Lansdowne Avenue room

Chapter 15

A New Year. A new diary, a five-year diary, brown and leather-bound, measuring four-by-five-and-a-half inches offered Vivian one-fifth of one small page for each day of the year. She'd have to write small, economize on words. She knew Billy adored her diary writing. Words from one of his letters stuck in her retentive memory, where he recalled the thrill of hearing her read excerpts to him from her 1946 diary before he left Halifax. "It was much like seeing flashback scenes at a movie," he enthused, "as though we were living through each of our past experiences again. You have all our yesterdays accounted for so beautifully in your diary that my feeble attempt at putting them in verse seems superfluous." His praise did wonders for her confidence. Billy's encouragement made her feel secure. In his eyes she was his linguistic equal and more prolific and constant in her writing regimen than he, save for poetry. Vivian, nevertheless, was a reluctant poet still insecure about sharing.

> January 1, 1947
> Billy & I left Mrs. Christian's as the clock was striking
> twelve midnight, went to Chinatown, returned around
> four a.m. Billy told my fortune. Went to bed at nine a.m.
> I slept in Billy's bed, and he was going to sleep in Doug's,
> but Doug came home just then. He lay on top of the bed

and didn't think he would go to sleep, but he did, woke at
ten, I at eleven. We had breakfast at three! Then I went back
to bed, and he wrote thank-you notes. Tonight we went to
see a good picture *Holiday In Mexico* at the Village Theatre
in Forest Hill. Had supper afterwards at the Casa Loma
Restaurant, a superior eating place. Walked home.

They couldn't behave like this down East, running full out, keeping ridiculous hours, coming and going as they pleased, being demonstrably close
and relaxed in public together, on the street or in a top restaurant, no questions asked, no strange looks to field – hardly any. Toronto was starting to
feel comfortable, Vivian had to admit. The Christians made it clear that she
should consider their domicile as her second home base. She was welcome to
sleep there, bathe there and drop in anytime for conversation. She and Billy
were free to cook meals there. Cleo set herself up as a self-appointed chaperone in charge of protecting Vivian's chastity, authorizing the chesterfield as
Billy's designated resting place when Vivian stayed overnight using his bed.

Fortunately, Vivian's landlords Margaret and George Phillips, were liberal whites, mirroring the Christians' welcoming, home-spun demeanor and
community thrust. They placed no restrictions on Billy's visiting. Having
connections to the Y, the Phillipses knew of Billy and his pivotal role in
social services at Home Service. They recognized his passion for people and
their betterment. He projected knowledge, exuded a lighthearted and engaged *joie de vivre*, signaled a likeable persona emblematized by his tuneful
and melodious whistling when waiting for something or other, hands in
pockets, rocking on the balls of his feet, always a tune in his heart ready to
escape through his lips.

The Phillipses were more relaxed than most Toronto landlords who
wouldn't dream of welcoming a black person into their home, let alone
renting to one.

But Toronto housed a swath of white progressives, Vivian discovered.
Surprisingly she was beginning to feel more at ease here than back home
where she'd had her brushes with intolerance. In Toronto with Billy as her
calling card, she met great people who accepted her immediately.

Chapter 15

One thing Vivian was extremely good at was listening. Vivian knew what questions to ask to learn all about new people who, without fail, were eager to share their backgrounds and personal profiles with her. A slew of venues and events were backdrops for her immersive life in Toronto. The Home Service Association, a hub and an office; a variety of temporary workplaces – presently Vivian was working for Mrs. Aitken, coordinator of the Kiwanis Music Festival; the Mary and Martha women's group; and a collection of downtown churches. All places where Vivian could meet other people like her who were free of racial prejudice. Knowing she wasn't alone cushioned the barrage of disapproval she was receiving courtesy of Jean's manipulations and protestations from afar.

Little pleased Vivian more, given her reserved personality, than being at the center of things and contributing without having the spotlight being thrust on her. Her fiancé was the showboating extrovert who would cast enough light for both of them as they carved out a new life together in Toronto.

The staff Christmas party at Home Service was the occasion Vivian would say sealed her arrival. Billy was attentive and wonderful, barely leaving her side except when he was called upon to emcee the speeches and lead a few carols with the children upstairs who were also being entertained by a clown and a juggler.

He introduced her with sweeping fanfare to all the board members and other guests as they mingled on the main floor, which had taken the guise of a party room, replete with red and white streamers and, tacked to the wall, a cut-out cardboard Santa's head, whose jolly face someone had shaded with a brown crayon. Snug in its metal stand in the corner was a spruce tree decorated with strands of popped corn and various colored metal balls, donated gifts for the kids underneath.

Vivian already knew Pauline, the office manager, and Vyola, the cherubic-faced executive director. But the room was plump with unfamiliar people.

What impressed Vivian that evening was the breadth of intellect and accomplishment and the blend of worldly wisdom that the board members collectively possessed. She was ready to acknowledge that she could settle comfortably in this city despite its faults. Such remarkable people all coming together for the cause of unity and charity – this was Vivian's cup of tea and she radiated interest and eagerness as she and Billy made the rounds. Guests seemed to mingle as one group, exactly as it should be, Vivian was thinking, confirming what she already believed. We are one race, the human race.

The directors clearly cared about Home Service. All of them attended the soirée, from the president Clarence Lightfoot and his wife, Nellie, to the esteemed Dr. Oscar Brewton and wife, Leona, whom one addressed as Madam Brewton, at her insistence. The Brewtons were pillars of the black community that peppered Toronto, he a soft-spoken podiatrist and leading figure in the British Methodist Episcopal Church, serving as its treasurer, and she a savvy hair salon owner and beauty consultant. Both were articulate speakers about the plight of their people. Together they owned the Brewton Comfort Shop on Yonge Street and served a loyal, mixed clientele. They lived in a stately red brick home on Kilbarry Road in Forest Hill, an enclave for the well-to-do.

Chatting with a small group standing with Vivian, Madam Brewton said she was once mistaken for a domestic servant by a local shopkeeper who couldn't fathom any other reason for a woman of her skin color to be in the neighborhood. "Out of the blue he asked me for the name of the mistress of the house I was employed at, and I replied, 'It's Brewton, sir, and I'm taking my business elsewhere.'"

Without skipping a beat, she turned to Vivian. "You must come to our home for dinner," she said. "We like to think ourselves responsible for your being here. I pushed very hard to get Billy here, you know. Now that you've arrived, the picture is complete. We can't wait to become more acquainted with you."

"The feeling is mutual." said Vivian, "Thank you."

The doctor, who never lost his American drawl, told her in his gentle, dignified rumble how much he'd look forward to their visit. "After dinner I'll ask Billy to play our piano and I'll join him on the 'hawn.'" That's how he pronounced horn, referring to his beloved tenor saxophone.

Making their way around the party, Vivian felt like a guest of honor, which seemed surreal given the stature of the people surrounding her, one of whom was Isabel LeBourdais, the journalist who had penned the magazine piece about Curley. About fifteen years older than Vivian, her vividly green eyes flashed like a champion's as she was introduced.

She was accompanied by her husband, Donat, an accomplished non-fiction writer and political activist who ran as a federal CCF candidate in High Park in 1935. During the course of small talk, he mentioned the local CCF office, the palatial Woodsworth House on Jarvis Street and urged Billy to reconnect with the Ontario wing of the party as soon as possible.

Billy already knew of Isabel's sister, Gwethalyn Graham. She had authored *Earth and High Heaven*, the novel he so revered. Telling the story of a love affair set in Quebec between a Jew and a Gentile, her book was thirty-seven weeks on the New York Times bestseller list, an unprecedented accomplishment for a Canadian writer. Surely its popularity meant attitudes in society were changing, Vivian ventured, and she mentioned the article and lesson plan she and Billy had submitted for the United Church national youth program.

"We have so much to talk about, Vivian," Isabel enthused and proceeded to itemize the interests she thought they could share: civil rights, humane treatment of the mentally ill, justice and equality for all and the CCF, a political party to which, like her husband, she wholeheartedly subscribed.

This was her second marriage. She met Donat, a man twenty-two years her senior, through CCF canvassing ten years ago; she was freelance writing while raising two children on her own at the time.

Vivian's innate inquisitiveness drew out basic details of Isabel's background: she was one of four children, the daughter of a successful lawyer, a known crusader who represented underdog cases for free. Her mother, a vigorous campaigner for such causes as compulsory vaccination and pasteurized milk, played host to international VIPs. She ingrained spirited, free and purposeful thinking in Isabel and her siblings.

Vivian soaked it all in: equal rights for women, compassionate care for those with mental illness, improved hospital care, ending corporal punishment in Canadian schools, human rights. Her head was full after the tete-a-tete with this amazing woman, who was reared in a multigenerational home in privileged Rosedale; educated at Havergal, an exclusive private school for girls, and the University of Toronto, a divorcée happily remarried to a much older man.

"We'll have tea, dear," Isabel said as they parted company.

They mingled with Billy's boss, Vyola Miller, and Goldie Redmon, the able and ever-chatty board secretary whose husband Nathan was the black owner of Redmon Haulage, a busy twelve-truck fleet, hauling bricks and lumber to an ever-burgeoning number of building sites. Vivian met Honorah Lucas, dynamo helmsman of the venerable Central Neighbourhood House, a core social service agency and settlement house on Sherbourne Street where she blazed a trail to address a postwar trend toward absentee fatherhood and bitter, family breakdowns, which fell on mothers to shoulder on meager wages.

Another new face belonged to Esther Hayes, a prominent member of the Bahá'í faith, her mother Inez a prominent proponent of the faith. Unlike the Anglicans who shunned her kind, Inez and Esther found the Bahá'í community carried no trace of bias against race.

Frederick Hubbard, a commissioner and one-time chairman of the Toronto Transportation Commission, was there too. Out of his earshot Billy candidly disclosed to Vivian that Mr. Hubbard, at the age of almost seventy, never alluded to his race even though he, the son of a groundbreaking council member, was the TTC's historic first non-white appointee and his grandparents were escaped slaves who arrived in Toronto in 1840 by way of the Underground Railroad.

Billy moved Vivian through the clusters, nodding, smiling, glad-handing and introducing his stunningly fresh-faced fiancée to a pocket of Toronto's elite that was committed to working for wholesale societal change.

Among them were Ben Lappin, of the Canadian Jewish Congress and Canadian Association of Social Workers; Ruth Hartman Frankel, a Princess Margaret Hospital benefactor who was on her way to founding a Toronto chapter of the Canadian Cancer Society, the wife of the CJC's vice-president, Egmont, a proponent of its Race Relations Day; Mrs. Peter Sandford, the influential wife of the head of the Ontario College of Education; Arnold Walter, a leading and learned Moravian-born Canadian music educator whose latest landmark was to found the graduate department of the Toronto Conservatory of Music and the conservatory's opera school.

A sea of first-time faces, Vivian could scarcely keep up. Her head spun. She knew she was in the midst of something special and significant around such people as Wilson O. Brooks, Mrs. Leo Chevalier, Aubrey Forbes, Shirley S. Jackson, Dawson Kennedy, Grant Hackley, W. A. Marshall, the Campbells, Fred and his wife, "call me Aunt Betty", who were best friends of the Christians, and Reverend J. T. Dawson. All of them had spectacularly interesting backgrounds, which were parceled out that night in snippets to Vivian as they rubbed elbows: Negroes, Jews and Gentiles resplendent in their readiness to build a community devoid of prejudice. The rebukes, protests and objections from back home stood in stark contrast to the holistic, multi-dynamic party scene she was witnessing.

Pauline, the Home Service office manager, was babysitting the record player cranking out symphonic background music from scratchy phonographs that seemed to help meld the directors, staff, donors and volunteers into one common assemblage of high hopes and morale. They munched on frugal sandwich triangles and cookies prepared by volunteers and sipped the watery fruit punch in their ceremonial toasting to a bright year ahead led by Billy.

Idling near Pauline was a young woman thumbing through a box of record albums as Vivian approached.

"Vivian, meet my replacement." Pauline rose from her chair and gestured an introduction. "Vivian Keeler, I'd like you to meet Tommy Swisoki, our new office manager. Tommy, this is Vivian, Billy's girlfriend."

"Fiancée," Vivian gently corrected as she and the girl shook hands. "How do you do, Tommy? It's a pleasure to meet you."

"An interesting name you have, Tommy. Is it spelled T-o-m-m-y?"

Tommy bubbled. "Vivian I am very pleased to meet you as well. It's T-o-m-i in Japanese, but I was told to change it, so I could blend in and make it easier for everyone. Still, it *is* a boy's name, so that adds confusion. Your Billy White, he is really something! I look forward to working with him here."

Vivian was struck that Tommy changed the spelling of her name to be more acceptable to others. Then she considered that Billy was in the throes of becoming "Bill" and wondered whether his reasons might be similar: a desire to fit in and be accepted.

"This may surprise you, Tommy, but Billy thinks his name is too girlish and he wants people to call him Bill."

"Bill White," Tommy repeated, followed by a smile and a quick nod. "I like it."

The memory of the party set the tone for the rest of December. On Christmas Day Vivian and Billy exchanged gifts in the Christians' living room. She gave him the recording of Beethoven's Ninth Symphony he'd been wanting, and he gave her a silver locket – one he hoped she would wear on their wedding day.

Only one additional letter about their impending marriage arrived in December. It was tame compared to the earlier ones. This one from Monterey, California, from a favored first cousin, Charles, Sgt. C.M. Riseborough, Elsie and John's military-minded son. He and Vivian were close growing up during her regular summer and weekend jaunts to North Brookfield.

> December 7, 1946
> Dear Vivian,
> Hello cousin, well here is that Yankee cousin of yours ven-
> turing on that tack of writing a letter, one that I never
> seem to have enough courage to tackle very often. I hope
> you are well, and I sure wish I could see you and have a
> good long talk, but I guess a letter will have to do for it's
> impossible for me to leave here now. Mary cannot travel as
> we are expecting the last of March. I sold my car the other
> day, while prices are high, as we seem to be settled here for
> a good while and don't really need it. Mary is fine and says
> she plans to write you soon. We have a nice place here so
> are very happy. I sure wish you could come out here and
> stay with us awhile. We'd really love to have you, believe
> me. The Army pays me well, so you wouldn't have to worry
> about what you'd do or where you'd live.
> I don't know how to ask you Vivian, but I've heard
> something about you that I don't want to believe. I sure
> wish we were closer so I could sit and talk to you. They say
> that you want to marry a Negro boy. I won't say I'm not

disturbed for I am, and I hope it's not true. If it is, I hope you will consider it for a long time and perhaps see it my way. I have nothing against any other races, and I've had a chance to work with them all. Mexican, Japanese, Chink and Negro, I have many friends among them. I am very fond of them, but I believe that marriage between races was not meant to be, and I have reason to. I think if you really love this boy you should leave him, for it can only mean unhappiness for him. At the time of your marriage, he'll be disavowed by the Negro race and that's the case even in France where the color line is the weakest.

Your children would be mulatto, which are accepted by neither race; and would bring great pain to you both. I hope you'll reconsider in the face of this and, if you need counsel, why not go to the nearest church regardless of faith and seek out the priest or minister there? He can give you honest clear opinions and advice. The intermarriage of races never bothered me much. In fact I never gave it much thought until I went to the Philippines. The people there are half-castes and some of the girls are really beautiful and very well educated. My pal, the closest friend I ever had, Ray Kath, fell in love with one of these girls and she loved him almost like in a book. When he asked her to marry him she refused for she knew that they could never be happy in the States or even in the Philippines for both their families would not have them. Ray loved her so much that he made a 3,800-mile trip back to the Philippines to try to get her to reconsider, but she still turned him down. That really took courage although before now I never realized how much. Ray will never marry and I'm sure Levinia will never be happy with anyone else, but she saw the impossibility of marrying, the hardship their children would have to face and the loss of their family to them forever.

I know it sounds like a yarn but on my d--n word of honor it's a fact. I seriously hope you'll think it all over. If you decide that it's wrong for you to marry that boy I sure wish you'd take a trip out here and stay with us awhile for I'm sure it would do you good and help you forget and find your sails of happiness once more. Please write me at any rate for I do love to hear from you and even though we always used to fight as kids I always thought the world of you and always will. I know to have control over emotions takes real courage and if "we trys and fails" it's no disgrace as far as I'm concerned. I've seen many boys break under fire and it's never any fault of their own. Well, hoping to hear from you soon and wishing you well.

A Merry Christmas & Happy New Year to you.

Charles

She was disappointed in her cousin's view, but unlike those of his father and mother, not left aghast. His parents were stuck like tar in their biases, but with her peer Charles, she deduced, she could guide him into a more modern way of thinking.

As the calendar flipped to 1947, Vivian sensed the opinions by mail on the subject of her marriage would stutter to a stop. She was wrong.

Six more letters were on their way to her. In order of appearance they came from "Aunt" Annie, Mother's girlhood friend; Aunt Doris, a Harlow; widowed Aunt Madge, a Keeler by marriage; Mother herself; Mrs. Keddy, another of her mother's long-time friends, and Mrs. A. B. Smith, Vivian's former Sunday school teacher, a pillar of the church.

As with the first round, Vivian routinely wrote back promptly. To ignore them would be rude. Holding her ground, stating her beliefs and adding some chatty news of interest somewhere in the body, she responded thoughtfully to each letter before carefully refolding it and adding it to the chocolate box collection. She tried not to let their opinions bother her, but they did. She was shaken, not broken, disheartened not angry.

Billy didn't know the half of it. Vivian felt an ongoing soap opera would interfere with his work. If at all, she preferred to unload on Mrs. Phillips. Better still was to keep busy to stymie any creeping uncertainty stirred up by the unsolicited missives. Vivian centered purposefully on what really mattered to her: preparing to be the wife of Billy White and throwing herself into her new job and community work.

He was going to be a prominent person someday, she envisioned, and she'd be behind him, supporting him, always, not burdening him with the whining, strident drama generated by her intolerant family circle. She'd square that circle on her own and spare him. In the meantime, Vivian and Billy exchanged love poems.

> January 27, 1947
> It's been that kind of day
> That makes me want to say
> "Let's get married right away,
> Not five months from today."
> I may as well reveal
> That that's the way I feel
> Let's make our living real
> By calling it a deal.
> I'll put you to a test
> And let you write the rest ...
> – Billy

> ... If you'd leave the 'writer here
> I might attempt it, dear,
> But I must have made it clear
> That I'm stupid while you're near.
> – Vivian

> To A Tall, Brown-Eyed Charmer with a Dimple in his Chin:
> You may think I'm rather simple

When I rave about your dimple,
But it is to me a token
Of a hold which can't be broken;
Of a faith which can't be shaken
A hope you only could awaken,
And, despite the world's endeavor,
A love that will endure forever.
– Vivian

January 28, 1947
Tonight, before I go to sleep,
This promise to myself I'll keep;
I'll write a line to you to say
Thanks for your poem of yesterday

The sentiments your words expressed
Left me indeed so much impressed
That I shan't – can't – hesitate
Your gesture to reciprocate.

Oh *chérie*, 'twas so nice to see
That you forgot your modesty
And put your thoughts for the first time
In well writ, balanced, – perfect rhyme.

To say what your love means to me
Would be sheer superfluity,
Because I tell you every day
In just the same ole corny way.

But yet, somehow, it seems tonight
That everything is, oh, so right
That if I tell you just once more

You won't think I'm an awful bore.

I love you; that you well may guess,
Because you've brought me happiness;
And with you in the months gone past
I've seen my love was meant to last.

And looking to the years ahead
I see pure bliss – unlimited;
Yes, you and I and ours will be
The perfect little family.

And so, before I go to sleep,
I'll send my love for you to keep;
And if 'twould do you any good,
I'd send my dimple – if I could.
– Billy

Young Jean Harlowe on Lake Banook

Chapter 16

January 19, 1947

Dear Vivian,

You will be surprised to hear from me, but you would not be if you knew how very much I have been thinking about you. I see your dear Dad – who loved you so very dearly. How proud he was of you, how he would take you on his lap and so patiently explain and reason out every little thing with you. I have felt so badly that you have been deprived of the companionship your dad would have given you – just what you needed to give you more confidence in yourself and a different outlook on life in general.

During the past months your dad has seemed to be haunting me just as though he was speaking to me, asking me to be "my brother's keeper."

Your grandma Harlow came to me in my dreams. It was so very real, Vivian. She walked in so slowly and so unlike the way she always greeted me – no smile whatever. But such sadness and looking at me in such a way. It made me feel so badly that I had not tried more to help you.

I plead with you Vivian to listen to those who are much wiser than you, through years of experience and learning. As Mr. Harris, a very good friend of your dad, said when he learned of your intentions, "Glenn would raise from his grave, if he could do so." Uncle Ralph was always a great friend of your dad, and all who knew him know that is true, dear. Listen to them Vivian, they are your friends and have had ever so much more experience.

Then think of your mother. She was very different from your dad. His going was a great blow to her. She just could not talk and reason with you as he would have. Neither could she go out and make new friends. She has just kept so alone. My heart has ached for her as well as you children. It would have been so different had Dad been spared. She just has you and Bernard, and the years are slipping away. Can you hurt her more and hope to be happy? Honor thy father and thy mother is still a great command, and not to be put aside lightly.

These are only a few points Vivian. There are many more I assure you.

Uncle Ralph joins with me in prayers that you may listen to those who wish so much to help you.

Will be glad to hear from you.

Lovingly,

Aunt Annie

January 23, 1947

Dear Vivian,

I've been thinking of you a lot these last few months. Of course I've heard about your affair with the colored fellow and feel very badly about it. That is not good enough for you, Vivian. Surely you won't marry him. They are all right in their place but certainly not a fit companion for a white girl of good family. If your father was living you know he would not allow it.

I can't understand how you can be so cruel to your mother and Bernard and in fact all of us. I'll dread to go home and face the gossip.

You know we are all very much opposed to it so how can you think you are right. It means all the rest of your life Viv. You realize that the only company you will have will be his tribe. No family or friends to come home to. How can you consider living with him especially after he has lived with a colored wife? It makes me shiver to think of it. Everyone who knows about it thinks it is a horrible thing for you to do.

Be our own Vivian and give him up. There is something better than that in life for you. We would all be so happy to hear you were through with him.

I haven't written Albert anything about this. You asked me where Deep River is situated. It is 125 miles NE of Ottawa. We were on the train six hours from Montreal to Chalk River, then drove six miles to Deep River.

Aunt Lou and I plan to go to Halifax tomorrow to spend the weekend.

Don't be so hard-hearted. Do as you know you should, for all our sakes. Write to me Viv.

Love,
Aunt Doris

January 30, 1947
My dear Vivian,
Recently I heard of your association with a person of another race. Two acquaintances, one woman my age and a girl of your own age, were horrified and asked me if I knew. I was terribly shocked and denied it. However, I have learned it is true and having known of a couple of very sad cases when I was in school in Halifax, I am hoping you may change your mind, as I would not like to think of your life being ruined as their lives were.

I realize of course that in a sense this is not my business. My decision to write to you is partly selfish as I wish to ask you to refrain from mentioning it to Evelyn if you should write and I hope it may be kept from her while she is so far away. I know it would be a terrible shock to her and she would probably brood over it. She always spoke of you with pride as a coming brilliant career woman.

I suppose you realize how this association would cut you off from your family because we just could not accept a situation of that nature.

With love,
Aunt Madge

January 31, 1947
My dear Vivian,
This letter will perhaps come as a surprise to you, but I hope it will be received kindly. You have been so very much in my mind and prayers during the past two weeks. Strange to say it was just about that time I heard you had gone away, and the story and circumstances connected with it.

Looking back to your baby days, it was in your mother's and daddy's home that Mr. Keddy and I used to visit as we were married just about the same time. Your mother and I belonged to the same Sunday school class taught by Mrs. Smallman. We started our homes together choosing floor plans very much alike and had the joy of each having a baby girl. How happy we were – our husbands each had served, and it was as if the sun truly shone in our lives again – just because we were about to establish a home.

I can't help but feel I have perhaps had more than my share of blessings in that I have had my husband and lovely family all through these years. They are my treasures, at least that is what my mother used to tell me, and I know she believed it her duty to lead us all in the Christian life.

How much we owe our mothers. I keep beside my bed a little book given to me by the Ladies Circle entitled *The Greatest Thing in the World* and on the fly leaf I pasted not long afterwards a little paper clipping "A Mother's Love." I read it often and nothing to me is greater, yet too tender to think of hurting.

I know your mother's heart is aching and about to break because of your decisions and I feel just as she does and my reaction would be the same, were I placed in similar circumstances.

Mr. Smith and I are praying for you each day and are confidently hoping that God will lead you to make the right decision.

We need each other's love all through the years and marriage is a tremendous step to take. God bless you Vivian,

Affectionately yours,

Reta Keddy

January 31, 1947

Dear Vivian

You will probably be surprised to receive a letter from me. But you have been constantly in my mind recently. I understand you are contemplating marriage.

You are now on the threshold of life, young, and ready to step forward. I know you want life to be full of happiness, of Christian living.

Take a look forward, try and think ahead into the years and try and imagine yourself in your home, surrounded by your children and friends. Any step you take now will determine your whole future for yourself, and children, and social life.

Every girl desires a nice, Christian home, lovely children to train and teach, and also while making many new friends their old ones from childhood are a part of life, all through.

When you get married, think of what kind of a church home you will have through life for yourself and children, what kind of a social life, will you have? What kind of an environment will your children be thrown into? In your marriage will your children be handicapped? The man you marry, to a great extent, determines these things. Don't ever let your mother down. She has lived for you.

I suppose by this time you feel like not reading more, but Vivian, do you really and honestly think that you will be happy with a social life among colored people? Now, I know, there are fine Christian colored people, and all races of the earth are God's family. He made some white and some colored. But I do not believe his plans were for inter-marriage. If he created them that way, don't you think he intended that the pure strain in each race should remain? Mixed marriages cannot be happy ones, all your bringing up does not harmonize with it. I enjoyed you in my Sunday school class. I often think of my girls. I loved them all and believe me this letter is written in a spirit of love and a desire to help.

Yours very sincerely,

Mrs. A. B. Smith

January 31, 1947

Dear Vivian,

After many vain attempts to answer your letter of November 23rd, I have decided it is only necessary to say a very few things. I had thought that in going to a large city, you would realize you had to establish high social standards and would see at once that a Negro could have no place in your life. As this hope died I wrote to him asking him to end matters between you. As you still continued,

I appealed to my brothers and sisters and they did what they could – shocked, hurt and horrified as they all were. When you would not listen to a wonderful person like Mrs. Abbott, or your fine uncles, you will pay no heed to me, but you should realize it is only those who really love you and are deeply concerned for your welfare, who will speak out and try to save you – many more, who care, will not say a word, and the strangers you are meeting there are not in the least concerned with your future happiness. They just put you in a class with Negroes and let it go at that. They do not know that your family is nearly foolish with worry and distress about it. Let it be one of their own, however, and it would be a very different story.

We have been given the precious heritage of a white skin and all that goes with it. How can you toss that away and mix with an incompatible race which will never be acceptable in marriage? You will be creating just another social problem, in yourself and your children for many generations, as it keeps cropping up to distress and embarrass. You will turn many against Negroes and their problems by your action. You are setting a bad example for other young people, and you are giving your church here, a very black eye.

I feel very, very sorry for Lillian.

Apart from race altogether, this fellow is most unworthy. He talks a lot and has a very smooth manner but there is no character behind it. He is not sincere or dependable. He sacrificed nothing in the war, as compared to the five, long years of service and bravery of your father. He has little more education than you have, a teacher's license and about a year of university as against your business training. Instead of being well established in life as he should be at thirty-one, he is just starting a new job proving that he will never amount to anything but will be a drifter all his life.

He earns about forty dollars per week, and as you cannot make ends meet on what you earn, how can you both live on his salary? A man has to earn the living and should be well equipped for it, not lazy and incompetent as he was in his job here, in need of constant prodding. He is erratic, keeping bad hours. He is still not legally free to marry you so he lied to you when he said you could be married last September. He made a mess of his marriage so that even a Negro did not want him, and his engagement was broken because he did not measure up to what he preached.

You must realize that you could never come home again if you married him. This seems a terrible thing to say as I know all that my home meant to me through the years, and although you think little of it now, you will see that you have made this stand necessary, as you are doing your best to ruin us. If you should change, I will do everything in my power to keep you, you know that, but in the meantime I can do nothing. I still have faith that you will see things differently before it is too late and shall hope and pray that you will.

You must stop charging goods to my accounts, you will return the key you have to this flat. You are not to use my name in any way in connection with any such alliance. Any of your belongings here can be sent to you. I believe you both know this thing is wrong and you are doing it for the sake of a crude passion which will expend itself in a short time and then you will see things as they really are. Cast it out now before it is too late. One who knows him said: "Surely she will see through him in time. Others did."

May God speak to your heart and mind.

Your Mother

Chapter 17

January was a month of melodrama. Even before the toxic volley of mail reached her in February, Vivian was on edge. Her Victory Bonds, her war savings certificates, Billy's divorce decree and related paperwork were missing from the drawer where she'd put them for safekeeping. After a thorough search she told Billy they were gone.

Billy insisted that she report it. He worried the disappearing divorce papers would delay the wedding. Moreover, he wanted the culprit held to account. He suspected Reg in the next room of the theft. He and Billy had been at loggerheads since their first encounter.

"You don't always lock your door when you're downstairs talking to Margaret," he reminded her.

Vivian had taken up smoking, a new trend among young adults. Billy smoked routinely, and she felt stylish and mature using cigarettes from time to time. She was smoking one when Detectives Corwin and Campbell of York Township came to investigate the theft in the early mid-January evening.

"The last place I saw them was in this drawer," she showed the officers. "Since discovering them missing, I have turned this room inside out. I even checked the most unlikely places like under my mattress and the throw rug."

"We're going to need the serial numbers for those bonds," said Corwin, the taller of the two, as he poked around. "Do you have that information for us, Miss Keeler?" She would write to Bern back home and ask him to track them down. Campbell made a note that those details would be forwarded. After interviewing Vivian, the officers took statements from Reg and Mrs. Phillips, whose natural nervousness was exacerbated by the police presence.

A hand-wringing Mrs. Phillips told the police Reg surprised her recently by indicating that he intended to leave town.

Reg told the officers he was leaving "because of the colored."

"I just can't be around them," he confided to note-taker Campbell. "It's a physical thing. It makes me sick. No Sambos or Aunt Jemimas for me, no siree! Races were made different and separate and were meant to stay apart. The little lady down the hall knows how I feel, and I make no apologies. I didn't do nothing wrong," he harrumphed indignantly to his impassive interrogators. "I'll stick around until this mess is cleaned up and my reputation is restored."

Reg specifically wanted to live in an all-white neighborhood although he didn't mind the Jews who had taken over St. Clair Avenue West.

"Whatever you're selling we don't want," he said disdainfully as he passed Billy waiting in the vestibule at Oakwood, their first encounter. "You're in the wrong part of town, buddy," he said over his shoulder as he strode up the stairs to his room. He almost bumped into Vivian at the top. "Watch out for that coon down there," he grumbled.

"I'm almost ready, Billy." Vivian called down as she paused to have a hushed word with Reg in the hall. She had lived there all of a week. "I see you've met my fiancé," she said as cordially as possible while facing the offense of his words and the alcoholic vapors on his breath. "And now you know his name, Reg. Please use it."

Tensions grew from there. Reg's negativity intensified. He complained to Mrs. Phillips about Billy's presence and tried, unsuccessfully, to derail visits.

Overlaying the difficulties with Reg and the theft, Vivian was completely out of money again, not that she wasn't working hard. Money was leaking out as quickly as it was flowing in. Without her securities to fall back on in a crunch, Vivian was scrimping and scraping as best she could.

The following day she met Billy for supper at the Pasadena, a popular College Street eatery.

"Bernie says a letter is in the works from the trade board which will confirm the serial numbers of the bonds. Then I can advise the police and the bank."

As they ate, Vivian raised her concern about money for the umpteenth time. That conversation was the usual pithy exchange.

"We have to cut back and start budgeting better," she said just before the check arrived.

"Don't worry," he said with a dismissive wave as he paid the bill.

"No, really."

"Don't worry. Everything will work out. It always does. I can always cash out my life insurance policy." Exactly what she didn't want to hear, that policy was their security.

His glibness made her want to press the issue of finances, yet she swallowed the urge with a forkful of cabbage. Going up against Billy's way of doing things was a challenge.

Instead, she filled the space with talk of the wedding – wanting it to be in Montreal, the symbolic birthplace of their new life together, where he sealed his bended-knee marriage proposal with a cheap ring (replaced that Christmas with the real thing), closer to the Maritimes for those easterners who would attend, close to best man Harold and maid-of-honor Helen, and a possible Quebec City honeymoon. Billy was about to pitch again for an accelerated knot-tying, a hastened, no-frills civil ceremony, until he remembered his paperwork problem.

They parted company for a while – he went back to Home Service, and she went home. He came up at nine o'clock bearing gifts – groceries he had purchased on his Eaton's charge account.

In the second-floor common room Billy and Vivian spent a few hours engaged in deep discussion about religion. They agreed to look outside the Baptist faith to find a religion that would marry them without hesitation. They should start looking for and booking their church of choice, Vivian decided, *tout de suite.*

As agreed, Billy left at half past ten.

Vivian's job working on Kiwanis Festival publicity was arduous but interesting. "Worked like a slave," Vivian confided to her diary, a remark that would return to haunt her.

Overwork, money worries, too many light meals, late nights – that had been her January so far. With the unresolved theft, Vivian was already on tenterhooks when she returned a local call from Dick's brother Chuck. Living in Toronto, he wasn't entwined in the Dartmouth grapevine, so he hadn't heard about her engagement to Billy. On being told, his first thought was of his older brother.

"Viv, I think this news is going to be a great shock to Dick," he volunteered. "I am sure he is still in love with you. Please write him. I owe him a letter. Don't let him hear this from me."

She hung up the phone to a sinking and settling sadness. Their conversation depressed her. Had she made the right decision? Her mother's words came back to her: "Your heart will never lie to you." Vivian vowed to write Dick soon like an author ending a chapter, committing to another.

It was comforting to connect with people from home. Chuck's voice pulled her back to memories of grand times. Nothing she loved better than calls, letters and visits from Maritimers, so it was with both openness and gratitude that she embraced a visit from Gordon Keddy, husband of Reta, Mother's childhood friend. "I've known you since you were a baby," Gordon bragged over a noontime dinner at Childs Restaurant in the University of Toronto, his treat, on her day off. A book seller, he was in Toronto for a trade fair. Vivian had him fill her in on all the news from home while she gorged herself on Swiss steak, mashed potatoes and new carrots, a roll and milk, then lemon snow pudding with custard sauce, trying not to appear too ravenous. Her diet that morning had consisted only of coffee. She described in detail the talk by Mrs. Paul Robeson on Africa she and Billy attended the previous evening at Shaw Street Church and what fun they'd had at the Christians' annual Christmas party.

A movie next, *Till the Clouds Roll By* at Loews Theatre, and then a stroll to Charles and Church Streets for supper at the fancy French restaurant La Chaumière, where Mr. Keddy made a confession during dessert, confirming Vivian's suspicions.

"Actually, your mother asked me to see you," he blurted out, causing her to look up from the plate where she was negotiating a chocolate éclair with a fork and knife.

After a few comments on both sides regarding "her situation," as he called it, "I suggested we not spoil our lovely day and he agreed at once. I think he was convinced that my mind was made up," she recounted to Billy later.

Bernie came through with successfully establishing Vivian's certificate numbers, information she immediately relayed to the police and the Bank of Canada. Vivian prayed for progress.

The first of February, a Saturday, began smoothly enough, no trace of trauma on the horizon, not a hint that Vivian would start her month with a breakdown. She had to work until one-thirty to complete an assignment for Kiwanis left unfinished from the night before, then rush to shop for a birthday present for Billy and reach her hair appointment with Louise at the Beauty Isle by half past two. She tried a new "do," a page boy – still long enough that Billy wouldn't object and enough of a change to satisfy her. Money burning in her purse, cash from a fresh payday, funded a visit to the post office, the delicatessen, dry cleaners and laundry. Arms full, she went home to tidy up before heading to Lansdowne. There she and Billy jointly composed a letter to Harold and Helen on the typewriter belonging to new tenant Sonny's girlfriend, June. Harold's birthday was on the third. In addition to sending salutations, Vivian was eager to confirm a Montreal venue and date for their wedding, with him and Helen as key participants. Time stretched with the ease of pulled taffy. By now it was three o'clock in the morning.

The house on Lansdowne was usually a constant hub of activity. This weekend Doug Christian and Sonny were in Windsor, so it was quieter than usual.

The incredible and kindly Cleo, a renaissance woman, fashionable, adventurous, creativity spilling out of her like an overturned can of paint, was so full of vim you wouldn't know she suffered severely from arthritis. She had a triangular face, deeply set, agate eyes, ample cheeks and a big chin, lifted by her ready smile, a nest of silvering hair happily crowning her head. They'd all had plenty of laughs earlier in the evening, with Curley now long asleep downstairs in his own room. Cleo, who often puttered well into the wee hours, had a bedroom on the main floor next to his. At this late hour she was just turning down the bed. She was truly the queen of hospitality right down to letting Vivian share her queen-sized bed so Billy could sleep in his room and avoid the punishment of the hostile living room chesterfield.

After a "good night" to Billy, Vivian changed in the bathroom into her white and blue flannel nightgown, ankle socks and slippers from her overnight bag. The smart thing for her to do upon entering Mrs. Christian's room would have been to slip quietly into the bed they were sharing with a simple "see you in the morning." Instead, she entered the room with a quip as Cleo was settling in, a springboard from the levity that arose earlier in the evening when Cleo had been describing working like a dog with the ladies at the Grant African Methodist Episcopal church to which she belonged.

"Your people may have worked like dogs, but I worked like a slave today," Vivian tried to joke with a stretch and a yawn. For Cleo the words hit the air with the slam of a shunting freight car just as she was settling in to rest her aching joints. She sat bolt upright in bed. Gone in a flash was the matronly tenderness, a humorless face Vivian had never seen before glowered in her direction.

"I don't call my people dogs!" Cleo shrieked in a whisper, gripping the mattress as though ready for takeoff, fists clenched. Her tizzy continued. "How dare you twist my words and insult me? What would you know about being a slave? You're white. You come from a privileged background. You know nothing of our struggle. I thought you were here to learn.

"You should know when to keep quiet," she snapped, the blistering, surprise attack winding down and Vivian spitting out repeated apologies, trying to explain in between bursts. Cleo wasn't quite done. Her tone lowered in volume and temperature. "I've had enough. I invited you to share my bed, but for tonight, that invitation no longer exists," she said frostily, pointing to the door.

Vivian stumbled out, her face hot with shame, breathing shallow, her heart beating like the wings of a flock of grackles in flight after a gunshot in a cornfield. She barely made it into Billy's room before the tears descended and continued to cascade. She cried and cried and cried. He tried to console her, gave up at five and sought refuge on the chesterfield. Nothing from his Dalhousie night school psychology courses was going to help in this circumstance. And being the sibling of six sisters, he knew better than to insert himself in a disagreement between two females.

Poor Vivian hit a raw nerve. How could she know Mrs. C. was a hard-liner forever angry about the theft of the African peoples, the legacy of enslavement, in which she felt her people were still trapped? Women as domestics and nannies, men as railway porters, slotted into a cogged wheel that holds them in one place no matter how many steps they take, Vivian's awkward attempt at humor provoked a hair-trigger reaction she didn't see coming. Billy predicted it would all blow over.

Though it pained him to witness her incurable emotionalism, he chalked it up to accumulated stresses, not just a startling outburst from the landlady, but also the unresolved situation back home with so many rejecting her most treasured life decision.

Drained and dejected, Vivian sank singularly into the misery of her thoughts, an echoing refrain of self-flagellating adjectives and never-ending replays of the incident rattling against her cranium. Eventually, her lullaby of deprecation and deep regret lulled her into oblivion until Billy awakened her at half past nine the next morning.

Again, he was right. Mrs. Christian apologized for being nasty and blamed sleep deprivation and body aches. Reflectively, Vivian drew several lessons from the episode. Think before opening her mouth or keep quiet. Toughen up and be strong. Don't let others upset her.

It's a good thing she girded herself before the next volleys of disapproval went from ink to paper through the postal system and into the Phillips' mail slot. Margaret became anxious over any out-of-province postmarks on letters to Vivian, sickened to be the bearer of news that was bound to upset her dear and gentle tenant.

Pausing at the bottom of the staircase, she inhaled fully as her reluctant feet began their begrudging ascent to Vivian's door.

"Some of those letters are here," Margaret called through the door between knuckle raps, gently offering the latest batch when Vivian answered the knocks.

Reading the contents was like a roller coaster ride. Sometimes her tummy would flip. A hard swallow, a tensing jaw, maybe a creeping headache, anger, sadness, the silent scream. Symptoms were physical as well as emotional.

In this collection, there was Mrs. Smith, acting like she was still Vivian's Sunday school teacher, and Mrs. Keddy, Mother's dear friend predictably aligning herself to the cause, Aunt Madge and Aunt Doris, working the guilt levers from both sides of the family tree. And Lillian, on whose letter Vivian had pinned some hopes that it would be a day-brightener, instead brought clouds. "I don't see how I could come to your wedding," she wrote. "I'm sorry, Viv, but that's the way I feel."

Owing to her recent expulsion from Cleo's room and the many opinionated missives in the mail to date, Vivian felt she was a student being schooled in the art of weathering rejection, a best friend's refusal to attend the ceremony simply another test. In her heart she knew she wasn't losing a friendship, just a wedding guest. Lillian didn't approve, but a difference in opinion had never divided them, ridiculous that a difference in skin tone could.

No time for brooding. Vivian was determined to change minds by example. She would prove everyone wrong.

Her mother's vitriol arrived on the day before Billy's thirty-second birthday. He had permission to come to Oakwood for dinner and the evening. Jean's first letter to her daughter since early December – disowning Vivian, asking for the house key, saying horrible things about Billy – failed to ruin their night. Clearly the woman's agitation had reached a new frenzy. She'd been on quite the tear in Halifax recently visiting his ex-workplace.

Billy received correspondence from his mother too. Lois had paid a visit. Since his departure from Halifax, Lois pined. She hadn't bargained on missing him so and her loneliness surprised her when the permanence of their breakup gradually sunk in. Sure, she had her job at the Y on account of him and yes, they were supposed to stay friends, but it simply didn't work out that way and now she was tapping into some residual anger. One acute change? When he disappeared, so did Lois's contact with his family. Izie was always so compassionate. A gentle, nurturing woman, she could comfort a person just by being present and listening. You could sit with her in silence too and be content away from the pressure of needing to talk, or equally could engage happily in conversation with her on any topic under the sun. She certainly got an earful from Lois, who arrived equipped with shears to give "Mom" a complimentary trim and dole out news she was bursting to tell.

"Your son's soon-to-be mother-in-law showed up at the Y yesterday." She rolled out the detail slowly, "She was in to see Les and wanted to see me too, but I felt I had nothing to say to her and I refused."

"I've not met your replacement," Izie said clumsily, not meaning to sound unkind. "Who wouldn't love my Billy? What's not to love? I know next to nothing about the new girl except her name because he played me the song he wrote for her. Even then I could see the writing on the wall."

Jealousy jabbed at Lois. He'd never composed a song for her in all their time together.

"Well she could hardly be my replacement, Mom," she laughed. "She's white!"

That detail caught Izie by surprise. She was glad Lois was working behind her and couldn't read her facial expression, which straddled between shock and disapproval. She wanted her sons to perpetuate their own race to strengthen it. Besides, she felt a soft spot for Lois and therefore was partial to her. Izie didn't oppose the kind of mixing that welcomed white parishioners into her church, and indeed there was white blood in her own lineage. Her children had a chromatic scale of skin tones from the richest Gabon Ebony to the faintest honey-tinged hue. Leave it to say Izie's preference was chocolate whatever the shade.

"I'm sorry it didn't work out for you two, dear," she sighed as Lois worked the comb and scissors. "Things happen for a reason. God only knows."

When Billy briefed Vivian on the contents of his mother's letter she immediately wondered what else Jean had left to throw. Her storming to the Y was an unexpected maneuver. What other surprises lay in store?

"As impossible as I find her to be, I can't hate my mother for being wrong. I'll never stop loving her. She will soon exhaust her arsenal."

Perhaps there would be a reprieve now.

• • •

At two minutes after midnight, February seventh, Vivian wished Billy a happy birthday and gave him one of his gifts – a scarf – before he left for home, saving the other two until the following day.

The most significant event for Billy on his birthday was a long-distance call from home during an early evening break at the Christians' between his day and night shifts.

Cheerful voices of sister June, niece Carolyn and Mom took turns crackling through the handset, then Cleo talked to Izie, and Doug talked to Carolyn. To make the phone call complete, Billy was nudging Vivian in pantomime to say hello to his mother. Vivian's frantically waving hands signaled "no," and she mouthed the word with a look of terror on her face. Too shy, afraid of saying the wrong thing to Mrs. Sealy, she let the opportunity slide. She hated herself.

One of the most distressing letters to date (it was starting to feel like a competition) came from William Elgee, the man of God who baptized Vivian while serving the Brunswick Street Baptist Church as minister.

> February 5, 1947
> My dear Vivian,
> I have today received a letter from your mother, so you will readily understand the purpose of this letter. We heard two or three days ago from another source of the tragic state of your mind, and I pondered the idea of writing to you. But I did not know your address, and I also hesitate to act on gossip.
>
> It certainly is tragic to think one has fallen in love with one of another race. So, if Mr. White is a Negro and that is your feelings toward him, you can have yourself the whole compensation of the martyr complex. Perhaps when I show you that that is what you are enjoying, it might help you to understand yourself. When Ignatius of Antioch, in the days of the Roman persecutions, was on his way to the lions at Rome, he enjoyed the thought of dying in the lion's paws for religion's sake, so much that he prayed the Lord

no one would interfere with his martyrdom. You are in the same state of mind.

If you and Mr. White marry, the real evil will not fall upon either of you but upon your children. They will be born into a world which has no society to receive them. If we had a definite inter-color society, that would provide for them somewhere to live. We do not have that. People cannot live alone. Your children will drift hither and yon. The suffering which will fall upon the older generation is a different matter. You can ignore that if you are hard enough.

But in consideration of your children, there would be only one step by which you could justify such a marriage. That would be to go to a hospital and have yourself sterilized ahead of time. Put your martyr-complex up against that as something to be done next month and see how it stands it. And do not tell anyone that I recommended it. I do not recommend it. I say it would be one degree less evil than to bring children of mixed blood into our type of society.

Did you ever read *All God's Children Got Wings*?

If Mr. White has divorced one wife and broken another engagement, you may think that you have great prospects of a very happy life with him. That is what the romance stories say. It is not the story told by the hard long years when you have separated yourself from any unified body of congenial human beings, bringing up a family almost alone. It is only palaver to suggest that Christian interracial goodwill requires or is furthered by inter-marriage.

Vivian, I have written hard, blunt, and without gentleness. This is no place for gentleness. I trust you will awake out of your dream before it is too late. If Mr. White has character he may withdraw himself. Of course another possibility would be that he would withdraw by another divorce leaving you with the care of your children. But I have written with deep desire for your welfare.

Cordially yours,

William H. Elgee

Chapter 18

One more letter for the chocolate box. That's how Vivian had to regard Elgee's letter. If this was Mother's idea of a final salvo, it was a dandy.

"Have yourself sterilized." Reading those words turned Vivian's spine to an icicle. This minister, who sanctified her childhood relationship with God, the man who preached from the Book of John, "Stop judging by mere appearances, but instead judge correctly" now counselled butchery? As for his suggested reading material, indeed she had read Eugene O'Neill's play about marriage between races. Vivian thought it out-of-date and poorly researched, and wondered had Mr. Elgee read Billy's favorite, *From Earth to High Heaven* or *I Married a Jew*, *The Atlantic* article from January 1939 that Billy found reprinted in *Chatelaine* last summer and gave her to read.

The whip of the backlash was wearying. Vivian identified with the railway porter, carrying the weight of heavy baggage he didn't own, hoping for validation and worth from people who would never oblige, having passengers from afar piling on and expecting instant servitude and compliance. This was her experience now.

With a note of resignation peppered with hope, she reasoned that where family had fallen away and failed her, her new community would fill the gap. Nowhere was the sense of community more evident than at Home Service. Everything Vivian valued resided there: history, cooperative activity, helping services, intergenerational connections, and a sense of belonging. The place welcomed all children, and Vivian observed that none of them discriminated. Here struggling moms found a nursery school and care for their kids. The outward manifestations of strain from hard life in the city were answered by caring people with knowledge of treating mental health. Pregnant women could find a volunteer to drive them to medical appointments. Boys who might otherwise feel aimless or disinterested were kept busy, by the king of busy, Billy White and his programming roster.

One focal point of the place was the well-functioning player piano in the huge dining room that could seat fifty. Youngsters routinely lined up to have a turn sitting on the piano bench, activating the roller with foot pedals to see the instrument play itself. Routinely they would gather around it while Mr. White conducted a singing lesson or impromptu singsong, summoning up tunefulness inside themselves they barely knew they had.

The piano was another way in which Home Service felt like home to Vivian. She could go there and refresh her faltering technique while waiting for Billy to wrap up, unless Mrs. Miller was sleeping, which was not unusual given her impossible working hours.

Vyola gave her all to her executive directorship. There was a legacy to keep, footsteps to follow, buttons to push to get things done – and getting things done wasn't easy. An American hand-picked for the job owing to her amassed professional training and knack for moving mountains, her specialization was advocating for people with special needs. Down there they nicknamed her The Fixer, an iron hand in a velvet glove.

Home Service took root as the Overseas Comfort Club in 1911, founded by the president of Grant African Methodist – Cleo's church – the Montreal Missionary Society, and a minister's wife with the aim of women volunteers bringing comfort and cheer in the form of socks, scarves, hampers of jams, jellies and preserves to black soldiers enlisted in the Canadian Army during the First World War.

Post-war it was renamed Home Comfort Club and then Home Service Association, an expanded hybrid founded to serve all black social welfare needs, not just those of military men.

A cornerstone of black self-help, allied with other groups and professional, civic and denominational networks, Home Service well-suited

Vivian, who would have seized a chance to work there, Billy or no Billy, pay or no pay.

The place was a hive of youngsters, reminding Vivian of how much she looked forward to having children of her own with Billy, and why William Elgee's words cut her deeply. Billy had a wonderful way with kids. The boys in his programs idolized him. You could tell by the eagerness that lit up their faces when he strode into the room, "Hi, hi, hi" his resonating rallying cheer upon entry, clapping his hands and rubbing them together vigorously as a gambler would before his lucky roll of the dice, indicating to his kids that something special was on the way. That could mean anything from games and sports to lessons on making bread or knitting a scarf, exploring the makeshift Home Service library and educational upgrading. And music, always the music, his key to harmony among people, his metaphor for his vision of the world. God is love, is music.

She was engaged to the handsomest of men – a most talented and uniquely skillful man. He'd make a superb father. Despite his previous marriage and his trysts with Lois, which irked Vivian like a tight ponytail, it was she who he would wed, she who would grace the Earth with his offspring. They would produce smart, beautiful children and they'd raise them free of racial bias.

Through Home Service, the church circuit, Billy's engagements and appearances, Vivian's varied workplaces and the network of transplanted East Coasters who had likewise migrated to Toronto, an array of people and possibilities materialized with each changing day.

Vivian and Billy ran into the much-admired Fran Wees, someone Vivian knew as a friend of her mother's youngest brother, Uncle Ralph, an unmarried psychiatrist living in New York City. Fran, forty-five and a public relations dynamo, was also a prolific mystery and romance novelist married to psychologist Dr. Wilfred Wees, a touted educator at the University of Toronto. During the war, Fran led the national clothing drive for the United Nations Relief and Rehabilitation Administration, which was how she came to know Uncle Ralph and the Harlows.

Most churches and hubs like Home Service held weekly fireside meetings, friendly drop-in chats where the topic was whatever people wanted to talk about. Mr. Gowans, minister of College Street United Church, hosted a fireside featuring Fran as a guest speaker talking about her career as an educational scribe and early Canadian female writer. This was ironic because she wasn't a Canadian. Although she called Canada home she never did renounce her American citizenship.

Frances Shelley Wees was born Frances Almeda Johnson in Oregon and moved twenty-six times before the age of ten, eventually landing in Saskatchewan and becoming a teacher at the age of seventeen. She wrote her first novel back then in longhand. Years later it was discovered by her husband, who typed it out, sent it to a New York publisher and secured a deal. Her inaugural book sold more than fifty-thousand copies. Besides recapping her literary path, Fran told of her eight years in the 1920s as the Canadian director of the Chautauqua traveling tent shows, adult education assemblies of speakers, teachers, musicians, showmen, preachers, and specialists of the day presented to the masses, which President Theodore Roosevelt declared to be "the most American thing in America."

Vivian took photographs at Fran's fireside with the camera she'd had the presence of mind to bring. Then Mr. Gowans invited Billy to speak briefly about his world brotherhood initiative for eliminating racial prejudice. A few people left before he got to the song leading. Those who stayed for the Bill White experience remained forever grateful for it. Singing in harmony with him was an emblematic and enduring lesson in human harmony.

Mr. Gowans, ever gracious, would be the perfect counsel for discussing William Elgee's letter, and her marriage, in confidence, Vivian was thinking. She made a mental note.

The Home Service annual general meeting was just before Valentine's Day. So many interesting people to meet. Billy's prowess as an organizer was on full display: attendance was robust. Vyola Miller was at her best. Prof. George Tatham, a geography specialist was the guest speaker. He painted his hoped-for picture of a country and world committed to fundamental human rights and freedoms. "Men and women of adult age, without any limitation due to race, nationality or religion, deserve the right to marry and to found a family. They are entitled to equal rights as to marriage and during marriage," he asserted at one point in his presentation. Whenever Vivian felt shipwrecked in future, she would cling to those affirming words like a storm survivor clinging to a lifebuoy. She thought of Reg and the bludgeon of Mr. Elgee's intervention. A nice counterpoint had been Dick's reaction to her intention to marry Billy, expressed in the letter she'd received from him the previous day.

February 8, 1947
Dear Vivian,
Thanks for your letter, which came last week. I was certainly glad to hear from you. Apparently, the rumors are flying thick and fast in Dartmouth, and someone is always telling me the latest. They all seem to think in the same terms as I gather Chuck does and seem quite surprised when I don't get all flustered. I have written to Chuck, by the way, but I doubt if it will do much good. Would you please set me straight though. Have you set a date for the wedding?

I'm glad you had such a grand Christmas. I had a very enjoyable one, but very quiet. I know Mum and Dad and Chuck all missed the grand crowd we used to have for Christmas in Dartmouth. Golly, when did I write to you last, anyway? I haven't the faintest idea. The last month has been hectic. Piles of work and more social dos than I ever remember for such a short time. Between now and March eleventh are six big dances, an operetta, and an evening of one-act plays. Last night was the Sadie Hawkins dance. What a time! We all really enjoyed ourselves.

Next Friday is the Junior Prom, which I hope to attend. *Trial by Jury* is in town the following week, and then comes the Boilermakers Banquet Hall. I must see *Trial by Jury* and of course I can't miss the Engineers' do. Then I think I'll try to get some work done. I'm doing distinction in March, but as yet haven't started to work on it.

You ask if I see Harry? I presume you mean Harry Zappler and I see him quite frequently at mealtimes.

The work you're doing certainly does sound interesting. Do you do different types of work at the various places, or does it all run along the same lines? One thing, you're not likely to get tired of having the same old boss all the time.

I must close now, and please write soon. I'll try to answer more promptly.

Sincerely,

Dick

He was a true friend. They would never lose touch.

Conscience clear, any worry about his feelings eradicated, uplifted by his understanding and support, Vivian carried no encumbrances into Valentine's Day save for the unsolved case of her missing bonds. In any event, surly Reg had given up waiting for police to wrap up and was gone until month's end. It was a reprieve from his daily diatribes around the Oakwood house. With him gone, restrictions on Billy left at the same time. Until further notice he could stay overnight if he wished, George Phillips decided, and Billy did a few times.

That's how he and Vivian were able to breakfast together and take the same streetcar into work on Valentine's Day morning, a crisp Friday.

She clocked in at nine-fifteen and out at five-forty-five. By six-thirty she had reached Home Service.

"Close your eyes," Billy commanded gently as they got ready to face a chilly confrontation with the outdoors and head home. "Hold out your hands. Okay, open!" In her gloved hands he had placed a small can of butterscotch candies accompanied by a plump envelope. Inside, a card with the words:

> I know it's not your birthday
> But somehow it just seems
> I had to buy this hankie
> For the lady of my dreams
>
> I thought it was quite pretty
> And wouldn't pass it by

Chapter 18

It would be such a pity
To let the hankie lie

I hope it comes in handy
For covering up a cough
Or taking either candy
Or sticky lipstick off

"Thank you, Billy. I love you," she said with a kiss. While juggling her holdings she unclasped her purse and dug into it to find the packet of photos. "Here, Happy Valentine's Day, my darling."

They were the photos from the fireside, excellent ones of Billy and great ones of Fran as well. "I'd like to drop these off to Mrs. Wees before we go home," she said.

"Sure," said Billy. "It's on our way. Let's go." He opened the door for her to exit to his finessed arm gesture.

"I don't think she'll mind if you call her 'Fran,'" he added.

At the door of the Wees's charming Victorian-style home, it didn't matter that they arrived unannounced. Fran was delighted to see them, and the photo delivery evoked an impromptu invitation to dinner.

"I didn't know I was so photogenic," she said theatrically, pumping her tousled short curls with her hand while striking a model's pose. "I can find a use for these in my portfolio. Thank you, Vivian."

Vivian reveled being in the company of sophisticates and learned professionals who fed her inquisitive mind and satiated her curiosity. At first she thought she would hate Toronto. She missed the ocean and landscapes of her east coast home, the colorfully painted frame houses, the familiar faces. Now amid Toronto's luminaries and the city's cultural largeness she conceded it was at least an even trade, not counting the Billy advantage.

It was their first-time meeting Dr. Wees, whose firm handshake conveyed a man very much in command, as warm and welcoming as his wife. Their daughter Margarita, an artist, was in her home studio with Len, her boyfriend, whose portrait she was painting as Fran led Billy and Vivian through for a tour. At their next stop, her workroom, Fran said she had two books coming out that year.

"The book that won me the highest acclaim from the critics was the only one that flopped commercially," she laughed. "And one of my most successful efforts came about when I decided to spite my publisher. He wanted me to write something I didn't want to write, so I deliberately based my plot on all the clichés I could think of. It was an instant smash!"

Vivian wanted to know about the craft of writing – how long it took Fran to write a book and was astounded to hear her answer, "Two weeks."

"By the time I sit down to write I've mapped out exactly where the plot will head, the turning points in the story and I know each character down to the last detail. The mapping of it is what takes the time. Then writing it is like I'm watching a film strip and describing each scene as it rolls out in front of me."

Before sitting down to a dinner of ham, scalloped potatoes, honeyed carrots, sugar beets and greens, Fran implored Billy to play and sing for them. Her husband had built a fire in the grate for them and saddled up beside Fran to listen.

Billy launched into an instrumental. "Bill, you must agree to let me interview you for an article I'm working on, and I think you should approach CBC about getting some work there, and I have another idea." While continuing to play, Billy looked over to indicate agreement by nodding his head in time to the music, eyebrows raised in anticipation of her next thought.

"I'm doing work on educational textbooks right now. Let's have some fun."

She thumbed through a stack of books and magazines on a nearby end table, found what she wanted and placed the open book in front of Billy.

"Here," she said. "It's a geography lesson. Let's hear you put this to music."

Ever the improviser, showman to the core, Billy's improvisation on Fran's assignment was deliciously entertaining and set the tone for the thoroughly enjoyable meal ahead.

After dessert Dr. Wees excused himself to go shave. He and Fran had a party to attend. Fran purchased a new dress for the occasion, a mint green, short-sleeved, brocade number with a matching jacket. She too left the table to change.

"Don't mind us," she told the two. "You stay as long as you like." Her guests began clearing the table in advance of doing the dishes. She was back to find them in the kitchen within five minutes, looking sheepish, the jacket folded over her arm. "Wilf's hands are soapy, I'm stuck." She sidled up to Billy and turned her back to reveal an open dress, a stubborn zipper halted just above her waistline. "Could you?" she asked him demurely.

Billy knew the correct procedure for working a woman's zipper, pulling it by the slider not the tab, and efficiently got the job done. Vivian found the scene a tad risqué but the freshly shaven Dr. Wees didn't seem concerned in the least when his wife later thanked Billy for zipping her into her dress.

When their hosts left for the party, Billy and Vivian played the piano and amused themselves in the comfort of the spacious, upscale Wees home until well after 11.

It was that night in her room after Billy had said goodnight (he stayed for tea and kisses before heading for home) that Vivian found the bonds. She cleared her purse of his Valentine handkerchief, card and candy and went to fetch the chocolate box on the top shelf of her closet to put away the letters from William Elgee and Dick, which she had shared with Billy before he left. The box was on top of two photo albums, and she got the idea to add his cute hanky poem to her latest album and she hauled that down too. In so doing she noted the protruding corner of an envelope sandwiched inside the cover of the second album, realizing with a "What the ..." as she tugged at it, that her securities and Billy's papers were intact. It defied explanation how she missed seeing the dark brown envelope during her thorough scouring. The photo album cover, also brown, had camouflaged it.

An initial reaction of relief was followed by one of sheepishness. She was in the humbling position of having to notify police of the find, inform Reg when he returned and admit to the Phillipses her stupid mistake of calling police in the first place and heaping more stress on poor Margaret, an anxious sort. Reg's propaganda campaign against Billy because of his race made the landlady's trembling hands jumpy. Vivian hoped to settle those waters. As she added the latest two letters to her Moirs collection an idea hatched: invite Mrs. Phillips to meet Mrs. Christian and let her see the fallacy of Reg's destructive talk. The Christians were respectable homeowners, the most popular family on their otherwise all-white street and block, Cleo famous for her festooned parties and neighborly good works and Curley a genuine Canadian hero and champion. They were her best hope and they encouraged her to plan Margaret's visit. With Reg away until the end of the month, Vivian longed to undo some of his damage while she could.

The first opportunity to speak to Mrs. Phillips about a visit didn't present itself until the following week.

"Any mail for me?" Vivian called down the hall. Emerging from the kitchen Mrs. Phillips quipped in feigned sympathy, "No. Nobody loves you." She smiled wanly.

"Well I don't really *care*," Vivian answered, feigning defiance.

"No, not the kind of love *they* hand out!" Mrs. Phillips laughed.

Vivian shifted gears. "On that note, there are some lovely people I'd like you to meet." She explained the invitation and watched her landlady's face closely. Margaret's smile had fallen. Her teeth bit her bottom lip as she considered the idea in an almost-trance-like fashion for a few seconds. "I'll think about it and let you know," she said, her eyes downward as her hands began to fidget. She started back to the kitchen, stopped and turned again, making eye contact – "Vivian, I can't." She sounded apologetic. "I'd like to, really I would, but it will be too hard on my nerves. I can't go into strange situations without upsetting my tremble. I don't even go to see *my* friends. Perhaps Mrs. Christian can come over here sometime first ..." her sentence trailed, realizing this was not in keeping with Vivian's vision.

"I'm sorry Mrs. Phillips. I was just hoping to dispel Reg's horrible ideas about race by introducing you to a lovely couple in their home."

It was one of the suggestions from Billy's world brotherhood essay: "Have several members of your group visit homes of members of minority groups, noting the similarities and differences in the ways of life as compared with their own."

She waited hoping for a change of heart.

"I'm sorry too," Margaret offered hastily before returning to her kitchen duties.

Vivian's disappointment shadowed her as she ascended the staircase to her bedroom. Anytime she couldn't bring people together she felt her destiny thwarted. Somewhere in her deepest beliefs dwelt an unshakable calling for community, camaraderie and social justice.

Sulking wasn't her style. As she was able to do with every roadblock and barrier to her bonding with Billy, she sidestepped the letdown by summoning her considerable store of gumption and resolve. What choice was there but to invest totally in the certainty that things would be okay? Even if it didn't always feel that way – things between them had been a tad prickly at times lately.

Ten years a bachelor, Billy was accustomed to being on his own and generally accountable to no one. Now he answered to Vivian, and her harping on his past had annoyed him. "Lois should move on. It's obvious Lois isn't over you," Vivian had told him.

He appreciated her frankness and honesty. Still he struggled with what he regarded as an unwarranted harangue.

"What do you want me to do – pretend I don't know her? If I hear from her I'll tell you, Vivian. I have nothing to hide. Why do you keep harping at me like this? Why bicker?"

And she'd never back down. She'd shift the debate to his inappropriate use of the verb "harp" when she was merely stating facts. "We're not bickering; we're debating," she'd say, holding her ground.

Billy wanted Vivian more than anything in the world, but this betrothal business was going to take some getting used to. The fact that his mind sometimes did venture to Lois made Vivian not entirely wrong.

Thank God his divorce papers were safe. If only she'd marry him right away he could shake the eerie foreboding that haunted his gut periodically.

• • •

Mrs. Christian's birthday party was coming up in early March. He'd propose again then. These were his thoughts as he rattled homeward on the southbound Oakwood streetcar after another night to remember with Vivian. Tonight, the second day of her period, it had been a *safe* night for lying together in bed.

Polarities softened; disagreements fell aside. They communed and talked and regained the intimacy they lost when arguing about Lois.

"Your immaculateness and purity mean so much to me, *ma* chérie," he purred as they cuddled. "On our blessed wedding night I will express to you the fullness of my gratitude."

She snuggled into his chest, knowing his stroking hands would not stray beyond their agreed-to boundaries, that their passion would be restricted to sensual caresses, embraces and touch.

They were happy again, like in Montreal. What seemed like years was less than four months ago.

Owing to work time forfeited by falling ill, Vivian's February was financially leaner than expected. When she couldn't cover her Tamblyn's pharmacy order, she cashed a bond. The presence of cash in her pocketbook at the end of the month relieved some of the pressure she'd been feeling and prompted her to purchase a black blouse, her first new apparel acquisition of the year.

This payday fell on a Friday. Billy and Vivian had supper at the Diet Kitchen, one of their dozen most-frequented downtown eateries. Then he had to go back to Home Service. They'd see each other at her place later.

As she approached home Vivian could tell from the glow of a second-story window that Reg was back after a two-week absence: a blissful fortnight, she thought to herself as she began preparing mentally for the ensuing interaction.

Was he waiting for her or was it mere coincidence that he presented himself in his doorway as her key triggered the clicking sound of her door unlocking? She put her bags inside her door and turned to face him.

"Reg, you're back," she said wryly, stating the obvious.

"I can tell you missed me," he said sarcastically. "Don't look so happy to see me." He paused. "Is that lover boy of yours still coming around?"

Vivian heaved a deliberate sigh and, hands on hips, leveled her most direct gaze at him.

"I found the bonds, Reg," she said, ignoring his goading tone. "I'm sorry for the trouble my actions may have caused you and I mean that most sincerely. It ..."

"I told you I don't want him or his kind around here. Nothing but trouble guaranteed. You're being led in a bad direction, kiddo. Wise up before it's too late. I say this for your own good." Reg, uninterested in accepting her apology, instead resumed fanning his flames of intolerance. Her glare was unmistakably cutting, and he stopped mid-stream. "What's with the dirty look?"

Vivian squared herself and took a few steps toward him. She spoke quietly and gravely.

"I want there to be no uncertainty about this, Reg. My hard feelings toward you are not occasioned by suspicion but by resentment at your remarks about Billy."

She felt her forthrightness surge. Every soliloquy she'd composed in her head about his conduct spilled out of her uncorked.

"Reg, I feel sorry for you. I know you've had your troubles and you carry around a lot of pain and anger. I can see it in how much you drink. You feel lousy much of the time and the only way you know to build yourself up is by tearing other people down. You have my sympathy, Reg, you really do. I hope you work on finding happiness for yourself, the kind of happiness Billy and I have found."

He went to reply, and she held up her hand to silence him.

"Now, Reg, if you really care about my own good, you can do two things for me."

At that point he lit a cigarette and blew a few smoke rings out of his mouth, leaning against his door frame, facing her, awaiting with an uncaring air.

"Two things," she said slowly. "One – I want you to stop harassing Mrs. Phillips – you're making her ill, and two – and this is equally important, Reg – any guest of mine is to be treated with respect. If you can't be pleasant, kindly just leave us alone. Don't drag the rest of us down with your uncharitable tirades. You'll be wasting your energy. Billy will be coming here later, and the new house rules are effective as of now."

Reg, who was using his hand for an ashtray, seemed stunned, unaccustomed to Vivian's assertiveness. He shrugged at her. "There's a word for girls like you and it ain't flattering. You want to ruin your reputation it's no skin off my nose," he said as he retreated to his room. It was time for a shot of Triple Crown. "Don't say I didn't try to warn you, kid. Have a nice life."

Vivian and Billy sitting on his front steps

Chapter 19

There was peace in the house after that. Vivian was amazed at the effectiveness of her hallway lecture. She decided not to breathe a word of their conversation to anyone to allow Reg the dignity of a fresh start, a second chance of his own making, not hers. The atmosphere improved vastly with his changed demeanor.

Still, Vivian was more acutely aware than ever of the importance of securing an acceptable place where she and Billy could live as a married couple free of Reg-style vexations.

With Reg keeping his opinions to himself, an easygoing atmosphere ensued at Oakwood as the season inched towards spring. Mrs. Phillips' tremors subsided. Billy's come-and-go privileges were fully restored. Tensions eased between Billy and Vivian, and much was accomplished in March, excluding Billy convincing Vivian to marry early. Again, she dashed his hopes after he broached the topic as planned on March fourth at Mrs. Christian's fiftieth birthday party.

Such a fun affair: it was a complete surprise to Cleo and a great success. She was decked out: a bold patchwork jacket over a cheery red floral dress that matched her lipstick, a cosmetic she was rarely seen not wearing. Her husband and son had tricked the unsuspecting guest-of-honor with an elaborate ploy to deliver her to the party unaware. Vivian was proud to have been in on the planning with 'Aunt' Betty Campbell and was particularly happy to be of use in the kitchen. "Imagine, *me!*" she enthused in her diary. Before the meal, Billy played the piano. The seventeen guests present enjoyed a buffet supper, after which Billy took command of the record player and entertained them further with his carefully selected playlist. His audience enrapt in his storytelling, he had his back to the kitchen when Vivian emerged and couldn't stop her from stepping on and fracturing one of his favorite records, a Jan Peerce, which he'd left on the floor.

By this time Curley had detached his legs and was wheeling around on his self-made platform, propelling himself using leather cups resembling toilet plungers fastened to his elbows, his height now that of a ten-year-old.

"C'mon, Cleopatra, let's dance!" Everybody roared when Cleo obliged, despite her chronically bad hips and quipped, "Curley, you know you dance better with no legs than I do with two!"

Later, when the last gushing guest bade goodnight and Billy retired with Vivian to his room, he implored her to accelerate their marriage timetable. Her predictable rebuff reduced him to shards resembling the vinyl LP that had succumbed to her shoe downstairs.

"I've been feeling more strongly now than ever that we ought to get married right away – I'm afraid of something but I don't know what," he confided as he sat dejectedly on the side of his bed.

She plunked down beside him and gave him a one-armed hug, as much to reassure herself as him. His words scared and unsettled her, but she refused to let it show.

Soothingly, she told him how sensible it would be to wait. They would find a place to live first and Vivian would save as much money as possible before "I become the enviable Mrs. W. A. White, your wife, helpmate and mother of your future children." Billy slapped his knees and sprung to his feet, reinvigorated.

"You can't blame a fellow for trying, *ma chérie,*" he said of his proposal. He checked his watch. "Let's get you home, speaking of sensible. The Christians are lending me their car."

The loaner car spared them a spotty transit ride and Billy was back at Lansdowne by half past midnight. Before parting ways with Vivian, he slipped a letter into her hands. He'd penned it twenty-four hours prior and formalized its delivery now at her door with a kiss and "I love you."

How she adored his letters. She soaked up his sentiments. A secret part of Vivian burst to proclaim: "Yes, I will marry you right away!" to be as spontaneous and carefree as Billy wanted her to be. It could never be that way though, not with her fixation on keeping her emotions in check and ensuring that pragmatism always governed.

The only thing she ever did that could be considered rash was to fall in love with a man of darker pigmentation.

Wanting to be truly ready when it came time to assume her housewifely duties, she would learn to cook, knowing she'd have to do better than that lumpy potato and chopped hotdog salad with canned peas she made for Billy recently from a recipe. He said it was good. She didn't believe him because he was a masterful cook but loved him for lying because it gave her impetus to strive. Mrs. Christian taught her how to make pastry and helped her bake her first pie.

Vivian resolved to shed her family's disapproval too – that phase was over now, the pangs of guilt, stabs of disappointment and the yoke of doubt. Detail by detail she'd start pulling together the wedding while working like a demon for the money to establish a secure foothold in her adopted city and create a dream environment to support her husband and his ambitions.

Vivian's work life was a mixed bag of bosses and supervisors with their assortment of peculiarities and temperaments. It was a collage of hard chairs, endless sitting, neck and back strain, typing pools, limited breaks, rigid rules and devaluing remuneration.

Sure, she had to contend with a few pompous, stiff shirts but there was an exclamation point named Billy to enhance the end of any day.

Notably in March Vivian found a dentist who believed in the concept of "freezing," a procedure she'd heard about for filling a tooth but had never previously experienced. "It was wonderful," she gushed to Billy when he met her there after the appointment. "Finally someone who can deal with my rotten teeth," said Billy, and a month later he had five extracted and got fitted for dentures. He also had the lenses upgraded in his round, gold, wire-rimmed reading glasses using an eye doctor Dr. Brewton had recommended.

Vivian was vexed about owing her mother money. The month of March saw her arrange a fifty-dollar loan through Billy's bank, using a bond as collateral, after deciding she would rather owe the bank than owe Jean a moment longer.

She rented a typewriter to keep up with her letter-writing and transcribe the notes she was keeping, detailing churches they visited, favorite restaurants, cultural events they attended, people they met, and recipes, including one for pancakes, which she made for the first time and didn't mess up.

Eight single-spaced typewritten pages to her mother among the myriad correspondences hastened to completion thanks to the machine. Vivian could never be faulted for losing touch. She was a connector and sustainer by nature, the power of her flying fingers on the typewriter keys her surest link to friends and family back home, and the device came in handy for taking Billy's dictation too as the pace of his work and extracurricular activities accelerated.

Word of his special talents spread through church and community grapevines like tendrils, and he was very much in demand. Vivian gladly played the role of private secretary, keeping him organized, remembering and recording schedules and particulars, recording his speeches as he ad-libbed them. He heaped so much on his plate he could be flighty at times, firing in all directions on a minimum of sleep. Being with him was to travel on the tail of a shooting star propelled by a blaze of energy fueled by his elevated inspiration, confidence and ardent hopes.

As embraced as Billy was by the community, Vivian still worried about his safety, worried that his skin color would give rise to prejudicial treatment and ugly reactions. She was trying not to fret when he was late for the Friday evening dinner she'd fixed before the much-anticipated Home Service fundraising *Rhapsody in Blue* concert. When she phoned Home Service Mrs. Miller said he'd left hours ago.

As Vivian ate alone, her mind sifting through every horrible scenario that would account for his extraordinary ninety-minute lateness, the phone rang. It was Billy calling from the Christians to say he had to walk home from work because he'd forgotten to bring money for bus fare. He'd be there soon. At seven-forty he was wolfing down warmed-over, canned corned beef and boiled cabbage upstairs at Oakwood.

He and Vivian arrived at the concert well past the appointed eight o'clock start but in time to hear the headline number which was the main thing. The star was Anne Brown, the Juilliard-trained, so-called "Negro soprano." Her role as Bess in George Gershwin's opera, Porgy & Bess, catapulted her to fame and headlong into a tight, musical bond with the composer.

In the afterglow of the ovations following the performance and as the crowds milled and thinned in the church hall Billy and Vivian remained seated on a pew. He was visibly pleased.

"A full house bodes well for a successful fundraising tally," he said as he scanned the room. "I see a lot of our donors are here."

As they stood up to put on their coats and head home, a voice called, "Billy!" It was Isabel LeBourdais. "Wasn't this splendid?" she beamed, looking up at them and not waiting for an answer. "You know about the reception for Anne Brown that my mother is hosting?"

She saw their blank looks. Billy vaguely remembered Mrs. Miller mentioning something. "You must come – 66 Dunvegan – I have to run. Don's out front already with the car." Isabel surveyed the hall. "Oh, there's Clive. Clive!" She beckoned to Clive Johnson, the church deacon who strode toward them. "You'll be taking Minister Wright with you to the reception, I understand. I'm hoping you have room for a few more."

Before long, six of them including Wilson Brookes, Phyllis Simmonds and the minister loaded themselves into Clive's car and he ferried them to Isa Brown and Frank Erichsen-Brown's house in Forest Hill.

On the ride there, feeling secure with Billy's arm around her, Vivian closed her eyes momentarily to absorb the banter, a variety of resonant voices, none belying a skin color. She wondered whether racial prejudice would exist if everyone were blind. A sightless person couldn't possibly hold that stunted a viewpoint.

"Our hosts tonight are magnificent supporters of the arts in Toronto." Vivian opened her eyes to Billy's words. "Isabel tells me they back the avant-garde movement, what would be characterized as modern art and experimental theatre, not just the traditional arts – the opera, the ballet, the Toronto Symphony and so forth. Her parents are well known for their philanthropy. It was because of them that Home Service secured a portion of tonight's fundraiser proceeds."

"I'm so looking forward to meeting them, especially Anne Brown," Phyllis gushed from the front seat, turning to face Billy and Vivian. "Anne Brown, colored Broadway star, meets Isa Brown, Toronto's white angel."

"Proof for white folks: there can never be too many Browns around," Clive ventured from behind the wheel as he signalled to make the turn into the moneyed neighborhood – laughter from both colors in the car.

"Anne Brown could pass for white," said Phyllis, whose skin was as dark as Portia's, "yet she was rejected from several schools because of her color. I read in Star Magazine that when she was accepted into Juilliard it was her father who held her back. He forbade her from leaving home to live in New York City – too dangerous. Anne's mother moved out and threatened to leave for good if he didn't capitulate."

"Well, we've certainly seen all the shades from light to dark in our church," said the minister.

"Sure have," Clive jumped in, "and the ones who pass, we call them the 'high yellows,' we only see them on Sundays with their families. The rest of the week they don't want to be seen with us folks and risk alienating themselves from their white friends."

Vivian was too astonished to speak.

They'd arrived. Clive dropped them off in front of the giant, three-story brick house and went to park. The passengers mounted the stairs leading to the slightly open oak door and spilled through into warm shouts of "Come in, come in!" from Isabel. They doffed their coats, and she ushered the new arrivals into the dining room where they met the hostess Mrs. Isa Brown, who was with her husband handing out flutes of champagne and urging guests to sample from the elegantly set table of party food: crackers and pickles, catered sandwiches and petits fours. "If you prefer mulled wine it's in the kitchen," she said with a gesture. "There are more guests in the study including our visiting star."

Nellie and Clarence Lightfoot, the Home Service president, were there, and Vyola Miller. Billy was over the moon to meet Gwethalyn, Isabel's sister, "call me Gwen. Everyone does." He'd heard she'd sold the film rights to her book. "It's true," she said. "Sadly, the studio canned the project and most of the earnings I derived from the sale I lost to income tax. My father is working with me, challenging the tax law. Such a large chunk gets extracted from struggling artists who have one good year, here and there."

Vivian inquired about Gwen's surname Graham.

"My *nomme* de plume," she explained, "a middle name that's been bouncing around among family members for the past couple hundred years."

An accented male voice called from a back room where a crackling fire danced behind a fireplace screen. "Billy! Billy White."

A barrel-chested, bushy-browed man approached, his arms extended in fond recognition as he greeted Billy, a kiss on each cheek.

"Dr. Vinci! May I present my fiancée, Vivian Keeler. Vivian, this is Dr. Ernesto Vinci, Portia's voice teacher, her mentor in Halifax and a major force behind her career. So good to see you, doctor."

"I'm delighted," the commanding maestro clucked as he repeated his welcoming ritual on Vivian and acknowledged the others with a nod and a gleeful smile. "Come. Grab your refreshments and follow me. There are some people I want you to meet. Will you excuse us, my dear Isa?"

The doctor's round of introductions included violinist Elie Spivak, concertmaster of the Toronto Symphony, Ettore Mazzoleni, associate conductor of the orchestra and principal of the Toronto Conservatory, flautist Joan Walter and Halifax-born soprano Elizabeth Guy, all of whom were among those clustered adoringly around Anne Brown, who was seated in a high-backed chair looking regal.

Vivian slowly drifted away from the group and seated herself on a velvet settee to consume her food and drink while taking in the scenery.

Billy was engaged in a side conversation with Dr. Vinci and his latest protégé, Elizabeth Benson Guy. Next month would mark her opera debut as Marie in the Royal Conservatory Opera School production of Smetana's *The Bartered Bride*.

"I've told Elizabeth she must enter CBC's *Singing Stars of Tomorrow* contest this season." The buxom brunette starlet blushed as Vinci waxed superlatives about her talent for comic opera.

Billy took her hands and looked straight into her bewildered eyes as he said, "You must enter. You will win that contest," he said very emphatically. "I'm psychic," he added with assuredness. The singer tittered.

Don LeBourdais had idled alongside them and was waiting to talk to Billy about CCF activities, having just reloaded the record player with another stack of classical favorites and temporarily freeing himself from his assigned duty. Several Home Service supporters moved in Billy's direction as well.

Vivian was watching a familiar scene unroll. Her fiancé never failed to attract a crowd. People found him interesting, and he loved an audience. Once in the same orbit neither one wanted to let the other one go. She'd then find a good vantage point, as she had tonight, and wait for someone she recognized, to make her feel truly comfortable. Before long, Isabel was striding toward her followed by a petite, smartly suited blonde woman walking with an uneven gait and obvious energy. "Vivian, meet Mrs. Avis McCurdy. Avis – Vivian Keeler, Billy's fiancée."

"How do you do Mrs. McCurdy?" Vivian extended her hand, mindful of the plate on her lap.

"Avis sit," Isabel directed, pointing to a fatly cushioned, gray, easy chair as she perched on the matching ottoman. "We're practically related," she said to explain her gently bossy tone. "My mother's a McCurdy and Avis here married one, my mom's cousin, Jarvis, over there. He teaches philosophy at U of T."

She pointed to a tweed-jacketed, tall and fit man now absorbed in Billy's circle. He held his lit pipe in one hand and a glass of scotch on ice in the other.

Avis and Jarvis, Vivian thought, unforgettable names. "I'm very pleased to make your acquaintance," she said to Avis.

"How does it feel to be marrying the most popular man in Toronto?" Avis queried playfully.

"Oh, you know Billy then?" was Vivian's reply.

I've had the pleasure of speaking to him in my role as a volunteer for a children's aid group. Don and I want him to open the upcoming CCF conference."

"Well, as the most popular woman of that most popular man, I will definitely put in a persuasive word for you," Vivian promised.

A few minutes of inquiring and Vivian had enough information about Mrs. McCurdy to write a bio: Avis Hunter Marshall McCurdy. Born in

Chapter 19

Goose Bay, Labrador, daughter of a lumber baron, moved to Stewiacke, NS, a graduate of Halifax Ladies College and Dalhousie University. In 1920 she was the only person in Nova Scotia to contract poliomyelitis – so-called "infantile paralysis".

It was only when she stood that the impact of the polio surgery at fourteen became obvious, her right leg shorter than the left.

Married two years in 1931 she and Jarvis spent a year traveling through Europe. But now they had two daughters and two adopted sons and were firmly rooted in Toronto.

"Billy and I look forward to starting a family of our own." Vivian waited for a reaction to her rare personal disclosure. Avis lit up with a smile. Isabel lifted her arms like a cheerleader and cooed, "You two will make beautiful children," with an emphasis on the ee-oo in "beautiful."

It made the soirée all the more wonderful to have these older women stepping in to do what Vivian's mother could not do: offer her comforting, maternal sustenance. Whether they knew it or not, Mrs. Christian, Mrs. Phillips, Mrs. LeBourdais and now Mrs. McCurdy were vital counterbalances to Jean Keeler's prejudice.

When the party wrapped, Billy and Vivian hitched a ride again with Oliver Simpson to St. Clair and Oakwood and walked the rest of the way home. It was past midnight and too late for Billy to come upstairs. He reached into his coat's inner breast pocket. "A poem for you to send you to dreamland, *ma chérie*" he purred, handing her the envelope after their farewell embrace.

She read it in her pyjamas, her back resting against her pillows.

Yesterday, Today and Tomorrow

My humble heart is searching for
The most appropriate way
To tell you, darling, just how much
I loved you yesterday
And every yesterday that's come
And gone these past two years

The yesterdays with tender smiles
And those with bitter tears
Those yesterdays when Spring had brought
New life to field and tree
I loved you then because I knew
You'd brought new life to me
And when, 'mid summer's fragrant warmth
We'd walk through wooded aisles
I found our later yesterdays
Brimful of sunny smiles
I loved you, oh I loved you then
For it was wondrous clear
That life for me had deeper warmth
Because of you, my dear
And when the autumn came with its
Majestic pageantry
It brought more glorious yesterdays
Than e'er I'd hoped to see
The falling leaves, all green and gold
All yellow, brown and red
Were carpeted beneath our feet
Where'er we chanced to tread
And when in time these myriad hues
Were turning dull and gray
Our love became more colorful
With each new yesterday.
The trees dropped all their leafy shade
The flow'rs fell fast asleep.
Then Winter came and softly spread
A blanket soft and deep.

Chapter 20

Overnights at the Christians' were becoming more customary. It wasn't unusual for the couple to press Vivian into staying rather than returning to Oakwood at a late hour. At Lansdowne she found hominess and a busy house, full of friendly people coming and going – Doug, Sonny and their friends had just wrapped up a card game, according to the clattering sound of dishes being placed in an empty sink.

Vivian was sharing Mrs. Christian's bed, memories of their earlier fallout completely by the wayside. Like true friends, they could laugh about it now.

"I'm sure my tirade must have scared you half to death," Cleo recalled as they sat with their backs against the headboard.

"I was a blubbering fool," Vivian admitted. "Poor Billy, he bore the brunt of it."

She shifted gears. A matter had been tugging at her mind since the ride over to the Anne Brown reception. "If I ask you something, will you promise not to get upset?"

"Go ahead," Cleo told her bedmate. "Shoot!"

"I wanted to ask you about the concept of 'passing.' I heard the term 'high yellows.' They were discussing it in the car after the concert and, well, I'd never heard of it before."

"And why would you?" Cleo wondered. "That ivory skin of yours is a passport to the world."

"You've never had to worry about where you shop or where you dine. When you ask to speak to the 'person in charge,' guaranteed you'll be facing a person of your own race. When we look in the history books, in children's magazines and picture books, all we see are people of your race, depicted on post cards and posters, reflected in dolls and toys and greeting cards.

"You've had all manner of choices and options at your disposal, be they social, political, travel, schooling or places of work. Can you honestly be surprised that those in our community with lighter skin would trade-in on their fair skin to gain privilege?"

"It seems discriminatory to me," Vivian said. "It's a caste system based on skin color. Regardless of which community engages in it, I don't believe in it."

Mrs. Christian sighed, "My dear, members of our community – we're always at the bottom. I don't fault those people for rising themselves up. Remember, being at the top of the ladder, you don't need to look up or worry about the climb. You get to admire the view.

"You will find our people in a range of hues – I don't pay mind to anyone's shade. You're born a certain way and you should be proud. A friend of mine found her daughter was using talcum powder to lighten her skin for school, thinking the teachers and classmates would treat her better if she was paler.

"Another told me about his young daughter wishing aloud that she had been born white, lamenting her dark skin. His wife wrote an article, and it wound up in the newspaper. After it was published and people read it, they started sending gifts to the newspaper office – gifts beyond the reach and dreams of any colored child arrived at their door in a newspaper delivery truck."

"But that's nice," said Vivian, "the kindness of strangers."

"What would be nicer is if her parents had opportunities and wages that would allow them to furnish those gifts themselves," Cleo countered.

"My theory is you're born, and you're born for a reason. Our paths are pre-ordained. My destiny was to become a nurse so that I could meet Curley and care for him, and we could advance the cause of our people and handicapped people. I believe we each have a destiny and an obligation to live up to our destiny. Unfortunately, for our people that's not always possible. They've mostly been relegated to domestic servitude and hard labor. They've not been allowed to be who they were born to be."

Vivian was skeptical of Mrs. Christian's determinism philosophy.

"I'd enjoy hearing you and Billy debate this 'you're born' theory," she said, suspecting he'd have a field day challenging his landlady's premise.

The topic changed to wedding plans – no, the Montreal location wasn't confirmed and no, they hadn't met with a minister, it was on their list, as was finding housing. Mrs. Christian suggested spreading word among the churches about their search for accommodation. "Be sure to make it clear from the outset that a Negro will be living there."

And from there the talk ricocheted to current events and then to recipes. Vivian then recited some of her favorite poems.

"It's superb – your recitation. How do you remember all that?"

Before Vivian could answer, a light rap sounded at the bedroom door. It was Doug telling them it was four-twenty in the morning. Playing the parent, he tucked them in, kissed them goodnight and told them to stop nattering.

When Vivian next saw Mrs. Phillips at Oakwood the landlady couldn't wait to tell her that Reg's estranged wife had visited and stayed the night, revealing the gossipy tidbit while handing off two letters that had arrived that day, one with a local postmark, the other from Deep River, Ontario. Vivian knew the latter would be from her Cousin Albert responding to the letter she had written to him. Ascending the stairs she wondered whether her talk with Reg had led him to some reflection. Something inside her hoped that it had.

In her room, she opened the envelope from the unknown local sender first. The return address said Park Road Baptist Church, home church of her friend Sally Spidell. This had nothing to do with Sally. It was a note from the Reverend Charles G. Stone, inviting Vivian to worship at his church.

"I was given your name by Mr. Elgee ..." was all she needed to conclude that this was one invitation she would not be accepting. This was probably some plot concocted to fix her thinking. She put the letter aside intending to reply indicating that although she had aligned to a church close by she wanted to introduce the minister to Billy's world brotherhood seminar and sing-along. Churches of different denominations were signing onto it, perhaps his would too. This, she felt, was a delicate and smart way around saying an outright "no thanks!"

She put her attention to the letter from Albert, twenty-six, Aunt Doris's firstborn, writing from the newly constructed northern Ontario company town of Deep River where he worked as a technician for Atomic Energy Canada.

> March 29, 1947
>
> Dear Viv,
>
> I hope you will forgive both the paper and the writing. I am writing this at five in the morning, in the laboratory using what paper is at hand. My mind feels rather foggy too, which is certainly not a help – I've had a headache the past several days – same trouble, I guess. I received your letter yesterday and was very pleased to finally hear from you Viv.
>
> I will admit I was very greatly surprised at the information it contained, for it was all news to me, as I did not know that you were even going steadily with anyone.
>
> No, Viv, I am not going to preach to you concerning your engagement to Billy, for I certainly am not qualified to say whether it is right or wrong. I wish you a contented and happy life Viv. I hope you can believe me when I say that you were, are, and will remain a favorite cousin Viv, and because of that I feel I must say a few words before passing on to other things. I grant you, Viv, you must make the decision – my wish and hope is that you will weigh the factors carefully before you make it final. I hope you will favorably recall the old days and permit me a few liberties without growing too highly annoyed – will you Viv?
>
> Brushing the cobwebs aside for a few moments, it would seem to me from the short-range point of view that it being your life, it is your own personal decision to make.

Basically, a Negro is equal to a white, but that is not generally conceded as you have already discovered and probably will not be for many years, probably, generations to come. From the long-range point of view however, Viv, the decision you make is not for you and you alone, for your decision will affect not only you but your children and their children after them – the flesh of your flesh, blood of your blood.

I presume of course that when you marry you will have children. To me life without them seems rather pointless. You were born into this world a female of the species and as such a mother-to-be. It seems to me that the female is the more important as it is only through them the species can be perpetuated – but now I am digressing. You say you and Billy are accepted as a couple by the important people: will your children be accepted likewise in the circles in which they may wish to move? I hope they will be, for a child's heart is a very tender thing.

You are probably feeling bitter toward your mother Viv – don't. She has had to be both a mother and a father to you for quite a number of years. I hope you realize that it must have been rather a difficult task for a possibly somewhat old-fashioned mother in this modern and sometimes rather crazy age. What she has done, she has done because she was striving to do what was best for you and remember Viv we *do* act rather crazy sometimes, don't we?

I do not consider myself to be a very good person and as you probably know I am not a particularly religious one – not in the orthodox sense at any rate, but I say and pray from the bottom of my heart God be with you to comfort and to guide you. Whichever way you finally decide I hope you may never have cause to regret it.

Unexpectedly a tickle in Vivian's nose tricked her eyes into welling up with a teary mixture of gratitude and wistfulness. She tucked Albert's letter into the inner sleeve of her purse as something to treasure.

Some of the discussions on racial prejudice and world brotherhood were better than others. The one at St. Clements Church was very good, in Vivian's opinion. She quoted part of her cousin's letter when it was her turn to speak, much to Billy's surprise because usually she wasn't so personally revealing.

"I agree with your cousin who says it is your own personal decision to make," said a woman named Doris, "We make way too much fuss about what someone looks like, or what religion is followed, when we should be looking at who that person really is and what that person has to offer."

Another successful evening, Derrick Bradbury, the junior minister who organized it, drove them home from St. Clements. It was then that he disclosed a surprise agenda.

"I wondered if we could use this time together to have a serious talk," said the young cleric to the two companions occupying the front seat with him. He cleared his throat. "I want to ask you both, have you considered the difficulties this marriage of yours could present to you? I ask this only because I care about you and hold you in such high regard. Have you opened your eyes to the possibly of hurtful consequences that may come your way from the bigoted and the intolerant? I'd feel so much better if you told me you are prepared for whatever may be."

Usually, Billy would be the one to respond to such questions, but Vivian jumped in first.

"Thanks to my mother, I am well versed in fending off negative reactions at this point," Vivian said. "There's nothing society can do to me that my own family hasn't tried to do."

She reached for Billy's hand and locked it in hers. "We decided long ago we weren't going to let bigots govern us."

"We believe love conquers all," Billy summarized, "but thank you for your concern, Derrick, and I mean that most sincerely. This is not a decision we have taken lightly." He gave her hand a squeeze.

Outwardly he and Bradbury were contrasts: Billy tall, dark-skinned, black-haired and the minister, slightly younger, just as tall, but a blanched complexion with blond eyebrows, lashes and hair. Inwardly the two men had much in common: their dedication to community development, societal betterment and the promotion of Billy's race awareness program in faith circles. The young minister was among its biggest boosters.

"God bless you both."

After depositing his charges at their respective addresses, the minister headed for home pondering their daring and the power of love, satisfied he had fulfilled his moral obligation to guide and counsel.

The month of March closed like the proverbial lamb, unusually temperate for the season. The birds' winter calls were changing to spring songs, free and melodic. Vivian noticed snowdrops and anemones poking out of waking front gardens on her extra-early departure to start her workday. After work she planned to head home to sleep after meeting Billy at the Pasadena for supper. But he had other ideas.

"You can never catch up on sleep, *ma chérie*," he told her as she yawned and tried to beg off. "Come back to Home Service with me. You'll catch your second wind on the walk there."

He had some dictation he asked her to transcribe while he ran the Cub group and then she could have unbridled use of the typewriter for her own purposes until the evening's music appreciation hour. Her own rented typewriter was recently relinquished, so Vivian was pleased for the trade-off. She had completed Billy's typing and was able to write a letter home before the show started.

Anyone could come to the music hour. There was no charge. This evening Billy planned to play recordings from his jazz collection. Almost ready to begin he sifted through his pile of thick black acetate, needle-etched, one-sided records housed in their paper covers, reordered them and stacked them by the record player, a wind-up gramophone. He surveyed the swiftly filling room.

Mrs. Miller, Nathan Redmon Jr. and Bill Carty were among those in the audience. Billy made a quick beeline to say a special word to Bill, one of the storied St. John, New Brunswick-born Carty boys – seven brothers. While two brothers joined the army during the Second World War, Bill Carty was one of five who pushed through barriers to get into the Royal Canadian Air Force as flight sergeants, aircraftmen: Bill was an aeronautical inspector.

Bill and Billy's fathers were together in The Great War. Mr. Albert Carty served in No. 2 under Pup, and he played tuba in the Second Construction Battalion Band.

The Cartys were a musical family too. Bill was staying on afterwards for orchestra rehearsal. He was pumped up about his latest invention and had a prototype in his satchel: the Carty "harmonic calculator and transposer," a figuring tool for music calligraphers to aid in the transposition and arranging of written music. Ingenious! Billy examined the cardboard panel and its built-in transition wheels held in place by grommets from the dime store. He scanned the instructional text, front and back, before handing it back to his friend. "Brilliant, Bill. You never cease to amaze me."

"I'm applying for a copyright," Bill grinned. "It could be the ticket to my million."

Vivian sat with Phyllis Simmons and Avril Shreve, a jolly-faced, honey brown, wise-cracking dynamo with brassy orange hair and wide, pink-coated lips, an agency all-star volunteer. Her brown eyes and broad, dimpled smile flashed a greeting as she extended Vivian her hand. "Your man plays a mean pee-yana," she drawled. "And I'm like him. I just love to sing. I'm aiming to recruit him to sing with Grace Trotman's choir," she said, referring to the revered choir leader and organist at British Methodist Episcopal Church.

Vivian couldn't imagine Billy taking on any more extracurricular activities. He or they were out practically every night of the week for work or a function.

Avril's face exuded impish good humor and genuine warmth. Vivian found her instantly likeable and was happy to learn more about Grace Trotman – musical leader, teacher, visionary and mentor – while Billy glad-handed before the show. When the music hour commenced, people applauded, and a few female voices cooed their sighs at the close of the dreamier Ellington numbers.

He switched from the phonograph to the piano in the room.

"I'd like to play for you now."

"This next song is one I wrote entitled," he paused slightly. *"Recompense,"* he announced before launching into the rendition.

Chapter 20

Vivian felt her face turn hot. An airing of her private song, he hadn't prepared her for this. But worse, he hadn't mentioned her in his introduction. She suddenly wondered whether he really wrote the song just for her. Or did he put her name on an existing work to impress her, a work perhaps written for some other girlfriend?

As his melody traveled and his voice crooned, notes cresting and diving with the prosody of his lyric, Vivian tightly clamped the beads of her necklace, bruising the beads in an effort to suppress any visible display of emotion. She was almost moved to tears. Feelings were threatening to take her hostage and place her in a horribly embarrassing situation in front of all these strangers.

The song carried her back to the seemingly distant days of rendezvousing with Billy back home: at Point Pleasant Park, Dingle Road, Halifax Public Gardens and the Garden View Restaurant. For some reason the music also conjured up imaginary pictures of Lois and thoughts of Billy's ex-wife.

She thought of all the outside influences that had contributed to the push-pull of her courtship thus far, outside influences striking like a sudden crescendo here and there, yet the song overall was one of sustained hopefulness.

Later, when she complained that Billy's introduction should have mentioned the song had been written for her, he told her not to be silly. "You're making a fuss over nothing," he said dismissively. She dropped the matter, recognizing that this was his stress talking.

The road to matrimony obviously isn't ever perfectly smooth and devoid of a hiccup. Coupling takes getting used to, they both were realizing. She was learning Billy was quick to take offense over even the slightest hint of criticism. He had begun to notice Vivian's proclivity for finding fault, rehashing and nitpicking, for which he had zero patience. Until someone could prove otherwise, he believed he was perfect exactly the way he was and didn't have to justify himself to anyone, which was a challenging stance to adopt with a perfectionist like Vivian, who couldn't resist the urge to correct if the opportunity presented itself.

Small ripples of disagreement surfaced but never amounted to much. Togetherness requires adjusting; that's a given.

Easter neared. Vivian ordered eighteen daffodils for her mother. She purchased an Easter card for Lillian. That evening she and Billy saw their first sunset together since being in Toronto, riding the Bathurst car at the right time of day, fingered streaks of apricot, pink and blazes of orange buoying their spirits. He had to go back to work that night. Vivian used her time alone to phone Fran Wees. They hadn't spoken since Fran's trip to New York City, where she had planned to see her old friend, Vivian's Uncle Ralph.

"Have you made any headway with your mother, Vivian?" Fran wanted to know. "After I gave your uncle all the information you wanted him to have about Billy and asked him to pass it along to your Uncle Walter, his first question was about her."

"We're corresponding by mail," Vivian replied. "I'm sure the reality of my situation is sinking in and it's only a matter time before she comes around. We still don't have a fixed wedding date. Maybe by the time we do her position will have softened." Her tone was less than convincing.

"Your Uncle Ralph doesn't think there's much chance of that. He says no one's more stubborn than a Harlow, and no Harlow is more stubborn than his little sister Jean."

"Then he doesn't know me as well as I thought," Vivian countered. "Thank you for being my liaison, Mrs. Wees. Whether my family agrees with my life choices or not, I'm determined to keep my lines of communication open. I can't be bitter. I'm too happy."

"Mr. Wees and I must have you over for dinner again soon, dear," Fran said. "Tell Billy I said 'hello' and do remind him to follow up with me about auditioning for the CBC."

On Good Friday Billy led singing at Carlton Street Church for the Easter fellowship. They arrived in time for the noon meal. One of the side benefits of Billy's musical trade was the availability of free dinners to two working people who frankly weren't eating enough and knew what it was to be short on food.

On Easter Sunday Mrs. Christian lent them the car so they could reach College Street United on time. Billy led singing. A church supper followed.

That was the weekend Vivian suffered the beginnings of a wretched cold, which she passed on to Billy within days.

Chapter 20

When his unrelenting pace got the best of him and he fell horribly ill, it was all anyone could do to make him stay home even as his temperature soared. Mrs. Christian summoned her nursing skills to baby him with mustard plasters, cold cloths for his forehead, blankets and hot lemonade, and fussed repeatedly over refreshing a hot water bottle for his icy feet; boiled water simmered on the stove for ready replenishment.

A worried Vivian came to him directly after work and stayed until midnight. He insisted he was well enough to return to work. Not in a million years did she expect to see him the next day striding through the lobby of the building where she worked. She tore out to the street after him.

"For heaven's sake, why aren't you in bed?" she semi-scolded him as he tried to conceal the shivering inside his tan overcoat.

"I went into work at one o'clock. Mrs. Miller took one look at me and said two words: 'Get home.' I'm going there now, boss's orders," he croaked.

When Vivian caught up with him later, remarkably, he was fast recuperating. Mrs. Christian attributed it to her chicken soup. An obvious sign he was feeling better was the prolonged argument he and Mrs. C. were engaged in on heredity and environment followed by a long discussion of her "you're born" theory.

She thought heredity governed what a person could become in life while he believed in a person's capacity to change.

"I've seen it with my own eyes, Mrs. Christian. I've seen destinies completely change course, positive attitudes emerge out of bleakness, character evolve when it seemed most unlikely, things that can't be credited to genetic determinants or sheer fate. We're only beginning to understand how the environment affects the degree to which potentialities can be realized."

"Only God knows," she said. "We are who we are."

Vivian hadn't been to her room at Oakwood for five days. On Friday night, after taking her out to supper at the St. Clair Tea Room, an exceptionally good place, and to a show at the nearby Paramount, *Three Wise Fools*, Billy brought her home.

A small stack representing five days of daily mail deliveries awaited her there on the magazine table near the foot of the stairs. Quickly leafing through on her way upstairs she could see there were no bad ones among the lot. Once settled in her room she tore into the one postmarked Lachine, PQ from Helen Kieran.

"I'm staying with my parents here in Lachine looking after my mother who is slowly recovering from a bad operation – intestinal. So we won't be able to have the wedding in Montreal unfortunately. We can come to Toronto though."

No Montreal. Vivian converted her faint tinge of disappointment to a sigh of relief. Their dear friends would be in attendance and with the location city settled planning for the wedding could begin in earnest.

Chapter 21

The plan on Saturday a few weeks into April was to meet Billy at Eaton's department store. Working nearby Vivian easily made the short hop to their noontime rendezvous inside the store's College Street entrance. She was feeling no pressure to return to the office in any haste. There was very little to do, her work was caught up. No one would miss her. Besides, this week Monday through Saturday, she'd arrived at work ten to five minutes before nine every morning and stayed past five on Tuesday.

She and Billy had business to transact with the credit department. Vivian wanted her own Eaton's charge account. She thought if Billy accompanied her, the Eaton's credit department might approve her application. Their major competitor, Simpsons, had rejected her because of her temporary work status and recent arrival in Toronto.

They ascended the steep, rickety moving stairs to the second-floor credit office to be met by a sign on the door saying closed for lunch until twelve-thirty, so they doubled back.

Vivian steered a strategic path through the bridal section with Billy captive, past the shoes and purses section, where she lingered a bit too long for his liking, stopping to admire a brown leather bag she couldn't afford.

"We might as well forget about waiting for the credit desk to reopen and go eat," Billy coaxed. A few minutes later, returning to the black and greasy escalator and down its precarious wooden treads, they were back on College heading toward Yonge Street to go north. Billy stopped to buy a pack of smokes from the shop at the corner. As they approached the Yonge Street Eaton's entrance an instantly recognizable figure exited the store: Portia! They nearly collided with her; their chance timing as precise as a metronome's. Behind her exuberant smile and delighted greeting, the revolving door had ushered out four others in her party onto the busy sidewalk to cluster at her side – her agent Katherine Whetham, Elizabeth Guy, the soprano from the LeBourdais's party and two gentlemen, Salvador Ley and Vic White. Portia made the go-around of introductions.

"Salvador," she announced in her fantastically theatrical voice, "I'd like you to meet my brother Billy and his fiancée Vivian. Mr. Ley is the Director of the National Conservatory in Guatemala, here on an exchange. We met when I performed in Guatemala. Coincidentally, he and Dr. Vinci go back to their days in Germany. And this is Vic – Victor White," she paused, "no relation." The group laughed uproariously, especially Vic, whose fair face blushed like a pomegranate, an unusual look for Vinci's star tenor who was usually as cool as a cucumber.

A series of coincidences had brought them all together. Portia and Katherine had broken from their rehearsal to shop for white gloves for Portia, cheaper here than in New York where she'd be returning in a few days. As a favor to Vinci, their singing teacher, Vic and Elizabeth were leading Salvador on a walking tour of the downtown when he decided to duck into Eaton's to shop for souvenirs and they followed so as not to lose him.

Two parties on different floors, surprisingly, they all wound up on the same elevator together and now were outside on the sidewalk marveling at the equally incredible happenstance of bumping into Portia's brother.

"We're on our way to the Royal Conservatory for lunch with Dr. Vinci. You must come," Portia said. It sounded like a gently spoken command.

Vic hailed a couple of taxicabs for the seven of them. Taxi rides were cheap due to the ongoing war for fares. Even so, a few available drivers slowed to look without stopping before a couple obliged Vic's beckoning hand.

The lively lunch at the grand stone building on Bloor Street left Vivian with a completely different impression of Portia, who was not a bit stiff or formal with her this time. She spilled over with graciousness and warmth,

perhaps her way of indicating approval of her brother's union and his departure from his previous playboy practises. He had found his *one*.

"Vivian will be turning twenty-two in a few weeks," Billy told the table.
A round of exclamations erupted such as one might hear at a baby shower:
some *ooohs* and a sigh of *so young*, making her feel like the baby of the family,
followed by a rendition of "Happy Birthday" as glorious as could be sung.

Twenty-two. Billy quoted the numerology definition of twenty-two: the
practical idealist, representing leadership and one who brings the forces of
life together.

"'V' is the twenty-second letter of the alphabet. It's very special,
and Vivian has two in her name. Twenty-two is a masterful builder,
foundational."

"And let me tell you what a peach my Vivian is," he told the table. "She's
giving up her birthday evening so that I can lead the world brotherhood
workshop at St. George's Anglican that same night. In fact, she arranged it."

Vivian picked up on the thread. "My birthday falls on the Sunday we
move our clocks ahead. I will only get a twenty-three-hour birthday as it is,
and I figure losing a few more hours to the church couldn't be a bad thing."
More chuckles. Vivian felt a surge of confidence that comes with acceptance.

The high spirits of the conservatory luncheon lingered through their
weekend. She and Billy saw Portia again the next evening at the Royal York
Hotel before she left for Union Station to catch the nine-thirty to New
York. Vivian wore her red suit with white sweater, gold earrings and choker,
a black coat over her shoulders to counteract what she considered her un-
prepossessing appearance the day before. Billy in his three-piece suit, Portia
surveyed them admiringly.

"You two are going to make it."

Vivian told her diary that night: "Tonight I was made more sure than
ever, if that were possible, about our marriage."

Sometimes in life events move from awfully perfect to perfectly awful
on a turn. The cold Vivian thought she had shaken came back with a ven-
geance. She went to work anyway, couldn't afford not to, and the unyielding
task of filing cards kept her on her feet all day. Each day by quitting time her
back ached, her eyes burned, and her head thumped in pain.

Among his diverse talents, Billy was a healer. It was as though his hands held some special power. Rubbing his hands together vigorously to warm them he'd proceed to place them over her eyes, or like a cap on the top of her head, on her forehead and temples. He'd use knuckles and fingers in his own brand of shoulder, neck and skull massage, always starting with the promise that he would make her headache go away. Maybe his cure had something to do with power of suggestion too. Over those congested, sinus-pounding few days he was doctor, nurse, comforter and cook.

Her stamina depleted on yet another evening at Oakwood, Vivian went to bed and Billy employed his body massage moves as she relaxed into his manipulations and found relief.

"Darling, will you recite me some poetry?" His elegant oratory carried her into sleep. He let himself out.

She'd be lucky to save two dollars this week. Last week, she was able to put away ten. In part Vivian's nuptials would be funded by her income tax refund. Finances were making her jittery again. They couldn't afford a reception. No mother of the bride to pay for this wedding.

A temperamental bout arose between Billy and Vivian over the issue of money. Predictably Billy didn't want to talk about it beyond offering his assurances that everything would work out. When his pat response failed to placate her, the discussion about credit and finances accelerated to a bickering match featuring two increasingly touchy, headstrong people. Vivian ended up in tears. Billy left in a huff after blistering her with his chilled brand of highhanded haughtiness. But their discords evaporated as quickly as they erupted. Neither party held grudges.

The day before Vivian's birthday her mother sent her a birthday cake.

This and other kindly maternal gestures of late had led Vivian to believe that perhaps Jean was relaxing her rigidity and was on the road to accepting current events. In addition to arranging deliveries to her daughter – summer dresses, pictures, Lux soap and a birthday gift from Bernard – Jean had enclosed a note, breaking a deliberate stretch of non-communication.

On the eve of Vivian's birthday Billy had Cubs, then was off to Danforth United Church, a snarly toothache notwithstanding, his dental appointment two days away. When his evening commitments were sealed, he dropped by her place, a store-wrapped gift in hand, which she opened as soon as he left at midnight. It was the luxurious brown shoulder bag she'd admired in Eaton's but would never have splurged to own. So she wouldn't worry about the cost, Billy's hand-doctored price tag of "twenty-nine cents" dangled from the strap. In the morning she would open her gift from Bernard.

Before retiring in her last hours as a twenty-one-year-old Vivian reflected on the journey of her life thus far: the distance traveled, choices she made, her destiny-altering decision and trade-offs, sacrifices willingly given for the sake of sticking to intentions and principles she could not and had no urge to shake.

Her Sunday birthday started with unwrapping Bern's gift: Pink Clover perfume – a dab on each wrist prior to leaving Oakwood en route to College Street United. She and Billy were traveling on the same streetcar, which she didn't realize until he whistled the first lines of "Begin the Beguine" to rivet her attention to his seat. After church they stopped by the Christians where Vivian received a silver cake-plate from the family, a kiss from Doug, and a comb and chocolates from Billy.

No lingering, Billy had to attend to his role at the Home Service membership tea that afternoon, first accompanying Vivian to her place and wolfing down a rushed bite before they both headed out.

The tea was one of those essentials inherent to running an organization like Home Service. The other service group in the city for the colored community was the UNIA, the Universal Negro Improvement Association, founded by entrepreneur and activist Marcus Garvey.

Their location at 355 College Street is where the politics happened, where table-thumping, hot under the collar debates on how to best achieve general uplift of their race resounded and manifested in action, where CPR sleeping car porters joined and found an organizing hub for their Brotherhood, and jazz cats jammed free-flowing riffs from the building's third floor.

UNIA's non-reliance on white people stood in stark contrast to the philosophy at Home Service, a difference as marked as the hues of the two organizations. UNIA attracted the dark complexions of the West Indies, people who believed in "Africa for the Africans" and doing for self as Garvey did. Home Service presented as an agency for the lighter-colored range of dark skins, the moderates: Canadian and American born individuals, or black-and-white combined, individuals pejoratively nicknamed after the sterile offspring of a horse and a mule – *mulatto*.

White philanthropists could get seats on the Home Service board, a practice unheard of at UNIA. The annual membership tea catered to the idea that working with whites and not apart from them was the surest route to improving the community. Billy was great at cozying up to moneyed prospects and getting the most out of them.

After the tea they went back to Vivian's to put an icepack on Billy's cheek to blunt his dental pain. Then they took the Eglinton bus to a fireside meeting at St. George's Church where he enthusiastically sold his concepts of racial brotherhood and equality.

Birthday blessings continued for Vivian the following day. Monday, more packages arrived. Stockings from Aunt Gladys (acknowledged immediately with a thank-you note to be mailed promptly), Coty-Styx perfume from Lillian and a shipment of Vivian's possessions from Jean containing a lampshade, more clothes, pictures, bric-a-brac and a box of *Pot of Gold* chocolates.

A first day with her new employer Imperial Oil, for a manager Mr. Grant who thundered at employees for lateness and insisted they arrive at eight-forty-five or earlier, meant Vivian had to stand all the way on an overburdened streetcar to get there on time when leaving to arrive just after nine would virtually guarantee her a seat. But these annoyances found counterbalance in the wonderful, after-hours social life she could anticipate. This evening it was a youth committee where Billy would lead the singing, followed by a music appreciation session on various classical composers.

Vivian met him at Home Service, and they walked over to the church together. They were head table guests. The room was inundated with people Billy knew. Goodwill seemed to follow him everywhere.

At dinner Vivian sat between Billy and Mr. Gowans. Tonight, she could seize on the opportunity to confirm the minister's interest in officiating their wedding. Halfway through the salad course, as Billy chatted up Mrs. Gowans to his left, Vivian grabbed her chance.

"We'd like to come see you about our June wedding soon," she said between bites of iceberg lettuce.

"That would be my distinct pleasure, Vivian," the minister replied. "I have time next week. The three of us will sit down and have a chat first. That's always my practice when a couple plans to marry. We sit down and draw a road map for your future together and then we discuss the particulars of the wedding itself."

He reached inside his jacket for his pocket calendar and found the desired page. "How does next Monday night at nine o'clock sound?"

Billy leaned in on their conversation at this point and eagerly confirmed the appointment. How long he had waited. In the coming days he would draw up a guest invitation list, identify possible dates and, with encouragement from Mrs. Christian, decide that he and Vivian could have a reception after all.

On May fifth they were comfortably seated with Mr. Gowans in his oak-paneled study for the conversation, ready to plan the rest of their lives.

"We're hoping for June twenty-third," Billy said. He and Vivian, occupying a small corner of the eight-foot couch, clasping hands as the minister listened from a matching chair positioned at a right angle to it.

He rose and strode to the church daybook on his desk to confirm the availability. "Consider it done," he said and with a flourish entered their names in ink. "You know it's up to you to supply the requisite paperwork, apply for and obtain your marriage licence?"

They nodded as he returned to sit with them.

"We know only too well. We were afraid we would have to redo some of the vital documentation," Vivian volunteered, and told the minister about the scare around Billy's "stolen" divorce papers, which led to the topic of his ex-wife.

"To be truthful Mr. Gowans, I'm uncomfortable with this other woman even though I've never met her.

Billy knew his past bothered Vivian. He was tired of defending his hopeless first marriage and wasting any words on it, but she kept bringing it up.

At this juncture in the discussion he jumped in to point out that Vivian's family had other reasons for objecting to their marriage. The three of them discussed the race issue.

"Racialism is contrary to the word of God," said the cleric. "As a man of God, I cite Mark, Chapter 12 Verse 31, 'Love your neighbor as yourself.

There is no commandment greater than this.' I salute you two for your brave and unblemished decision. You seem to be entering this marriage with your eyes and hearts wide open."

"Yes we are." Vivian answered definitively for both of them.

There was a pregnant pause. Mr. Gowans trained his eyes on Vivian.

"You raised with me the point about this being Bill's second marriage. I would counsel you to think of it as his first just as it is your first. This marriage is a fresh, new start for both of you. Open the window and let it breathe. My advice to you, Vivian, is very simple and I think it will be helpful in relieving your dilemma."

Billy had an internal hallelujah moment when Mr. Gowans offered his solution.

"I seriously suggest that you promise not to refer, ever, to the former wife or the first marriage. This goes for both of you. The subject will never again divide you. She has no relevance to your present or your future."

For Vivian, it was much needed and welcomed advice. For Billy it was a bit of a godsend. He could see a common source of bickering ending. Now, if she'd only stop mentioning Lois, he thought.

They headed to Oakwood on their usual transit route, finished up some leftover fruit salad at her place, then worked on their invitations and wedding announcement lists.

Reg didn't live there anymore, having reconciled with his wife, and the atmospheric difference was palpable. Billy was free to come and go, treat the place as his own home-away-from-home just as Vivian had quasi-familial privileges at the Christians.

She hadn't told Billy about the birthday letter from Uncle Roy yet and wasn't sure she would. At this point she'd been sitting on it for days.

> April 27, 1947
> Dear Vivian,
> Today is your birthday I believe. I miss you from the church, and the odd greeting we exchanged, miss you a great deal more than you realize.

Chapter 21

I would wish for you happy birthdays and happy every days, but I don't see how you are going to have them if you follow the plan you seemed determined to carry out. Just recently I saw in a magazine a list of questions for young people who were considering marriage. The questions were supposed to have a favorable answer to indicate a fair chance for happiness. One of them was "Are you both of the same race"? so even an impartial observer would discount your chances for happiness. Why do you consider your chance for happiness any greater than the girl who did marry him and has now been cast off?

The Ten Commandments, the civil laws which we must obey or else, that set of laws of conduct we call conventions; the unwritten laws of society: If we have the wisdom to heed them we have the greater chance for happiness. If we ignore them we are almost sure to suffer. Perhaps the suffering will bring years of sorrow, regret, and remorse.

Why risk this for yourself, as well as bringing sorrow to those who love you and cared for you through the years? Why risk being the next one to be cast off, when he is tired of you? You are such a fine girl; you should be striving for the highest ideals in life.

One thing I want you to remember always. If you ever feel you have need of me, I will still be your loving,

Uncle Roy

Was it starting again, round two of the pummelling, her crusty, puritan uncle firing the next in a series of shots across the bow from the East Coast juggernaut?

His letter was like a can opener on all the fears she had neatly lidded far back in her mind. They were out in the open again and haunting her mood. She would see how long she could keep this latest letter from Billy. These past few days since their meeting with Mr. Gowans he hadn't been his pleasant old self. Why add to whatever was bothering him? To feel better she went to Simpsons and ordered wedding invitations, came home and got ready to welcome Billy for supper, creamed asparagus on toast. He had the night off.

All evening he was bent on picking on her, a combination of interrogation and teasing. Had she done anything about finding them a place? She had nagged it was so important, why hadn't she done anything? Don't complain about something you're not willing to do anything about. He had to count on her to keep up her end. "Vivian, you'll just have to do more."

She burst into tears.

"You've been nasty ever since we began talking about our wedding plans," she sobbed. "Why are you being so mean?"

He had pushed her too far. Her tear-streamed cheeks, her anguished brow, her hands now covering her face, her head hung low, woeful sobs. Now he had to manage the situation, find an excuse beyond blaming his frustrating, forced chastity, the sexual drought that was his engagement. He confessed to a hidden agenda.

"Vivian. Please don't cry. Forgive me. I've deliberately been at my worst because I wanted you to be absolutely sure you wanted to marry me. I was giving you a way out if you wanted to change your mind. 'For better or worse' I gave you my worst."

He wrapped her in a hug and let her cry like a river until she exhausted her well of emotion. In between hiccupped breaths she expressed her worries about the wedding – the expense of it and getting everything right – and the knowledge of her mother's grief and the arrival of Roy's latest letter. She let it all spill. He listened and acknowledged with a soothing low "hmm."

"My darling, I would do anything to relieve the pressures being applied on you for making this unorthodox choice, even if it means releasing you to the comfort of safe norms. Tell me you'll forgive the wicked way in which I tested your resolve. You know I'm desperately in love with you. I dream of our wedding night, but I would surely let you go if it would make you happy. That's how much I love you."

His sweet unselfishness, which she had so misinterpreted, lifted her despondency.

"Let's put you to bed," he said, scooping her in his arms. He promised to "magic away" her blues and did so, gently, rhythmically and wonderfully with caresses and massage, before seeking a late streetcar home.

> May 7, 1947
> Dearest Vivian,
> I'm taking just a minute or so at nine-fifteen this morning to start the day out right by dashing off this note to you. It's a gloomy morning but I'm certainly not in a gloomy frame of mind. In fact, darling, I'm so deeply engrossed with thoughts of my love for you that I just have to write this note. Otherwise, I'll never settle down to do some work.
>
> It's such a relief to know that my "campaign," which made you so miserable during the past couple of weeks, has been brought to an end. After our talk last night, I'm sure that you understand the workings of the mind of your future husband better than ever before. To state the situation more specifically, you should now have the assurance that I shall never again resort to the use of applied psychology for the express purpose of making you unhappy. You understand, of course, that I did so this time only because I knew that the success of our future together would depend largely on your reaction to me at my worst. Don't forget for a moment, my little sweetheart, that I made myself pretty miserable too.
> I love you,
> Billy

"As long as I keep my face toward the sunshine, the shadows will fall behind me."

The sagacity of poets had underpinned Vivian since childhood, had saved her as a girl housebound with TB for a year. An infection control measure she saw as both unfair and unnecessary, they took away her doll and toy chest. Books became her refuge from boredom. Poetry and verse were precious gems adorning her lonely days, days that could have been as boring as gray flannel. She discovered Walt Whitman and cherry-picked his sunshine quotation during that period of illness and did the mental equivalent of tucking it in her pocket along with myriad other jewels for a rainy day to extract motivation from as needed. This morning was such a day.

Purged of her doldrums she found wind in her sails. She composed and placed a notice advertising their apartment search and put the word "Negro" in it, using the Christians' phone number for fielding inquiries. Besides a classified in *The Tribune*, she hunted down church newsletters and bulletin boards and inserted it there as well. She got some shopping done and drew up a task list.

One glaring task stood out: finding a substitute father of the bride, someone to walk her down the aisle and give her away. A substitute father, there could never be such a person. Vivian had been missing her father. Despite what her family wanted her to think, she inherently knew he'd have been on her side and at her side. Vivian aspired to Glenn Keeler's best qualities: kindness, intelligence, honesty and fairness.

A few difficult moments couldn't detract from her countless hundreds of good days with her husband-to-be. Marriage was a fresh start, she recalled Mr. Gowans as saying. He'd counseled on the give-and-take and ups and downs of wedded life, perfectly natural for couples to encounter bumps along the road.

They were two very busy people juggling too few dollars at times, and late nights, on several occasions until five a.m., once because Billy forgot his key and locked himself out of the Christians. He and Vivian conversed for three hours on the porch until he felt he could knock on the door and disturb his landlady at five. The other time they were simply having too good a time to end it early. There were many late nights she couldn't decline, like when Billy and fellow tenant Sonny Bell called on her at one in the morning to take her on an exploratory night drive. She was not about to refuse to see the city showcased in a way she hadn't seen before.

Fatigue could be transcended, she learned. Second winds were real. She proved it time and time again. Earlier in the week she headed to Home

Service at the conclusion of her workday to undertake volunteer work for the agency. As tired as she was after the meeting adjourned Billy insisted she stay for tea. They left around midnight on the last bus and said their good-byes at the Lansdowne Loop.

Vivian was dismayed when Mrs. Miller sent a check home with Billy the next day as payment for her work. As broke as they were, she didn't want to accept payment from the non-profit. She and Billy argued about returning the check while she was penning a note to Mrs. Miller explaining why she couldn't accept it. Billy won. Vivian kept the money.

Weekends were for errands and sleep, if lucky. Saturday Vivian shopped at the new A&P grocery store at Eglinton and Oakwood and allowed herself some rarities such as salmon, ketchup and laundry soap, having decided again to borrow fifty dollars against her one-hundred-dollar Victory Bond.

Sunday afternoon at the Christians stuck out for Vivian because she and Sonny exchanged turns playing the piano while Billy slept peacefully on the couch. Sonny brought butter and Vivian was able to borrow some of it to tide her over since her war-time ration for the week was depleted. Make it last or go without was the way it went. Starting in 1942 in Canada each adult had a weekly entitlement of one-quarter pound of butter, one cup of sugar, and twenty-four to thirty-two ounces of meat. Most basic foods and staples were restricted – no chance of eating anything that wasn't Canadian-produced. The war had ended nearly two years ago, but the rationing continued; maybe after they're married it will be over, Vivian hoped.

Billy's irritability now vanished, replaced by buoyancy over the progress being made: he had sewn up arrangements on the phone with Harold and Helen, Vivian had ordered the wedding cake, tended to the housing search, tried on a few bridal gowns and begun drafting the wording for their announcement in the paper.

Somewhere during that spree she found time to purchase and mail a Mother's Day gift to Jean. Soon she would receive something horrible in return.

Jean and Vivian, Dartmouth, 1927

Chapter 22

Sunday, Mother's Day, was the first really warm day of the year. Their tiff of four days ago an evaporation of pent-up steam, the air had cleared figuratively and literally. Today Billy was most intent on talking to Vivian and giving her the full focus of his attention. He sat on one of the padded chrome kitchen chairs watching her like a tennis game as she bounced between the cupboards and the icebox of her Oakwood kitchenette, compensating for her sparse diet of yesterday – four bowls of Rice Krispies – by eating everything in sight.

"Why do you love me, Vivian?" Perhaps his behavior of the other night had jeopardized her affections. He needed reassurance.

She paused between finding the soda crackers and stirring the pot of alphabet soup on the hot plate.

"You don't have time to hear all the reasons why, dear. You'll be late for your appointment." He was supposed to be at the A.M.E. church soon. "Tall, dark and handsome doesn't cover it?" She smiled over her shoulder.

No, he genuinely wanted to hear more about the whys of her affection, to listen and absorb her expression of thoughts and feelings.

If she had one criticism it was that Billy didn't treat her like this when they were together in a crowd. He only acted like she was the only person in the room when she *was* the only person in the room.

But she kept that observation to herself and told him some reasons – exceptionally clever, considerate and charming, endlessly talented, his wisdom, his humor.

"You've opened up a whole new world to me, Billy. I love you and I love that you love me."

Their conversation made him late for his church date. For once Billy didn't mind not being punctual. Unlike Vivian he held himself to the preciseness of the national time signal broadcast from Ottawa over the radio, to which he set his watch to the second. She had forced him to learn more patience since tardiness was her trademark, being on time was a constant struggle.

On Monday Underwood dispatched Vivian to Spruce Falls Power & Paper Co. in the Canada Life Building. A good typewriter, a big desk, a nice group of gals – still, the big office environment wasn't Vivian's cup of tea. She could hardly wait to beetle over to Home Service after work and later attend the choir and banquet at College Street United. She and Billy had two helpings of everything. He spoke on the event's theme of racial prejudice and led the singsong. Then a pleasant surprise: dancing upstairs, the final complement to a very satisfying evening.

He swung her with such an able light-footedness and deft steering that the floor felt like cotton batten underfoot and her head felt like it was packed with the stuff. She was stupid in love with him. On her transit ride back to Oakwood she coasted on the memory of their twirls and glides around the dance floor.

It was a good thing she had that vision to recall as she lay awake that night troubled over the thick letter she found awaiting her arrival home. Her Mother's Day gift to Jean was enclosed, returned to sender unopened, a note enclosed set with a purple pansy motif. Hope of her mother's opinion softening wholly dissolved. The accompanying letter was fat with vitriol.

Jean wrote it on Mother's Day.

> Dear Vivian,
> My intention was to write to you on Mother's Day to appeal once more to your better judgment regarding your future. When I received the gift this morning I saw the

hopelessness of saying anything to one with so little con-
ception of the tragedy hanging over us.

What a Judas you are – betraying your own mother
– crucifying me every time you allow that _____ to touch
you. Why you permitted his first insidious touch I shall
never be able to understand. Don't you realize you are betraying everyone who has ever taken any interest in you?
Why should you do what no mother can approve? You say
you do not advocate such marriages on a wholesale scale,
but by doing it yourself you are advocating them in the
most convincing way possible. You are opening the way
for any rude colored fellow to make advances to any white
girl which is a crime now as always. If such marriages are
not right in principle they are not right for anyone. Such
love should be "cut out." It offends! When you told me
you would rather you were both black or both white, you
were so near the truth, which is that you both must be
one or the other. Nothing but tragedy could result from
such a union. One sees it in the eyes of the children of
such marriages. They will ask you "why couldn't we be
one thing or the other." If you were really broad minded,
Vivian, you would see that the way to help Negroes is in
developing their own race to its highest and best, not by
mixing them up with white people, causing embarrassing,
agonizing situations. Do you not realize that no one who
has the best interests of either race at heart approves of such
unions? There are many ways you can help them if you are
really interested, but marriage is not one of them.

I am surprised that you quote the Bible to me and that
you dare to say it is God's will for you to marry a Negro. It
is your own self will and nothing else. Does he unite different animals? You may be very brazen and force yourselves
on people but there will never be real acceptance of you by
them. The time will come when you have to face what you

have done and discover how you have demeaned yourself. Nobody cares what you do with your life except those who really love you and you would do well to listen carefully to what they say.

You quote "God hath made of one blood all nations to dwell in unity." Paul meant unity of purpose as Christians, certainly not intimacy on which marriage is based. When Negroes stop their horrible rowdyism, their love of being obnoxious to everyone, we can dwell in unity as we do very well until someone like you gets a foolish idea and disrupts that unity. The Baptists have done more for the Negro than any other group around here, and as a sample of how they repay us, we will remember the Rev. Kenneth Tines of Dartmouth who expressed a desire to become a minister. He was sent to Acadia by the Baptists and received a license to preach. The first thing they knew he was arrested for stealing! The Negroes are noted for taking all and then asking for more, giving nothing in return.

You of course know nothing of Negroes in general. If you had Bernice's job for a while having to deal with the loathsome creatures every day, it might give you pause. Every time I meet one now I have to think of you and wonder how you can love one.

Real respect will be lost to you if you persist in this ghastly mistake. What a horrible thing to do to Bernard, your father's memory and to me. The one thing I cannot accept!

We realize fully what we are losing in you, and it seems a ghastly shame. We will never cease loving you and missing you deeply. To say that God meant for a pure and lovely young white girl to marry an old, divorced, colored man is sheer blasphemy. Would you approve it in anyone else?

It grieves me to my soul to think how little you are getting – worse than nothing – that you are losing all – when you could have everything desirable in life. What a colossal failure I must be as a mother.

If you know of a case similar to yours, a Negro man and a white girl, not a white man and a Negro woman, study it carefully. Find out exactly if she would recommend such a marriage to you, honestly.

You are being most unreasonable, reckless and fool-hardy to say the least, to step as far out of your accepted pattern, against the wishes of your mother and all those who love you and know you best.

You know it is a social disgrace, gloss it over as you will, and you are making us the laughingstock of the country. Any way you look at it, it is just too mean and senseless. I would want my mother to hammer this into me with a sledgehammer, as it were, to keep me from doing such a thing. I was often mean to my mother and hated her for correcting me but at least I never brought disgrace on her and did bring her a little comfort at times, just by "dwelling in unity" with her and realize now how wonderful she was in every way.

Remember we can do nothing for you once the die is cast, he can *creolize* you as much as he likes, and we cannot say a word. He would not know how to treat a white girl.

I do not believe you really care anymore for colored people than I do and if you have to live in close contact with them long enough, as you may have to do, you will be more than fed up. If you can be happy with them I would say it is nothing to your credit.

The fact that white people are so revolted by such marriages, conceal it as they may, should show you that it cannot be right. What has so changed your personality that you do not feel the natural revulsion which might have kept you normal? What we know by instinct, you will have to learn by experience.

You may feel inordinate pity – they do not need it – they are very happy among themselves, fat and well fed, having a wonderful time. You have just glamorized this one, romanticized him, fastened your ideas on him, while you are really in love with the ideas.

Do not commit this outrage, it is unworthy of you. Even at this late date I still believe you will not.

With tenderest love,

Mother

Horrible. Sickening. "Her mind is so poisoned." Vivian tossed the scorching letter beside her on the bed where she sat on the edge, numb with disillusion.

With a measure of hesitation as if in slow motion she picked it up and reread it as was her habit, lingering over certain paragraphs, shaking her head at the tragedy of misinformation and meanness throughout. She smiled wryly at Jean's salutation of tender love, remembering Mrs. Phillips saying, "not the kind of love they hand out!" concerning the last bout of nasty letters.

Vivian was glad to have moved a thousand miles away. Despite all Toronto's faults Jean couldn't touch her here. Her objections, diluted over the distance, were having no effect. Her opinions rooted in all that is wrong and ignorant, while initially upsetting to Vivian, lost impact in their absence of evidence and validity.

When Billy came up for a quick supper Friday before rushing back to another evening meeting, she made passing reference to her mother's latest parcel but didn't dwell on the matter. The letter was now the top layer of the chocolate box of commentary that represented her home circle's view of interracial relations. She would prove the detractors wrong. As long as she had Billy, that's all she needed.

• • •

Chapter 22

Their ad for housing had elicited responses. Once back at Home Service Billy phoned her and dictated a reply for two of them. Fingers crossed one would bear fruit.

Saturday the bride-to-be journeyed downtown to Simpsons and Northways and tried on wedding dresses. She arranged for a photographer recommended by the chatty, helpful bride's counsel at Simpsons. There was something therapeutic about continuing with the wedding plans the day after the bruising of Jean's letter. Not exactly an act of defiance from Vivian, more a "life goes on" sentiment of pushing past her mother's static interference and carrying on as normal. Opinions change. In spite of everything to date Vivian held hope that Jean's would.

Arriving home she had to go right out again to meet Billy at High Park United Church where he led the singsong at the annual Young People's Banquet, *Feast of the Full Moon*. She left the event early to arrive late at the Paul Robeson concert at the Coliseum down by the waterfront. For Vivian the timing was perfect. Hearing the renowned Robeson's flawless vocal renderings emitted with his insignia volcanic depth, titanic resonance and butter-rich textures erased any of her niggling worries. In his art, just as in his life of activism for social justice Robeson was "all in", unrelenting and unapologetic and uncaring of the price of holding to one's convictions unbowed. So too would she be. In the audience that night she found Billy's truth resonating in her head: music is a teacher, a bridge and a healer.

That melodious night portended pleasing developments on the horizon. Four days later Vivian proclaimed, "Miracle of miracles and joy of joys!"

They found a place, a beautiful, self-contained four-room apartment in swanky Rosedale surrounded by breathtaking valley scenery. A Miss Dorothy Anderson answered their ad in *The Tribune*, Billy relayed, and they wasted no time seeing her that evening.

"You understand it's a sublet until at least the end of September, possibly longer. I'll give you plenty of notice," said Dorothy as she gave them the tour. "You can move in any time after June the first. I'll be on the Island by then."

Her well-to-do parents kept a place on Ward's Island, which was about to open up to full-time residency. A short ferry ride from the docks of Lake Ontario, the easternmost in the cluster of Toronto Islands, she was moving there to spend time with the family. In the fall her fine arts studies would resume but during the summer she augmented her father's financial support by selling watercolors to Toronto Islands' visitors. In appearance she looked very much the artiste, adorned in a smock over a mid-thigh-length floral-patterned dress with a full skirt, her blonde hair swept up in a bun. Vivian felt an instant bond to Dorothy. The young woman not only solved their housing dilemma, readily pocketing their deposit, she accepted them warmly and was sympathetic when Vivian described her housing search difficulties due to racial discrimination.

"I'm sorry those attitudes exist," Dorothy said. "I'm an artist. I embrace all colors. Each one is an integral part of the palette. Every color in the rainbow has a uniqueness of purpose, just like human beings. I can't imagine someone wanting a rainbow that's all orange." She gave a carefree laugh.

"Anyway, the place is yours." She handed them the keys.

Billy and Vivian left, ecstatic and relieved. "You see? I told you everything would work out, *chérie*," Billy boasted as they trundled up Lansdowne after exiting the streetcar. She faked a poke to his ribs with her elbow and gave him a nudge with a smile.

"We were extremely lucky. This relieves some pressure but we're not out of the woods yet, Billy. It's only a sublet, don't forget."

She could always find something to worry about. Being practical, having and following a plan, meant a lot to her. Billy put his arm around her and told her not to think about it.

Now she was planning a wedding and a move. There also was a road trip north in the works to rural Flesherton, near Collingwood with Dr. and Madam Brewton for Victoria Day weekend where Billy would be giving three performances in Grey County, two at St. John's United and one at Rock Mills.

In May Vivian used her temp worker status advantageously. She devoted time to wedding planning between assignments. One morning, rather than arrive to work late and get yelled at, she booked off and walked from Bay and Bloor to Yonge Street, below Adelaide, stopping in every shop that looked as though it might sell wedding-gowns. Midmonth was the tightest time for Vivian's finances. No breakfast, nor a midday meal, nothing in the house to eat and no money summed up her situation neatly. That evening she borrowed two dollars and twenty cents from Mrs. Phillips, used fifty cents of it for a hairdo at Beauty Isle, and spent most of the rest on groceries.

When Billy came by at ten o'clock he shared with her that one of the respondents to their "housing wanted" ad turned out to be Reverend Al Cooper.

"Never let it be said that we don't have the church on our side," he commented jokingly to Vivian during his short stopover.

They talked about their itinerary for the next day's trip, with Oscar and Leona Brewton driving them up in their touring car. They were to be house guests of Reverend and Mrs. White in Flesherton, a few hours' drive north on Highway 10.

They were to be picked up from Home Service at six by the Brewtons. Vivian rushed from work to get there on time. Ironically her uncommon punctuality didn't matter. Madam Brewton had phoned to say the doctor was caught up in his work. They'd be "a little late." They arrived four hours later ready to roll.

Billy had been anticipating the car trip with the doctor as an opportunity to soak up the mentor's wisdom. The city limits were barely behind them when serious talk began.

"Doctor, let me ask you something," Billy began. "In Toronto there are many cleavages I've noticed – divisions based on differing national backgrounds – American, West Indian and Canadian – to say nothing of the many subdivisions in each of these groups. When I came here, I expected to find a substantial and cohesive Negro community and an outstanding center for our people's progress in Canada. In reality, our population, fewer than six thousand, is scattered pretty well over the city. My question is, how do we deal with the need for spiritual unity, race consciousness, or any other such common denominator which will serve to draw our people together?"

Dr. Brewton filled the car with his cool Floridian drawl. "In our case, Leona and I made something of ourselves and as soon as we had something to give, we gave."

"We were inspired by Professor Merl R. Eppse when we met him at A & I State College in Nashville in 1937," his wife elaborated. "He presented us with an inscribed copy of his ground-breaking book, *A Guide to The Study of the Negro in American History.*"

"'As the chasm of ignorance narrows, the mountain of prejudice and hatred will crumble and gradually fade into level land,'" said the doctor, quoting from memory a phrase from the book's foreword.

"Amen," said Billy.

Vivian listened, fascinated to learn about the couple. He had graduated from the Tuskegee Institute in Alabama, where he studied under Booker T. Washington and Dr. George Washington Carver and followed school with a stint in the US Army Reserve – the only role he could get in World War 1 because of his color. After the Armistice jobs were scarce. He and Leona thought it would be easier to find work in Toronto than Chicago. They moved north only to discover they were wrong.

"I worked as a porter for two years and I don't regret it," the doctor said. "I got a real nice taste of racial discrimination Canadian-style, and it gave me the impetus to follow through on what I already knew: I could do better."

He traded the indignity of his job on the CPR trains for enrolment at the Illinois College of Podiatry. While he studied in Chicago for his degree, Leona stayed in Toronto to study beauty culture.

"Graduating from a beauty school was one thing, finding clients was quite another," she said. "I knocked on doors until my knuckles were sore, and finally someone let me in. The door opened, and out of that job I got a dozen more. Soon I wasn't knocking anymore, it was them coming to me."

Vivian couldn't recall a single instance of knocking on someone's door and feeling unwelcomed.

"You've contended with barriers I've never known. I feel so ashamed of my race," she anguished from the back seat.

Madam turned her head to utter a reassurance, "No, dear. You're not part of the problem. You are part of the solution, and we love you for who you are."

She recounted her founding of the Young Men's Bible Class to teach young black men about their culture and history.

Vivian could hardly fathom the idea of people not knowing their history, her scrapbooks bulging with genealogy records and family history.

Dr. Brewton re-entered the discourse. "We put ourselves in situations where we can do the most good for the most people. We have successful side-by-side businesses, and we use them to fuel community good works."

"Like your picnic," Billy said.

In 1930 the Brewtons co-founded the annual community Emancipation Day Picnic in High Park to celebrate August the first – the date slavery was abolished in 1834.

"Yes indeed we love our picnic," the doctor said, "but giving doesn't always have to mean money. We put high stakes in giving time, experience and commitment too. I dove into UNIA and our churches.

"You didn't dive, you cannonballed," his wife inserted with obvious pride. "You joined two boards, took over the finances and fundraising and worked on clearing their debts."

The doctor left a little pause. "Billy, you say you want to bring the community together. I'll tell you how. Use the basic lessons of podiatry: put one foot in front of the other."

He smiled from behind the steering wheel to the sound of laughter in the car.

Rounds of reminiscences filled in the miles. The party arrived at the town of Flesherton and reached the manse of the Reverend and Mrs. White at half past midnight. The Brewtons continued on a little ways to stay with the Hutchinsons, their friends nearby.

Vivian and Billy and their hosts stayed up talking until three-thirty in the morning. It was obvious from their robust hospitality they thought the world of Billy, doted on him as so many of his admirers did.

The next day, Saturday, started with a trek over to the Hutchinsons to retrieve the camera Billy forgot in the Brewtons' car.

Later on Mr. White took them to view the local splendor of Eugenia Falls. In the evening he and his wife opened their home to a carousel of people dropping in to welcome the out-of-towners.

During one conversation, Vivian overheard the Whites reveal that they sided with cottagers at a nearby private resort who had passed a restrictive covenant barring Jews from purchasing property there. "Open the door and they'll take over. We have our Christian values to protect."

"Was disillusioned to discover that the Whites, with all their fine free-dom from racial prejudice, are subject to *religious* prejudice," she told her diary.

She thought of the scenario in their world brotherhood text where a Jew is denied membership in a club. "They need a fireside here," she mused to herself. Their anti-Semitism made her realize the level of undoing needed even in the seemingly nicest people, just as within her own family.

Hallmarks of their sojourn were restful sleeps, time for Vivian to write a letter to Dick and one to Lillian who had recently written to say she was traveling to New York, lunch with Deacon and Mrs. Betts, supper at the par-sonage and an after-church gathering at the invitation of new acquaintance Mrs. Milligan.

Madam Leona sang a spiritual at the Sunday evening service. Billy played and sang at all services and the doctor played his sax.

An idyllic weekend was drawing to a close. With the clinching of good-byes to the Whites on being dropped at the Hutchinsons, the Brewtons were still packing and in no hurry. Billy filled the gap by teaching the ingénue daughter Katherine Hutchinson songs and recitations and thrilling her with feats of magic. By the time the Brewtons were ready to leave it was after mid-night. Billy and Vivian landed at Lansdowne at three. She had a bath, was in bed by five and set the alarm for seven. Billy woke up when she kissed him goodbye before leaving bleary-eyed to face a Monday she would not soon forget, not because of what happened at work but because of what awaited her at home after work. Another letter had arrived to add to her collection, this one from her mother's friend Mardie.

> Dear Vivian,
> You will no doubt be surprised to hear from me, but I am so anxious about you, felt I must write, and I'll type the letter as I am afraid you would throw it in the wastepaper basket were I to write long hand.
> First of all I want you to know that I believe in equality of races. We are all God's children, and one race is just as precious as any other. I have shed tears when I have heard of

cruel remarks thoughtlessly spoken which brought heartache to one of another race. I knew the late Rev. White. He used to come in the Dominion Life office when I was there to see Mr. Griffin the manager. They had been friends of long standing, both having at one-time lived in Truro. I remember Mr. Ripley the cashier used to address Mr. White as "Captain," and I, not knowing at the time of his service in the First World War, resented the title, thinking he was using it as a nickname, so to speak, but later learned of his very splendid record overseas from the same Mr. Ripley. I also knew Mr. White's daughter Helena, now married and living in Wolfville, and a very nice girl, musical too. She was stenographer for Mrs. Durand.

However, although I believe in equal rights and opportunities for all people, I do not believe in mixed marriages – and I believe I learned this from my father who used to go to sea and had been in countries where the Negro race formed the majority of the population – that the full-blooded Negro would not recognize, and held in contempt, their people who had mixed with other races (the mulattoes). They felt it a dishonor to their race.

Following are the reasons I oppose this union:

1. Billy White is ten years older than you. That is too great a difference when you are only twenty-two. If you were fifty-two and he sixty-two, as far as age is concerned, that would be all right.

2. He is a divorced man, and regardless of whose fault it is, you have never talked with his wife, have you? I would be a bit timid marrying a man who is divorced. They must have cared for each other at first, and surely she must have had some reason for changing her affections. The Bible condemns divorce, but of course you both know that.

3. Your future children will suffer. Supposing you have
   two daughters, one white just like you, the other very
   black. How will they feel when they look at each other?
   I would think the black girl would find it hard not to be
   envious of her white sister, and I should not say envious,
   but would not a feeling of sadness come over her? I could
   imagine her feelings. And will the white sister enjoy the
   companionship of the Negroes? The same would apply
   to your sons. To me, their future seems heartbreaking.
   This may sound like crossing bridges before one comes
   to them, but in the natural course of events you will have
   children.

4. Your mother is the best friend you have or ever will have.
   She is more interested in your happiness than anyone
   else. Your mother has had a lot of sorrow, and if you go
   through with this marriage I do not need to tell you, you
   will be adding to her suffering. Can you do that to your
   mother Vivian?

5. Are you sure you are in love with this man or is it the
   cause? You are twenty-two, why not wait for two or three
   years? Twenty-five is a good age to be married, and don't
   worry, he will live if you do not marry him.

   I was so interested in you going to Toronto, little did I
   know the attraction there.

   I do wish you would postpone the wedding for a few
   years Vivian. I feel Billy White is being selfish, considering the differences in your ages, and are you not being a
   bit selfish when you consider your family? Remember the
   glamour disappears weeks after marriage. You will not care
   as you think you care now.

   I want to tell you, if I had followed the inclination of
   my heart, and had not fate intervened when I was around
   your age, I would today be a very unhappy person. What

at that time seemed a disaster, now I know was a blessing in disguise. We understand so little when we are young.

Vivian dear I want to see you happy, but I beg of you think this over carefully, and on your knees. I am praying for you.

With much love,

Mardie

Far more meaningful to Vivian than receiving yet another opinion at this juncture was the message slipped under her door to phone Aunt Gladys at the Royal York Hotel. Her aunt's presence in Toronto represented an unexpected turn into the unknown. Vivian phoned her at the hotel, and they set a date to meet in a couple of days.

"I'm so looking forward to seeing you, dear," Aunt Gladys demurred. "I've made some plans."

Vivian ignored the tickle of nerves that usually served as her early warning system and dove into a good night's sleep.

Jean and her sister-in-law Gladys Baker

Chapter 23

"**W**hy don't you look into that crystal ball of yours and tell me what to expect tomorrow from Aunt Gladys and Uncle Don?"

Vivian gazed expectantly at Billy from across the table at Peter's Restaurant.

"As I recall she was intent on 'grabbing you back from the precipice of destruction,'" Billy said between swallows of his shish kebab platter. "I can't imagine her agenda has changed."

He paused to do a mental calculation while chewing on a forkful of seasoned rice.

"Do you really want to know what the numbers say?"

He was hesitant to disclose his numerology findings unless she said she could handle it. His caution made her all the more curious and she insisted on full disclosure. No matter what he said it wouldn't interfere with her enjoyment of her hot chicken sandwich.

"Tomorrow, the twenty-eighth of May, is a *nine* day, telling you to be prepared for some emotional ups and downs. Stick to your principles of universality and humanitarianism because that's what the number nine stands for. It won't be an easy day, *chérie*."

"That rings true," she affirmed.

They put the topic to rest, finished and paid for the meal and continued on with their evening plan to visit Ida Hunt, the Home Service supporter who volunteered to coordinate their wedding reception. The two women worked on details while Billy played Mrs. Hunt's piano, and much was accomplished to the cadence and flow of his music in the house.

After that they hiked over to 1421 Lansdowne to find nobody home and Billy hadn't his key. So they proceeded to the B.M.E. Church on Shaw Street to hear a piano recital. Unfortunately, the church was cold, the piano tuneless and they both preferred to be asleep. Back at the Christians the lights were on now and Vivian swung in to say hello before heading home on her own after eleven, very tired.

Bright and early the Phillipses' phone was trilling for Vivian.

"I know it's early, but I wanted to catch you before you left for work."

Gladys's voice reached through the phone. "Can you meet us for lunch, dear?"

Vivian replied, "I only have forty-five minutes for lunch. I couldn't possibly. I can come by after work. I'll call for you at the hotel desk."

A few minutes after the desk clerk's call to their room Aunt Gladys was in front of her but no Uncle Don.

"Where's Uncle?"

"Come, come …" Gladys scooted her toward a waiting taxi and slid into the backseat beside her. "There's somewhere we have to be," she said matter-of-factly. "We have an appointment."

It must be some kind of surprise, Vivian thought. Her aunt revealed nothing more than "you'll see when we get there" in answer to her niece's queries. She had to execute this intervention carefully. Had she told Vivian they were off to see Dr. Richardson, a neurologist, there was no guarantee Vivian would have boarded the cab. Riding north on Yonge past the landmarks and buildings, in tow with her aunt, she felt like a kid again, suddenly small, tongue-tied and powerless, like a doll engulfed by an oversized chair. She let her aunt control the conversation.

Twenty minutes later they were in midtown, the cabbie pulling over to the curb. "This is the place, Ma'am." He gestured toward the red brick office building.

Following her aunt down the ground floor corridor and noting the clinical nameplates, Vivian found her voice again, "Aunt Gladys, I demand to know what's going on." By that time, she was being nudged into an office, "Dr. R. Richardson, By Appointment Only."

Clearly, she wasn't being led into a surprise party.

"I've found someone who may be able to help us with our situation," Gladys whispered as they entered the waiting room.

A young woman behind a counter looked up and smiled. "I'll tell Dr. Richardson you're here." By the time they'd hung up their coats on an oak coat tree a bespectacled older man in grey trousers and a blue cardigan buttoned over a white shirt had opened his office door with a sweeping "Come in!" He had a nametag pinned to his sweater, slightly askew, Vivian noticed. With an exaggerated smile he extended his hand first to Gladys and then to Vivian, whose eyes were drawn to the ring on his left hand, gold forged into the initials RR. "And you must be Vivian," he said.

Manners mattered. It was impossible for Vivian to do anything except be polite and respond "pleased to meet you."

He had prominent eyebrows ceding from black to grey, elongated rogue hairs sticking out randomly like pins in a cushion, and a bit of a wave in his black hair, greying at the temples. A nick on his chin suggested he had too close a shave that morning.

"Sit down, please," he said as he led Vivian to a cozy seating area.

Gladys had been holding back, closer to the doorway.

"Doctor, do you think it best if I leave now so that you two can talk privately?"

Dr. Richardson agreed she should as Gladys knew he would. They had rehearsed this over the phone.

"Vivian, dear, I'll be back in a while. Just remember we're all here to help you. Relax and let the doctor do his work."

Relax? Vivian felt numb as the doctor rose to close his office door behind her departing aunt. Then, after grabbing his pen and notepad from the polished leather blotter on his desk, he took a seat opposite Vivian, who nervously waited to see what would unfold.

Dr. Richardson studied her for a moment then opened his notebook. Such a young, pretty thing, looking all mixed-up, understandably confused in her unplanned whereabouts, he owed her an explanation.

"I've heard so much about you, Vivian. You must be wondering why you're here."

"I feel like I've been kidnapped," she quipped.

He made a note in his book. "I can understand how you would feel that way."

"Your aunt requested that I meet with you, Vivian. And what I'd like to do with you today with your permission, of course, is perform an assessment to answer her question of whether there might be some ... clinical explanation for your behavior."

"Behavior," Vivian repeated.

"Yes. Your family fears this decision of yours to marry a Negro indicates a neurological problem."

"That's ridiculous," Vivian retorted.

The doctor continued. "The assessment entails a few non-invasive tests and measurements and a deeper discussion. Your family is seeking comfort and understanding during what is a difficult time for them, Vivian. They'd like me to report on what's happening up here with you." He pointed to his own skull.

"I was retained to examine this with you, and I wonder if you wouldn't mind if we commenced with the evaluation."

He looked at his watch and back at Vivian.

"I am entirely confident there's nothing wrong with *my* brain," Vivian sighed, already the weary hostage. "All right, let's get on with it."

Their session began with the administration of his mental status exam.

In rapid succession the doctor asked her to smile, raise her eyebrows, stick out her tongue, and shrug her shoulders. He asked her to close her eyes and indicate when she felt his pen tip on her arms, legs, fingers and face. Eyes open, she followed the tip of his pen as he moved it through her visual field and finally toward her face. Next was a strength test in which he provided resistance against her arm while she tried to lift it.

"That wasn't so bad now, was it?" Dr. Richardson settled back in his seat, notebook in lap. He made a few more notations.

"Compared to what?" Vivian wanted to know.

She could have laughed but was afraid she'd cry. There was the hilarity of this ridiculous scene of stupid exercises and neurological testing for a problem she didn't have against the humiliation of being treated like a laboratory rat or someone with an unsound mind.

Ignoring her rhetorical question, the doctor added extra scribbles to his book.

"The prefrontal cortex is responsible for the functions responsible for planning and making decisions. Vivian, in this part of your mental status exam, I look at problem-solving, interpretative ability and word similarities and your ability to complete certain tasks in those areas. It's a subtest that assesses judgment and reasoning directed at three aspects of frontal lobe function."

"You'll see I do very well at this," Vivian told him.

The tests completed and feeling confident in her answers she then gave him a "what's next" look.

He asked about the death of her father and how she felt about her mother, her brother, the loss of her grandfather, her relationships with family and friends before and after deciding to marry out of her race. He bandied words like "complex," "attachment," "hysteria" and "abandonment" to hear her reaction, then asked a series of what-if scenarios. He followed by espousing the view, which Vivian was now very weary of hearing, that races ought to be separate for the betterment of both races.

The exhaustive session was over. Aunt Gladys was there in the waiting room and had a taxi outside ready to whisk them back to the hotel.

Vivian was tired. But Gladys had another zinger that jolted her into alertness.

"Your mother arrived to Toronto today and will be at the hotel any minute to have dinner with us. Your Uncle Don said he'll escort her to the dining room and meet us there."

This was the final straw for Vivian, beleaguered by all the gamesmanship and unwanted interference, the sneaky, underhanded nature of it all. She snapped at her aunt: "You planned all this behind my back. I want you to know I don't appreciate it, Aunt Gladys. I will play along for the good of the family, but I'm terribly annoyed by your secrecy and you manipulating me to see Dr. Richardson."

Her aunt had come prepared to take a few punches, it seemed.

"Forgive me, Vivian. It's just that we love you so much. We're all in shock over what's happening. I know it was wrong of me not to tell you beforehand but we're at our wits' end. I think we could all benefit from professional help over this. Maybe if we'd had that lunch I would have been able to prepare you."

That was enough of an apology to settle Vivian for the moment. In the hotel dining room she greeted her mother with a hug and a kiss. A thin layer of ice coated the cordiality of their embrace. Jean could sense Vivian was miserable and saw she was thin as a rail. This added to her worry about the marriage, three undesirables: unhappiness, insufficient income, Negro status the absolute worst. She said nothing about Billy that night, bit her tongue and didn't criticize her daughter either. In fact, they had quite a pleasant time pretending there wasn't a problem. Around ten-thirty Gladys and Don walked Jean to the King Edward Hotel where she was lodging. Vivian hopped on a Bay streetcar to Lansdowne. Curley and Cleo were demonstrably glad to see her, and Billy had been home all evening pacing. He gladly walked her home – for him, both ways, four miles.

She had survived her *nine* day.

When the phone rang early the next morning Vivian swore the quality of the blare identified it as her mother's ring.

"I'd like you to come stay at the hotel with me while I'm here, dear," she said doing her best to make it sound like an enticing proposition.

"We'll see," Vivian offered, buying time.

What would Billy think? He phoned her at work that afternoon and asked her not to go.

"I worry for your wellbeing, Vivian. I'm afraid your mother has become a termagant. Yes, I know she's your mother. Still for your sake I'd like to see you maintain a comfortable distance. Before you go to the hotel meet me after work."

She did, and they walked around in the wind for a while, clutching each other for stability, the gustiness temporarily sweeping their minds free of cares. But the turbulence around them also mirrored the internal swirling they felt as they said goodbye at the doors of the King Edward Hotel.

In Jean's well-appointed room – a suite, actually – Vivian silently decided the King Eddy is where she and Billy should spend their wedding night.

Usually a detail an eager bride-to-be would be bursting to share with her mother; not this mother, not this anticipant bride.

"I phoned Fran Wees yesterday, Mother. She was hoping to get to see you but she's having a serious operation tomorrow and can't now. She suggested we visit Margarita while you're here." Vivian strode to the window to gaze down to the street.

"I went to see your Mr. Gowans this afternoon," Jean said coolly as she smoothed the wrinkles in her skirt in advance of Gladys's arrival, the three of them destined for dinner and a show. Vivian turned.

"Mother, I was going to arrange a meeting for you with him, but I didn't think you would go. What did you say to him?"

"Well, naturally I implored him to withdraw from the ceremony. He told me he was contractually obligated, said the matter was out of his hands."

"And did he tell you no legal reason exists that would prohibit me from marrying the man of my choice?"

"I contest this marriage on moral grounds, Vivian. You know that. Look around. You see whites with whites and only whites, and why do you think that is?"

Vivian opened her mouth to reply, then realized the pointlessness as Jean answered her own question.

"We stick to our kind because that's the way God planned it, creatures in like pairs – two by two. I can barely hold my head high in church these days because of the ungodly thing you're proposing to do. I'm praying Dr. Richardson will sort this out. I pray to God you will come to your senses before it's too late."

"Well, Mr. Gowans saluted our decision, Mother. Not everyone agrees with your interpretation of the Bible and that's something I had hoped you would realize."

If Vivian wanted hers to be the last word, it wasn't. Throughout dinner, unlike when Uncle Don was present, Gladys and Jean raveled a prolonged discussion about Billy into their conversational strand.

How little they know him, Vivian was thinking. Their opinions gave offense. The advantage to attending a movie after dinner was they couldn't talk, and she didn't have to listen.

She'd escaped staying over at the King Eddy, spent the night in her own bed and before leaving the house the next morning entertained a phone call from Aunt Gladys.

"Doctor Richardson would like to see us, by *us* I mean you, me, your mother and Billy. Tonight at six forty-five."

Initially resistant, Vivian reminded herself of her pledge to play along for the faint hope of familial reconciliation. Scheduling the parties fell to Vivian. Luckily she had very little to do at work in the afternoon. Her entire day was peppered with phone calls, incoming and outgoing, to nail down the arrangement for which she and Billy were twenty-five minutes late, entirely Vivian's fault. Billy was on a tight time frame, required at his office by eight. As they entered Dr. Richardson's office Vivian was thinking of the worried look on Mrs. Phillips' face as she asked her roomer not to go back to the doctor's.

"There's no need," she said. "There's no need."

The meeting didn't last long. Mrs. Phillips was right, there was no need for it, not a chance the polarities in the room would dissolve. Billy showed himself to be as smart and articulate as the doctor if not more so. The meeting truncated by time constraints Dr. Richardson soon jumped to his point. He seemed quite nonplussed by Billy's layman knowledge in the field of neurology.

On the surface everything was cordial. The doctor advised that while he could find nothing neurologically wrong with Vivian, he did believe in the science that said her children would be born inferior in intellect and ability. In a situation such as this Mr. White should take steps to ensure that children will never be a by-product if this marriage does proceed.

"I strongly disagree with you, Dr. Richardson, with all due respect," Billy said in a tone that was inarguably authoritative. "There are emerging anthropological studies that dispute what you say unequivocally."

He trotted out a few. "My fiancée and I reject the thinking that has caused the races to divide. We are intent on bringing them together and of course children are a large part of that."

He looked at Gladys, then at Jean, and stood up.

"I think we're done here, and as you know I have another engagement. I look forward to seeing you both under more conducive circumstances.

Dr. Richardson, I'd like to thank you for your time. We'll have to agree to disagree, and then leave on good terms all around. Are you coming as well, Vivian?"

He had disarmed them using dignity. She was so proud of him.

"I'll telephone you later, Mother. Thank you, doctor, for your time," she said, hastily retreating as Billy held the door for her and tipped his hat to them.

No special goodbye for Aunt Gladys, Vivian still smarting from the original blindsiding, cloaked her perturbation about her aunt in blithe indifference toward her, which was definitely unsettling for Gladys and out of character for her niece.

The Phillips house was quiet when Vivian got there. George was away. Margaret was out. She appreciated the silence. Ironically it spoke to her louder than words ever could for it enabled her thoughts to echo with a clarity that can be masked in the mumbo-jumbo of other people's opinions. Here in the calming peace and tranquility of her own space she allowed herself to put the past few days' events behind her like one waves aside a bad dream.

Billy was coming up around at half past ten and they'd have something to eat together.

She phoned her mother. They talked, mostly news of home. And much to Vivian's relief, Jean dropped her push to have her daughter stay at the hotel.

"It wouldn't be worthwhile. I'm leaving Monday or Tuesday."

"Well, tomorrow's Saturday. We have all weekend together, Mother."

Three more days, what she wouldn't give to know what they held in store. She made a couple of sandwiches and did some ironing while waiting for Billy.

They heard when Mrs. Phillips come home, went downstairs, and talked to her till just past midnight.

Here was comfort, reassurance, openness, acceptance, love in fact. All the cozy attributes Vivian hoped for from her closest kin she found readily in the kitchen of a landlady she'd known just over six-and-a-half months.

To outside onlookers Jean and Vivian were a mother and daughter enjoying time together on a Saturday afternoon, the hotel their meeting place, lunching at Diana's, roaming in Simpsons debating fashion styles and scrutinizing price tags. In reality, tension lingered.

Jean wanted to buy her daughter all sorts of things: a fetching blouse, sensible shoes, toiletries, decorative combs for her hair. Vivian wouldn't let her, having sworn to be neither indebted nor beholden to her.

"I won't have you buying anything for me, Mother. What I want from you is something money cannot buy: your blessing."

"You're asking me for the one thing I cannot give," Jean grumbled despondently. "I want to speak to Billy later. He left Dr. Richardson's office so abruptly I had no opportunity to respond. Surely as your mother I'm owed that."

Robbed of the fun of shopping, Jean was pouty and tired and headed back to the hotel to rest. Vivian grabbed the opportunity to find a phone booth. She called Billy to update him. Then she continued shopping, bought her wedding-gown and going-away dress and had them set aside before returning to the hotel.

She and Jean dined that evening at Little Denmark, the Tudor style restaurant and tavern at 720 Bay Street.

"Billy's home tonight and quite happy to speak to you, Mother. The Christians went to the movies with their friends the Campbells, so he's there on his own and you two can talk about whatever you want to talk about."

"You know what I want to talk about, Vivian. If you won't listen to good sense, maybe he will."

"That's between the two of you. Please, Mother, let's put this aside for now or it will ruin our evening."

After dinner they made their way to 1421 Lansdowne and Billy was ready for them, very relaxed, keeping a polite distance from Vivian so as not to upset her mother. Jean opened her handbag to retrieve the report from Dr. Richardson and handed it to him, requesting he read it and do what's prescribed. Outwardly she was so nice. She could have been requesting his presence at a society tea.

"I will read it, Mrs. Keeler," he promised. "I will read it to make you happy, not because I intend to follow any of its recommendations. I have to be honest. If the meeting I had with Dr. Richardson was the starting point, this report stands for everything Vivian and I are working actively to change and to prove wrong. You ask too much of me. All I'm asking of you is to be happy for us."

At that moment thumping on the porch sounded the arrival of the Christians and the Campbells home from the show. A little earlier than expected.

Cleo's graciousness instantly sprang to the fore when she saw Jean and was introduced, not stymied by what she knew of the woman's backward thinking and anti-African bias. "Kill 'em with kindness," her own mother taught her.

"You must stay for tea, Jean," Mrs. Christian insisted.

That tea turned out to be a banquet. Jean again advanced an idea she'd dismissed days earlier.

"Vivian, on second thought, it would be nice to have you stay with me at the hotel for my last few days here," she said.

As suspected, in front of a crowd – Doug, girlfriend Gerry, Sonny and his gal June had joined the gathering – there was no wiggle room for escaping the invitation. Doug was an unwitting facilitator. He offered to drive them to the hotel with a stopover first at Oakwood to get her things.

Sunday morning Billy phoned the hotel inviting both Keelers to join the carload going to Waubaushene for the day, but the women declined in favor of their pre-laid plans. They attended a service at Metropolitan Church, exiting into a downpour which ceased to let up. That meant meals confined to the hotel, although not entirely an indoor day. Gladys and Don liaised with them there to begin a touristy outing to Casa Loma, followed by a trip to the Swansea neighborhood to visit Margarita Wees.

That evening, on her side of the hotel suite, Jean positioned herself in an armchair to read and listen to hymns from the gospel program on the radio.

Vivian seized the opening her mother's preoccupation created. She could slip out to see Billy for an hour. Earlier on the phone he told her he'd be stationed at the hotel coffee shop trusting she'd appear. She did. They stole some time together.

Breakfast in the cafeteria on a rainy Monday in early June, Jean's departure day on a ten-fifteen morning train from Union Station just across from her hotel, there was outward calm masking inner turmoil in both of them. Neither let it show throughout a cordial breakfast and then, goodbyes.

Vivian had to leave the hotel directly for work in the rain. She hadn't brought an umbrella to the hotel and was totally unprepared for the downpour. Arriving at the office drenched but punctual, looking silly and soggy, she felt deeply saddened realizing she may never see her mother again. And that yucky sensation clung like the morning's stubborn, unrelenting clouds.

Billy was waiting for her at the Phillips, when Vivian, soaked again, sloshed her way through the front door at half past six struggling with a misbehaving suitcase. Everything today so far had been difficult right down to the suitcase latch. He rescued the broken baggage from her clutch and set it down in the anteroom. He handed her a thick bath towel that he had draped over his arm. He prepared tea and reheated leftovers for her. And hated that he had to leave for his night work.

"I'll come up later and we can talk about everything that's happened. Okay, *chèrie?*"

He kissed her and cupped her cool face in his hands. "We can address those wedding invitations while we're at it."

When he did return, she opened up to him about her mother's farewell and it triggered a letting go of all the tears Vivian had been holding back. He held her in his arms as she released a torrent of pent-up grief and loss.

Addressing envelopes for their wedding invitations after that was as cathartic as purchasing her bridal outfits had been on the weekend. The postman had delivered a letter from Harold that day, which Billy and Vivian read together. It confirmed the Kierans' arrival date, and the letter achieved something else significant. It helped crystallize Vivian's thoughts around priorities, moving in thirteen days, marrying in three weeks.

When Billy reached home, he wrote her a letter.

> My *chérie,*
> It may seem silly of me to say that I'm thinking about you so much that it's hard to stop and write to you. Silly or not, it's true, so I'm not going to try to stop. Instead, I'll go right on thinking of you and writing what I think – as I think it. Gee, it would be so much nicer, *chérie,* if you were here with me, as I'm imagining you are, close to me, with your hand resting on my arm. Then I could whisper

countless I love you's to make up, in a measure, for the time you've been hammered at during these past several trying days. Thank goodness we have only three weeks of waiting for what will be the happiest day of my life. Oh, my darling, I'm so happy that you'll be my wife – just think – Mrs. W. A. White! What a thrill it gave me to read our announcements last Friday night. They look so right, and my name seems to bear real importance when I think of yours being there with it.

Oh darling, I thrill at the thought of seeing you as my bride. I'm so lucky – so, so lucky!

We'll be gloriously happy – even in our moments of after-dishwashing-fatigue, we'll be happy because we love each other so.

Chérie, my darling, I'll be so good to you, not only because I know you'll be the most wonderful wife in the world but also because you'll always be my *chérie* too. You have been, and are, good for me in so many, many ways. I'll always love to show you the goodness in my life for which you're responsible.

June 23rd, please hurry and come!"

Elm Avenue

Chapter 24

The day following Jean's departure from Toronto, after seeing Billy at lunch, quite by accident Vivian met him again on the Queen streetcar on her way home from work. He had a group of boys with him.

"There's a baby kangaroo at Eaton's. I took these boys to see it. All in a day's work, how did you like it, boys?" A swarm of cheers rose up from the seats they occupied.

"Boys, I'd like you to meet Miss Keeler. In exactly nineteen days she will be my wife, Mrs. White!"

The boys received the news like a weather report. They didn't care what color she was. No odd stares, over-the-shoulder looks, head shakes, insinuations or whispers.

Billy was heading to College Street Baptist Church, Vivian to get a perm. They parted ways and reunited later at Oakwood to do more work on invitations.

Each day Vivian crossed out more done items on her task list. Surging to the top was the need to find someone to give her away. She called Margarita, advancing the idea that her dad, Dr. Wees, would be a wonderful candidate, and seeking the best way to approach him.

Margarita thought it a grand idea and felt her mother should arrange it. Fran, who was recovering well from her gall bladder surgery, told Vivian, "Leave it with me."

Billy's impromptu dinner with Portia at her hotel had sidelined the idea of him coming over that evening. They'd both be seeing Portia in concert the next night, performing at The Promenade on Bloor Street with the noted Czech-born American maestro Victor Kolar.

Vivian made efficient use of Billy's time away. She cleaned her room, wrote a few letters, ironed, cleaned four milk bottles, and made her phone calls including one to Avril Shreve, her cheery, budding friend and fellow volunteer at Home Service.

Portia's concert the next day was predictably glorious, but the seats were uncomfortable. They went backstage when it was over to be lifted by the inimitable glow of Portia's greatness. Vivian cast back to the August concert two years ago when she first met Portia and felt out of place. She felt fully embraced as family now.

Billy wanted to stop by the new apartment after the concert. Vivian slipped off the shoes that were strangling her sore feet and walked in her stocking feet. It felt great to stretch her legs and savor a taste of summer.

"I received a nice letter from Mother today," Vivian told him en route, with a note of optimism.

"Careful," said Billy, "it's probably another trap."

He hadn't intended to sound pessimistic. In truth he too was feeling the effects of being put through the ringer by Jean. One day she would apologize to them, he predicted on a more positive note, as they approached the wrought iron gate entrance to a virtually private road.

Number One Elm stood out to Vivian like an east-facing, yellow-brick castle, masonry pillars, columns and balconies complementing its floor-to-ceiling windows that yawned their welcoming to a flood of natural light. Situated at the end of a cul-de-sac, the backyard was a living ravine down the verdant valley slope canopied by trees.

After poking around a bit, they indulged in their first luxury in many months, treating themselves to ice cream sundaes at Peter's on Sherbourne.

Always nice to have a sweet memory to recall when a sour taste visits your tongue like it did for Vivian the next day.

Dr. Wees's response was not favorable.

"Vivian? It's W.R. Wees speaking. Yes, I'm fine thank you, dear."

She couldn't pinpoint the exact tone of his voice – tentative? Uncomfortable? There was a shifty uneasiness to it.

"You have news for me?" Vivian prompted. "Fran spoke to you about the favor I'm asking?"

"Yes, she did, Vivian, she outlined your request to me exactly as you put it to her," replied Dr. Wees, so haltingly she wanted to yell *get to the point* through the telephone.

"It was sweet of you to want me to give you away, but to do so would be to condone your marriage so I must refuse, as I agree with my good friend Dr. Richardson."

His response floored her. Flabbergasted she managed to spit out the words, "You know Dr. Richardson?"

"Yes, I was the one who recommended him to your mother and facilitated your appointment. I thought you knew, my poor dear. Well, then, this must be a shock for you, but I make no apologies, you understand."

The conversation ended with Vivian believing that in seeking out Dr. Wees she'd punched herself. Another clumsy move by V. Keeler had set her up for injury. Well, she'd have to behave like a prizefighter and shake this off like any of the other blows delivered to her over the course of her courtship with Billy.

If not Wees, they'd find someone else. They had to.

Mr. Bradbury! The name leapt at Vivian in a neon flash. How had she missed the obvious? He was a natural choice. She felt safe asking the cleric. Knowing he'd be difficult to reach she wasted no time trying.

Next to knock off their things-to-do was obtaining the licence, and for this Vivian willed herself to wake up early and alert, to attack the job fresh in the day on Saturday, stopping first at Simpsons for her pre-arranged appointment with the bride's counsel to discuss flowers. Only when she neared her destination did she realize she had forgotten her birth certificate and had to double back.

She made it to City Hall at eleven. Billy was waiting for her at the Clerk's counter with the form in front of him, his portion of it already filled out and his other vital documents close at hand. Vivian scanned his answers. Of the three choices, Bachelor, Widowed or Divorced he had ticked the latter. He handed her a pen and she surveyed her multiple choice: Widowed, Divorced and, reluctantly, she ticked the remaining option for a female, Spinster. Nevertheless, success! They had their license.

Sunday, fifteen days and counting, truly was a day of rest. After church, a noontime meal at Oakwood and an afternoon of reading and an eruption of play-fighting, where Vivian proved to be quite the formidable wrestler. The fun and physicality of their horseplay opened a portal that moved Vivian to disclose her innermost feelings.

Just before he left for a fireside at Home Service she broke down and told him how she'd been feeling, or rather not feeling, this past week.

"Instead of elation and excitement leading up to the happiest day of my life I mostly feel dead inside, like you could stick me with a pin, Billy, I wouldn't feel it. Like I'm sleepwalking, I'm numb. I go through the motions and my mind isn't there. It goes to thoughts of all those people who wrote me. Mother, Aunt Gladys, Uncle John and Uncle Roy, Reverend Elgee ..."

Billy empathized. "They don't treat you like a person. They treat you like a problem."

She was weeping now, and the sorrow caught Billy in the throat. He was sobbing too.

"I can't even trust my own mother," she sniffled, and he immediately regretted disparaging Jean the day before, fearing his words might have primed Vivian's outcry.

Vivian was standing now at her dressing table with a hanky. He reached for his own, wiped his face to compose himself.

"You've been subjected to so much, darling. I'm guessing everything you are going through is a reaction to the stress of your mother's visit."

"That must be it," Vivian said in recovery mode. "I think I'll be all right now."

Prophetic words, the next evening gleamed like the silver tea service that Mrs. Christian was lending for the reception. Vivian polished it before leaving for a show, on Billy's arm.

They saw Noel Coward's *Brief Encounter*, a powerful and witty piece that mirrored in many ways their own relationship.

"That was a wonderful picture, especially for us, Billy. I am sure we understood it better than anyone else there. We are so lucky."

They walked home in a state of exalted happiness, talking all the way.

• • •

Exactly two weeks to go, and Vivian squeezed every ounce of advantage out of the time she had left. On this day, luckily, she was able to steal away from the office in order to get some errands done: the wedding ring at Birks, the veil and headdress acquired, a gift for Helen secured. She even managed her way to The Prom's record store to purchase a Jan Peerce record for Billy to replace the one she destroyed on Mrs. Christian's birthday.

The streetcars looked so crowded she was afraid the record album would break if she rode with it among the compressed, jostling and lurching horde. She opted to walk back to the office to avoid the risk. No one missed her.

At ten that evening, twelve days before the wedding, when Billy came up to Vivian's, he tracked down Derrick Bradbury by phone. The young minister was in at last, and Vivian put her request to him.

"Oh my," Bradbury said regretfully. "I'm being married myself on June twenty-first so it's out of the question, unfortunately. I would have loved to do it, Vivian. I would have been proud to. Perhaps I can find someone for you."

Another wrinkle! How fitting that her first wedding gift was an iron from the Phillips, which they gave to her the next day. Vivian held faith that their pastor friend would come through with someone suitable.

Billy surprised her at Oakwood with dinner made, flowers on the table, a tablecloth and everything set, delicious. He had a meeting at the museum. Vivian accompanied him there, then continued on to survey their new apartment, awaiting his arrival later. She visualized incorporating their possessions into the already furnished surroundings. Moving day, a Sunday, was about to unfold.

It started for them at six a.m. on empty stomachs.

Bless the Christians, they provided the car to transport the assembly of items. Billy and Vivian filled every available space in it with most of Billy's possessions. His boxes of books and heavy phonograph folios, bulging suit-cases, a wardrobe bag of suits, and assorted sundries crammed the vehicle. On the road by half past seven, Vivian's load would necessitate a second trip and likely a second day.

"Come on! Let's get this over with." In his rush to do everything as quickly as possible a naturally impatient Billy was close to burning out by late afternoon. They anticipated going to church in the evening but slept instead. They had their first meal at nightfall. Billy's search to find a place open to buy bread on a Sunday further tested his patience. Once he'd eaten, he found his good temper again.

Their first night in the new place, he slept in the bedroom, she slept in the living room. In eight more days, they'd be sleeping together in matrimony.

For the next number of days, they would gradually transition from their former residences, escaping the customary pressure on tenants to vacate by a firm date. They had the world's best landlords.

Oakwood would be home to Vivian a while longer. She was there an-swering another letter from her mother when Mrs. Phillips called upstairs: "someone to see you." It was Lillian, smiling, arms outstretched. Vivian was ecstatic. They hugged.

"I flew in from New York this morning. My friend Charlie is outside in the car."

Vivian waved him in from the door. A few minutes of chit-chat later Charlie volunteered to drive them over to the apartment so they could see it. That meant a trip to Home Service first to get the key from Billy. Charlie made them laugh when he pretended to be a limo driver. The women sat in the back seat, bantering the way reunited best friends do, as if no time had passed, while he chauffeured them downtown. Vivian bounded in to retrieve the key from Billy, who dashed out to say a quick hello.

After popping into One Elm for an admiring tour, Charlie and Lillian drove Vivian home.

Billy could hear sunshine in Vivian's cadence when they talked on the phone into the night. When they met for lunch at noon the next day as planned, he asked whether she was going to talk to Lillian about her snub-bing the wedding. He was mind reading again.

"Yes."

Vivian and Lillian had arranged to meet at Yonge and Dundas for dinner and a show after Lillian, Charlie and his mother returned from a day trip to Niagara Falls.

When the girlfriends did connect at the designated intersection Lillian accompanied Vivian to finalize the wedding flowers. Then for dinner they chose Little Denmark and ordered duck, which neither of them had tried before, another one of those things best friends do: share inaugural experiences together, along the lines of pinky swears, exchanging confidences and paddling their first canoe ride of the summer. Lillian's company felt like a final jigsaw puzzle piece had been snapped into place: satisfying and complete.

"Flowers, shoes, dress, veil, hat, going away dress, announcements, invitations, hair appointment is set," Vivian recited in the lead up to what she really wanted to say. There was the right pause.

"Lillian, I want you to know I forgive you for not coming to my wedding. You know Mother has been doing everything in her power to stop me from marrying Billy."

Lillian nodded.

"Mother mentioned you in one of her earliest letters. In fact, she was more concerned about how you were feeling than how I was feeling," Vivian said.

"Your news came as such a shock, Viv, but I accept it now," Lillian replied. "Your mother's campaign did influence me in the beginning, and how we were raised as well. But I've had time to reflect since then. I know how much in love you are with Billy. I see it in your eyes. I read it in your letters. Your happiness is what matters to me."

"It's only a matter of time before my mother sees the light," Vivian said determinedly. "Her frenzy must be petering out by now."

The train would be taking Lillian home to Nova Scotia in a few days.

"I'll be thinking of you on your wedding day, my friend," she said. "I wish you the best."

Well wishes shared by many, evidently. Vivian returned home to a bounty of parcels, letters, and messages, ending the day on a sustained high note.

The next day Billy came to see her after work with news. "Mr. Bradbury came through. He found someone to walk you down the aisle: Johnny Rumball. He's available and he'll do it."

The name struck her like a timpani mallet. Johnny Rumball looked to be barely out of high school and bore a strong resemblance to Mickey Rooney, a good three inches shorter than she.

She had no personal connection to him other than having sat next to him at a church supper. Despite his junior looks, he was a third-year pharmacology student at U of T and talked incessantly at that dinner about his personal ambitions and drive for success. In her mind he was wrong for the part. She felt awful about it, and she struggled to respond.

"I'm relieved we have someone," she said. She dared not share her opinion about Johnny as the choice.

Mr. and Mrs. Christian called for them in the car. A team effort moved most of her things over to the apartment then spirited her home. She'd be in for a jolt when the postman delivered the next day's mail.

It wasn't the letter from Fran – that was a surprise, her writing to apologize about her husband, saying she had not been aware of the Dr. Richardson business or that Dr. Wees would decline her request. Short, sweet, and somewhat surprising, but not like the jarring letter from Jean.

Dear Vivian,

If on your wedding day, even to the last second, you should feel that you want do something else with your life – that a long life of raising Negroes is not a good future for you – all my offers are more than open to you. I would do anything to save you from so ruining your life.

I feel that God placed in our hands, through Dr. Richardson, the means for stopping this marriage and the fact that Billy White deliberately refused to follow the medical findings, shocked me very deeply and proved how utterly selfish, relentless and cruel he is. I trouble for you Vivian and I hope you will not go through with it. He has never done the right thing by you, or your family and he never will.

He knows that all your family and friends think it is the very worst thing you can do with your life. It has been denounced by ministers, doctors, mothers, fathers, and other people well qualified to know what is right.

I can see nothing to justify such a course. I feel that you are being forced into it in some way. It is not natural. How can he say he has not influenced you when he insisted upon seeing you every day without exception?

You have done foolish things in your life, have you not? Then you should be willing to be guided by those who have lived a little longer. This race question is a very old one and there is an unwritten law that most people accept and observe and which you felt in the beginning. You will have to get back to that and give up this idea. Twenty-two is very young to decide on such a marriage. The fact that it makes you capable of turning your back on all your family should show you it is wrong.

If you could have known Daddy in your adult years you could never be satisfied with such a marriage. I think you were very mean to Aunt Gladys who did all she could for Daddy's sake and her love for you.

We know you could have a wonderful time with people of your own age and kind if you were not tied to him. He has kept you from that for over a year now and will continue to do so.

Think once more before you take this awful plunge into the darkness from which there is no way out.

Fly home to me and we will map out a program. I will furnish the money and gladly.

Lovingly,
Mother

PS I will draw $100 so that I can wire it at a moment's notice.

Vivian's adrenalin ramped up to overdrive as she plowed through her mother's letter.

"She is still hoping I will change my mind at the last minute," Vivian lamented.

In real time the wedding was fifty-four hundred minutes away.

As a twosome she and Billy shopped together for groceries and remaining items for the reception. It was Friday, Vivian's last day with her current employer Spruce Falls Power & Paper. She'd be working her next job as a married woman.

Harold and Helen were due to arrive that evening, by train. For efficiency Billy suggested he and Vivian divide and go separate ways. Using transit, he would take the last of her stuff from Oakwood to the Elm apartment and she would go directly to the train station. He would meet up with her there.

By the time he got there the train was just pulling in and Vivian radiated on the platform in all her loveliness. When she saw him, she clasped him in an enthusiastic hug. Helen and Harold were moving in their direction. Their joyous reunion had begun. They piled into a taxi and headed to Elm Avenue. Billy and Vivian were about to host their first house guests. The four of them talked into the early hours.

They went in separate directions the next day, Saturday, Billy to work, Vivian for a hairdo and Harold and Helen went shopping. They reconnected at suppertime and chatted into the wee hours before retiring.

Just one more day until Monday, The Day.

After a morning of final arrangements and an afternoon drive with Curley, Cleo, Harold and Helen, they went to church Sunday evening for the rehearsal.

Then it was back to the Christians for merriment: Fred and Betty Campbell and their daughter June, Vic Craven, Doug Christian, his girl-friend Gerry, Harold, Helen, and the soon-to-be newlyweds all hammed around, with juice and snack refreshments. Billy played the piano and he and Harold did their operatic version of "Mary Had a Little Lamb." At one minute to midnight the older women whisked Vivian home to Oakwood to ensure that Billy wouldn't see her again.

If you can judge a marriage by the weather of that day, June twenty-third was beautiful, hot and sunny. Billy phoned to say they'd be going on a honeymoon after all – to Waubaushene – so Vivian packed a few more things before Mrs. Christian, Mrs. Campbell and Helen came to call for her in the car.

The ceremony was beautiful, the wedding, the reception – perfect. Even Johnny Rumball. Vivian had misjudged him. He was steady as a rock, mature in his official role, the enthusiastic life of the party at the reception.

Fifty-three guests, every one so earnest with their good wishes. Toronto wasn't perfect – far from it – but it was birthing something essential and important that had helped them along their path. Like a nesting place, a seed in soil, the city into which they had tapped was an environment for incubating and exploring these concepts of equality and civil rights and putting them into practice, with love.

Their friends from Home Service, the Brewtons, the Lightfoots, the Redmons, the Simpsons, Isabel and Don LeBourdais, the Christians, of course, the Campbell and Phillips families, Avril – all of them formed a cast of precious Torontonians committed to change and the percolation of progress.

"May your ocean always be calm and your rudder steady," Honorah Lucas wrote in the wedding guest book.

· · ·

"Mr. White, your suite is ready."

The desk clerk at the King Edward Hotel passed Billy the key and flagged for a baggage attendant to escort the new Mrs. White, her husband, Harold and Helen to the elevator and onward to the room. Harold tipped the porter two bits. "I'll get this, Billy." He and Helen had seats on the twelve-thirty overnight train to Montreal. They took a few pictures with Billy's camera before they left.

Billy and Vivian talked a while before going to bed. They luxuriated in the plump, lavender-scented bed linens, sleeping in until eleven and having lunch sent up to the room.

What happened that night was their business. Vivian recorded nothing about it in her diary, not so much as an editorial comment. Burned from when Jean read her diary years ago, she self-censored when it came to writing about anything as personal as having sex.

When Mrs. Christian saw Vivian two days after the honeymoon, she had to remark, "You're dead on your feet and weak as a kitten. You look as though your husband beat you."

Vivian went red then hinted a smile.

"I hardly eat at all these days. My malnutrition is beginning to catch up with me. And we're not getting much sleep."

"I bet you're not," Mrs. Christian laughed.

Chapter 25

Legally bound in holy matrimony, no one could try to obstruct now. They were free to love as they had dreamed. He had his muse and she her handsome hero. Winged by love, he was the sail to her cool, refreshing breeze.

The night train to Waubaushene stirred up Vivian's thoughts of her last train ride, the one that carried her from Halifax to Billy in Montreal – was it just last November? It felt a lifetime away. She likened their journey these past seven months to the climate of the changing seasons. The cruel chill of winter's barbs and spring's frostiness the emblems of those who harassed and shunned her, moving into the growth of summer's warmth and promise reflective of those who supported her and fostered her happiness.

Curley and Cleo were absolute angels, lending money, advice, and their cottage, including arranging for a Mr. Archer to meet them at the station upon arrival. Four days on Georgian Bay...

At the cottage she adored the water pump that spilled forth its clean, fresh well water. She experienced long-recalled joys of being in nature. They relaxed in the sun, went for a swim – Billy always close to shore – visited a bunch of local folks and acquired fresh cream from the Walkers across the road. Billy was going to make butter once back in Toronto to bolster their strictly rationed allowance.

Strawberry time was at its prime, berries so ready they perfumed the kitchen as they laid down in sacrifice atop the mountainous shortcakes enveloped in cascading whipped cream, an absolute luxury.

"I feel overfed," Billy groaned after devouring his. He wasn't yet dressed for the day and was rubbing his stomach as the richness of the dessert settled there. Vivian sent him outside in his pyjamas to run around the cottage three times to work off the bloat.

They had so much fun. An added treat, the train car on their ride home was air-conditioned. Four days of honeymooning all too soon came to an end.

When the taxi deposited them at One Elm at the end of their sojourn, Billy carried her over the threshold – but not up the stairs!

These were the frames of remembrance that sent a smile to Vivian's lips as she started with Mr. H. C. Powell, Insurance, in the twelve-story Temple Building at 62 Richmond Street West on the second of July.

"Will you continue to work now that you're married?" he inquired. "Some girls are you know, even with the war being over."

"I think I will need to be married a little longer before I can answer you, Mr. Powell," she replied.

He was a very nice boss, went out of his way to get Vivian a duplicate key made for the apartment.

"If you do want permanent employment, I think you would be an excellent addition to our secretarial staff," he said when he handed back her apartment key and the copy.

"Thank you," she said, genuinely unsure at that moment what her future work-life entailed.

At home, she delved energetically into the box of wedding gifts and discovered some she hadn't seen before, including brass candlesticks from Avril, and an eight-sided, floral-patterned, metal, lidded tea canister from Portia, for which she immediately wrote thank-you notes.

Supper would be waiting for Billy. Now he could come home in between his days and nights at the agency knowing his wife would be there to generate sustenance, harmony, comfort, stability and support to help him to the ambitious heights he planned to climb.

And the meal wasn't half bad. Her culinary skills were advancing. Still, he preferred his own cooking. "I'll be back around ten and tonight let's re-read some of our old letters and love poems. I have a new one for you too."

When he arrived home from evening duties at Home Service, he entered the apartment to find Vivian sifting through a stack of his loose photographs which he'd placed on the armoire.

"Harboring memories of your ex-girlfriend, are we?" With a mock look of disapproval, she held up a particularly cozy snapshot of Lois melded to Billy.

She was startled when he took exception to the remark. She was only kidding, but he put on an exaggerated display of sorting the pile of photographs, theatrically discarding about half, whistling cheerfully all the while, the black-and-white glossies fluttering down tauntingly to the wastepaper basket, as she watched, feeling miserable about having said anything. She would fish them out of the trash tomorrow when he was out.

In truth Billy had been in touch with Lois. Once Les suggested she phone for advice about a troubled boy. The other time it was to tell Billy that her cousin Lindy had died. No point in telling Vivian about those calls. He didn't want her to read more into it and he certainly didn't want to be held to answer any questions about Lois. He would slot her name into the same category as his ex-wife's, covered by the promise they made to Mr. Gowans. Never discuss her.

He was confident after tonight's exhibition that Vivian wouldn't be raising the topic of Lois again.

Being a Friday night, they stayed up late, then next morning he let her sleep in while he got breakfast ready. When not assembling the household in July's oppressive heat, they had baths together – a mad scramble ensued when Vivian's childhood friend Muriel phoned in the middle of one. They read aloud to each other, grocery shopped, ran errands, and romped in the sack when it cooled down after dark. He wooed her with his latest poetic creation, inspired by the cotton dress she had worn in Waubaushene, a corny verse but cute, she loved him for it.

One look at you
Did make me think
How wonderful
You look in pink
And even now
That day has gone
The simple thought
Still lingers on.
"You're wonderful"
To you say I –
I say to me
"You lucky guy!"

Saturday night they were up until the sun rose. They knew the impossible pace couldn't be sustained and yet they did.

The effects on Vivian were evident on the job. One day she kept falling asleep whenever Mr. Powell paused in his dictation. When he went out, she had difficulty transcribing it and made stupid mistakes. A few days later he lectured her about punctuality which she silently and begrudgingly deemed was justified, and she worked an hour of overtime unbeknownst to him. Ah, to be a wife and mother ... her aspiration was ripe.

Marriage is the art of adjustment, Vivian was learning. Two people coalescing under the same roof soon will spot the differences among their similarities: habits, quirks, personalities, approaches. Vivian, an astrological Taurus, the bull: stubborn. Earth sign: grounded, rooted, devoted to growth, practical, inquisitive and opinionated with judgmental tendencies. Billy, the airy, Aquarian, man of the universe, independent and accustomed to having his own way and, like the wind, being the force that controls events and floats freely on his own terms.

As soon as the place was set up, they planned to entertain, a custom they were ideally suited for. They chose the date of July fifteenth to host their first party as a couple.

Billy was also counting on a robust summer camp circuit to be another welcome sideline for supplementing his income.

Chapter 25

Early in the summer they were driven up to Lake Couchiching, where Billy directed the music at the annual CCF conference. His connection to Don LeBourdais and Avis McCurdy, and routine drop-ins to the political party's Woodsworth House headquarters on Jarvis Street, where he established a vocal quartet and a choir, *Woodsworth House Music Guild*, had reintegrated him into the sphere and led to a paid offer to lead conference delegates in singing on Saturday evening and again later around the campfire.

At the conference retreat Billy was introduced to a leading party figure, Howard Conquergood, a hulking, former Toronto Argonaut football linebacker turned labor organizer, CCF adviser and campaigner. Down the road he had plans for Billy, took him aside for a chat and told him he'd be in touch.

The Irwin brothers drove them to and from "Couch." Returning, a carload of six passengers sang most of the way home. When she wasn't singing or revelling, Vivian was thinking about the entertaining they'd be doing in their new place as a married couple and began formulating plans.

A phone call the next day from Dorothy Anderson to Billy at his office sent those plans tumbling. Dorothy was in trouble with the building's management.

"They're very angry that I sublet the apartment to you. It's true they told me no sublets, but now they've given me my notice to move out by the end of September. I'm sorry, Billy, and for Vivian too, I feel horrible. Miss Breithaupt, the owner, is an absolute witch."

Billy wasn't relishing relaying this development to Vivian. She wasn't eating enough as it was and blamed the oppressive heat for robbing her of her appetite. This would be one more worry for her basket. When Billy reached the apartment after work, Vivian received the bad news predictably downheartedly.

The next day Howard Conquergood drove him to Couchiching directly after work and, driving Howard's car, Billy returned home at two-thirty in the morning. Vivian had only just retired when his key entered the lock.

He took her for a spin later that day and brought her up to date.

"Howard sees a future for me in politics, and he sees a grand future for this party." Billy said,

"CCF governs Saskatchewan. There are twenty-eight members in the House of Commons now. He's telling me this is the time for candidates to get involved. What do you think, Vivian?"

"I certainly stand with the party's values," she said. She was a keen admirer of the CCF premier in Saskatchewan, Tommy Douglas.

"I'm not in the least bit surprised that Howard wants to recruit you."

Howard Conquergood attended Queen's University, became a professional football player, a Grey Cup winner, married a Hollywood movie star, and now was heading the Canadian Congress of Labour's Department of Education and Welfare. His sheer size was both intimidating and persuasive.

"Howard told me of one time he spoke at a union meeting. He entered the room standing on his hands and walked down the aisle that way, wearing his hat on one foot before proceeding to speak to union members about the ins and outs of labor organizing and teaching young people solidarity," said Billy. "Obviously a two-hundred-and-fifty-pound lineman had no difficulty grabbing their attention and interest."

"I think he looks a bit like Walt Disney," Vivian said.

"Well, he certainly animated that meeting," Billy joked. They laughed.

"He wants me to think about running in the 1949 campaign, Vivian."

"Politics suits you," she told him. "You will be wonderful at it, and I'll do anything I can to help, but let's find our new place and pay our debts first.

"By the way, a Dr. Allen was at my office yesterday to insure his car and informed me he's known you for five years and just saw you at Couchiching. Turns out he is the financial secretary of the Ontario CCF. Is there anyone you don't know, Billy White?"

He gave her a lift to work, door-to-door service, rushed around to the passenger side with the engine running to assist her exit. When he kissed her goodbye, a couple passing on the sidewalk slowed for a double take.

Billy received an update about the apartment from Dorothy by phone the following Monday.

"It appears that you do not have to move September thirtieth – they say you can stay if you're prepared to pay almost double the rent for the place unfurnished as you're paying now furnished." She sighed. "I don't know whether to call it bigotry or piracy."

"It could be both," Billy said. "They hope we won't accept their offer. They must figure they can freeze me out using price rather than my race. Maybe they are afraid of court action, although there's no law against discrimination in this country. Listen, Dorothy. Vivian and I appreciate everything you've done. Don't for a minute think we blame you for this. We don't. You are a treasure."

She recited the number for the housing company, Wakunda, where the owner Miss Breithaupt ran the show, which he recorded on a scrap of paper destined for his wallet. He hung up the phone, groaning at the prospect of facing a housing search and moving again so soon. Then he put the matter out of his mind and did what he always did: put his faith in a lucky star.

It was that laissez-faire tendency of Billy's that spurred Vivian to visit Dominion Bank and open a personal account without telling him. Any mention of money, debt repayment and budgeting never went well with Billy. For all his charismatic niceness and imitable charms, he could be prickly to a fault.

She could broach finances another time, Vivian concluded, and they proceeded to have a hoot that night. She changed into slacks and a plaid shirt and Billy put on his moose jacket, and they laughed and carried on like clowns whooping it up until she upset a cup of tea all over the kitchen table and floor.

Tomorrow they'd be one month married. Wedding gifts and congratulatory letters continued to trickle in, each one politely acknowledged by Vivian with promptness.

Saturday was the annual Home Service picnic at High Park. Many guests were late arriving, so instead of starting at two under sunny skies the event began at six with a thunderstorm threatening. Still there was a good crowd, exuberant participation in the races, a long lineup for ice cream. But Vivian, who booked off from H.C. Powell's that afternoon to be on hand to help, realized she probably should have just gone home to sleep. She was dead on her feet.

A loud knock on the apartment door Sunday morning returned the issue of their evaporating sublet to the front burner. It was a Wakunda Housing agent with prospective tenants to whom he wished to show the apartment.

"Come back in fifteen minutes," a bleary Vivian instructed the agent through the barely open door. Hardly prepared, just out of bed, she flew around and cleared the place up in that interval and concentrated on waking up and getting dressed. The prospects revisited, surveyed the space and left. Their presence reawakened Vivian's undercurrent of anxiety. However, she buried her nerves. Why not try Billy's approach and trust that a solution would soon present itself?

She committed to enjoying the rest of the summer; long strolls around Rosedale, reading time on *their* rustic bench at the edge of the ravine, discovering Severn Street, and scaling the ramparts by the southern approaches of their Elm Avenue building. They also trekked by Rosedale Valley Road and instead of going the long way around by the steps on the south side, she and Billy climbed the steep hill on the north and vaulted the bridge out onto Huntley Street.

They both enjoyed baking special treats that summer, Vivian perfecting blueberry muffins just like Aunt Doris used to make and Billy baked scrumptious peach pie with fruit he brought home from Normandale, near Camp Ryerson, one of his summer engagements. He loved making Vivian his cinnamon cartwheels too.

And music filled that apartment, a loan of the Home Service's record player in August. On one special night, they were listening to recorded music at midnight, augmented by the crickets outside, the living-room illumined only by the heat lightning, followed by a terrific thunderstorm all night.

There were also silly moments, when Vivian thought she bought a ham for dinner until Billy informed her it was lamb, and a moment of joy upon receiving their long-lost ration book from the King Edward Hotel in the mail. That's where they left it!

Camp Nagiwa in Severn Falls was a summer highlight. With Billy usually soloing on the camp circuit and Vivian spending those weekends alone, this time it was a trip for two by train, departing Friday, preceded by lunch in Union Station.

At camp Vivian caught up on hours of sleep, wrote cards to her mother, brother, brother-in-law George and Lillian while Billy worked. There was a concert and dancing the night of their arrival, and dancing again Saturday night, but not with Billy: he was at the keys playing the dance music.

Billy tried to show her how to handle a baseball and bat and ignored her claim of being hopelessly unsynchronized. The canoe was a different story. It was blissful to paddle again, her blade deftly cutting a watery path. A quick swim was equally reviving. They were in the company of kindly Reverend Parks of Sherbourne United Church in Toronto, who was presiding over the religious service at the camp chapel and would give them a ride home after lunch. That lunch was the first time Vivian had eaten with an appetite in a long time.

They were given a rousing Nagiwa farewell as they left in the motorboat for the mainland and their ride home with the minister.

On one of her weekends alone Vivian attended an evening service at Reverend Parks' Sherbourne Church.

They spoke afterwards.

"You should have been here this morning, Vivian," Parks smiled. "My whole sermon was made up of Bill White's stories."

She relished relaying this latest compliment to Billy and laughed to herself imagining his inflated head rendering him airborne like a hot air balloon.

As her husband intended, more people were calling him "Bill" now. He wanted her to call him that in public. It sounded more professional.

She missed him terribly when he was gone. Time seemed so long.

One time in particular Billy went out to dinner at the home of some old acquaintances and Vivian guessed he had a good time. He didn't get home till quarter to two. She thought he should have told them he was married and included her in the invitation. Of course, she never said anything about it, and neither did he.

She wished she had more energy. Her cigarette smoking was supposed to give that lift. She wished she could be like Tommy, Billy's office manager, who played tennis and ping-pong in the evenings, instead of just collapsing as soon as permitted to do so.

Vivian's diary revealed her deep-seated desire to be all that Billy wanted her to be. "I prayed last night that God would give me the strength to do my daily tasks as I should, and I believe He has done so," she wrote.

She got a bang-up dinner ready, screened the kitchen window with mosquito netting, mended Billy's leather suspenders and ironed. Although she didn't feel good, she at least had the satisfaction in knowing she'd accomplished those tasks and to Billy's satisfaction, she hoped.

They were finding their way, their love underpinning the pushes and pulls, ups and downs of intimacy.

Sometimes what she considered innocent comments or questions he considered badgering. She had a certain tone of voice that could rankle, and bluntly honest remarks that cut – unaccustomed to criticism as he was. Couldn't she see he was working day and night to be a provider, to pay off Campbell Finance and clear their other debts? He didn't need to be reminded.

He assured Vivian he was "on the beam, on the ball and on the nose."

As they grew into each other the impasses dissolved, best amplified on the Saturday he had to be at Trinity Park at six-thirty. With one look she could see he was overtired, so she sent him for a nap and made tea and cheese sandwiches for him while he rested. Awake again, he went out. She had dinner ready when he returned.

"So good," he said of the dinner. "The rest and lunch did me a lot of good too and made me feel like a million dollars. Thank you, my darling *chérie*."

For the second time in two days, she was moved to tears, this time tears of happiness at the realization that she had done the right thing for once.

He pressed his suit. She packed his suitcase for his weekend in Severn Falls. The poem he brought home from there was about how he missed her.

Where had the summer gone?

Vivian started a new assignment, a happy office at Monahan Sales, 191 Queen Street East, as September beckoned. On her second day she asked a colleague, Marjorie, to recommend a doctor: she'd had awful pains almost constantly all week.

Almost before she knew what was happening, Marjorie had an appointment arranged five days hence with her own doctor, Dr. O'Leary, in the Medical Arts Building.

"He's grand. You'll see, Vivian."

The bespectacled, diminutive Dr. O'Leary performed a routine examination, elicited her medical history, and invited her to talk about herself. He listened thoughtfully and without interruption as Vivian summarized her life since arriving in Toronto. So unlike Dr. Richardson, this doctor genuinely seemed to relate to her and care about her.

"Well, Miss Keeler, all your vital signs are normal. There is nothing wrong with you, actually. I recommend more sleep, exercise, food and diversions. Your body is crying for your attention. Frankly, I think you haven't recovered from the emotional strain which preceded your marriage. I guarantee you will feel better if you follow my advice."

She felt validated. This doctor wasn't branding her neurotic or suggesting she have her fallopian tubes tied. He was agreeing she'd been through the wringer and was feeling lingering effects. A healthier lifestyle was an easy pill to swallow.

September brought with it the special delights of the Canadian National Exhibition and two opportunities to follow doctor's orders. Vivian had the day off and Billy booked off the afternoon to meet her at Bathurst and Adelaide Streets and escort her for the first time through the monumental Princes' Gates archway onto the CNE grounds. There was plenty of walking. They started in the Electrical and Automotive Buildings, all the newest cars a wistful reminder to Billy of how much he missed his car, and how little he could afford a new one. When he had to scoot back to Home Service for a meeting, she made her way to the Coliseum, heard a male choir, and a talk and dissertation on "Charm" by Pasquale D'Angelo in the Women's Theatre before heading home on her own.

She and Billy revisited the exhibition three days later. Billy had his portrait sketched. Reaching home after midnight they amused themselves trying to draw each other.

He introduced her to a live baseball game at Davisville Park, Home Service vs. Mercury, which she found exciting despite not knowing the rules.

Dr. O'Leary said exercise? Vivian was getting plenty of it in the carriage of daily errands. Household management entailed weightlifting and marathons. For example, lugging heavy laundry to Spick & Span Laundromat one day, only to discover that they don't do customer laundry anymore despite their sign, and hauling dry cleaning to the Rosedale Hand Laundry on Church Street to find it closed, tested her mettle and muscles especially when she had to carry the whole load home again. She splurged six cents on a Coke at the drugstore to relax and recover before the trek back.

There was never a day when she wasn't burdened with packages. One Saturday in particular, she could hardly carry her grocery load plus Billy's shoes, which weren't accepted for repair. A man in a red truck gave her a lift to Elm and Sherbourne, then just as her paper shopping bag began to tear and tomatoes to splatter her skirt as they hit the sidewalk, a young chap in a battered coupe picked her up and drove her right to the door. Thirty minutes later she set out again, for Eaton's, and returned with another heavy load, having decided to buy a set of dishes.

Fresh air, more activity, she hadn't abandoned late nights and all-nighters quite yet. She threw herself into entertaining and welcoming visitors while they still had the apartment. Tommy and Nelson Abraham, a visiting Indian scholar from Pakistan on a work-study exchange program who had quickly become a good friend, Shirley and Paul, friends who had just moved into Sixteen Elm, Ken Whitby, also a neighbor, Mr. Clarence Johnston, the Financial Secretary at Cornwallis Church visiting from Nova Scotia, and his son Noel, were beneficiaries of one of her best parties as hostess.

"You have a wonderful wife," Nelson told Billy.

That was the night Vivian inaugurated her new mop for cleaning the floor when the guests were gone. She and Billy got gut-splitting silly with antics and carried on till four-thirty a.m. Never had she seen him laugh so much and it was wonderful.

The next day Billy paid off the Campbell Finance debt. In another month they could start repaying Mrs. Christian at a rate of fifteen dollars a month. They were turning a corner, but one never knows what's around the next one.

For Billy there was troubling news. Mrs. Miller called to say that Portia had been trying to reach him from Moncton. He phoned her and learned that their mother was in hospital in Halifax with bronchial pneumonia, further complicated by her heart condition.

"She has been in an oxygen tent for four days and is not responding to treatment and the doctors do not hold any hope," Portia relayed with concern. "I flew in from New York this morning and I'll be flying to Halifax this afternoon."

Vivian didn't know how they would manage it, but Billy had to go home.

Chapter 26

H e would leave for Halifax to his mother's bedside the following day, a Friday, a morning that began with Billy and Vivian sleeping through two alarm clocks and not waking until nine. She phoned work to say she'd be in at one. He went to Home Service, and they gave him his check for the month two weeks early so he could afford the trip, a one-way plane ticket there and a train ticket back.

He came to meet her after work so they could go home together. They had dinner around seven-thirty, and she could see he was worried. There was a chance his late-night flight would be too late by the sounds of it.

On a corner table in the living room, Vivian had vases positioned and filled with flowers which had been discarded from St. Paul's Church a few days earlier when she rescued them. They wrote a special prayer for his mom and had a beautiful communion service.

She traveled down to the bus depot with Billy. "I'll call you from the airport," he promised.

"I'll miss you," she said.

While he was gone, she visited Household Finance and squared that account. Subsequently she went for her delayed trip to Eaton's second floor to open a new charge account. She was proud of her successes that day.

She was anxious for word from Billy and, guided by advice from Mrs. Christian and Doug, she phoned the telegraph office to check with CN.

A telegram from Billy had come through saying Izie's condition had been upgraded.

Two days later Billy phoned to report that the doctors said his mother's improvement was a miracle. He was anxious to get home but would stay one more day. Vivian agreed with that decision although she ached for his presence.

Out of loneliness she attended a Mary and Martha Society Christian volunteer group meeting at College Street Church, which turned out to be boring. With him away she smoked more cigarettes than usual thanks to a supply from office colleagues. She would have been too proud to ask, but they offered them as freely as mints. In Billy's absence she went to work breakfastless, something he would dissuade. Dr. O'Leary would cringe if he knew her first meal of the day was dictation and a cigarette from her boss.

She chose her red suit and white sweater to wear for meeting Billy at Union Station. There was an unrecognizable dark man disembarking and he wasn't a porter. It was Billy with a haircut! He looked so different she hardly recognized him for a split second and then embraced him exuberantly as his handsome new look sunk in.

He pushed a box of Moirs and a pair of stockings into her hands and produced from his pocket a lipstick from George.

"You like my hair?" he asked, seeking affirmation. She assured him she did and wasn't the least bit flapped when he said, "Lois cut it."

He saw so many people they both knew in Halifax and of course Lois was one of the many. Despite her status as a former girlfriend, she was first and foremost a family friend. Vivian completely accepted that.

She was so excited to have Billy home she couldn't eat the meal she had prepared for them and was more than happy just to listen to his recap and share her own.

"I saw Harold at the Montreal train station during a brief stopover and phoned Helen from there," Billy began. "They send their love. George is manager of Fader's now, and there was a case of race discrimination at the Sword & Anchor which he took up with the mayor. You know George: he's dogged when he sets out to do something. He's convinced he can be the squeaky wheel that gets the problem fixed. By problem, he means the white people who allege we don't belong or can't come in."

He rattled off a lengthy string of other familiar names and gave updates including a detailed account of his youngest brother Lorne's trip to England.

Then it was Vivian's turn.

"I phoned Mrs. Miller with the good news about your mom. Tommy called and I told her too. Then I phoned Mrs. Christian. They're leaving for Vancouver tomorrow night. She's invited us there for late afternoon, for Doug's birthday before they leave. We can't stay long, mind you. We have the Camp Nagiwa reunion corn roast at George and Isabel Smith's in Thorncrest. Ed and Molly Christie are picking us up, and before we head to the Smiths we have to collect Peggy and Peter Schwartzkopf at St. George Street."

Vivian talked a mile a minute.

"Oh, also I spoke to your Aunt Wil, who sounds like quite the character over the telephone. She'd like us to visit," Vivian related,

"Did I tell you she's not my aunt? She was in love with my father before he married Mom. She told all us kids to call her "Auntie Wil" as she had come close to being our mother. She's quite the character, alright. Gee, you're going to get a kick out of her."

"Speaking of 'kick,' I had to buy new shoes, an absolute necessity. They cost me eleven dollars," she groused, then paused. "I missed you so much," she said and melted in his direction.

They were awake till four a.m. and slept through both alarms the next morning.

The Smith's corn roast was lots of fun, a blend of people who seemed like old friends and many new ones being introduced. A feast of corn, a feast of singing together under the stars in the expansive backyard of the couple's beautiful, ultra-modern home could not have been more picture perfect, right down to the toasted marshmallows and coffee.

One week to go until month's end but Billy seemed quite unconcerned about finding a place to live. He had tracked down company agent Mr. Hansen and made an appointment for them to go see him at Wakunda House at Bloor and Sherbourne after work.

He met them in paint-splattered coveralls in the front office, smelling vaguely of turpentine and rum, and seemed truly compassionate to their plight although he said his hands were tied.

"I'm sorry. I can't do anything until Miss Breithaupt returns and I can't say when that will be. She was supposed to be back on the seventeenth."

Vivian tried not to project panic.

"What if she doesn't come before the end of the month? What will become of us? Surely to goodness you're not going to throw us out on the street."

Billy intervened with calm words as if effecting hypnotic suggestion.

"I have every confidence given our circumstances that you will secure us appropriate lodging, Mr. Hansen. We leave it with you, sir, and thank you very much." The two men shook hands.

The way Billy strutted out of that rental office one would think they'd just signed a lease. Vivian wasn't convinced Wakunda would come through. Miss Breithaupt had come across as decidedly hostile toward their tenancy.

"You should start calling some places, maybe call a few on your lunch hour today," she suggested to Billy.

"I don't want people at the office to know my business," he sniffed. "I won't phone during the day, but tonight I will, after dinner and before my meeting."

True to his word, he did, consulting the advertisements and calling the prospects. All were taken. They now had five days to find an apartment. An evening concert featuring the Leslie Bell Singers at the Prom with their neighbor Ken interrupted the pressure of house hunting. Ken chose the occasion to tell them he was reporting for duty in two weeks in the Royal Canadian Air Force.

"This is my greatest accomplishment since the Globe and Mail made me their very first paper delivery boy in my good, old hometown of Niagara Falls," he joked.

The next morning Billy did not have to go to work and Vivian was late to hers. It was her payday, but there was no joy of enrichment, with debt and expenses on her mind. Finding lodging warranted all the time she could spare. Buckling down at home after stopping for groceries she phoned the numbers she had jotted down from the papers she'd perused at noon. They went to see one place: $12.50 weekly plus one half of light and telephone bills for a bedroom and kitchen in the extreme east end of town, tastelessly furnished.

Billy was okay with it. She was having none of it. "It's atrocious and is more than we can afford to pay right now."

He was quite annoyed with her fussiness and went back to work into the wee hours.

One-half day of working on Saturday, then they devoted the entire afternoon to home-hunting. After many unsuccessful viewings the only possibility was on Havelock near Bloor and Dovercourt. They met Mrs. Selou, who was Jewish and very nice. She showed them a bedroom and kitchen, with a sink for fifteen dollars a week, but someone else had first right of refusal: she was waiting to hear back.

Feeling very optimistic about it for no good reason, they called off their search for the day. The deal didn't materialize. There were three days to go and counting, actually two because they couldn't hunt on Sunday.

All the possibilities Vivian contacted on her lunch hour Monday were already taken or to be rented to the first comers, with whom they couldn't compete. Tapped of leads an anxious Vivian prayed this would be their lucky day, September twenty-ninth.

Billy had to work until eight. They ate late and then packed. The mood was completely spoiled by something Vivian found in an old coat of his. As she folded or hung their coats and sweaters, she systematically inspected each pocket, an acquired laundering habit. Her fingers locked on something tiny and hard in the left pocket of a rarely worn winter walking coat of his.

"What's this?" She pulled out the item for a closer look. It was a ring, a gold ring, his old wedding ring. He had saved it. Why?

"It's my old ring. It's nothing." He dismissed her.

"Well, it must be something if you've saved it all this time," she countered.

"We promised Mr. Gowans we would never speak of her," Billy was quick to play the card and knew his wife would never break a promise.

Vivian seethed inwardly at the caginess of it all.

"We're broke and you have gold in your pocket you could have hawked?

"I forgot about it, for Pete's sake. I'll sell it if that's what you want."

The truth about the ring was that he had given it to Joan at one point when she needed money, but she returned it to him and in the pocket it stayed. He didn't want to talk about Joan either.

Needless to say, they were both miserable working through the night until four in the morning, getting ready to move to who knew where?

The answer lay with Mr. Hansen. Billy could hardly wait to phone Vivian at her office after a call from Dorothy.

"Hansen told her he would put us up for a couple of weeks until we find a place. I'm going to see the place now at 338 Bloor East one block from Mount Pleasant Road. He's meeting me there."

It was a bed-sitting room and kitchen one floor above ground. Once Billy got there, Mr. Hansen told him they could stay longer than a fortnight and that he would pull a few strings to make it happen.

"Actually, the place is not supposed to be rented except as a studio so on the Wakunda records you're a *musician*. You can stay here as long as you wish as far as I'm concerned."

"What about Miss Breithaupt?"

"She can be difficult, but you let me worry about her."

They moved into their new place that night. Meanwhile, The Elm Avenue apartment was a complete madhouse. Dorothy was packing her things with the assistance of two new friends; the new tenants were moving in, and Mr. Hansen was in and out several times. Vivian had a violent headache and was sick to her stomach for the first time in years.

Mr. Hansen turned out to be a champ, loaned them a blanket for their first night there and stopped by the next day to see how they were doing in their new second-floor abode.

Now they could start organizing their new space and socializing again.

They went to the Prom with Ken to see ten-year-old prodigy Patsy Parr at the piano. They'd be saying goodbye to Ken, who was leaving for the air force in eight days.

"I'll be back in Toronto in a couple of weeks. Why don't we tentatively plan to go to the Prom Ball?" he suggested.

Vivian longed to go. Knowing she couldn't afford the new dress, the must-have stockings in the new darker shade, and having her hair done she guessed it was out of the question. Besides, Billy was ambivalent, saying a "yes, yes" that sounded like a "maybe."

He reminded her of the upcoming party in a couple of weeks for the young married couples of College Street Church, sponsored by her Mary-Martha group.

One way or another she was going to get her evening of dancing, he said.

Their place on Bloor was beginning to look like home, although there was no phone, no refrigerator, and no stove, instead a hot plate and pressure cooker. They parked books in the bookcase, devised a record cabinet and put all the LPs inside with a lamp and magazines on top.

Ten days after moving in they went over to see Mr. Hansen to settle accounts.

"I'm busy for another twenty minutes or so," Hansen said. "Why don't I take you down to the book shop? You can amuse yourselves till I finish what I'm doing."

Besides his role with Wakunda, where he lived in a unit near them, Mr. Hansen was the proprietor of the used books and antiquities shop in the basement leased from the company.

Being bibliophiles, they delighted in passing time, poking around the shelves and stacks. Billy wanted to purchase the set of Shakespeare's works he found. When Mr. Hansen came, it was added to the ledger. He went to a specific shelf, ran his finger along the spines aligned in the row until he came to a red-covered book. "Aha!"

"Here, Mrs. White, a gift from me." He handed her the book, an 1880 edition of *A Christmas Carol*. "God bless us everyone." She thanked him warmly, still adjusting to hearing the name Mrs. White. "You want to put a piano in your studio, that's fine by me too," he said.

He gestured to furniture crowding the back of the store and offered them a chest of drawers and a round mahogany table.

"I want you two to be comfortable. If Mr. White will fix up the kitchen with shelves and cabinets, I will hunt around for a larger sink to install."

He then invited them down to the basement of 346 Bloor. He had another chest of drawers for them. It needed a wash but would clean up nicely. Vivian was more than happy to scrub it down.

"You can have anything you want," Mr. Hansen said with a sweeping hand gesture.

She explored and found several useful items, including some material for kitchen shelves. Billy wasted no time constructing them. At four in the morning Vivian awoke to find the project finished, complete with their new dishes and supplies organized atop.

Day by day, piece by piece – Mrs. Christian offered them furniture too – bit by bit, they made the best of what they had while living on a shoestring. Billy ably undertook chores, repairs and showed exceptional zeal for waxing floors. They had so little, but it felt like a lot.

Vivian waxed philosophical in her diary.

"I suppose someday we will look back and laugh at the time when we made toast over the hot plate holding it speared on a paring knife, and when we had so little cutlery, we had to wash it all several times during a meal. And now Billy has decided to give up our last luxury – cigarettes."

They had much to be thankful for this Thanksgiving. They were married, moved, and managing, making good friends everywhere.

Oscar and Leona Brewton came to call and took them to their house where the doctor and Billy practised their next performance piece. From there it was "the meal of our dreams" at the Golden Dragon in Chinatown where an involved discussion of heredity and environment ensued, Vivian absorbing opinions in a new way.

She suspected she was pregnant.

Another in a string of ridiculously late nights, this one landed them in bed at two-thirty in the morning. Fatigue was still an issue for them. As much as Billy touted his theory that one can never catch up on sleep, he napped to sustain his schedule of hours that worked him every night in October except the twenty-ninth, and late into the evening.

Vivian was fatigued half the time, tired-looking enough that Billy excused her from going bowling with him several times.

Bowling night conflicted with the married couples' dance party at College Street Church, and they'd never really settled on going. Vivian had a black dress she could lengthen so it would not look too indiscreet in view of current style trends. While she altered, he went and bowled with the

Queen Street Church crowd. They would meet at the party. Sounded like a plan, but when Vivian arrived Billy was already there. He had been roped into every imaginable task: playing the piano for the square dances, judging games and generally assisting in a lively and engaging manner. Vivian hugged the sidelines all evening in the company of the pregnant Mrs. Foster and the pastor's wife.

The only time she and Billy were together was at the table for dinner afterwards.

"Why didn't you tell me you planned to be occupied all night?" she inquired as he was taking his first bite, and he was instantly rankled.

"Please Vivian, let me have an hour's respite at least." So she didn't say another word to him until they got home.

They had a real old-fashioned quarrel: tears, accusations, protestations, and later, when they found they couldn't sleep, the reconciliation.

Vivian had a gift for forgiving. During low points she would remind herself of the good times. She worked on herself too, reflecting on how to better herself and learn from her mistakes. There was nothing superficial about Vivian. She was a deep deliberator and a careful planner.

On budgeting, wouldn't she relish that role? Their Eaton's debt – still a meteoric $100 even after the sixty-dollar post-dated check Billy took there the other day. Wednesday, the day after their fight, she had only fifteen cents for lunch. Her workmate Eleanor lent her an unsolicited seven cents for a coffee.

For all their bickering and differences, she could not fathom a world without Bill White. Fun, fascinating, handy – he fixed the broken toaster she'd scavenged from Mr. Hansen's and restored it to like-new condition – brilliantly intelligent and talented, he had opened a whole new world to her in so many ways and opened her heart wider than she knew it could be. Her love for him was infinite.

She finally got her dances with Billy, two of them, at the open house at Home Service on Friday night, which made her long all the more to be going to the Prom Ball the next Monday, but he just didn't want to go and that was that.

On the day of the Prom event, Billy had the morning off. She came home to find the place immaculate and a poem on the kitchen table about his cleaning achievements, ending with the statement that he didn't want thanks, just a smile. When he came home, she didn't say anything, she just looked at him with her broadest grin.

"We're crazy but it's fun," she told her diary that night.

When a couple can't laugh together, it's over. Billy and Vivian were broke, mostly exhausted and sometimes hungry and cranky, but at least they had humor, and now maybe an extra reason to be happy: a baby on the way. Billy was certain of it when he woke up with a toothache.

"That's a sure sign you're pregnant," he pronounced.

"Sounds cockeyed to me," she said.

"Tell that to my tooth," he smiled and pointed to a left molar.

So-called old wives' tales were embedded in Nova Scotia culture, legends and folklore. Some people swore by them.

October's winding down brought a surprise visit from his sister Mildred, stopping over en route to Buffalo from Halifax. The entire month had been decorated with memorable moments: with Billy on Thanksgiving Day, after their delicious dinner – he was "chef du chicken" and she made the cranberry sauce – they walked down Sherbourne and Church and up Yonge, looking in all the windows, both homes and stores; visiting Tommy after canceling once during their chaotic house-hunting period; a party at the LeBourdais residence; a nice evening at the Beresford Avenue home of Irene and Harvey Halbut, a Halifax crowd that included Les Vipond and his wife, Helen; a Nagiwa Reunion at Sherbourne Church, a Pops Concert and Halloween dance at Wakunda Center, both on the same night.

Mrs. Christian on her way home stopped by for a rare visit one day. Billy out as usual, she and Vivian chattered sixteen to the dozen. It was only the third time Vivian had seen Cleo in the almost four months since the wedding, compared to the previous November to June when they spoke practically daily.

"I tell you, child, I was so mad at Billy on Sunday," his former landlady chirped.

"Why, what did he do?" Vivian asked, surprised.

"Oh, he wastes so much of his time. He should be here giving more of his attention and consideration to you. Not that I'm interfering, you understand." Cleo looked down studiously to inspect her fingernails having said her piece.

"I assure you, Mrs. Christian, I don't feel neglected at all."

About that conversation, Vivian confided to her diary that night: "I would say this anyway whether true or not, but I think it is true – am not going to probe too deeply as I know I have a tendency to feel sorry for myself with very little cause sometimes."

Ball players on the steps of Home Service Association, Bathurst Street

Chapter 27

Was a baby on the way? Billy tossed around the thought excitedly. One thing obvious about Bill White was that he loved kids, delighted in their open-eyed looks of new discovery and wonder, as their learning expanded with his input. He was a born teacher, coach, and leader, who encountered few discipline problems with his youngsters due to the firmness of his voice and determined instruction, and the promise of fun and rewards for their attention.

It tickled him to see children transfixed as they leaned-in to hear one of his many stories, especially his ghost stories which were always punctuated with a startling ending that made them jump, yelp and titter after being spooked.

He derived great pleasure from seeing them respond to musical activities and the benefit they got from learning songs and singing them, sometimes with actions, or sitting behind a full-sized drum kit and banging the tubs or learning how to play the ukulele or harmonica.

Billy's Woodsworth House vocal quartet rehearsed at Home Service with a makeshift band consisting of piano, drums, guitar and Dr. Brewton on saxophone. With the kids, he paralleled the example of a four-piece band to the concepts of cooperation and community, illustrating to them that distinct and different instruments working in harmony were essential to the success of the orchestra as they are in life.

He'd been waiting a long time for a family. He viewed the pending arrival of a little White as a testament to the beauty of interracial relations.

During a five-minute break between meetings, the ringing bell of his office phone jolted him from his ponderings on fatherhood. No surprise, it was Vivian.

"I was just thinking about you, *chérie*. How is your day?"

"I'm about to finish typing my fifth of twelve copies of a comparative price chart," she said dryly, and then on a more upbeat note. "Did you mention something about going to the Christians on Sunday?"

Billy assured her that plan was still in play. They were invited to meet a special friend of Cleo and Curley's.

"Don't mention anything about my maternity, agreed? I want it to be confirmed by the doctor before it's announced."

"Mum's the word," he punned.

"Seriously, Billy."

"Not a word," he clarified. "I promise. It's your news to tell when the time is right."

They went there after church on Sunday. As expected, the Christians doled out warm, rich, and abundant hospitality, concluding with a lunch like times of old.

Billy and Vivian fused an instant connection with the special guest Umilta McShine, in 1936 the first locally appointed principal of the esteemed Tranquility Girls' School in Trinidad, here to study music and other subjects at the University of Toronto. Her native island was steeped in reverence for the historic McShine family, whose contributions included education, the medical arts, and the founding of a bank.

Her musicianship was unbeatable, Curley said. His comment fired up a friendly duel between Billy and Umilta as they took turns trying to one-up the other at the piano. She was a large woman in charm and size, with chocolate skin, and laughing eyes.

"Next time we shall do battle on the steel drum," she laughed confidently since she was an accomplished composer on the instrument.

"They're opening the new veterans' hospital to the public for the first time on Tuesday, November eleventh. It's touted to be the largest in Canada, possibly in the world, when fully built." Curley announced. "You must come, Umilta, Billy and Vivian, it will be historic."

Vivian flashed a pout.

"I can't join you, unfortunately. Remembrance Day isn't a holiday for me. I'll look forward to hearing all about it though."

The plan laid, Umilta bade them a good day and left.

Continuing with the Christians, Billy played checkers and chess with Curley. Cleo spent the evening making drapes for Vivian, being unable to stand idle while the girl muddled through with them herself. Vivian concentrated on hemming a tablecloth and made out alright. At midnight they all ate again, and talked volumes, another 4 a.m. night for the visitors.

November eighth marked a year since her life-changing train ride from Halifax. Vivian and Billy marked it with a dinner at the Golden Dragon, compensating Vivian somewhat for missing the Remembrance Day outing.

In some ways November made her forget her possible pregnancy. Stimuli abounded; the Athletic Club Dance at Belvin Hall on College Street was among them.

The place jumped and swung to the tunes of Cy McLean's Orchestra. Canada's only all-black, full-scale orchestra was governed by the baton of Cy McLean, a Sydney, Nova Scotia transplant living in Toronto. A child prodigy schooled at Hamburg Conservatory studying the Russian classics in 1933 when he was seventeen, he was the first of his race to be invited to join the Canadian Musicians Union. Rhythm Rompers, his amazing dance band, fresh from their gig at the Colonial Tavern, had just shattered the age-old edict against black musicians playing the Yonge Street clubs, Toronto's heart of live music.

Vivian chummed around with Tommy most of the evening as Billy flitted and hobnobbed, part of his job assignment that evening. As she had predicted, she didn't get to dance with him till eleven-thirty. Shortly afterwards, a buzz traveled the room and there was a parting of the seas when the cast of *Anna Lucasta* dropped by after their show. The play at the Royal Alex starred an all-black cast and had attracted considerable attention for that reason, as well as for its artistic merit. The crowd opened the way for the party to move through to meet and greet. Here they were in the flesh and being introduced to Vivian personally. Feeling like a celebrity, she danced with the two leading men, Sydney Poitier, who played Lester, and Ralf Coleman who played Eddie. The latter was an especially nice dancer, to the tune of "Sentimental Journey."

She felt like a star. When she had children, she would keep the story fresh by retelling it to them. Their mother had danced with Sidney Poitier, a moment that confirmed for her that she was in the right place at the right time.

Exactly mid-month and synced with the first snow of the season, going to the Santa Claus Parade with Billy presented a feast for the eyes and ears. There they soaked in the color with a sea of people, young and old, enchanted by the fairy tale floats, marching bands, madcap clowns and larger-than-life mascots, courtesy of Timothy Eaton Company.

Free tickets were an occasional perquisite of Billy's job. In this case, a pair to a matinee of *Anna Lucasta* at the Royal Alex. By complete fluke their tickets in the twelve hundred-seat theatre positioned Billy and Vivian directly behind the Christians and Umilta.

"Mr. Coleman invited us backstage," Billy informed them as the house lights came up after the curtain call.

"And then you will all come as my guests to Diana's," insisted Umilta, referring to the popular eatery on Bloor Street near Avenue Road.

These diversions were as welcome as punctuation marks in a run-on sentence, which is what Billy's average week could resemble, a collection of projects and obligations that ran him like a wind-up doll.

Vivian seldom accompanied him now. She welcomed the solo time away from Billy so she could work on learning to knit him a sweater, a surprise for Christmas. The wool, needles and instruction book she purchased were hidden for use at opportune times.

In passing she had said to him, "I wish I could knit," never imagining he'd go acquire his own wool, needles and a knitting book offering to give her a first lesson. "I learned how when teaching, and my pupils really wanted to learn," he said as he demonstrated the stitches to all ten of her thumbs.

There was no getting ahead of that husband of hers.

Santa's parade and the knitting project put Christmas very much top of mind for Vivian. "How about spending it with Harold and Helen?" she suggested to Billy.

"Harold says the idea of spending Christmas without us, after missing us last year, is like 'looking forward to a trip up the river to Sing Sing,'" Vivian read from their friends' newsy letter. "Look at all the funny diagrams and sketches Harold made." She put the enclosures under Billy's nose. Surely, they would arouse some enthusiasm in him, Vivian thought.

His silence said, *not now.* He was thinking: What did she want from him, debts diminished or, with money so tight, a trip to Montreal they couldn't afford?

It wasn't until late that night that he finally commented. His emphasis was on asking her what she wanted to do.

"I want to go." Her statement was emphatic and matter of fact.

"All right," he said cautiously, his terms at the ready. "I'll not give any presents or send anything home and then we can afford to go."

The way he chose to answer rather siphoned the joy out of things. At least she had the answer she wanted. She'd already started her Christmas shopping.

December was designed for memorable moments. She and he were sure to derive their share.

Billy bounced back to his good-natured self. He brought her a rose the night of the Home Service social for students, pushing for her to join him. She begged off, not wanting to overdo it, plus she wanted to work on the sweater. So far, she did all of two rows, the first one took her fifty-five minutes and the second thirty.

Quality calendar moments punctuated the month. But two developments stood out above all others: Dr. O'Leary confirmed she was pregnant on December eleventh, and beyond her wildest dreams her mother sent her a letter, a normal letter, absent of vitriol, in response to Vivian's.

It arrived five days before Christmas, the day Vivian purchased train tickets to Montreal. Jean's letter tiptoed around anything contentious and concentrated on safe subjects. It alluded to Princess Elizabeth's recent marriage but not Vivian's.

"I suppose when Mother learns I'm going to have a baby she will disown me all over again," she predicted.

"Then don't tell her," Billy replied. "Leave that to Bernard," which is how Jean eventually found out.

Vivian viewed a week away with her husband and their best friends as just what the doctor ordered. She hoped Billy would relax and have a good time as well.

As newlyweds they were gradually acclimatizing to each other's moods and idiosyncrasies and learning to laugh at them on occasion. That's not to say it was easy.

One night as he was dressing for an engagement to sing a couple of solos at the West End Y, Vivian offered her offhand assessment.

"Getting a little carefree with your appearance, I see," she said. The remark crawled under his skin, and he reacted with considerable drama. He pressed his suit with great ostentation and insisted Vivian pick out his shirt and tie, and kept plucking at his knife-edge creases, awaiting her inspection. Not until they nearly reached Frank and Viola Simpson's for a post-perform-ance dinner did they break down and laugh about it.

That night they had to agree it's easier to laugh at foibles than to stew over them.

Christmas with the Kierans came in the nick of time, in Vivian's opin-ion. Vivian watched the true Billy emerge in the welcome change of scene and company.

By the time they arrived at the Kierans' house in Beaurepaire, a bucolic area of the West Island where a fledgling community was sprouting from former farm fields, Billy was back to his old self. For the next seven days they rollicked and romped, reminisced, and relaxed.

Vivian swore she'd never forget those sleeping arrangements. Harold, Helen, Billy and she slept on the studio couch.

The vacation bore all the festive markings. Wrapped presents, a decor-ated tree, the snow-washed landscape ideal for smooth sledding, and the music, hearty singing. To pass the time everyone took turns at the piano, ex-cept for Harold who was wedded to his clarinet. Harold and Billy hammed it up. Billy and Vivian recited funny poems they'd all written to each other.

There were visits from Harold's family – his parents, brothers Al and Dave, and their wives with young kids in tow on several occasions – a ton of fun.

At the children's insistence Billy talked like Bugs Bunny and did *Thue* for everyone, his narrative peppered with "s" words, a comic story about Sue, aged six, the girl with a "lithp" because she was missing her two front teeth.

One morning the bunch of them took the nieces and nephew out coasting. Again, they all nearly froze and had to stop at Johnny's grocery store on the way back and thaw out. Then the men insisted that their wives get on the sleds with the kids and pulled them home. Billy made up a crossword puzzle for Helen and Vivian to do while Harold slept. When he awoke, the men traded stories while the women had oatmeal facials.

"Billy says it's a boy," Vivian told Helen under the mask. "We have a name picked out already: Romney after Billy's older brother who died at ten."

"That's a lovely tribute and a unique name to keep alive," Helen said. "I'm happy for you, Viv."

It felt good to talk about expectancy and motherhood with her friend, who assured her from all she'd read that Vivian's nagging pains could no doubt be blamed on baby "Romney."

"We'll name our second one Laurie," Vivian said. "I think it's a beautiful girl's name. It's a salute to my wonderful great uncle Laurie Harlow. He died at Passchendaele, bless his beautiful soul."

As they rinsed and patted dry their reconditioned faces, Vivian felt her holiday rejuvenation was complete.

"Helen, thank you for the wonderful time. It's exactly what the doctor ordered."

The vacation unwound.

> Darling, je vous aime beaucoup,
> Je ne c'est pas what to do.
> Vous avez completely stolen my heart.
> Matin, midi et le soir.
> Toujours wond'ring how you are
> That's the way it's been right from the start.

Et, chérie, my love for you is très, très fort.
If my French were good enough
I'd tell you so much more.
Et j'espère que tu compris
All the little things you mean to me.
Darling, je vous aime beaucoup –
I do, I do love you.

From your husband Billy, December 31, 1947, written as
you slept on the train.

Quite a quantity of mail awaited Billy and Vivian upon their Toronto homecoming, including fruit cake from Billy's mother and stockings for Vivian from Aunt Gladys (the inevitable half size too large). From One Elm, a redirected Christmas card and a note from Miss Blackadar. It still struck Vivian with amazement that the missionary friend on her side of the family was the very woman to steer Billy's father to Canada and help open doors for him at university in Nova Scotia. Vivian owed her husband in part to this woman.

Full hearts, high hopes, empty pockets, empty pantry. New Year's Eve was all of that. One can of beans the only food left in the house, Billy traipsed the wider neighborhood for an open eatery and found fish and chips and bread. They snuck downstairs at two in the morning to get a closer view of Mr. Hansen in one of his towering rages causing uproar in the laneway. By day he was a completely different person, a mild-mannered moderate. He and alcohol were terrible friends. Good people will have flaws though. Vivian had seen first-hand proof in her own family, bigotry, the diminishing trait. Mr. Hansen didn't suffer from that.

January was as lean as the weather was mean. Their building's maintenance system failed to deliver reliable heat and hot water throughout the winter – an understatement. At minus twelve outside, no heat inside and cold-water bathing only, their neighbor alerted the Health Department. The nascent thrill of pending motherhood couldn't be suppressed in Vivian, not even by these less-than-ideal living conditions.

She was eager to share news of her maternity with her adopted families: the Christians and the Campbells. She told them separately two days apart, anticipating much joy and enthusiasm after she disclosed the blessed event. Not to be.

"So soon? Goodness gracious, how will you manage? This is so sudden. You've only been married six months." Aunt Betty sounded more sympathetic than glad.

The Christians greeted the news as a calamity: "Whatever will you do for money, Vivian? Raising a child is terribly difficult when you can't afford it. You have our blessings, of course, but I worry about the timing. I don't think the two of you are ready," Cleo said pointedly, with Curley nodding.

"I don't have any choice in the matter. We'll make the best of this. You'll see."

Vivian was not to be daunted. This was a generally accepted fact among all who knew her.

When she told her boss Mr. Burn about the baby, she was met with a contrast. His congratulations and assurances nearly took her breath away.

"The financial angle will work out okay," he said. "It always does."

*Young Portia White, circa 1930, at home in
Halifax*

Chapter 28

L ess than two months later, Billy was enlisted to seek out and confront discriminatory practices at a local club that had been reported to the race relations committee of the FoR, the Fellowship of Reconciliation, a non-sectarian pacifist group aligned with CCF's push for a universal bill of rights.

Only too willing, Billy and a team – Roy Clifton, Lloyd Sawyer, Betty Bradley and two other girls – went to Player's Society Hall on the southeast corner of Broadview and Danforth Avenues. All the big bands played there including Guy Lombardo. If the rumor held true, they had their evidence. If false, they'd get to take in a good show.

They proceeded to the lobby ticket wicket. "Here for the dance, six of us." Roy plunked down the admission fee pretending not to have seen the sign they all passed at the door.

The dark-browed attendant sized them up from behind the cage. "You, you, you, and you ...", he pointed to the whites in the group, "yes."

"You," he pointed to Billy, "no."

"Read the sign," he droned unapologetically. "No Jews. No Negroes. No Orientals. No Indians. Not allowed on the premises."

"We want to speak to the manager," Roy said.

"I am the manager," the man sniffed. "I don't allow any of them here."

He directed his remarks to Roy as if Billy wasn't standing there. Not slighted, almost buoyed by the rejection, Billy spoke.

"It may interest you to know that we are part of an investigation into racial prejudice. We found what we came for and our business with you has concluded. You have given us far more than we expected in the way of evidence. You can expect to be reported."

They left satisfied with their fact-finding exposé. Vivian filed her husband's account as a diary item: "Billy went to the dance hall to confirm the FoR report. It was true and he wasn't admitted. The manager, who was a Jew, said he did not allow non-whites on the premises — the only time Billy has been kept out of any place.

FoR sponsored Billy to appear at York Memorial Collegiate the next morning where he led his largest four-part harmony group ever, eight hundred students.

The United Church of Canada also sought a follow-up piece from him for their program annual. He and Vivian worked on his essay "Interpretation of the Negro Spiritual" for three consecutive nights. Odd hours were still an everyday occurrence. Thank God for naps. One night he made hot cross buns while she slept for a couple of hours, and then woke her up for dictation to the smell of cinnamon and sugar. They managed.

Just before Easter Vivian's long-awaited and very-much-missed, cherry wood writing desk arrived by CN freight thanks to Bernard's handling. Now she could rattle off her considerable correspondence in comfort.

The desk had belonged to her Gram. Separately its contents and other items arrived from Jean: the return of *Color Blind*, a book Vivian lent her last summer, Vivian's 1941-45 diary, plus a box of chocolates, Pot of Gold, in Easter wrap, and a pair of Mohawk pillowcases.

The pillowcases mystified her. They were indeed badly needed for their home but represented a joint gift, not one just for Vivian alone. Was there even the remotest chance her mother would soon hold a grandchild in her arms? The resumption of two-way communication served up a sliver of hope.

The CCF convention entailed a pleasant but bouncy trip to Brantford, catching a ride with Harry Gilbert, who arrived in his car for Billy and Vivian at nine then picked up Eve, a Woodsworth House employee, and Al Watson of the FoR.

Chapter 28

After hearing CCF president Andy Brewin speak, Vivian knew she had found her political nesting zone. Vivian found inspiration in the party's vision of co-operation, racial equality and enhanced rights for workers and the poor. This was further reinforced by a speech from Ted Jolliffe, who was on the comeback trail for the CCF as the former opposition leader in Ontario.

Both she and Billy left the conference feeling part of something larger.

Certain situations were beyond her power to fix. Vyola Miller's suggestion that Billy curtail his outside work and put his efforts to Home Service exclusively was an attempt to corral and cage him, perish the thought!

The conversation with his boss bothered him. Vivian was downright indignant when he recounted the substance of the discussion.

"I told her about the CCF summer school. That's how it started," he began. "She launched into this speech about how I needed to focus and do more for the agency. She wants more programs, more this, more that. She feels my extracurricular activities are getting in the way of innovations. She doesn't want me doing any outside work, speaking, leading singsongs for young people's groups, YMCA, the camps ... I had to point out to her the number of hours I work for her for which I receive no remuneration, and she said, 'Welcome to the club.'"

Vivian was miffed.

"I'm no expert, dear, but I'm fairly certain she has no authority to dictate how you spend your free time. Your raise is coming due soon. Maybe you can have another conversation with her about it then. Your community work is important. Through it, you introduce people to the agency.

"Well, she also told me I shouldn't spend so much time away from home when my wife is pregnant."

"And another thing, commercial rent controls have been lifted. Home Service received notice to vacate the 556 Bathurst offices and will have to find a new building somewhere."

He saw from her confused expression that she was trying to make sense of it all.

"They terminated our lease so they can bring in a new tenant and charge more. We can't afford what they're asking," he elaborated.

Vivian had an empathy streak a mile wide. "That must be weighing on her mind," she said.

Billy's $100 raise came through in mid-April, adding three dollars to each paycheck, a pittance in Vivian's view but welcome, nonetheless. Vivian was working mornings-only now and was quitting work for good May fifteenth. Every extra dollar was crucial now.

Vivian had been emotionally fragile lately and Billy wasn't helping. Their misunderstandings drove her to crying jags where she was practically hysterical, raw emotion spouting to the surface, scenes always righting themselves eventually.

As she embarked on the remainder of her half-days, three girls from the Mary-Martha group showed up one afternoon with baby gifts. In her tender state she didn't trust herself to open and inspect the packages until her friends left. With no one watching she laughed and cried at the same time, being quite overcome by their generosity and thoughtfulness. They gave towels, facecloths, baby soap and powder, four pairs of booties, two jackets, two bonnets, two pairs of socks, three handmade nightgowns, one dozen diapers, two size-two shirts, a flannelette blanket and an adorable cuddly toy.

Billy's *Alumni News* arrived with lots of interesting items, including news of their own marriage and an item about Portia setting sail from Halifax July fifteenth for a two-month European tour.

Professor Klein at the University of Toronto asked Billy to substitute for him and give two lectures to the School of Social Work, news that thrilled Vivian, but Billy didn't seem to think was any big deal.

Money arrived in the form of a twenty-dollar money order from Jean suggesting her daughter buy a blouse or slip with it for her birthday. Vivian used part of it for a new lipstick.

On her birthday, her twenty-third, "Sunshine and showers and spells of indecisiveness, paralleling my temperament," is how she described the weather.

She successfully assembled an intimate dinner for them both: breaded lamb chops, whipped potatoes, mashed turnips, tiny peas, for dessert – lemon snow with custard sauce and whipped cream.

Chapter 28

Fate dealt her a nice surprise – hot water and heat in the radiators both at the same time, a rarity indeed, so she had a luxurious bath and a good night's sleep for a change.

On the last evening of April, she made a point of retiring early but couldn't sleep. Billy was out. Before going to bed, she had answered an ad for a four-room, self-contained apartment over a store in the St. Clair district, a larger apartment necessary with a baby on the way. Doing that last thing at night was a mistake. Head on the pillow, her mind raced and of course sleep eluded her.

Finally at midnight she got up and sat in the rocker. Fifteen minutes later Billy came home. Fifteen minutes after that a knock sounded on the door. A woman around Vivian's age, accompanied by two men, smiled at Billy as he greeted the unfamiliar threesome.

"Billy?" the woman guessed. "I'm Phyllis – Phyllis Frangooles, Vivian's pen pal. This is my husband Jimmy, and his cousin, Jimmy: me and two Jimmys" She laughed. "We were in the neighborhood."

"Come in, come in," Billy said as Vivian rushed to the door with an arms-open call of "Phyllis!"

They'd known each other since childhood and had continued correspondence into adulthood when Phyllis moved to the U.S. They married around the same time and now they were both pregnant. In her letters Vivian never mentioned Billy's race and was gratified that Phyllis and the two Jimmys accepted the situation as though it was completely normal.

"We were staying in Buffalo with my aunt and uncle and decided to drive up and see you since we were so close," Phyllis explained. "I know it's late. I took a risk."

"I'm so glad you did," Vivian said.

"Late is early around here," Billy chuckled.

The visitors stayed until two comparing notes on life in Canada and the U.S.: prices of food, cars, cigarettes, rentals, as well as laws, viewpoints and sensibilities.

Vivian and Billy continued talking until four. She bowed out of work the next morning and yawned her way into May. Tiredness was pretty much a constant. And she cried too much, usually out of lonesomeness when Billy was out or away for a weekend. It was then that all the worries and problems seemed to gang up on her, and she anguished over her muddling incompetence at not being able to solve them all.

Her new physician, Dr. Noonan, assured her that these emotions were perfectly normal in expectant mothers and in women generally, he said.

"We know women are prone to emotionalism. I'd be concerned if prolonged, but this sounds fleeting. You weigh 134 pounds. All your vitals are functioning well. I recommend you eat, exercise, and keep busy. Try a cup of warmed milk before bed to aid your sleep."

The warm milk didn't help the night Billy was expected to be back from the CCF weekend in Belleville by eleven-thirty. He didn't walk through the door until two in the morning.

"Where have you been? I've been worried sick," she confessed, relieved nothing horrible had happened to him.

Billy was pumped.

"Howard Conquergood took me to a late dinner at *Larry's* to talk about the summer school, then we talked in his car for quite a while. He's as convinced as am I that the CCF is going to break through in Ontario this election. He's quite adamant that I will be a candidate for the party federally next year. He thinks I can win."

She hadn't seen him this enthusiastic in some time. "What did you tell him?" she was eager to know.

"I said 'yes'!"

"No one of my race has run in a Canadian election before. Even if I stood no chance of winning, I believe my candidacy is important symbolically and I have a duty to oblige."

"We can do this, Vivian, you and I, together. I haven't a prayer if you're not in this with me."

Music to her ears those words. All her cares eased. There were always pivot points like this to set her mood right again, events to keep her busy like the doctor ordered.

Early in May she went to see the Toronto Negro Choral Society's presentation of *Pirates of Penzance*. Avril stole the show from the rainbow range of all-black talent on the stage. Avril had long wanted them to witness the magic of director Grace Trotman and her ensemble in action. Billy arrived late but Avril was still able to fulfil her long-held desire to get those two collaborating.

"Pleased to meet you, Mr. White," said the elegant and gracious Mrs. Trotman.

Avril, ever the wisecracker, jumped in with, "Heck, Grace. I've just brought you your next recruit."

The choir leader took her cue.

"We're doing *The Mikado* next year and Mr. White you are going to be in it."

"I'd be delighted," Billy responded without missing a beat. Again, Vivian didn't see where he'd find the time to give to another project.

She stuck to Dr. Noonan's prescription of keeping busy and eating as best she could. Her afternoons were free and mid-May seemed the perfect time to invite workmate Millie and neighbor Victoria Collins to supper with her and Billy, a farewell for Miss Collins who was packing, on her way to moving to a new place. The sweet and sour spareribs were steaming on a plate alongside a big bowl of rice when Portia dropped by.

"No, thank you, I'll not be able to stay for supper," she declined after her introduction to the guests. "Can you and Billy have dinner with me at Little Denmark tomorrow night? Carly Sullivan will be there."

"It's a date." Billy worshipped his older sister and was worried for her. She was in town for throat surgery. Her voice was at stake. Medical technicians at Toronto General would be incising her money-making instrument. That their work be flawless and fully restorative was imperative. Carly, one of Portia's many Toronto friends, wanted to be her care companion in recovery.

"It will be the last time we see you before you go into hospital," Billy said.

"Well," said Portia in her drawn out, musical way of speaking, smiling broadly, "at least it won't be the last time you see me. I'm going to be perfectly fine."

It wasn't the last time he would see his sister before the operation. She dropped by his office the next day with a check for one hundred dollars, about a third of what she owed him from way back when she was a struggling novice and as broke as a shattered sugar bowl.

Their dinner at Little Denmark, scheduled between Billy's afternoon and evening shifts at Home Service, put Vivian in the position of walking partway home alone. She walked with Carly and Portia to Yonge and College before separating from them when they boarded the southbound streetcar.

Dressed smartly in her white shorty coat she happily walked north on Yonge towards Bloor but grew more and more distressed on being the recipient of macho whistles, comments and catcalls that screamed disrespect and sunk her morale. She didn't know where a woman could go to talk about such harassment but was determined to ignore the unwelcome attention.

The girls at work asked her to have tea with them on her second to final day. "Surprise!" Marg Philpott and Adelaide McGivern carted in a bassinette filled to the brim with gifts from the whole office. "And this is for you!" Marg thrust a soft bundle toward Vivian. It was an embroidered blue satin bed jacket that she and Adelaide handmade. Quite remarkably, Vivian didn't cry.

Her final day, a Saturday, Mr. Burn wasn't in, but phoned to tell her he had enjoyed having her work for him, a compliment to end her working life. Very tired, she went home to lie down. Later, feeling better, she went with Billy to see Portia in the pavilion of Toronto General Hospital.

Stitches would come out in a week, and she'd be discharged on day eight. It was recommended she not talk. "Finally, I get the last word on my big sister," Billy cajoled. "Sorry it had to be this way, Portia. I know there's nothing you'd like better than to recover quickly and give me my 'what for' like you used to when we were kids."

She nodded and gestured for a pen and paper. Vivian obliged.

"Just wait!" Portia wrote in a mock threat.

Vivian was due in roughly three weeks. Now that Billy was sole breadwinner, discussions about money were unavoidable.

He had tried on a suit from the previous September, only to discover from its snug fit that she wasn't the only one gaining weight. He wanted to look sharp for the world brotherhood discussion he was leading at Dentonia Park United Church that night.

All Vivian did was suggest he have his suit altered rather than buy new and put his windfall from Portia into savings. He perceived it as three swipes in one: criticizing his money management, his sartorial suitability, and his weight gain, which was defensive and silly of him but led to nothing being settled. Having separate bank accounts, hers depleting, and no budget was not Vivian's idea of preparedness.

June first, eighty-five degrees, feeling like a beach ball, she was happy to receive a parcel from her mother containing two old, flannelette sheets for making diapers, and baby clothes, plus a pillow and perfect pillowslip with tatting done by Nana.

Jean's birthday on the horizon, Vivian made a note to wire her a dozen yellow roses on the ninth. Then she broke a piece of her tooth while eating one of the cookies she baked the previous day.

Their building was alive with activity related to the provincial election days away. With an election office located in another unit of their building, Vivian felt like an information kiosk redirecting people to the returning officer, Mr. Yeomans, and once signing on his behalf for the delivery of a registered letter.

On June seventh after all votes were tallied much to everyone's surprise the City of Toronto went CCF gaining eleven of the seventeen seats in Toronto and the Yorks.

The Progressive Conservatives were still in power, but with a much smaller majority and George Drew, the premier, was defeated in his own riding by CCF candidate Bill Temple.

Any thought that Billy would alter his patterns for fatherhood was pure notion. If before, his schedule was wall-to-wall it was about to run down the hall. The Saturday after election day his weekend plans caught Vivian unaware: he worked that morning, rushed home at noon to eat, washed up and dashed off to a Central Neighborhood House picnic at Linbrook Park in the Town of Whitby, then to a CCF party in Toronto to celebrate young Reid Scott's victory. She stayed home feeling disturbed because he was so late, and she didn't know his whereabouts. To his benefit she did quite a bit of mending while worrying. On Sunday he changed all their plans without telling her. She found out only after dragging herself out of bed in the morning and undergoing the usual long, painful process to get Billy up that he wasn't going to Dr. Perry's church after all. Oh, by the way, he'd be going out that afternoon and to Home Service that evening. Much to his annoyance she burst into tears and went out for a long walk.

Why couldn't she understand? A man has to be where a man has to be and do what he has to do if he's going to get ahead in the world. She and the baby were his overriding motivation now, his foremost concerns. His success would depend on the level of sacrifice she was willing to make, just as her happiness would be dependent on the sacrifices he was making in striving to provide for them.

A new place to live would give them a new leaf. Billy thought he had a good lead.

"Three unfinished rooms we could have for $27.50 a month – at Isabelle Lucas' home. We can go see them next Saturday."

As wonderful as it would be to live with Isabelle, the talented and confident melody maker who was blazing her way to establishing a stage career, after viewing the rooms they decided against it. They would have to spend more for furniture than the lower rent would save them. Besides, Vivian finally had the studio apartment arranged satisfactorily, and in three months there was a possibility of moving to Montreal where Billy had a job offer to do similar work at a community center there!

In the morning two days later – a show of blood on the sheet.

"She should stay quiet," Dr. Noonan instructed when Billy called from the home telephone, just installed last week.

Billy made her lunch and went to work. The pains kept coming though. Vivian managed to catch some sleep eventually.

"We're here to kidnap you. Billy sent us." At first Vivian thought the words came from a dream. She awakened at three o'clock to find Mrs. Christian and "Aunt Betty" standing at her bedside.

"You and Billy are staying with us tonight," Cleo said. "He'll come up after work."

The older women took charge, helped pack her bag and chauffeured her to Lansdowne. Umilta and a friend dropped by to visit. Billy brought home a nosegay of pansies for Vivian from Isabelle Lucas. Mrs. Christian had the guest room, Billy's old room, ready. Both Vivian and Billy were awake all night with her pregnancy pains and by four-thirty in the morning Mrs. Christian decided it was time to notify the doctor, who said they should shepherd his patient to hospital.

In a way Vivian felt cheated though. Billy could have stayed while Vivian's nurse prepped her, but he left with Mrs. Christian to grab at least a few hours of rest. Vivian was alone with her pains all morning. Up to the delivery room at noon, she gave birth to Romney at one o'clock on June twenty-second, a Tuesday. The ether knocked out all memory of the event but coming out of the fog Mrs. Christian was standing by Vivian's bed. Not Billy, he had a luncheon to attend. Tommy at Home Service took the phone call from Dr. Noonan: a healthy, eight-pound boy, William Romney White, mother and baby doing well. Billy got back to Home Service and was showered with choruses of congratulations.

A new mother stayed in hospital for ten days. Billy popped in for visits when he could, between his CCF meeting, choir practices and Home Service.

There were lovely surprises and sporadic visitors: Cleo and Betty with an anniversary card and a bouquet of peonies. Vivian figured she must be the only woman in the maternity ward marking her wedding anniversary the day after giving birth.

Visitors included Umilta, Millie, Avis McCurdy and daughter Jan, with roses, Miss Collins, Mrs. Gowans and others, never for long enough in Vivian's eyes.

Beautiful carnations arrived from her mother to mark Romney's birth. Along with her now- regular letters, another good sign that Jean might be seeing some light.

Home Service staff sent Vivian a sterling silver porringer.

The lush gift basket of cookies, fruit, crackers, nuts, and jams with a card from the Christians and Campbells said, "to the bravest person in the world from Curley, Cleo, Doug, Betty and Fred."

"What a tribute," Vivian thought, laughing at the exaggerated sentiment.

To the senders, though, this lily-white young woman was an egalitarian heroine.

Perhaps this was the level of admiration Billy wished to express in the carefully selected gifts he brought for Vivian five days into her hospital stay. Maybe the necklace and matching earrings were a belated anniversary present or a happy birthing day offering. In any event she didn't want them.

"We need the money so badly to pay the doctor and hospital bills, Billy.

Just to know that you thought of getting me a gift is enough. Please, please return it," she begged. "That can be your present to me."

He wouldn't hear of it. "I'm just going to refuse to agree," he said with a note of defiance.

She continued to prod, until finally she said, "Well, I don't like them anyway."

He was hurt, like the rejection of a first date, and left with jewel box in hand, resigned and unfulfilled, while she self-flagellated over her wretchedness, feeling so miserable about having hurt him. The next day he made a special third trip to the hospital to bring her ice cream to share with her roommate who'd just had twins.

"This act of thoughtfulness on Billy's part made me feel one hundred percent better both mentally and physically," she told her diary.

She was so glad to come home with Romney on July second. There was more to infant care than she'd read about in the *Canadian Mother & Child*, both physically and emotionally.

Billy was great with the baby and with her. He cooked, cleaned, laundered diapers and had his own resourceful way of responding when baby Romney didn't behave according to the rules – and their baby was a crier.

As Billy dove into his summer work schedule though, Vivian felt besieged and beleaguered despite home visits from Miss MacMillan, her assigned Victorian Order of Nurses (VON) nurse.

It was less than a month after coming home with Romney that the biggest break of their married life presented itself in the form of Avis McCurdy.

Freshly returned from the CCF summer school in Couchiching for a debriefing with Billy, Avis visited on the sweltering final day of July. She mentioned that she and Professor McCurdy had a basement apartment.

"Come for tea and see it on Sunday," she encouraged.

"Emancipation Day," Billy said, "I've got the A.M.E. Church radio program that night. We definitely have time to see the place. It may be an emancipation day for us too."

On August first they sealed the deal with the McCurdys for the basement: a large living room and two small rooms, fireplace, gas stove and phone for only thirty-five dollars a month.

Chapter 29

They moved into their storybook Forest Hill home near Bathurst and St. Clair on August ninth.

Their place, 239 Lonsmount Drive, rimmed by a knee-high picket fence, had the appearance and warmth of a grand cottage: an estate house of twenty rooms, one hundred windows, leaded-paned glass, a sunroom welcoming rays on three sides, ivy climbing the stuccoed wall of the entranceway, sprawling lawns stretching down to a virgin ravine, oak tree sentinels and robust gardens next to a vacant lot. It had been well-loved and cared for by the previous owners, the Bertrams, Avis explained as she and Jarvis helped move the couple in.

"We told the Bertrams we couldn't afford it on our salary of four thousand dollars a year and regretfully said 'no.' Later our real estate agent called to say they wanted us to make an offer, asked us to set our own price. Seven thousand was our absolute top limit. They accepted.

"The agent said they liked us – people with a large family starting their family life as they did in that house twenty-five years before. They also liked that we didn't spend the entire inspection time complaining about what was wrong with their beloved home."

Two years later Jarvis was able to purchase the vacant lot to the west, also from the Bertrams, with the eighteen hundred dollars he inherited from his father. The purchase fulfilled Reverend James F. McCurdy's dream that his son own the adjoining lot as well.

Billy noted that he and Jarvis were both sons of ministers.

"PKs – Preachers' Kids."

Such different landlords they were, Jarvis and Avis. They had refreshed the basement suite and promised more improvements to come, a new kitchen sink being the most immediate one and new wallpaper in a pattern of Vivian's choosing.

They had four children, Dorothy, Janet, in their teens, and David and Donald, boys adopted as infants in 1939 and 1940. In 1945 they fostered Amy Shimizu, a sixteen-year-old Japanese Canadian, upon her release from a BC internment camp.

Their home's ambience, sectioned into suites, was crazy with activity: a melting pot of characters and crusaders, who brought campaigns, critical thinking and culture to the home.

There were musical evenings – Alan Sangster and Ingham Sutcliffe sporting a fancy new stereo – attended by a hundred people every second Sunday. Square dancing in the dining room, bridge in the library, euchre in the sunroom every other Saturday night to raise funds for Joe Noseworthy's comeback campaign, local Joe, the first CCF member of parliament, a schoolteacher who gave up his pension to run.

Joining the McCurdy family was a friend of the Bertrams, Pat Shiels, a tidy, polite, Irish gentlemen, a retired Standard Life Assurance executive. The Pulley family, Madge, her machinist husband Brian and their baby, Christine, also lived in the house. Isabel and Jack Smaller occupied another unit. Needing shelter badly, Isabel learned about the McCurdys through Avis's CGIT friend. Husband Jack, ex-writer for the communist *Clarion*, was hiding and on the run, writing comics for money.

Wholly CCF, Avis intended to run as the party's candidate in Danforth-Beaches in 1949's federal contest. "We'll be running mates," she said enthusiastically to Billy.

One day, shortly after moving in, an unexpected guest wired Billy – Bernard! He would be arriving from Ottawa on the five o'clock train. His last writing to Vivian was that he would be working on an Ontario farm all summer.

"I fell in the barn, broke my wrist. I've been in hospital for eleven days," he told her on the phone after reaching Toronto. "Obviously they couldn't keep me on the job. So I came here."

Fate had handed her a two-week visit with her brother. It could have been longer had Jean not written and ordered him back to Nova Scotia. Bernie's visit was a lifeline, no question. Welcome company, yes, and she knew if she asked him for money, he would lend it to her. She was right. His loan would sustain them temporarily.

Even with an immobilized right hand, he was helpful during his stay, in the one-armed rearranging of furniture and assisting Billy's unpacking and shelving of his voluminous book collection, including his set of 1946 Encyclopedia Britannica.

In a private moment Bernie apologized to Vivian for his letter in opposition to her marriage. He described the scene on the Dartmouth church steps almost two years ago when he witnessed white prejudice blocking the darker man's way.

"I knew it was wrong. I can still see the hurt in that man's eyes. If it happened again, I'd say something. I would. I'd take action and let the chips fall where they may, like you did."

Vivian hugged him. He sounded proud of her.

She and Billy threw a party so Bernard could meet their friends. The previous evening, at Vivian's suggestion, he invited Dorothy McCurdy to a movie. Of course, impossible for them to know then, eight years later they would marry each other.

He booked a night bus ticket home. Vivian and Billy accompanied him to the terminal. "Be a good wife and mother," was his parting advice to his sister.

She took his words as a show of his confidence in her life choice and felt a surge of sisterly love for his staunch support and acceptance. "I'm going to be as good and decent as our mother," she replied.

"But I'll make sure my children know that Mother's thoughts about race were wrong, just as you and I know them to be."

With her brother gone, she had to be creative about survival. In a long conversation with Mrs. Christian, she recapped events of the past two weeks and mentioned borrowing from Bernard to buy groceries and existing without money since he left.

Cleo came over with some peaches, sausages, cookies, jam, and other things she had on hand, including more to add to the story.

"Obviously that husband of yours didn't tell you I offered to lend him some money, but he refused, saying he had enough," she disclosed. "If he didn't tell you this, I have to wonder what else he isn't telling you."

"Well, I'm not telling Billy the whole truth about your generous gifts, Mrs. Christian. I'm sure he'd think me disloyal if he knew I'd said anything," Vivian confided to her elder, whom she always addressed formally out of respect. "My own hunger would never have made me tell you, but I was thinking of the baby, who depends on me for his nourishment."

Billy came home at midnight with fresh corn, cake and a loaf of bread he purchased with borrowed money along with lots of free ice cream left over from an event.

The late August days leading up to the CCF summer school at Deer Lodge in Haliburton were so hot Vivian's jelly dessert wouldn't gel.

Four oppressively humid scorchers topping one hundred degrees ended the month and disagreed with infant Romney. He had to be kept inside. Billy fell violently ill from the heat. To help organize things she typed notes and letters for him and the summer school program for Avis. Despite the thrill of having a typewriter at hand, the job felt arduous. She couldn't wait for the holiday at Deer Lodge to come and was counting on it as a curative.

They were able to see Billy's visiting "baby brother" Lorne before leaving for Haliburton.

On August thirtieth six of them including Romney piled into Jarvis's car at three o'clock and set out for Deer Lodge, picking up Dorothy at CGIT camp on the way. They reached Haliburton railroad station around nine-thirty to fetch the baby carriage shipped ahead, Mrs. Christian's idea. The station was closed but the station master offered to open up for them and they reached camp around ten, Jarvis, Avis, Amy, Dorothy, Billy, Vivian and baby, to the welcoming facilitation of the camp manager, Mr. Handscombe.

CCF Canada's national secretary David Lewis was an exceptional speaker. Vivian, captivated, dared not miss a single well-articulated word of his daily lectures: "Socialism & Freedom," "Socialism & Compassion" and "The Future of Socialism."

She heard Joe Noseworthy and Ted Jolliffe speak, heard elite professors Eric Havelock and Jean-Charles Falardeau, the latter opening her mind to the distinctness of Quebec in his series of lectures, "What is the Quebec problem?," "Social Movements in Quebec" and "Political Parties in Quebec."

A time of jumping in a car with Billy and a "let's go" was impossible now with a baby to consider so Billy drove on his own to the town of Peterborough to meet Professor Falardeau the day before the academic was to arrive at camp. Vivian stayed behind caring for Romney and trying the electric washing machine, hailing its invention with every load.

While up there Vivian got to know Bee Reiter whom she sat beside at the talent night. She and her husband, Adam, were furriers, German Jews helped by the Workmen's Circle to escape their country, both of them ardent CCFers, living north of Toronto with a young son, Johnny, in Thornhill. Vivian and Billy would be seeing much more of them.

Back in Toronto, one of the first things Billy and Vivian did was argue about money. Clearly their time away hadn't been that relaxing for either of them.

"I'm going to turn my check book over to you to handle, so that I won't have to hear anything about money," he sniped petulantly. "You imply you can do a better job of managing than I have done? We'll see."

It occurred to her that Romney was very much like Billy, crying when not the center of attention, all smiles with an audience.

All she had wanted was a joint bank account, which they did eventually open in November at Bank of Toronto.

• • •

At Home Service Mrs. Miller instructed Tommy not to disturb her as she and Billy would be "in conference."

"Come in, Billy. Please close the door," she said. She was clearly not happy.

"You shouldn't have gone away while I was away too," she started, but he jumped in.

"Mrs. Miller, I cleared this with you. I've had this engagement booked for months. I sat in this very chair, and you indicated your consent."

"I have no recollection of that," she denied, "and this agency cannot afford to pay for your political work, as I've stated before. We can't compensate you for unscheduled time off when you were needed here. There were problems in your absence."

She launched into listing them.

"I take my holidays at the same time every year and I absolutely would not have condoned you going." She held fast to her position even though she was wrong.

Billy was miserable about the whole thing. Leaders don't like being subordinates. He hoped his deciding against the job in Montreal had been the right one.

At home, breaks seemed to be coming their way, though. A friend asked them to store her Heintzman piano. It arrived on September twentieth necessitating another rearrangement of the furniture with pleasure.

Jean continued her flow of baby gifts and letters, opening the door in increments, not fully ready to accept the interracial situation. These things take time, Vivian reminded herself.

She was worried about Romney; how unhappy he had become since Billy attempted to break him of sucking his thumb. Vivian thought the habit a blessing: it quieted Romney. He used to laugh and smile, now all he did was cry.

Billy believed the popular theory that thumb sucking was injurious to children and vowed to cure his son. Billy's deterrents made things worse. Now Romney was putting his entire fist in his mouth all the time, causing frequent vomiting.

Of all people, Billy should know that to succeed in achieving a change, the method matters. Vivian couldn't convince him to abandon his controlling ways despite sharing that May Etkin's doctor recommended against intervening in her baby Carol's thumb sucking.

In the autumn of 1948 events flew by at the rate of resplendent falling leaves.

The browns, russets, yellow-gold and crimson, each leaf uniquely colored, cascading on a common breath of wind but to its own pace and tune.

If so for leaves, why not for people – the question floated like leaves over the ravine as Vivian contemplated the onset of fall at her desk, writing letters.

She broke from her correspondence to go upstairs with Billy to a gathering for an address by Dr. Lotta Hitchmanova, director of the Unitarian Service Committee. The speaker gave eyewitness accounts of USC's humanitarian efforts internationally, showed a movie *Children's Republic* made in Sèvres, France, and also played some slides.

The Unitarian Church in Toronto was a denomination Billy and Vivian hadn't known let alone visited. First Unitarian Church minister Bill Jenkins stayed after everyone else had gone and he, Jarvis, Avis, Billy, and Vivian talked until well past midnight.

Billy attended two subsequent Sunday services with Avis at First Unitarian on St. Clair. He realized Unitarians were natural allies in the fight for a bill of human rights.

It was the cusp of the CCF convention when all these concepts were converging; equality, dignity, economic justice, fairness. A rare night off, at Avis's suggestion Billy headed down to the Barclay Hotel to rub shoulders with David Lewis and many who had convened at Deer Lodge, including Bee and Adam Reiter. The mood was hopeful for a breakthrough in 1949. Voters in Saskatchewan had recently re-elected a CCF government under Premier Tommy Douglas. Returned with a reduced majority it was still a shining example of the possible.

Through Avis, the Reiters became fast friends and welcome visitors. Adam snared Billy to go golfing with him and Bee. He wanted to help plan Billy's campaign. Bee and Vivian bonded instantly over their mutual love of nature. Invitations and rides to and from the Reiter home in the unspoiled outskirts of Toronto were added to the Whites' bulging calendar.

Meanwhile Billy formalized Woodsworth House Music Guild by developing a constitution for the CCF singing group. Adam and Bee joined. Also, the CCF Youth Movement welcomed Billy's energy, leadership, and counsel, which he freely gave.

His quartet continued while Home Service projects ramped up as well. Firesides and church affiliations cultivated meaningful community connections and respect for Billy. He and Vivian started to become an identifiable and known couple in Toronto. Everywhere they went it seemed someone knew one or both of them.

One advantage of a houseful of people was Vivian had babysitters now. Madge or Brian willingly minded Romney knowing Vivian would do the same for their little Christine, and Dorothy McCurdy was babysitting age too.

The arrangement freed up Vivian to attend the annual Home Service social for students from Pakistan, Ethiopia and British Honduras, where she met many old friends, Sonny and Tommy included.

The Whites went to Kay and George Livingstone's crowded housewarming at 391 Bedford Park. Avis lent them her car. Kay Livingstone was the spark that lit up the party. Conservatory trained in music and elocution, fresh from Ottawa, host of *The Kathleen Livingstone Show* on CBC and now CKEY, she was on her way to becoming one of Canada's best black actresses, not to mention a powerhouse social activist. Her parents founded *The Dawn of Tomorrow* newspaper in London, Ontario in July 1923, a national weekly "devoted to the interests of the darker races."

Billy and Vivian saw many people they knew and met many others for the first time. The two had much to report when they returned from the housewarming to Lonsmount and found Don and Isabel LeBourdais, Avis and Jarvis, some of Jarvis's students and their wives, seated around a dining room table that could seat twenty-two comfortably.

"What a surprise at tonight's housewarming, I ran into an old schoolmate, 'Bunny' McElum," Vivian reported. "She took me aside and said for all the fuss about my marriage back home, she agreed with my actions, thought I was spunky and was always cheering for me from a distance."

"There's more of her type than the other, I hope," one student commented. "Our generation wants to build bridges, not walls."

A hopeful sign of a crumbling wall came in November: Jean Keeler sent her first letter to both Vivian and Billy. In it she included a descriptive scene from her trip to Pleasant River.

Vivian drew symbolism from nature. Childhood days in North Brookfield ingrained in her an appreciation of the diversity inherent in the intricacies of the natural world and that differences are appealing, interesting and awe-inspiring, that each component needs the other. She would be a lifelong subscriber to social and environmental justice.

Winter ushered in moments to remember, treats, such as meeting music-ologists Frank and Edith Fowke and listening to stories and selections from their outstanding record collection and her vast array of Canadian folk music, catching the December concert by Paul Robeson and the Jewish Folk Choir at Massey Hall, taking Curley and Cleo with them for a fun day with "Auntie Wil" MacKerron, champion of routine, two-hour telephone conversations with Vivian, known to talk on the phone so long Vivian got a kink in her shoulder.

One particular godsend, as Vivian and Billy were still very short of cash, was a week's worth of leftover noodles and meatballs they inherited from Avis after she made enough for one hundred people and only thirty-five showed up. Variations on a theme never tasted so good.

In November they learned Umilta was cutting her stay short, returning to Trinidad as her father's health had failed. Fran Wees called to say Margarita had a baby boy. Vivian counted backwards on her fingers. She was only married this summer. I'm sure Dr. Wees still walked her down the aisle.

Sadly, Mrs. Christian needed an operation to remove a tumor. As for her hips, little chance of a cure.

Romney threw a beautiful tantrum because Vivian wouldn't let him put his hands in his mouth while having his cereal. He must have cried for about an hour altogether. Finally, she relented as he refused to eat otherwise. His loud lungs would come in handy very shortly though.

The baby was as amusing as he was strong-willed. Vivian laughed intro-ducing him to strained vegetable soup, watching the faces he made with every bite and all his other cute baby manoeuvres.

The Reiters were extremely hospitable. Bee made suppers, dispatched Adam to chauffeur them both ways, had a guest room for them when they wanted to stay over, coddled Romney, got Billy out on the greens with Adam, who considered himself quite the sportsman and lady's man. Several inches shorter than Billy and always well attired, he had a serious, almost stern face due to a vertical squint line above his bony, aristocratic nose and brooding eyes, below dark brows that matched his moustache.

One week into December Adam dropped in for a visit. Billy wasn't home, a Tuesday, a weeknight, why would he be?

"I don't know when he'll be home Ad," Vivian replied to Adam's unasked question as he sat in a living room chair watching her from behind while she extricated a cake from its pan and transferred her freshly baked and cooled cookies from the rack to a tin.

He was watching her intently like a cat, and then noiselessly approached. Suddenly she felt his hands slip around her waist as he pushed his torso against her back to lean over her shoulder.

"Do you want some help putting those away?" He was breathing heavily through his nose onto the side of her face and neck.

She removed his hands and sidestepped, frozen. Guess he had a few drinks, she thought, although there was no discernible alcohol smell.

"You must be lonely with Bill leaving you alone so much. I can give you what you need." He drifted toward her this time tracing the side of her jaw from her ear to her chin with his forefinger as he spoke directly into her eyes.

"You're so beautiful. I could make you so happy, and it would be our little secret."

She was in shock when he went to pull her close. Just then, baby Romney's wails erupted from the bedroom. For once Vivian was glad Romney was crying since it diverted Adam's attention.

She waited until the next night in bed to tell Billy about the incident. He didn't think it serious.

"He must have had one too many. He probably doesn't even remember. If it happens again, I think you simply tell him to stop."

It didn't happen again the next time she saw Adam when he dropped by with a bottle of cognac and Billy was there. Knowing nothing about brandy, Vivian poured a healthy double serving for the gents and for herself, straight, having not eaten much all day. Neither of the men enlightened her, preferring to get a kick out of seeing her drunk. The most interesting effects had worn off before they began hosting a carol party for fellow residents that evening.

This Christmas season was vastly different from last – they had a place that felt like home. Billy's Christmas gift to Vivian made it more so, a beautiful combination radio and phonograph in a cabinet. Their days of borrowing the Home Service record player were over.

Billy went to lead singing at B'nai Brith on Boxing Day. On New Year's Eve the Whites hosted a party: Nelson, Madge and Brian, Avril and her sister among the guests. Bee, Adam and Johnny planned to bring a turkey and logs for the fireplace, but a terrific storm left them snowbound. The next time Vivian saw Adam alone was the middle of January.

This year followed the previous year's theme of activity and the happy adjustment to life in Forest Hill Village. Vivian discovered a new difficulty with winter was pushing a baby carriage in the snow.

Home at Lonsmount, they had a place where anyone could (and did) drop in night or day, the choral group could rehearse, and the campaign could start brewing. The place seemed constantly alive. For noise at night, it was an address known to police.

Brand new Forest Hill Collegiate went wild in approval for Billy when he went there to do some song leading to kick off the year. He was even offered a position on the staff.

Woodsworth House and A.M.E. had become a regular part of Billy's Sundays now and he was out as usual when Adam arrived at the door. He had firewood with him.

"Is Bill home?" he asked. She assumed he was asking whether he'd have help carrying in the logs, but that's not why he was asking. As soon as he transported the woodpile to the fireplace, he started making small talk, pacing the living room-kitchen.

"Where's Romney?" he asked.

"The baby's sleeping," Vivian said, aware by the way Ad was posturing that he was about to make a move. He began to molest her in a fashion similar to before. This time he rubbed up against her and said, "Don't play innocent with me. You know you want it."

Vivian blew up.

"Adam, stop it. Touch me again and it will be Billy you'll be talking to, not me. I'll go talk to Bee. Is that what you want?"

It worked. He left peaceably and without further incident.

On his birthday, February seventh, Billy awakened to a record Vivian had purchased for him, "Don't Burn the Candle at Both Ends." In the evening she set up a candlelight dinner and a two-layer white birthday cake with coconut chocolate filling and frosting for dessert, with seven candles atop (three plus four). He opened gifts from her – a scarf and money for gloves, and two combs and a pack of razor blades wrapped in a diaper liner from Romney. They planned to take in a community concert. Then Howard Conquergood called from the Guild Inn in Scarborough.

"The Chief Information Officers winter school is being held here. Please, Billy, come out."

They did and what a lovely place the inn turned out to be. Dr. Stan Allen was dispatched to give them a lift and Howard drove them home. Billy insisted on staying up until two in the morning to hear if the event made the news.

All roads were leading to the election now. June was not that far away.

Chapter 30

"Eve Silver tells me I've been suggested as the candidate in Spadina riding. I saw her at Woodsworth House last night."

It was May thirteenth, and he'd awakened Vivian in the middle of the night to talk about a wrinkle in his candidacy.

"Mrs. Miller is adamant that if I accept the nomination, I will have to resign from Home Service. It's a Community Chest policy. The agency must be non-partisan.

"I don't know how we're going to live on nothing," Billy worried.

Frankly, neither did Vivian. She was pregnant again, adding to Billy's nervousness about money and job security. He asked what she thought about him running.

He'd be without a salary leading up to the June twenty-seventh federal election. The period June thirtieth to September tenth was covered. He had signed a contract with Taylor Statten to be Camp Music Director at Canoe Lake in Algonquin for the month of August, Vivian and Romney included, and he'd be solo at Camp Wabi-Kon in Temagami for the month of July.

Though not as much pay, Vivian approved of a change.

"I think you should run," she said. "Everything you've done has led you to this point. I can find some work with the elections office. You have steady work for the summer. Surely the party will have something for you after that. What does your numerology say for 1949?"

She was seeking the quickest route to a decision so that she could return to rare and precious sleep.

1+9+4+9=23, 2+3=5, "Its value is five. A *five* year is risk, travel, adventure, sacrifice, family, community ..." The nouns stopped flowing as Billy realized he had his answer.

"Vivian, I love you more than words can say. I will be confident in taking this risk knowing both you and the numbers are with me."

They survived the lean May days through the courtesies and kindnesses of friends. Free rhubarb and a basket of asparagus from Bee, fish Brian caught at Honey Harbour, free food at events, care packages from Mrs. Christian.

Both Vivian and Madge Pulley landed jobs as enumerators, a liberating experience that both mothers appreciated: to be out, productive and making money, facilitated by having people in-house at Lonsmount to babysit. Vivian started thinking about a part-time return to the workforce once her baby daughter (it was sure to be a girl) arrived and using the earnings to pay for babysitting.

Billy snagged the loan of Frank Fowke's 1929 Chrysler until after the election since Frank and Edith had just purchased the McCurdys' Studebaker. He hungered to buy it for the $150 asking price and eventually did. He had two choral groups on the go in Forest Hill now, one for teens and one for adults. Coupled with his engagements and election travel he was grateful for wheels and equally thankful that they had so many friends.

Much happened in the months leading up to nomination day in May. In February there was a scare that Billy's mother had died. Jarvis brought the telegram from Halifax downstairs at eleven-thirty at night.

"Bad news," he said. "There's only one kind of telegram they don't phone in first."

It was addressed to Billy. He wasn't home so Vivian didn't feel proper opening it and fretted until he finally got there at just after one. It proved to be from his mom, with news of Mr. Sealy's death. Vivian felt relief. Billy reacted spontaneously.

"Well, Mom's a widow for the second time and I hope she stays that way!"

From then on, Vivian had blanket permission to open all telegrams.

There were five unforgettable days Vivian and Romney spent with the Reiters in mid-March at their invitation – unforgettably dreadful. She saw behind the curtain of their troubled marriage and concluded that Adam was thoroughly rotten.

Fortunately, events the day after her return from Thornhill erased the Adam-induced enervations. Esther Hayes, a founding member of the Negro Youth Council, was their dinner guest at Lonsmount. Like her mother Inez, a member of the Bahá'í faith, quiet, reserved, thoughtful, brimming with ideas at twenty-six, Esther wanted to work on bridging the gap between races.

"I encounter many who are ignorant of other races, and they ask embarrassing and often rude questions," she told them. "I describe this attitude as ignorance born out of innocence. It's really a hunger on their part to become informed, so I answer their unknowns and bridge their understanding that way."

That night Madge and Vivian went to the Community Concert Series of the Volkoff Ballet debuting Jack Weinzweig's new dance work, *The Red Ear of Corn*. In the audience sitting next to her was Jack Weinzweig, whom she hadn't seen since the LeBourdais' party. She felt honored.

On April first she saw Billy perform in *The Mikado* as Pooh-Bah with Grace Trotman's impressive all-Negro cast. He was outstanding and she was proud of him, right down to the fan of hand-painted birds he created to accompany his costume.

Occasions with Portia were always highlights. In town until Easter, she took Billy and Vivian to see the Ballet Russe de Monte Carlo perform three ballets – *Pas de Quatre*, *Gisella* and *Madronos* – with a Chinese meal afterwards joined by her long-time friend Ruth Wilson.

Pre-election preparations for Avis and Billy were underway. They would run the campaigns out of Lonsmount sharing the sole telephone in the house.

Home Service moved operations up Bathurst Street past Bloor. Technically, June first would be Billy's last day there. Howard Conquergood hinted at a job as his assistant opening up in the fall that would have Billy's name on it.

Nomination night was Wednesday, May eighteen. Two other nominated candidates – Jack Freedman and Herb Orliff – declined so that Billy could be acclaimed. The Toronto Star phoned at midnight while he was still out. Vivian said a photographer could come the next morning to get a family picture of the CCF candidate for Spadina. She also agreed to an interview on the intermarriage angle with Miss Marjorie Earl, the Star reporter, who arrived Thursday afternoon.

Coverage of Billy's nomination appeared on Thursday in multiple newspapers, prompting phone calls from Auntie Wil and a deluge of others.

One headline read: "Spadina CCF Names White First Negro To Seek Seat."

"I don't expect my color to come into it at all. The big issues are principles. Torontonians are mature enough to cast their votes on that basis, not because of color," Billy told The Toronto Telegram. "The main issues involved in the campaign are housing, living costs, health and social security."

Overly wound and unable to sleep, Billy got out of bed at ten and changed his wife's plans for sleep. He dictated a speech and press release to her and accompanied her upstairs where she typed them up. These efforts resulted in generous media coverage for the campaign. True to form, Vivian kept a scrapbook of it all.

"'Never Knew Discrimination' Wife of Candidate Says" headlined the Star story.

Miss Earl's story was quite long and nicely done, Vivian thought, and she phoned the reporter and complimented her on it. All the quotations were accurate.

On prejudice: "I think discrimination exists largely among people who are not satisfied with themselves and have to feel superior to someone."

On friendships, "One of the nicest things about my marriage is that it has brought me into contact with so many interesting Negro people whom I would never have encountered had I not married Billy."

On facing problems: "Before I got married, all kinds of dire predictions were made about the difficulties I would experience and for all I knew they might have come true. But it now turns out I'm just a happily married woman leading an ordinary, normal life."

Billy's campaign manager was twenty-year-old Joan Easser, daughter of passionate socialist stalwarts, Sarah and Sam, who raised all three of their well-educated children, Ruth, Percy and Joan, on CCF ideas and ideals of a fairer and more inclusive society. Joan pioneered the Cooperative Commonwealth Youth Movement and had a well-honed organizational skill set. There were two Syds on the team, both sharp, outspoken young lawyers: Syd Harris was co-manager and Syd Midanik of the Jewish Labour Congress was the campaign's official agent. Adam Reiter helped with publicity and leaflet design.

A photo shoot was arranged with John Steele, who insisted on doing a second session for better results. The team had a strategy: young voters, immigrant minority voters, women voters, labor muscle, community endorsements and personal appearances. Getting Billy out there was crucial. Public appearances made more sense than door knocking.

From the outset their candidate was attracting fertile media. Articles appeared. His speeches were basis for commentary. He was imminently quotable. Vivian kept track.

"Progressive Conservative promises to fix the housing problem," he said, were "as ridiculous as trying to cross the Atlantic in an Island ferry – They just don't go that way. Cocktail bars seem to have a priority with them."

As for past Liberal promises to create housing for as little as nine dollars and fifty-eight cents a month, "You just have to look at the people right in Spadina riding living in garages and temporary housing camps to know how poorly the Liberals have carried this out."

His campaign was not without controversy. The Communists alleged Billy was a token candidate because he made it a gentlemen's contest by speaking well of his formidable Liberal opponent, incumbent David Croll, a respected figure in the Jewish community. There was also a brief controversy in CCF ranks on Billy's nomination night in the packed committee room. Given Croll's popularity in the riding, David Stein, an official of the Amalgamated Clothing Workers, early in the meeting suggested the CCF party not field a candidate at all so as not to split the vote of labor. But once the room cemented Billy's candidature, Mr. Stein stood up again to congratulate the party on Billy's nomination.

"Our union in Spadina definitely will not work against the CCF. I do not want to leave the wrong impression. We are going to support the CCF candidate," he said.

Billy responded, "I know in choosing a candidate from the ranks of the Negro citizens of Toronto you are turning the spotlight of the nation on Spadina. I know the responsibility I bear will be many times greater than it otherwise would be, but I am determined to carry it to the best of my ability."

One hundred Japanese Canadians in the riding were denied voter registration. Billy railed against such routine and systemic abrogation of human rights and articulately echoed the party's push for a Canadian Bill of Rights.

Across the country, Frank Calder, the first-ever native Canadian candidate, was making history in a provincial election running for the CCF in the riding of Atlin, British Columbia.

Native Canadians were voting for the first time. The Toronto Star, while endorsing Croll and Louis St. Laurent (Liberal Prime Minister) for the federal election, praised Calder and White for "blazing new trails in the forward march of their respective races."

Candidacy is a marathon for everyone involved and every candidate is a believer. Joan ran Billy through his paces. His itinerary required almost superhuman stamina. He was built for it, felt like he'd trained for the rigors all his life. Vivian hadn't known what to expect. In her eyes the best gift to the campaign was from Bee – a genuine typewriter table. She felt insecure about her role as the candidate's wife, uncomfortably gawky at the obligatory socials that politicking entails.

Her diary spilled the truth. "There is a party at Mrs. Easser's next Sunday. I dread these things – I'm just useless socially. No asset to Billy, in fact I'm afraid I'm a liability," she wrote.

Would annals record him as the first Negro Member of Parliament? He had to believe the answer was "yes." No election candidate runs to lose. Although the numbers suggested no chance, Billy was out to defy the odds. In the last election of 1945 the CCF had 2,769 votes to Croll's 17,978.

Billy worked the circuit like a standard bearer, not a sacrificial lamb. Head held high at every function, he pitched the party's push for rights, freedoms and a better quality of life for minority groups, fair wages, and pensions for workers. An effective canvasser one-on-one, his true prowess was public speaking.

Both the Globe and the Star among others covered his bill of rights speech at the Universal Negro Improvement Association.

"The CCF presented a petition in the House of Commons, signed by over six hundred and twenty-five thousand Canadians who asked to have a Bill of Rights passed. The response, in the traditional Liberal manner, was to pass the buck by saying that Mr. Pearson, Minister of External Affairs, would make a public statement. That statement has not been made yet. And now, in the midst of an election campaign, the Liberals are being true to form by loosely throwing around countless promises which they can never fulfill," he intoned to refrains of "shame, shame!" from the crowd.

After Miss Earl's Star article appeared Vivian received a letter from Jemma Jones identifying herself as a Negro girl from British Guyana going to school in Orillia. She shared that she was meeting with lots of prejudice. Vivian wrote to her immediately.

It closed: "I commend you for your grace and courage, Jemma. Please don't let those mean and hurtful people define you. You're too good for that."

Billy, the candidate, was superb. Billy, the husband, was verging on insufferable.

Their first contact since he left one morning, he phoned her at seven o'clock in the evening. He'd had dinner at the Eassers.

When she saw him face-to-face later that evening she merely inquired why he hadn't let her know he wasn't coming home.

"I kept your dinner hot for several hours, waiting."

He blew up.

"I'm in a campaign, for Pete's sake, and you want me to worry about a burner on the stove? I don't have time to handhold. Come on, Vivian, stop complaining. You'll just have to adjust."

Luckily his moodiness was fleeting. The pressures of his heaping-full plate and his unemployed status were real, but the good times easily outweighed his histrionics, Vivian reminded herself.

Campaign or no, Romney's first birthday party was not to be missed. The perfect weather on June twenty-second wooed the party outdoors for eighteen guests, including seven kids, abandoning the indoor crepe paper streamers Billy had stayed up installing in the wee hours.

Then it was back on the trail.

A major election meeting at the Labour Lyceum, an important cultural hub for Jewish labor groups, teemed with the curious, the committed and the undecided. At least half were new Canadians speaking no English. The audience was a checkerboard of colors. Vivian deposited herself inconspicuously in a back row. She overheard two women seated in the row behind her assessing Billy when he spoke from the platform.

"Oooh, mmm," purred one to the other in obvious approval. "I could go for him." The other enthusiastically agreed.

Vivian turned around and told them with a smile,

"He's already taken."

As the commenter blushed crimson, her friend hastened to whisper back, "Well, he's got our votes!"

David Lewis was the guest speaker and spoke mostly in Yiddish. His wife, Sophie, sat next to Vivian and translated, later saying how impressed she was with Billy's speech, high praise considering the source. No doubt Mrs. Lewis had heard her share of speeches.

That event was the high point in the campaign in retrospect.

On June twenty-seventh the Liberals swept the nation and locally David Croll achieved the largest plurality of anyone, 23,652 votes to the Conservative's 9,407, and Billy's 5,969. The only CCFer in Toronto to win was Joe Noseworthy in York-South.

Vivian worked as a district returning officer at the fringe of the riding and was home by nine. Billy arrived around ten with his visiting sister June in tow, and they all went to Woodsworth House. Vivian never saw such a collection of tired-looking people.

The sorry part about a career in politics isn't in the losing, it's in the not trying, Billy believed. He and Vivian were satisfied that he more than doubled the CCF vote from 1945. Of course, Billy noticed his vote count in numerology added up to eleven – a good sign: the idealist, the great messenger, the great psychologist, the great teacher.

Three days later Billy and Jarvis were eight hours at CBC scripting and recording a radio program about civil liberties and the bill of rights with producer Allan Anderson.

Then it was off to northern resorts for Billy, July in Temagami without Vivian and Romney and then most of August with them in Algonquin where they would stay in the pleasant one-room chief's cabin in the center of Camp Ahmek.

It was always the first few days following his departure that Vivian missed Billy the most. She felt as lonely as an empty closet at times. During July they communicated through letters, resuming their well-honed tradition of the past.

She was most distressed over two successive, disastrous attempts to make blueberry muffins to send him. The first batch tasted okay but looked embarrassingly ragged. Enough batter remaining to make four more, they came out of the oven perfectly puffed and golden brown. Ten minutes later each muffin had a large hole in the top of it, revealing a center which was still gooey batter.

"So, is it any wonder that I am thoroughly disgusted with myself?" she wrote to him. "I'm left with the demoralizing certainty that I am as much of a failure as the muffins, that I can never do anything right, that it is useless for me to hope that I will ever learn. I ought to be able to take it by now."

He replied: "Whether or not your muffins turn out well, it's much more important to me that you remember that I love you more than anyone else in the world. When you're despising yourself, you're despising the person I love, and I won't put up with it."

> Don't you worry 'bout a muffin
> 'Cause a muffin's really nuffin'
> That's for sure.
> Go ahead an' show your stuff an'
> Call the silly muffin's bluff an'
> Make some more

After the camps Billy was on the road again, this time with the McCurdy family to Meadville, Pennsylvania for the McCurdys' treasured ritual Week of Work sojourn presented by the National Council on Religion in Higher Education. It stimulated an epiphany in Billy: he desired further study.

"Unless I can find a fairy godmother somewhere, or I win the sweepstake, darling, I am very concerned about my present no-degree, pseudo-professional status. Tonight, I have the feeling of having missed the boat and am speculating as to the possibility of catching another at this stage," he wrote his wife. "Whether in education, music or social work, I must contemplate the urgent necessity of permanent establishment in the professional field. I must do this or resign myself to mediocrity and possible eventual failure."

Mid-September was crunch time. Little Laurie could arrive anytime now, although Dr. Costain estimated early October.

The Monday after his Meadville trip, Billy sought out Howard Conquergood about the CCF job and learned, if he got it, it wouldn't start until October fifteenth.

"Nothing definite, the election results set us back," Howard acknowledged.

During the depths of their financial bottom, Billy's mom visited from Halifax with her new husband, who once had visited One Elm, the financial secretary of their church on Cornwallis Street, Clarence "C.H." Johnston.

Auntie invited Billy, Vivian, his mom and C.H., the Perrys and Inez Hayes to a gathering. Vivian's labor began the night of the party.

"I feel just the way I did the night before Romney was born," Vivian whispered to Billy on their way into the gathering.

The actual labor pains didn't start until they got home, and they kept Vivian awake all night.

The next day mostly seated and taking breaks for the pains, she prepared dinner for Billy's mom and C.H. She felt rather proud of her ingenuity in producing a meal from her meager supplies.

Jarvis drove Vivian to Grace Hospital that night. She was admitted but the baby wasn't born until the next morning, Sunday's child. They hadn't imagined another boy let alone a name for one.

This time Billy had been with her all night and was able to visit the afternoon and evening of the birth.

Chapter 30

Despite her preference Vivian was moved out of the lively but crowded ward and into a staid semi-private room, limiting visitors to two at a time. For this birth, Vivian was up walking virtually right away, not waiting for her doctor's permission. For a few days it seemed Dr. Costain forgot about her anyway. She was out in six days, coming home to the spotless floors Billy had washed and waxed.

They named the new guy Christopher David. Romney saw his new brother and said "doll." When Vivian was burping Christopher, Romney trotted around burping his teddy bear in tandem.

Shortly after Vivian's release from hospital, Billy departed on an evening train to Ottawa for a religious education conference.

Before he left, they'd argued about Romney's thumb-sucking again. She slept poorly and woke up to a fussy, restless Christopher crying at six in the morning. She nursed him three times before ten o'clock when Romney woke up and had breakfast.

The door-to-door photographer who showed up peddling his services to moms of toddlers seemed to Vivian like a good way of occupying Romney for a while. She agreed to a photo session, invited the man into the McCurdy living room and left Romney with him so she could go downstairs for a small slice of respite.

A few minutes later, the photographer called down the stairs. "Pardon me ma'am please, I need your help up here." He was insistent and she felt impinged, the unwilling assistant.

Too many directives, an empty stomach, exhausted, fragile, Vivian felt the bottom dropping out of her. She broke down completely, could not stop crying. The bewildered photographer took a pause while tenant Audrey Newton, hearing the distressed mother, brought her back downstairs to lie down. She did Vivian's dishes and straightened up the place until Vivian, still feeling wan, gave Romney lunch before his nap. Soon afterwards, Madge came and did the laundry. Women helping women. In her low state, Vivian silently bemoaned that one of them wasn't her mother.

As much as Vivian wanted to sleep after nursing Christopher, she couldn't. She resisted the impulse to phone Bee and ask her to come over, but finally relented. Bee arrived around suppertime laden with groceries and got dinner ready. She gave Romney his bath and generally took over. By then Adam had arrived to pick her up. After they left, Vivian took her quinine pill for leg cramps and went to bed completely spent, praying things would be better when Billy arrived home, which was at eight-forty the next morning.

"Really felt the effects of my overdoing it since I've been home," she confided to her diary. His arrival kiss and first words, "I love you" and his soft words and comforting embrace soothed her battered nerves. Her bad day was now just a yesterday.

Billy zealously pursued an outside itinerary that rivaled his campaign schedule. He couldn't wait for the speculative chance of CCF employment. His nose was in the hunt for a real job and fast. Meanwhile, they secured a two-hundred-dollar loan from Household Finance Company to pay off their debts.

Their joint social calendar was a saving grace as always, the restorative equilibrium of friendship giving balance to the mad pace of life with two under-twos.

Edith Fowke's folk song listening group at Woodsworth House was, predictably, a pleasure and delight. Woodsworth House continued to be a nerve center for social, political and union activity.

Attending the first Forest Hill community concert of the season, featuring Leslie Bell Singers and Oskar Morawetz, was facilitated by Avril babysitting.

Events like the lovely party at the Rackham's, where an evening's discussion on arrogance was featured, served as well-placed steppingstones through a nerve-wracking October.

Parcels and letters from Jean represented a further sign she was ready to thaw relations.

Exactly two months after Christopher entered the world, Billy landed a new job and was glad for it, even if it was new terrain in the receiving department of John Inglis, the famous Canadian company that rhymed with "mingles." It moved from making weapons like Bren machine guns for the Allies to manufacturing washing machines and other home appliances after the war ended and families boomed. Hours eight to five and Saturdays off, it was steady work, decent pay, Billy was told there was room for advancement.

"I'll give it a *shot*," Billy joked.

When the shutters closed on the year 1949, Bill White was cutting a new path, proceeding with everything he needed to succeed: a track record, a strong résumé, skills and finesse, no allergy to hard work, a charming personality, a community that hailed him, adherence to excellence and a devoted wife.

As he and Vivian greeted the New Year – his *five* year in numerology, for lovers of change – they were happy in the embrace of their adopted home, Toronto.

Just as they hadn't married to prove naysayers wrong or to challenge convention, they hadn't set out to be trailblazers either, but indeed they were. Theirs were early faces in what grew to become the most diverse city in the world, all because they married for love.

Billy with Laurie, 1951

Epilogue

Miss Portia White (Singer)
63 Alma St., Moncton, New Brunswick, Canada

October 29, 1948
My dear Miss White,
I've been clipping from the papers every mention of the singer from Halifax ever since I was a member of the First Baptist Church in Halifax and first heard you sing there. Since I moved here I've heard all the great singers, including Marian Anderson, Dorothy Maynor, Paul Robeson. I would like to add your name to the list, but chiefly because last year your brother Billie White married a relative of mine, Miss Keeler, whose father was my nephew. My niece Gladys Keeler wrote me about it, was quite distressed thinking she had wrecked her life and quite surprised to learn that I did not agree with her.

 Will you make an effort to have Long Beach in Los Angeles put on your schedule if you can manage coming to America as I would like to have the pleasure of hearing you sing and also of meeting you.

 Sincerely,
 (Miss) Bessie Hume
 Long Beach, California

December 12, 1949

Vivian Dear,

I have been planning to write you for a long, long time. I have thought of you many times, but after writing you as I did before your marriage, it's rather difficult. However, I have tried to put myself in your place and consider what I would do if I were actually in love with one of another race and have come to the conclusion I would probably do just what you did. In any case it is your life, and if you and your husband are satisfied and feel that you could not be happy apart, why should friends interfere? As I wrote you before, I have the greatest respect for your husband's people and I do feel and told your mother long ago, that you two will likely someday surprise us. After all we are old fashioned, belong to the old school and we must remember this world is marching on and things are changing every day.

I would like to hear from you. Is your baby good and how old is he now? You seem so young to be married, but not so. I do hope you are both very happy.

Your mother is looking well. Saw her in Mona's the other day and told her I was writing you. Do write me Vivian when you have time.

Best wishes to you and your husband for a Merry Christmas and Happy New Year.

Love Mardie

My parents Vivian and Bill White finally got their girl, Laurie, on February twenty-eighth, 1951. They paid tribute to Jean Keeler with the baby's middle name. Mom wasn't writing much in her diary by then but did squeak out this entry: "Laurie Jean born 2:20 a.m. at Women's College Hospital. Weight seven pounds six and a half ounces. Dark hair (lots of it) and dark eyes. Billy came in to see us both this p.m. He is allowed only one visit on account of the flu epidemic."

Epilogue

I came along in 1954 and brother, Tim, followed in 1967 when Mom was a month shy of forty-two.

Nana Jean enlightened herself, accepted, then embraced Mom's decision to marry Dad. If sending the flannel sheets for diapers was her surrender flag, having Mom, Romney and Christopher visiting her in Dartmouth in May 1950 was armistice.

Was there an exact "aha moment" when she put to rest and apologized for her racist views? If so, we kids were never told about that. We didn't think to ask. The important thing was that she did banish her nonsensical views about race. It was water under the bridge for us and clearly for her too. She lent my parents $1,500 interest-free for one year for the purchase of their forever home in Agincourt.

Nana first visited after Laurie was born. She faithfully sent each of us birthday cards with money orders enclosed and well-wrapped packages from Nova Scotia at Christmas. We received special occasion cards and letters and Nana visited Toronto when she could. She hosted us each summer during the family's annual car trips east. Nana and my Grandma Johnston became friends. When Nana was dying, siblings of Dad's in Halifax – Lorne and Yvonne – came and sang hymns for her.

Growing up I never detected a hint of racial intolerance in Nana. I only know about it because that was a key part of my mother's earliest narrative to me and my siblings regarding our origins: Nana didn't want our mother to marry and have children with Dad because of his color, believing he and we wouldn't amount to much.

Collectively, my father, mother, siblings and I couldn't have proven Nana more wrong. Romney's a veteran computer systems genius, Chris an award-winning folk music writer and performer, broadcaster and organizer, Laurie a revered family doctor, Tim a bass-playing Canadian rock star and music producer, and me, a creative politico, musician, and now author.

Around the time Laurie was born, the John Inglis company promoted Dad to personnel manager at its new plant in Scarborough, east of Toronto. He sprang into action. The idea of a consumers' cooperative association as a community economic empowerment tool had been percolating in him since 1949. Now he had the milieu for it. He co-founded an employees' credit union for which, as a volunteer, he recruited, kept records, designed and wrote a newsletter complete with an original cryptic crossword in every monthly issue. He revitalized the company's recreation committee and, as its head, made it his business to spread his brotherhood around, whether it was in the boardroom, around a negotiating table, on the shop floor or at a company Christmas party, picnic or staff outing.

Three children now, Dad's posting in faraway Scarborough, and Avis and Jarvis deciding to sell Lonsmount were indicators it was time to move.

My parents began house-hunting. A choice of two homes remained after their whittling: a fieldstone beauty with its cheery red door and trim near the railway tracks at Sheppard Avenue and Leslie Street or a farmhouse built in 1888 in the quaint, self-contained Village of Agincourt with its own post office, general store, railway station and skating rink. My parents opted for the Harris farmhouse and its trees, which stand today designated under the Ontario Heritage Act as the Harris-White House. The home they didn't pick was expropriated and leveled long ago for a railway overpass.

Along the way my parents changed religions coinciding with Avis landing a job as secretary of the First Unitarian Church in 1952. A friend suggested to Avis that Unitarian Universalism suited her ideas. She went to investigate and was sold.

Mom and Dad chose a religious path divergent from their embedded Christian roots. Neither felt the same about Christianity after Rev. Elgee's letter of long ago.

Influenced by the McCurdys, Mom and Dad became Unitarians in the mid-1950s. In 1960 they joined with others to co-found Don Heights Unitarian Congregation in Agincourt, closer to home. Theirs were the first names in the official registry on opening. They remained members and contributors for the rest of their lives.

Dad was devoted to becoming the definition of a great Canadian. He stayed with John Inglis for ten years, the last two in the industrial relations division at head office. By then he had become a charter member of Scarborough's Golden Mile Kiwanis Club in 1953 and its president in 1956 at age forty.

Kiwanis elected him as Lieutenant Governor of Division No. 6, Ontario, Quebec and Maritime District. He was the first black to serve in a leadership role in Kiwanis. He was a continuing, active member of the YMCA and on the Canadian Council of Christians and Jews board of directors, "symbolic of the melting away of religious and racial differences in a common desire to serve the community," he said.

Dad was definitely hooked on accomplishment to the highest degree. He was driven to serve and shine.

From our north Scarborough home base in Agincourt, Dad accelerated his community involvements adding to his roster Scarborough Area Social Planning Council chair, Metropolitan Toronto Social Planning Council member, Neighbourhood Workers' Association public relations advisory committee, Forest Hill Glee Club, Agincourt Girls' and Boys' Glee Club, Scarborough Centennial Singers (a.k.a. the Bill White Singers), who sang at the opening of Ontario Place, Toronto's waterfront park.

In 1961 he became General Manager at Toronto Cast Stone Company Limited, later named Beer Precast after its founder Fred Beer. Located on Manville Road in southern Scarborough, this was the company that manufactured and supplied Toronto City Hall with its unique concrete exterior.

Dad changed jobs again in 1974 to assume the post of director of safety education for the provincial Workers' Compensation Board.

He sat on boards of the Canadian National Institute for the Blind (CNIB), Toronto Arts Foundation, the Industrial Accident Prevention Association, and was a president of the Construction Safety Association of Ontario.

In 1962 Dad and Mom championed a Scarborough fundraising canvass of sixty-six thousand households for the national Peace Research Institute, dedicated to studying the causes of war, to mitigate future risk of war.

We wouldn't see much of our whistling Dad through the week: home for supper, home late at night when he'd head to the piano at midnight, out the door in the morning. Saturday was baking day for Glee Club, the night when all the children would receive a homemade cinnamon bun or a crunchy, buttery, taffy-laden popcorn ball. Besides baking and cooking, he had many hobbies, singular pursuits like golf, rug hooking, needlepoint, winemaking, music arranging with superb notation (never smearing the India ink), flawless calligraphy, poster painting, photography and the big one, song leading. Leading, always leading, Dad warmed to his podium roles where he was most comfortable, stationed at the front of the room, as emcee, public speaker, lecturer, conductor, auctioneer, voice production coach and team leader.

At home he was our musical director. Routinely he assembled my three older siblings and me to learn all the harmonies for the songs he and his siblings grew up singing. We would perform them for company and in concert on demand. We were de facto members of his glee club, which he started in our living room and later moved to Agincourt Community Center due to its popularity and rapid growth. (Despite begging to belong at age six, I wasn't allowed to join until I was eight.) Mom ensured that exposure to music and culture was part of our regular diet. She was musically talented herself, abashedly, because she felt dwarfed in ability next to Dad. Musically, she was our biggest booster.

Weekends in the summer Dad covered his camp circuit. On the odd occasion he took a kid or two with him.

Mom tended to the administration of his life and children in a setting she instantly loved: a treed, expansive yard in a tight knit neighborhood anchored by a public school and rich with history. Morris Shiff, who had subdivided the farmland as building lots, and his wife Rae sold my parents the farmhouse for fourteen thousand dollars on November 12, 1952. When Mr. Shiff told a neighbor he had sold the farmhouse to a Negro, the man's face clouded. "Oh, Morris, how could you?" was the response.

That bigot aside (my parents were never aware of the comment), the community embraced the Whites.

Dad allotted Mom an allowance to run the house and she got to keep the government's monthly baby bonus. When I was four, she took a local secretarial job to have money to enroll me in nursery school to overcome my overt shyness.

Mom delved into community and church affairs doing good works, which eventually earned her medals of recognition for lifetime voluntarism. She minded all the household paperwork, kept up her correspondence forte in all areas, including Dad's bookings, acknowledgments, confirmations and itineraries and her ritual personal correspondence. Her annual process of handwriting Christmas cards and letters took a good month – their recipient list was that long.

Avis and Jarvis McCurdy likely would have been fixtures in my parents' lives regardless, but Uncle Bernie ensured it when he and Dorothy McCurdy married in a 1957 Unitarian wedding and her parents became his in-laws. From then on our families were inextricably linked.

The bestowal of awards and honors began for Dad in 1966 with a Human Relations Award from The Canadian Council of Christians and Jews along-side fellow recipients Max Enkin, Charles Gundy and Claude Ryan. As a director he relished declaring he was neither Christian nor Jewish.

Seventeen years after running against him, Dad's award presenter was David Croll. Uniquely true to form Dad accepted his award in song. The audience of twelve hundred in the Royal York Ballroom joined with him in the Jewish folksong "Zum Gali, Gali" and he sang his penned verse: "Men are intended to live in harmony."

On Canada Day 1967 he received the federal Centennial Medal "in recognition of valuable service to the nation." In 1970 he was invested with the country's highest civilian honor, the Order of Canada. This was followed by the Order of St. John in 1975 and the Scarborough Civic Award of Merit 1976 and, posthumously, a Bicentennial Award.

"What I am or will become is not determined by the color of my skin, but by what I have done and will do," he once said.

He urged the practise of a new concept of brotherhood. "Rise to the occasion and do everything in your power to create a new understanding in the community."

By so doing he was convinced "minds would be properly developed along the correct lines of thinking."

"The world is full of virtual dynamite points that could explode at any moment causing untold destruction. If man is to survive, brotherhood must become a living reality," he said as National President of Brotherhood Week in 1967.

"The world is shrinking to a virtual neighborhood, and we can no longer close our eyes to what happens in other parts of the world. We are neighbors whether we like it or not. What happens to 'Joe Blow' in Africa is now of our deepest concern."

If there was one person in his sphere who understood that concept better than anyone it was the woman who married him. My mother pioneered the kind of activism that never took a rest.

It earned her a Queen's Jubilee Medal for Voluntarism, civic honors and the admiration of her church, community, family and copious circle of friends.

Her life revolved around bringing people together, involvement in causes, keeping in touch and working for improvements.

My parents threw wonderful parties and family gatherings: corn roasts, sing-along "dos" and holiday dinners, parties for the choir, hosting friends from their earliest times in Toronto, some of them, to remain unnamed, rather odd, somewhat needy sycophants in deep hero worship of Dad.

Part of mom's talent was documentation. Her avid chronicling and archiving of our family history and genealogy made the telling of this story possible.

She was the impeccable editor of elaborate community and church newsletters for many decades, valued member of the Canadian Unitarian Council, the Unitarian Service Committee (now SeedChange) and helped found the C. D. Farquharson Community Association in 1972.

Mom was the intrepid environmentalist before the word was coined. The day in 1977 when municipal crews clear cut trees for a soccer field in our local woodlot without consultation she stood in front of heavy equipment to stop more from being razed. She was light years ahead of the recycle program. Retail stores resented her bringing her own shopping bag and refusing their plastic back then. Growing up we boycotted Loblaws because they sold produce from South Africa during apartheid. Believer in boycotts, the doer, the marcher, the giver, and oh did she give. As a charitable donor at age eighty-eight she was subjected to a painful government audit because the revenue agency questioned that she was honestly that generous.

Mom was famous for hosting house concerts for almost three decades, selling tickets and CDs to help Canadian musicians, freely billeting them as required.

Her thirty-five years of daily diary writing became the basis of a published study presented internationally by University of Toronto linguistic researchers called the *Vivian White Project*. Dr. Sali Tagliamonte, PhD candidate Katharina Pabst and team were amazed to find such a comprehensive, continuous collection of diaries that enabled them to analyze the changes in written language in someone with Alzheimer's disease, the illness that ended Mom's life in 2016.

Shockingly, Dad died far too young at sixty-five in January 1981 in hospital in New Zealand while on holiday with Mom and Tim. He was admitted on day four of their vacation with gastro pains, received emergency surgery and went downhill over the ensuing days, sepsis. The autopsy was inconclusive. Doctors couldn't identify what prompted his sudden death.

He died without a will.

Mom organized a grand celebration of life at First Unitarian Church six weeks after his death. He has no marker or grave. At some point mom tossed his ashes in the garden, I learned after the fact. She didn't invite anyone. I know now there was a lot going on under the surface despite my parents' obvious profound, visceral connection. Inside our very happy household there were secrets simmering between parents, I have no doubt. But that's another book. My childhood was joyous and carefree.

Tim, their final child, Jarvis jokingly referred to as their "happy accident," a newborn for mom at forty-one and for Dad at fifty-two, the by-product of a convention in Chicago. He was born into a completely different scene as a Canadian centennial baby arriving when the nation was celebrating every race and culture at its world's fair, Expo 67.

When Portia died tragically at fifty-six of cancer in 1968, Dad formed *White House Records* to cast to vinyl the vintage recordings of her historic, nineteen-forties concerts from Town Hall, New York, and called it *Think On Me*. He frequently told me not a day went by that he didn't think of her.

Long before Toronto became the cosmopolitan city it is today Bill and Vivian White were pioneers, two early influencers for diversity, inclusion and the eradication of color barriers in the fledgling movement for the acceptance of all people as equals.

Obviously I couldn't be more glad they didn't back down from marriage and having children in the face of prejudice, that they held to their convictions.

Looking around today it's hard to imagine that mixed relationships were considered verboten or strange. I overheard Dad being interviewed in 1963 for a CHUM Radio talk show about the novel fact that he was married to a white woman. He boasted that we, his children, were so popular it wouldn't have mattered if we were pink with purple polka dots.

On their thirtieth anniversary I asked Dad to reflect on his marriage, thinking he might propose a toast or pay tribute to Mom. He didn't take the lob, replying instead that we, his children, were his proudest accomplishment.

Among the enduring friendships from my parents' earliest days in Toronto I think fondly of the visits from ever-happy gamer Avril, the very cool Dr. Brewton (who chose Dad as his executor), scholarly Nelson Abraham, super friendly Dick Hill, famous author and rights-fighter Isabel *("The Trial of Stephen Truscott")* LeBourdais and community stalwart Cleo Christian. I did not fully appreciate their weighty significance to my parents' formative Toronto days. Now I feel very thankful for people like them. Incidentally, Bee Reiter divorced Adam.

The White family was present in our lives, Grandma Johnston and those many aunts and uncles, Helena, Portia, Nettie, Mildred, George, Jack, June, Yvonne and Lorne, and cousins galore. Naturally Mom had a hand in organizing the two biennial White family reunions that took place in Toronto in 1999 and 2010, welcoming abundant kin from the US and Canada. The first reunion to connect Whites from both sides of the border happened in Baltimore in 1984.

I had no bond with the Harlows. Being told young that they wrote letters disapproving of the idea of my existence, I must have turned off. I wholly identified with the White Family. When I was growing up I had no curiosity about Harlows. Nana was my only connection to them, and I wasn't particularly close to her. My mother's relatives Elsie, Doris, Charles, Ralph and Albert to me were merely names on letters she was mailing to them. Staunch loyalty her trademark, Mom always kept in touch with her Harlow side. Only one family member (a Harlow in-law) clung to racist notions and refused to see her ever again, her loss. Vivian became a nurturing life member of the enduring, international Harlow Family Association. Now I'm a lifetime member too.

She had a huge capacity for forgiveness, was trusting and saw the best in people. Like Dad she regarded racism as a correctable flaw.

In the words of Bill White, "It's not people themselves who are right or wrong, but what they do."

Afterwords

I first met Vivian and Bill White in 1960 when they joined Don Heights Unitarian Congregation where I had been a member for five years. They quickly became very involved members, Vivian using her formidable secretarial and archiving skills for organizing and storing church records and Bill as music director, ever the contributor to dialogue, and a facilitator of thoughtful and new approaches.

Bill had the unique ability to lead large groups in four-part harmony. He did so at Don Heights, of course, on many occasions. The antique Steinway grand piano, which Bill found for Don Heights and which Sheila's older sister Laurie painstakingly and exquisitely refinished, is still a treasured part of the congregation. I experienced the unique demonstration of Bill's ability in Edmonton in the summer of 1978 during the Commonwealth Games. The opening ceremonies were taking place in the new stadium with a full house of 42,500 people. After a few minutes of explanation to the crowd, he led the whole stadium singing several numbers in perfect four-part harmony on national television and in the presence of Prince Philip!

One personal reason for my fellowship with Vivian and Bill's story is that my own husband, Dr. Wilson Head, before his death in 1992, was also well-known for his work as a black activist in race relations and human rights both in Canada and the United States, bringing me closer to these issues as well.

Nearly three decades after Vivian was condemned by family members, her church and her community for her decision to marry a person of color, my husband was asked to spend a year interviewing the Nova Scotia community to ascertain the degree of discrimination felt toward natives and blacks. He accepted, as long as they agreed to publish the results of the study. His co-authored study entitled "Discrimination Against Blacks in Nova Scotia: The Criminal Justice System" did in fact find extensive discrimination felt by many levels of the community.

It is remarkable to me that Bill White always said discrimination never personally affected him or held him back, which his life bore out. If he were alive today, I know Bill would be leading workshops on how to address racism, and I know his solution would involve the universal language of music.

As forerunners, my friends Vivian and Bill were champions and leaders in this cause when there were but few.

– *Sandy Macdonald, educator, human rights and race relations expert*

• • •

If Vivian and Bill were here today, I wonder what they would think about people's attitudes and the direction the world is heading. Yes, there is greater awareness than there was seventy-five years ago – in some circles, at least – of the systemic racism and injustice that are built into our society. However, it is not clear that significant progress has been made in confronting and dismantling those systems. Our systems of commerce, education, justice and information are founded on subjugation and enslavement in ways that are deeply ingrained, widely accepted and still largely invisible.

I do think Vivian and Bill would be proud of the way their children have carried on the struggle for social, economic and environmental justice over the years. They would be pleased by our ongoing work to tell the truth about our family's history and this country's history in a variety of ways.

From Vivian, we learned the importance of respecting all others and being both consistent and persistent in attempting to do good, not harm, through our words and actions. She refused to believe that skin color or cultural background made one person more worthy of respect and inclusion than another. She showed us the power of love to transcend barriers and bring out the best in others.

From Bill, we learned that a society that includes and respects everyone is stronger, healthier and more vibrant than one that is based on exclusion and disrespect. He explained that the ongoing effort required to enforce systems of injustice has a soul-destroying effect not only on the oppressed but also on the oppressor. He showed us the power of community dialogue and group singing to uplift people's spirits and unite them in the struggle for positive change.

Vivian's family – our ancestors – thought they were acting in her best interests when they begged her not to throw away the "precious heritage of a white skin." In fact, they were reflecting the deeply entrenched attitudes of the day that allowed a privileged class to increase its power and wealth by oppressing others on the basis of visual and cultural differences. I'm not sure how Vivian had the fair-mindedness and courage to resist those pervasive attitudes. I'm not sure how she had the wisdom to ignore the desperate pleas for her to refrain from having children on the grounds that they would be outcasts, but I'm pretty sure that all five of those children are grateful that she ignored that advice.

Here's to Vivian and Bill! Their many talents, their ground-breaking leadership, and their love for each other and for the larger community have enriched us all.

– Chris White, author's brother, songwriter,
radio host and community builder

Vivian on a swing at Camp Owen

Vivian photographs dapper Billy walking in Halifax, 1946

YMCA band at Camp Owen in 1946 l.-r. Herman Seltzer, Don Scott, Billy, Les Vipond, Earl Findlay, George Coffin

Dick Hill, Vivian and Billy at Camp Owen in the summer of 1946

Aunts and uncles front row l.-r. John and Elsie Riseborough, Lloyd Colp;
back row l.-r. Walter "Wal" Harlow, Doris Colp, Lou Harlow

Vivian and Billy sitting on a bench during their trip to Moncton, September 1946

Vivian at her desk at the Wartime Prices and Trade Board

Vivian walking on Yonge Street, 1947

Cleo and Curley Christian on the front porch of their home at 1421 Lansdowne Avenue

Curley, Doug and girlfriend Gerry

The wedding day was perfect, Vivian told her diary

Billy songleading, 1965

Bee Reiter, Vivian and Billy with David Lewis, National Secretary of the CCF, at a party conference at Deer Lodge near Haliburton

Bringing Romney home from the hospital, July 2, 1948

Bernie Keeler holds baby Romney in the yard of 239 Lonsmount Drive

At the Hills' place in Lunenburg, front row l.-r. Laurie, Chris, Sheila, Romney White, "Nana" Jean Keeler; back row l.-r. Dick's parents, Harry and Emma, Billy

Bernie, Vivian, Billy and George reunite at 33 Murray Avenue in Agincourt

Bill White in action, leading singing in July 1965

Billy and his siblings, Mildred, Jack and Portia, at the Whites' home in Scarborough

The great Canadian sprinter Harry Jerome poses with Vivian and fellow Order of Canada recipient Bill White at Rideau Hall for the investiture ceremony in 1971

1917 photo of Billy and his siblings and mother l.-r. Helena, Portia, Billy, Nettie, Mildred on Izie's knee, Romney, who died in 1919 at age ten

Brothers Billy and George, Halifax, 1953

About the Author

SHEILA WHITE hails from a most-noteworthy Canadian black family on her father's side, the White Family of Nova Scotia, and from prominent white colonists on her mother's side in the Harlow and Keeler families. Sheila is the granddaughter of famed Nova Scotia Baptist minister and First World War hero, the Rev. Capt. Dr. William "Andrew" White. She is a niece of the iconic black concert singer Portia White and daughter of Order of Canada recipient Bill White and Vivian Keeler, whose inspiring story is told here. Sheila won an African Canadian Achievement Award for Politics in Toronto in 2014 and a Queen's Platinum Jubilee Medal in September 2022 from the Province of Nova Scotia for her work in anti-racism. Sheila also received a Canada 150 medal in 2017 and an Urban Hero Award in 2020. A lay chaplain, Sheila is an accomplished songwriter, serving as music director at Don Heights Unitarian Congregation. She and husband Alex reside in Agincourt, the Toronto neighborhood where she was born and raised.

Printed in the USA
CPSIA information can be obtained
at www.ICGtesting.com
JSHW010953190923
48733JS00002B/4